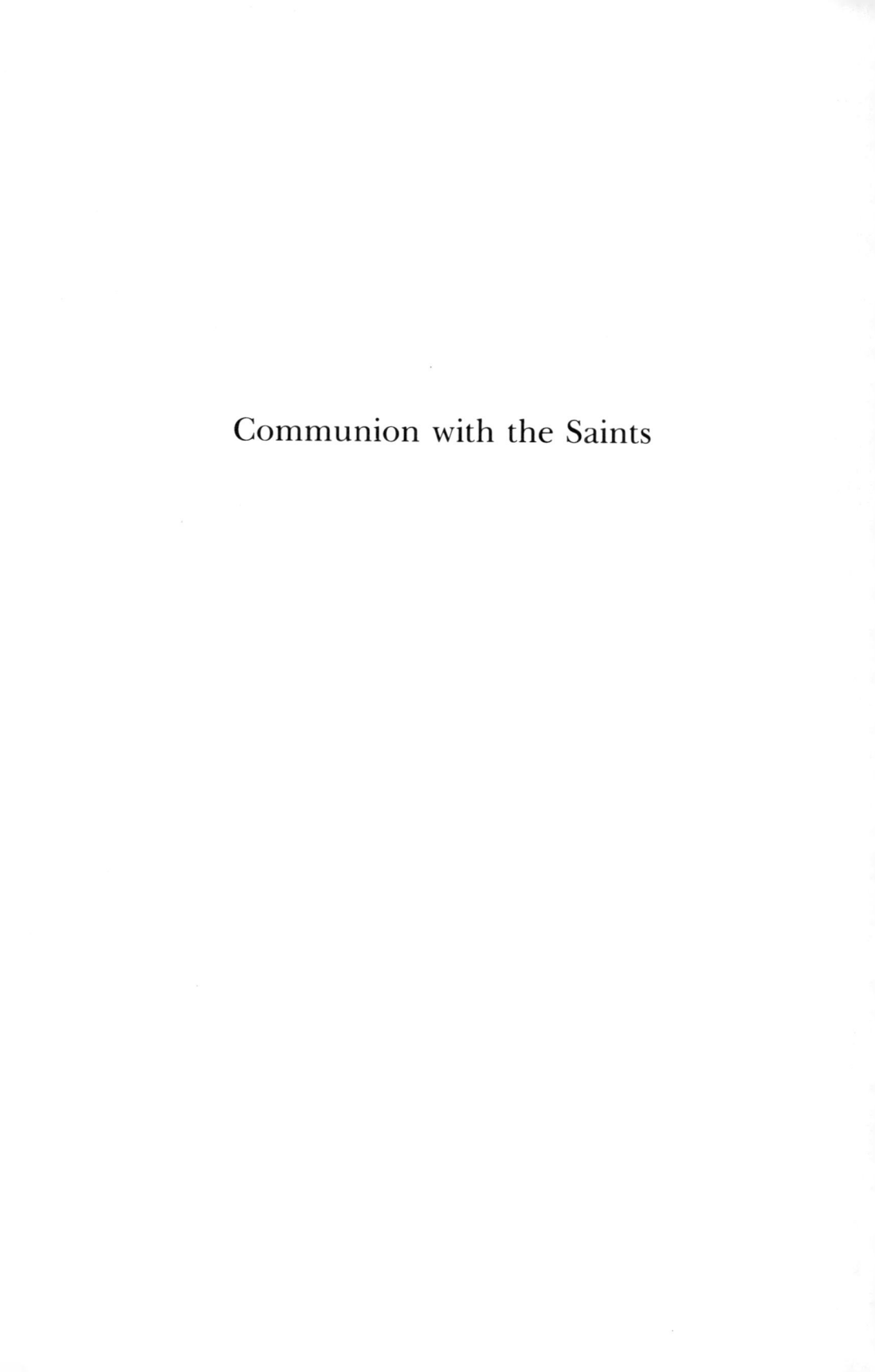

Communion with the Saints

COMMUNION WITH THE SAINTS

HOMILIES FOR FEASTS AND MEMORIALS OF THE SAINTS, WITH INTRODUCTIONS, PENITENTIAL PRAYERS, AND GENERAL INTERCESSIONS

By
Albert Schneider O.M.I.

Translated by
Paul Duggan

FRANCISCAN HERALD PRESS
Chicago, Illinois 60609

Communion with the Saints by Albert Schneider O.M.I., translated by Paul Duggan from the German *Gemeinschaft mit den Heiligen,* Wurzburg: Echter-Verlag. Published with permission. Copyright © 1983 by Franciscan Herald Press. All rights reserved. No part of this book may be reproduced, stored in retrieval system, or transmitted, in any form or by any means, electronic, mechanical, photocopying, recording or otherwise without written permission of Franciscan Herald Press, 1434 West 51st Street, Chicago, Illinois 60609.

Library of Congress Cataloging in Publication Data

Schneider, Albert.
  Communion with the saints.

  Translation of: Gemeinschaft mit den Heiligen.
  Includes index, p. 579
  1. Christian saints—Prayer-books and devotions—English. 2. Christian saints—Sermons. I. Title.
BX2166.S3613   1983   252'.6   83-11723
ISBN 0-8199-0816-9

Published with Ecclesiastical Permission
MADE IN THE UNITED STATES OF AMERICA

CONTENTS

Foreword xix
The Saints as Exemplars xxv
The Saints as Intercessors xxix

January

2. Monk and Bishop in the Midst of the Church—**Basil the Great**
   (Suggested Readings: Reading I, Eph 4:1–7, 11–13; Gospel, Mt 23:8–12) 1
6. Men before Christ—**Epiphany of the Lord**
   (Is 60:1–6; Eph 3:2–3, 5–6; Mt 2:1–12) 4
7. Patron of Canonists—**Raymond of Peñafort**
   (Suggested Readings: Reading I, 2 Cor 5:14–20; Gospel, Lk 12:35–40) 7
13. A Bishop for the Period of Transition—**Hilary**
    (1 Jn 2:18–25; Mt 5:13–16) 10
17. Radical Christianity—**Anthony**
    (Eph 6:10–13, 18; Mt 19:16–26) 13
20. Caretaker of Christian Burial Places—**Fabian**
    (1 Pt 5:1–4; Jn 21:15–17) 16
20. A Soldier as Patron Saint—**Sebastian** 19
21. Risking Everything for the Sake of the Kingdom—**Agnes**
    (1 Cor 1:26–31; Mt 13:44–46) 22

22. "Hunted, Yet not Overtaken"—**Vincent**
    (2 Cor 4:7–15; Mt 10:17–22) 25
24. Christian Life in the Midst of the World—**Francis de Sales**
    (Eph 3:8–12; Jn 15:9–17) 28
25. Threefold Conversion—**Conversion of the Apostle Paul**
    (Acts 22:3–16 or 9:1–22; Mt 16:15–18) 31
26. Paul's Co-workers—**Timothy and Titus**
    (2 Tim 1:1–8 or Ti 1:1–5; Lk 10:1–9) 34
27. Far Ahead of Her Time—**Angela Merici**
    (1 Pt 4:7–11; Mk 9:34–37) 38
28. "Kneeling Theology"—**Thomas Aquinas**
    (Wis 7:7–10, 15–16; Mt 23:8–12) 41
31. A Saint's Educational Wisdom—**John Bosco**
    (Phil 4:4–9; Mt 18:1–4) 44

February

2. Jesus Christ—Light Like the Light of a Candle—**Presentation of the Lord**
    (Mal 3:1–4; Heb 2:14–18; Lk 2:22–40 or 1:22–32) 47
3. The Apostle of Northern Europe—**Ansgar**
    (Is 52:7–10; Mk 1:14–20) 50
3. Blessing Throats with Candles—**Blase**
    (Rom 5:1–5; Mk 16:15–20) 53
5. "God Has Chosen the Weak in this World"—**Agatha**
    (1 Cor 1:26–31; Lk 9:23–26) 56
7. The Church Under the Cross—**Paul Miki and Companions**
    (Gal 2:19–20; Mt 28:16–20) 59
8. A One-month Imprisonment with Results—**Jerome Emiliani**
    (Tb 12:6–13; Mk 10:17–30 or 17–27) 62
10. She Had the Greater Love—**Scholastica**
    (Sq 8:6–7; Lk 10:38–42) 65
11. "Where Heaven Touches Earth"—**Our Lady of Lourdes**
    (Is 66:10–14; Jn 2:1–11) 68

Contents vii

14. God Has Made All Languages for His Praise—**Cyril and Methodius**
    (Acts 13:46–49; Lk 10:1–9) 71
17. Detour Through the Desert?—**The Seven Holy Founders of the Order of the Servites**
    (Rom 8:26–30; Mk 10:17–30 or 17–27) 74
21. Interior Renewal—**Peter Damian**
    (2 Tm 4:1–5; Jn 15, 1–8) 77
22. The Pope: Teacher in the Church—**Chair of Peter**
    (1 Pt 5:1–4; Mt 16:13–19) 80
23. A Follower of the Apostles—**Polycarp of Smyrna**
    (Rv 2:8–11; Jn 15:18–21) 83

March

4. Responsibility of Christians to the World—**Casimir**
   (Phil 3:8–14; Jn 15:9–17) 86
7. Joy in Faith Unto Death—**Perpetua and Felicity**
   (Rom 8:31–39; Mt 10:34–39) 89
8. Late Vocation—**John of God**
   (1 Jn 3:14–18; Mt 25:31–46 or 31–40) 92
9. Forty Years Married—**Frances of Rome**
   (Prv 31:10–31, 19–20, 30–31; Mt 16:24–27) 95
17. Irish Catholicism—**Patrick**
    (1 Pt 4:7–11; Lk 5:1–11) 98
18. Pastor and Catechist—**Cyril of Jerusalem**
    (1 Jn 5:1–5; Jn 15:1–8) 101
19. Joseph the Just—**Joseph**
    (2 Sm 7:4–5, 12–14, 16; Rom 4:13, 16–18, 22; Mt 1:16, 18–21, 24) 104
23. A South American Bishop—**Turibius of Mongrovejo**
    (2 Tm 1:13–14; Mk 1:14–20) 107
25. The Incarnation—**Annunciation of the Lord**
    (Is 7:10–14; Heb 10:4–10; Lk 1:26–38) 110

April

2. Silence for God's Sake—**Francis of Paula**
   (Phil 3:8–14; Lk 12:32–34) 113
4. The Last Father of the Church—**Isidore of Seville**
   (2 Cor 4:1–2, 5–7; Mt 23:8–12) 116
5. On the Wrong Side?—**Vincent Ferrer**
   (2 Tm 4:1–5; Lk 12:35–40) 119
7. Educational Reform in the Seventeenth Century—**John Baptist de la Salle**
   (2 Tm 1:13–14; Mt 18:1–4) 122
11. In Defense of Human Rights—**Stanislaus**
    (Rv 12:10–12; Jn 17:11–19) 125
13. A Pope in the Political Arena—**Martin I**
    (2 Tm 2:8–13 and 3:10–12; Jn 15:18–21) 128
21. Faith Seeking Understanding—**Anselm**
    (Eph 3:14–19; Mt 18:1–4) 131
23. Soldier of Christ—**George**
    Rv 21:5–7; Lk 9:23–26) 134
24. For the One Church—**Fidelis of Sigmaringen**
    (Col 1:24–29; Jn 15:9–17) 137
25. The First Evangelist—**Mark**
    (1 Pt 5:5–14; Mk 16:15–20) 140
28. Patron Saint of the South Sea Islands—**Peter Chanel**
    (1 Cor 1:18–25; Mk 1:14–20) 143
29. Doctor of the Church—**Catherine of Siena**
    (1 Jn 1:5–2:2) 146
30. The Pope of the Tridentine Missal—**Pius V**
    (1 Cor 4:1–5; Jn 21:15–17) 149

May

1. Life and Work—**Joseph the Worker**
   (Gn 1:26–2:3 or Col 3:14–15, 17, 23–24; Mt 13:54–58) 152
2. His Strength Was Also His Weakness—**Athanasius**
   (1 Jn 5:1–5; Mt 10:22–25) 155

Contents ix

  3. On the Path of Faith—**Philip**
     (1 Cor 15:1–8; Jn 14:6–14) 158

12. History Lived by Men—**Nereus, Achilleus, Pancratius**
     (Rv 7:9–17; Mt 11:25–30.–Rv 19:1, 5–9; Mt 11:25–30) 161

14. The Replacement—**Matthias**
     (Acts 1:15–17, 20–25; Jn 15:9–17) 164

18. Condemned to Failure—**John I**
     (Rv 3:14, 20–22; Lk 22:24–30) 167

20. A Great Preacher—**Bernardine of Siena**
     (Acts 4:8–12; Lk 9:57–62) 170

25. Author and Teacher—**Bede the Venerable**
     (1 Cor 2:10–16; Mt 5:13–16) 173

25. For the Independence of the Church—**Gregory VII**
     (Acts 20:17–18, 28–32, 36; Mt 16:13–19) 176

25. Concerned with the Lord's Business—**Mary Magdalene of Pazzi**
     (1 Cor 7:25–35; Mk 3:31–35) 179

26. A Comical Oddball?—**Philip Neri**
     (Phil 4:4–9; Jn 17:20–26) 182

27. Withdraw into Isolation?—**Augustine of Canterbury**
     (1 Thes 2:2–8; Mt 16:15–20) 185

31. "He Whom You, O Virgin, Brought to Elizabeth"—**Visitation**
     (Zep 3:14–18 or Rom 12:9–16; Lk 1:39–56) 188

    Friday Following the Second Sunday After Pentecost: Redemption
    through Love—**Feast of the Sacred Heart of Jesus**
    *(A - Dt 7:6–11; 1 Jn 4:7–16; Mt 11:25–30. B - Hos 11: 1, 3–4,
    8–9; Eph 3:8–12, 14–19; Jn 19:31–37. C - Ez 34:11–16; Rom
    5:5–11; Lk 15:3–7)* 191

    Saturday Following the Second Sunday After Pentecost: "She
    Has a Heart for Us"—**The Immaculate Heart of Mary**
    (Is 61:9–11; Lk 2:41–51) 194

June

  1. Witness for Christ in a Philosopher's Robe—**Justin**
     (1 Cor 1:18–25; Mt 5:13–16) 197

2. Martyrdom in Life—**Marcellinus and Peter**
   (2 Cor 6:4–10; Jn 17:11–19) 200
3. The Uganda Martyrs—**Charles Lwanga and Companions**
   (2 Mc 7:1–2, 9–14; Mt 5:1–12) 203
5. Apostle of Germany—**Boniface**
   (Acts 26:19–23; Jn 10:11–16) 206
6. Playboy, Preacher of Penance, Prince of the Church—**Norbert of Xanten**
   (Ez 34:11–16; Lk 14:25–33) 209
9. Teacher, Writer, and Poet in a Restless Time—**Ephrem**
   (1 Pt 4:7–11; Mk 3:31–35) 212
11. Friend and Co-worker of Paul—**Barnabas**
    (Acts 11:21–26 and 13:1–3; Mt 10:7–13)................... 215
13. The Saint with the Child Jesus on His Arm—**Anthony of Padua**
    (Is 61:1–3; Lk 10:1–9) 218
19. "Let Me Be Formed into the Pattern of His Death"—**Romuald**
    (Eph 6:10–13, 18; Lk 14:25–33) 221
21. Patron of Youth—**Aloysius Gonzaga**
    (1 Jn 5:1–5; Mt 16:24–27)................................. 224
22. "Sell What You Have . . ."—**Paulinus of Nola**
    (2 Cor 8:9–15; Lk 12:32–34).............................. 227
22. Gentlemen—**John Fisher and Thomas More**
    (1 Pt 4:12–19; Mt 10:34–39) 230
24. God's Instrument—**John the Baptist**
    (Vigil - Jer 1:4–10; 1 Pt 1:8–12; Lk 1:5–17. Day - Is 49:1–6; Acts 13:22–26; Lk 1:57–66, 80) 233
27. Theological Squabbling, or Defense of the Faith?—**Cyril of Alexandria**
    (2 Tm 4:1–5; Mt 5:13–16) 236
28. "Father of Catholic Dogmatic Theology"—**Irenaeus**
    (2 Tm 2:22–26; Jn 17:20–26) 239
29. Peter, "Christian with Us"—**Peter and Paul**
    (Vigil - Acts 3:1–10; Gal 1:11–20; Jn 21:15–19. Day - Acts 12:1–11; 2 Tm 4:6–8, 17–18; Mt 16:13–19)................. 242

Contents   xi

30. Outsiders as Scapegoats—**First Martyrs of the Church of Rome**
    (Rom 8:31–39; Mt 24:4–13).............................   245

July

3. "Blest Are They Who Have not Seen and Have Believed"—
    Thomas
    (Eph 2:19–22; Jn 20:24–29)   249
4. Christian Life in a Difficult Marriage—**Elizabeth of Portugal**
    (1 Pt 4:7–11; Mt 25:31–46).............................   252
5. In the Spirit of the Apostle Paul—**Anthony Mary Zaccaria**
    (2 Tm 1:13–14 and 2:1–3; Mk 10:13–16)   255
6. The Result of Deficient Clarification—or More?—**Maria Goretti**
    (1 Cor 6:13–15, 17–20; Jn 12:24–26)   258
11. Father of the West, Patron Saint of Europe—**Benedict**
    (Prv 2:1–9; Mk 10:17–30)   261
13. Queen and Empress—**Henry and Kunigunde**
    (Mi 6:6–8; Mk 3:31–35).................................   264
14. A "Mother Teresa" of the Sixteenth Century—**Camillus de Lellis**
    (1 Jn 3:14–18; Jn 15:9–17)   267
15. The Second Founder of the Franciscan Order—**Bonaventure**
    (Eph 3:14–19; Mt 23:8–12)   270
16. "Feast of the Scapular"—**Our Lady of Mount Carmel**
    (Zec 2:14–17; Mt 11:27–28)   273
21. The Capuchins and the Counter Reformation—**Lawrence of Brindisi**
    (2 Cor 5:1–2, 5–7; Mk 4:1–10, 13–20)   276
22. Called by Her Name by the Risen One—**Mary Magdalene**
    (Sq 3:1–4 or 2 Cor 5:14–17; Jn 20:1–2, 11–18)   279
23. Noble Lady and Prophet—**Bridget of Sweden**
    Gal 2:19–20; Jn 15:1–8)   282
25. "We Can"?—**James**
    (2 Cor 4:7–15; Mt 20:20–28)   286

26. Legend of the Miraculous Birth of Mary—**Joachim and Ann**
    (Sir 44:1, 10–15; Mt 13:16–17) 289
29. The Believing and Serving Woman—**Martha**
    (1 Jn 4:7–16; Jn 11:19–27 or Lk 10:38–42) 292
30. To Proclaim the Unfathomable Richness of Christ—**Peter Chrysologus**
    (Eph 3:8–12; Mt 5:13–16) 295
31. God Above All—**Ignatius of Loyola**
    (1 Cor 10:31 and 11:1; Lk 14:25–33) 298

August

1. Christ, the Law of Our Life—**Alphonsus Mary de Liguori**
   (Rom 8:1–4; Mt 5:13–16) 301
2. Faith Overcoming This World—**Eusebius**
   (1 Jn 5:1–5; Mt 5:1–12) 304
4. He Had Compassion for Them—**John Mary Vianney**
   (Ez 3:17–21; Mt 9:35–38 and 10:1) 307
5. Mary, Archetype of the Church—**Dedication of St. Mary Major in Rome**
   (Rv 21:1–5; Lk 11:27–28) 310
6. A Law of Life—**Transfiguration of the Lord**
   (Dn 7:9–10, 13–14; 2 Pt 1:16–19; A - Mt 17:1–9; B - Mk 9:2–10; C - Lk 9:28–36) 313
7. "In the Eyes of the Foolish, They Are Dead . . ."—**Sixtus and Companions**
   (Wis 3:1–9; Mt 10:28–33) 316
7. In Contrast to the Renaissance—**Cajetan**
   (1 Cor 2:1–10; Lk 9:57–62) 319
8. His Desire: Solid Preaching—**Dominic**
   (1 Cor 2:1–10; Lk 9:57–62) 323
10. A Match for Any Situation—**Lawrence**
    (2 Cor 9:6–10; Jn 12:24–26) 326

Contents xiii

11. For the Sake of Poverty—**Clare**
    (Phil 3:8–14; Mt 16:24–27) 329
13. Trials—The Most Normal Thing in the World?—**Pontian and Hippolytus**
    (1 Pt 4:12–19; Jn 15:18–21) 332
15. Assumption, not Ascension—**The Assumption of Mary into Heaven**
    (Vigil - 1 Chr 15:3–4, 15, 16 and 16:1–2; 1 Cor 15:54–57; Lk 11:27–28. Day - Rv 11:19 and 12:1–6, 10; 1 Cor 15:20–26; Lk 1:39–56) 335
16. Using His Talents—**Stephen of Hungary**
    (Dt 6:3–9; Mt 11:14–30) 338
19. Understanding the Love of Christ—**John Eudes**
    (Eph 3:14–19; Mt 11:25–30) 342
20. A Monk Who Left an Imprint on His Age—**Bernard of Clairvaux**
    (Sir 15:1–6; Jn 17:20–26) 345
21. "For You Became Very Dear to Us"—**Pius X**
    (1 Thes 2: 2–8; Jn 21:15–17) 348
22. "Hail, Holy Queen"—**Queenship of Mary**
    (Is 9:1–6; Lk 1:26–38) 351
23. Patroness of Latin America—**Rose of Lima**
    (2 Cor 10:17 to 11:2; Mt 13:44–46) 354
24. "A True Israelite"—**Bartholomew**
    (Rv 21:9–14; Jn 1:45–51) 357
25. Holiness on the Royal Throne—**Louis**
    (Is 58:6–11; Mt 16:24–27) 360
25. Yes to the Will of God—**Joseph Calasanz** 363
27. A Mother Waits—**Monica**
    (Sir 26:1–4, 13–16; Lk 7:11–17) 366
28. God Stands at the End of the Road—**Augustine**
    (1 Jn 4:7–16; Mt 23:8–12) 369
29. Can We Trust in God?—**The Beheading of John the Baptist**
    (Jer 1:17–19; Mk 6:17–29) 372

September

3. The Last Roman on the Papal Throne—**Gregory the Great**
   (2 Cor 4:1–2, 5–7; Lk 22:24–30) 375
8. "Dawn of Salvation"—**The Birth of Mary**
   (Mi 5:1–4 or Rom 8:28–30; Mt 1:1–16, 18–23 or 1:18–23) 378
13. One Who Stands Up for Something Sets Himself Apart—**John Chrysostom**
    (Eph 4:1–7, 11–13; Mk 4:1–10; 13–20). 381
14. In the Cross There Is Salvation—**The Triumph of the Cross**
    (Nm 21:4–9; Phil 2:6–11; Jn 3:13–17). 384
15. To Suffer Out of Love—**Our Lady of Sorrows**
    (Heb 5:7–9; Jn 19:25–27 or Lk 2:33–35). 387
16. Bishop in Time of Transition—**Cornelius and Cyprian**
    (2 Cor 4:7–15; Jn 17:11–19) 391
17. Theology Professor and Papal Adviser—**Robert Bellarmine**
    (Wis 7:7–10, 15–16; Mk 4:1–10, 13–20). 395
19. Against Weariness and Resignation—**Januarius**
    (Heb 10:32–36; Mt 12:24–26) 398
21. From Tax Collector to Apostle—**Matthew**
    (Eph 4:1–7, 11–13; Mt 9:9–13) 401
26. Helpers to the Sick and Suffering—**Cosmas and Damian**
    (Wis 3:1–9; Mt 10:28–33) 404
27. Saint of Charity—**Vincent de Paul**
    (1 Cor 1:26–31; Mt 23:8–12) 408
28. Germans and Czechs—**Wenceslaus**
    (1 Pt 3:14–17; Mt 10:34–49). 411
29. Creatures of God—**Michael, Gabriel, Raphael**
    (Dn 7:9–10, 13–14 or Rv 12:7–12; Jn 1:47–51). 414
30. A Difficult Contemporary—**Jerome**
    (2 Tm 3:14–17; Mt 23:8–12) 417

October

1. My Vocation Is Love—**Theresa of the Child Jesus**
   (Is 66:10–14; Mt 18:1–4) 420

Contents

2. "Let Angels Always Attend Us . . ."—**Guardian Angels**
   (Ex 23:20–23; Mt 18:1–5, 10) 423
4. "Praise to You, My Lord"—**Francis of Assisi**
   (Gal 6:14–18; Mt 11:25–30) 426
6. In Solitude for the Sake of Christ—**Bruno**
   (Phil 3:8–14; Mt 9:57–62) 429
7. Meditating with Mary—**Our Lady of the Rosary**
   (Acts 1:12–14; Lk 1:26–28) 432
9. To Be a Light to the World Here and Now—**Denis and Companions**
   (2 Cor 6:4–10; Mt 5:13–16) 435
9. From Pharmacist's Assistant to Fisher of Men—**John Leonardi**
   (2 Cor 4:1–2, 5–7, Lk 5:1–11) 438
14. Yes, to the Church of Sinners—**Callistus**
    (1 Pt 5:1–4; Lk 22:24–30) 441
15. "When Partridge, Then Partridge . . ."—**Teresa of Avila**
    (Rom 8:22–27; Jn 15:1–8) 445
16. Duchess of Germans and Poles—**Hedwig**
    (Sir 26:1–4, 13–16; Mk 3:31–35) 448
16. Devotion to the Sacred Heart—**Margaret Mary Alacoque**
    (Eph 3:14–19; Mt 11:25–30) 451
17. Bishop and Martyr in Passage—**Ignatius of Antioch**
    (Phil 3:17 to 4:1; Jn 12:24–26) 454
18. A "Painter of Mary"—**Luke**
    (2 Tm 4:9–17; Lk 10:1–9) 457
19. Mission Among the Indians—**John de Brebeuf, Isaac Jogues, and Companions.**
    (2 Cor 4:7–15; Mt 28:16–20) 460
19. The Word from the Cross—**Paul of the Cross**
    (1 Cor 1:18–25; Mt 16:24–27) 463
23. Envoy in God's Stead—**John of Capistrano**
    (2 Cor 5:14–20; Lk 9:57–62) 466
24. Missionary to the Common People, Bishop, Confessor to the Queen—**Anthony Mary Claret**
    (Is 52:7–10; Mk 1:14–20) 469

28. The Call to Discipleship—**Simon and Jude**
    (Eph 2:19–22; Lk 6:12–16) 472

November

1. The Saints, "God's Children"—**All Saints**
   (Rv 7:2–4, 9–14; 1 Jn 3:1–3; Mt 5:1–12) 475
2. But She Is Still Dead—**All Souls**
   (I - Jb 19:1, 23–27; 1 Cor 15:51–57; Jn 6:37–40. II - Wis 3:1–9 or 3:1–6, 9; Phil 3:20–21; Jn 11:17–27 or 11:21–27. III - 2 Mc 12:43–46; Rv 14:13; Jn 14:1–6) 479
3. A Saint of Brotherly Love from the Third World—**Martin de Porres**
   (Col 3:12–17; Jn 15:9–17) 482
4. Bishop of the Council of Trent—**Charles Borromeo**
   (Rom 12:3–13; Jn 10:11–16) 486
9. "You Are God's House"—**Dedication of the Lateran Basilica**
   (2 Chr 5:6–10, 13 and 6:2; 1 Cor 3:9–13, 16–17; Lk 19:1–10). 490
10. Successor of Peter—**Leo the Great**
    (Sir 39:6–11; Mt 16:13–19) 493
11. The Other Martin—**Martin**
    (Is 61:1–3; Mt 25:31–46) 496
12. One Lord, One Faith, One Baptism—**Josaphat**
    (Eph 4:1–7, 11–13; Jn 17:20–26) 499
15. The First Modern Scientist—**Albert the Great**
    (Sir 15:1–6; Mt 13:47–53) 502
16. She Tamed Her Husband—**Margaret of Scotland**
    (Is 58:6–11; Jn 15:9–17) 505
17. A Strong Personality—**Elizabeth of Hungary**
    (1 Jn 3:14–18; Lk 6:27–38) 508
18. The Church in the Steps of Peter and Paul—**Dedication of the Churches of Peter and Paul**
    (Acts 28:11–16, 30–31; Mt 14:22–33) 511
21. "For Whoever Does the Will of My Father . . ."—**The Presentation of Mary**
    (Zec 2:14–17; Mt 12:46–50) 514

Contents   xvii

22. Patroness of Church Music—**Cecilia**
    (Lv 19:1–2, 17–18; Mt 10:28–33)................... 518
23. From the Life of the Early Church—**Clement**
    (1 Pt 5:1–4; Lk 5:1–11)................................. 521
23. "The Foxes Have Lairs . . ."—**Columban**
    (Is 52:7–10; Lk 9:57–62)................................ 525
30. Fisher of Men—**Andrew**
    (Rom 10:9–18; Mt 4:8–22).............................. 528

December

3. "How Could He Do All That?"—**Francis Xavier**
   (1 Cor 9:16–19, 22–23; Mk 16:15–20)................ 531
4. Christian Veneration of Images—**John Damascene**
   (2 Tm 1:13–14 and 2:1–3; Mt 25:14–30)............. 534
6. Comical Figure or Saint?—**Nicholas**
   (Is 6:1–8; Lk 10:1–9).................................... 537
7. The Christian Grows with His Duties—**Ambrose**
   (Eph 3:8–12; Jn 10:11–16).............................. 540
8. God Gives Grace for Service—**The Immaculate Conception of Mary**
   (Gn 3:9–15, 20; Eph 1:3–6, 11–12; Lk 1:26–38)............. 543
11. Pope in a Turbulent Time—**Damasus I**
    (Acts 20:17–18, 28–32, 36; Jn 15:9–17)............. 546
12. An Extraordinary Woman—**Jane Frances de Chantal**
    (Prv 31:10–13, 19–20, 30–31; Mk 3:31–35)......... 549
13. "Betrothed to One Husband"—**Lucy**
    (2 Cor 10:17 to 11:2; Mt 25:1–13).................... 552
14. Forerunner in the Sign of the Cross—**John of the Cross**
    (1 Cor 2:1–10; Lk 14:25–33)........................... 555
21. The Second Apostle of Germany—**Peter Canisius**
    (2 Tm 4:1–5; Mt 5:13–16).............................. 558
23. "Yahweh Has Had Mercy"—**John of Kanty**
    (Jas 2:14–17; Mt 25:31–46)............................ 561
26. The World Accepted Him Not—**Stephen**
    (Acts 6:8–10 and 7:54–59; Mt 10:17–22)........... 564

27. A ''Son of Thunder''—**John the Evangelist**
    (1 Jn 1:1–4; Jn 20:2–8) 567
28. How Can God Allow That?—**Holy Innocents**
    (1 Jn 1:5 to 2:2; Mt 2:13–18) 570
29. Murder in the Cathedral—**Thomas Becket**
    (2 Tm 2:8–13 and 3:10–12; Mt 16:24–27) 573
31. Pope of Transition—**Sylvester I**
    (Ez 34:11–16; Mt 28:16–20) 576

Index.. 579

FOREWORD

In this work Short Talks and—with few exceptions—texts for the Greeting, Penitential Rite, and Prayer of the Faithful for all feasts and memorials of the General Roman Calendar are provided. A series of these texts have already appeared in an annual for preachers (*Gottes Wort im Kirchenjahr—God's Word in the Liturgical Year*) during the years from 1975 to 1978. The favorable reaction to their publication has encouraged the author to compile this complete collection.*

Memorials of the Saints during the Liturgical Year

This work is not intended to make the structure of the liturgical year once again overloaded by an excessive cult of the saints. It is based on the primary intention of the revised liturgy and the corresponding rubrics of the "General Introduction to the Roman Missal." It is intended as a help to all who, out of pastoral considerations in daily Eucharistic celebrations, want to proclaim the Good News in relation to the memorial days of the saints, as well as to the other feasts of the liturgical calendar.

---

*The publisher also recommends two other recent volumes of daily readings based on the new Calendar and the lives of the saints—*The Franciscan Book of Saints* by Marion A. Habig, O.F.M. and *Lives of the Saints* by Augustine Kalberer O.S.B. Both of these titles are available from Franciscan Herald Press.

Diocesan directories supply general information on the options of the saints' memorials for workday Eucharistic liturgies. For the sake of an overview, let us have a brief look at the general regulations (cf. the "General Introduction," nos. 313–34):

—On all weekdays, with the exception of Ash Wednesday and Holy Week, the Prayer may be taken from the corresponding obligatory or optional memorial day (no. 316 a).

—On weekdays throughout the year, with the exception of the time from December 17 through January 6, and of Lent including Easter Week, the entire Mass formulary of the saint of the day may be used (no. 316 b).

—On all these days, it is also possible (even when the memorial day of the day's saint was supplanted) to celebrate the memorial of the saint in the form of a votive Mass, "as long as genuine need or a pastoral situation calls for it" (no. 333); this can be true, for example, in the case of a specially emphasized weekly liturgy, in which particular categories of saints are to be presented.

Choice of Readings

Preaching on feast and memorial days of the liturgical calendar is not possible without a reference to the particular Scriptural passages (from which one can surely depart now and then). There is a certain precedence enjoyed by the current weekday pericopes, but there is also the possibility of choosing at will from the selections in the saints' lectionary. With this in mind, these short talks, for practical reasons, correspond to the Scriptural readings prescribed or suggested in the official lectionary for the specific feasts and memorial days. These readings are also the ones that appear in various missals for congregational use, e.g., *New St. Joseph Weekday Missal*, 2 vols. References to these readings have been added in the Contents.

This choice is also justified by the Introduction to the Sanctoral Lectionary, when pastoral reasons apply. Reasons of this kind are present when it is desirable to point out how the particular saint lived in the imitation of Christ by the power of the Eucharist. Moreover, the possibility is never ruled out in the "General Introduction to the Roman Missal" that a change be made even during Advent and Lent from the current daily readings.

The Short Talks

The short talks in this book are an attempt to help bring forth fruit for preaching (and thus for our Christian life) from the saints' days. This is accomplished, with various combinations of elements, through imparting historical information, through singling out particular aspects of each saint's life and work (or the history of his or her cult), or else through reflecting on the suggested Biblical pericopes. The relation to the questions and problems of today in the life of the Church and in personal Christian life is thus constantly brought out and set into clear arrangement. The way in which the individual celebrant will use the material offered will depend on specific situations. It may be in the form of a somewhat long introduction at the beginning of the Eucharistic celebration, or as a talk, or as a "station" prior to Mass, or else as part of a service of the Word.

The Other Texts

There is no need of reprinting the daily orations; they are available in the various editions of missals, both for altar and congregational use. Special introductions to the readings, introductory texts for the orations, for the dismissal, and so forth—while at times good in themselves—are not included here, lest the daily liturgy be encumbered with too much talking. Suggestions for song selection also are found in other publications. Besides the talks, however, we present for each feast or memorial, an Introduction, prayers for the Penitential Rite, and petitions for the Prayer of the Faithful or General Intercessions.

The Introduction creates an awareness, with varying emphasis, of present-day problems; it also awakens interest in the saint of the day or even makes a brief presentation of him or her. Great importance is thus given to variety of expression.

Now and then the suggested text invites a reflection and examen of conscience or makes evident the direct relation to the eucharistic celebration. Normally, of course, it is left up to the celebrant to point out the relation with the proper forms from the missal or with his own composition.

The proffered prayers for the *Penitential Rite* generally give a call to awareness along with a period of silence, and lead to a closing deprecatory exhortation for forgiveness by the priest ("May almighty God have mercy on us . . ."). These are understood as options and are not designed to push aside Form A (which is nowhere especially mentioned) for general confession of sin ("I confess . . .").

In part they illustrate a broadening of Form B through the insertion of psalm texts. The latter have either the format of a confession, or else give expression to trust in the forgiving and saving God. Others take the construct of a developed Kyrie-litany along the lines of Form C.

Those texts display a particular literary style that ties the threefold call of the Kyrie with a Biblical stimulus to reflection, drawing mostly upon the readings of the given memorial day. One should make sure that a helpful silence be observed after each Biblical call; in this case, a single foregoing silence is not necessary.

The petitions for the *Prayer of the Faithful* or *General Intercessions* are developed mainly out of the theme material of the short talks. They diverge from the rule given in no. 46 of the "General Introduction to the Roman Missal." Since the prayers of petition in the canon normally direct the assembly's attention to the whole world, it is defensible—for the purpose of concretizing and varying prayer in the daily Eucharist—to formulate "one-sided" petitions occasionally (and sometimes even "we" prayers).

With respect to the habitual (or else newly introduced) responses of the congregation, it is worth noting that both the introductory prayer and the congregation's petitionary response should be addressed to the same divine Person. A more frequent silence following individual petitions would be especially fitting in weekday liturgies.

Sources

The author has gratefully employed as sources of historical information the already mentioned work of Peter Mann and also the short biographies in the missal and in the *Schott-Volksmessbuch*. A number of petitions and a series of Kyrie-litanies are texts reproduced from *Gotteslob* (their numbers are always cited).

Albert Schneider O.M.I.

THE SAINTS AS EXEMPLARS

In recent years the veneration of the saints has receded in the Catholic Church. In the official liturgical calendar, the number of saints' feasts has been reduced. Our modern church buildings offer little space for saints' images. Devotions to specific saints (May devotions, novenas, and others) have diminished or lost meaning altogether.

Reasons for the Decline: The Theological Situation

This decline must first be seen in relation to the fact that central questions of our Christian faith have become problems for us in an entirely new way. Our theologians must deal first of all with urgent questions of God, Jesus Christ, and the Church. The whole Church moves in many experiments on a painstaking path into the future. In this context, the effort expended toward shaping a liturgy effective for our times involves many forces. There is consequently little spare room or energy in our theology and in our practical ecclesial life for any intensive concern with the saints or with the development of their particular veneration.

Sensitivity toward Possible Inadequate Forms

It is also from a broader standpoint that we have become more reserved about venerating saints. Even in the Catholic Church, we have in recent decades become aware of the central meaning of Christ's redemptive act. Moreover, we have had encounters with non-Catholic Christians in greater measure than ever, not without effect. Our critical judgment became more and more developed, and we saw more clearly that many specific forms of veneration of the saints had grown up near the core of our faith. Saints, however, are not independent titans possessing redeeming power and might apart from God and Jesus Christ.

Still, a veneration of saints that is rightly understood and correctly subordinated theologically has its justification even in our day and a practical meaning for our Christian life.

Honoring Exemplars

In all ages, people have held exemplars in high regard with the effect of aiding the shaping of their own lives. In all peoples and cultural spheres, great figures of the past are honored, and people see in exemplary lives models for conducting their own.

We Christians act in a way like other peoples. For us, the saints are people who, in their faith and Christian mode of life, in their toil and struggles, are examples for our own lives.

In this veneration of great Christians of the past, all Christian confessions are at one. It is possible to imagine a book series: "Saints of Undivided Christianity." And it is not seldom that one finds in Protestant churches, where in Catholic churches one finds statues and pictures of saints, statues or images of great characters of the Reformation, of great people of piety in the history of Protestant Christianity, or of former pastors of a community.

Patron Saints. It is in line with this veneration of saints that we bear the names of great figures of the Christian past. We read about their lives in order to learn from their exemplary practice of Christian life. It is to our purposes to be able in our day to lead a life of faith and of dedication to the Kingdom of God.

The Saints as Exemplars

"Modern Saints." The image of canonized saints of past times and centuries can be surprisingly current in many aspects. And yet, our interest should also be directed toward model Christian figures of the most recent past and of the present (such as Carl Sonnenschein, Alfred Delp, Abbé Pierre, Mother Teresa. . .). From those "contemporary saints," impulses stream forth in a special way for the shaping of our lives, since the problems of their lives lie close to us.

God Has Done Great Things for Them. We know that we are in agreement with all Christians when we see God himself at work in the lives and deeds of saints or of other great Christian figures of the past and when we praise God in them by reason of their deeds. The words that sacred Scripture places in Mary's mouth—"My soul proclaims the greatness of the Lord," for "the Almighty has done great things for me" (Lk 1:46,49)—are words that every saint, as well as every Christian, must apply to himself.

What the saints were, how they lived, and what they accomplished in the Church, they did in the power of God's grace. A rather romantic comparison can illustrate this: just as a dewdrop in early morning holds all the sun's radiance that is mirrored within it, so is God's grace mirrored in the lives and deeds of the saints.

This absolute dependence of the saints upon God's sovereign grace alone redeems us (this we must emphasize again and again in our time), and their example stands out once again. Whatever we are and can do for the Church, we are such totally and solely by the grace of God. The saints are, first of all, gifted. So are we. We ought never to forget this in all our strivings toward a contemporary mode of imitating Christ.

THE SAINTS AS INTERCESSORS

To venerate great personalitites of the past, and to see them as models for one's own life, is a trait common to humanity. To concern oneself with great personalities of the Christian past, and to draw strength for one's own course of life from reflecting upon their lives, is also normal among all Christians. To call out in prayer to the saints, exemplary Christians of the past, about the worries and problems of oneself and of the Church, and to trust in their intercession: in this we are followed by Orthodox Christians; in it we run up against critical reservations on the part of Protestants; and we Catholics as well have our own difficulties about it today.

It is a fact that the Catholic Church since early times has seen meaning in petitionary prayer to the saints. Would it not be appropriate in the light of all reservations to inquire more precisely how we should understand the intercession of the saints (as well as our prayers of petition to them)?

Salvation in Jesus Christ

Holy by the Grace of God. In our petitionary prayer to the saints, our premise is that they have their being dependent upon God. They are whatever they are by God and his grace. They do whatever they do in God's power, dedicated to his will.

Partnership with God in Salvation History. We are, of course convinced in faith that God has called man into natural and supernatural partnership with him. Man's action (understood as dependent upon God) enters into the history of divine salvation for the whole world. He cooperates in a mysterious way in the world's salvation. It rests entirely upon God and entirely upon man, without mutual exclusion of God's grace and man's cooperation.

Action for Others. The life, suffering, and death of Jesus Christ are, according to our faith, of fundamental meaning for the salvation of each individual human being and of the entire world, without removing the individual's responsibility for his salvation. In the imitation of Jesus Christ we are certain that the personal action of the individual Christian has a salvific effect in other's lives (without diminishing their personal responsibility for their lives and salvation). This is the theological basis for all prayer for one another in the community of the Church, and for all sacrifices that we undertake in order to bring benefit to others.

Living Communion with the Saints

Communion with the Dead. According to our faith, our fellow Christians who died in Christ have passed into fulfillment with the Father. In Jesus Christ we, as the "Church militant," make up with them—as the "Church suffering" and "Church triumphant"—the one Church of Jesus Christ. Earthly death has not destroyed this bond.

Life Completely for God's Kingdom. We know that the saints, during their earthly lives, work with all their power for the coming of God's Kingdom. They live more and more in the fulfillment of God, with clear purpose: that God's Kingdom come, that his Name be held holy, that his will be done in heaven and on earth. They dedicate themselves not merely with words, they live entirely for this goal.

God Is a God of Fullness. We are bound together with the saints in Jesus Christ. They live in fullness with God for one main goal: the coming of God's Kingdom, for which we also pray. We know in faith that the action of the individual Christian can have a salvific result in the lives of others (although the *how* remains a mystery).

Thus it is possible and meaningful, in "conversation" with dead fellow Christians (prayer to the saints), to speak out our concern for the things of God in this world. We can therefore draw strength from the conviction that they dedicate themselves along with us with all their power for the fulfillment of God's will. And, since we human beings vary and the saints also vary, it is also understandable that we turn to specific saints, who stand closer to us in a special way.

One can, of course, object that this form of petitionary prayer is a detour. Indeed, it all leads back to the truth that we live entirely by the grace of God. Yet this God is a God of fullness. He wills men's salvation not without their cooperation. Rightly understood, petitionary prayer to the saints and theologically correct trust in their intercession are therefore expressions for acknowledging the greatness of God, who takes men seriously as his partners and has granted them the dignity of co-workers in salvation history.

Personal Difficulties

With this reflection, perhaps the theological background of prayer to the saints becomes clearer. Whether personal difficulties also become cleared away is another matter. Even if the approach to the veneration of the saints along the lines mentioned above is not possible for us at present, we still stand in imitation of Jesus Christ in the communion of the Church when we live with the convictions: that the grace of God comes at the beginning before all things; that God wills our salvation only with our cooperation; that our action has meaning for the whole Church; that the action of others mysteriously influences our own lives, without interfering with our own individual response.

St. Basil the Great (January 2)

MONK AND BISHOP IN THE MIDST OF THE CHURCH

Introduction

". . . His brotherhood [his 'order'] remains open to the world; moreover, contact with 'seculars' is stronger, a school for youth is attached to the community, and various social works such as hospitals and guest houses are maintained by the brothers." These lines tell of the community of monks that St. Basil the Great founded around 370 while bishop in Asia Minor. In his religious community, he sought to realize his ideal of life.

Penitential Prayer

Lord Jesus Christ: we are not humble, peaceable, patient; we are often pround, hostile, and impatient: Lord, have mercy. . . .

We do not put up with one another; we try to shake off the other's burden from us: Christ, have mercy. . . .

We do not cherish the Spirit's unity and peace; we stress our contrary opinions and our differences: Lord, have mercy. . . .

Talk

A Second Conversion. Cappadocia, a region in what is now Turkey, was largely Christian around 330 (the year of St. Basil's birth). The saint's family confessed the Christian faith. Since the father was wealthy, he was able to afford an appropriate education for his son. Basil thus studied in his home town of Caesarea, in the capital city Constantinople, and in Athens which at that time still attracted fine minds.

Upon completion of his studies, Basil returned to his home town. He had offers for a brilliant career. All doors were open to him. Yet in all his studies, the religious question had not let go of him. As a hope-filled young man, he made a conscious decision for Christ. He had himself baptized and became a monk.

From Monk to Bishop. The monastic ideal attracted many people in those times. However Basil, with his decision, did not just coast on the wave of a passing fashion. He was serious about it. Together with some like-minded types, he withdrew into a remote valley. He drew up rules of life for his community (which are still followed by monks in the Eastern Church). Life is divided between prayer and work, between manual labor and spiritual concerns. His confreres were above all to study the sacred Scriptures deeply.

Basil loved solitude. Yet he loved the Church more. As the Church slipped into internal difficulties, he determined to relinquish his solitude and become a priest in his home town. At the age of forty, he became bishop of that city. Up until his death—he was only forty-nine then—he labored untiringly for the faithful of his diocese. He sought to be the servant of all [Gospel]: he watched over Church discipline; he fought against error; he intervened in the theological controversies of his time. In this context, he had contacts through a great number of letters with other bishops and communities east and west.

Monastic Community for the Church. Even as a bishop, Basil sought to remain true to his monastic ideal. He brought his companions out of solitude into the episcopal city. He continued to live together with them. However, he opened his fraternal community (in addition, he also founded a similar community for women) to the needs of his diocese. He saw his monks not so much as world-fleeing hermits

St. Basil the Great (January 2)

(although prayer to his mind was essential), as a kind of ecclesial "special troop," a core group to enliven the whole community. The cloistered community was to live after the pattern of the primitive Church. It was not, however, to seal itself off from other Christians, but was to place itself consciously in their service. Accordingly, he entrusted to his monks (and nuns) the care of the poor and the education of young people. They were to serve in hospitals and guest houses, and were to be an example in their lives and works for the whole community.

Basil, "worthy of the call he had received" (Reading), as a Christian, who as a monk "seeks God" as the "servant of all" [Gospel] in his diocese. At the beginning of his Rule he raises the question: What distinguishes the Christian? He provides an answer: faith that is effective through love. In this phrase is summarized the life of this holy bishop. The same is true time and again in our lives.

Petitions

Lord Jesus Christ, you are the Lord of your Church. Hear our prayer and listen to us.

Let us lead a life as Christians that is worthy of the call we have received. . . .
Help the varying groups in the Church, in all their difference of opinion, to hold fast to the one faith in you, the one Lord. . . .
Be with our bishops and priests, our pastors and laity, that they might fruitfully work together in common cause for your Kingdom. . . .

For you desire to be recognized in the Church in the midst of the world, who live and reign forever and ever.

Epiphany of the Lord (January 6)

MEN BEFORE CHRIST

Introduction

Children in many parts of the world call this day "Three Kings' Day." The official liturgical designation is: Epiphany of the Lord. It is not the visitors, but the Child in the crib who is at the center of this feast day. The story of the adoration by the Wise Men ought to proclaim that the Child in the crib is Lord and Redeemer of the whole world. He is the star that shines for all people and leads them to salvation. Do I too acknowledge in him the light that brightens all human darkness? The star that lends hope and guidance in all human distress and entrapment?

Penitential Prayer

Lord Jesus Christ, splendor of the Father, prototype of creation, Son of the Virgin: Lord have mercy. . . .

Light of mankind, source of grace, way to the Father: Christ have mercy. . . .

King of the nations, King of the ages, King of glory: Our Lord, have mercy. . . .

Talk

Is the Child in the crib, is the *risen* Lord Jesus Christ light and star for me, Lord and Savior? The answer to this question is something I give

Epiphany of the Lord (January 6)   5

not in a theoretical confession of faith, but rather only my relationship to him. Am I like the scribe and high priests—or rather am I like the men from a foreign land?

Dead Knowledge of Faith. The high priests and scribes in Jerusalem were religiously interested and pious men. They occupied themselves intensely with scriptural study, prayer, and worship services. They could provide the most exact account of their creed and religious hope.

Yet their creed was only a dead letter. It did not touch them within. Their hearts did not beat to it. They taught and discussed religious questions, without keeping themselves inwardly ready for the truth that they handled. Because of this, even with all their knowledge they did not come to the recognition and acknowledgment of the Messiah.

Do we recognize the danger that threatens our faith too? Do we know only the "dry truths" of our creed in the same way that we have picked up phrases in foreign languages? Or do we live in the awareness of Jesus Christ and of his message of the Father's love? Are we only performing religion (whether as a performance of piety, like the high priests, or as a performance of theology, like the scribes), or is a genuine religious concern alive in us? Before God, theological knowledge and religious performance count for nothing. What counts before him is living concern for Christ and an aware life with him.

Openness to God. The "Wise Men from the East" remained until this time outside of Biblical revelation. They knew little about God or his covenant and his promises. Yet they were inwardly unquiet. They had longings, desires, hopes. They were searching men who made their way in interior openness.

Into this readiness for truth, the light of Christ shone. They allowed themselves in their longing to be led by the star. They sought the Messiah, the world's Salvation, and they recognized him "with exceedingly great joy." They acknowledged him by falling down in adoration, and presented him with their gifts.

All this is written "that we might know." Christ gives himself to those who seek him. When it is a matter of finding him, what counts first is not the religious tradition within which one has grown up; rather, what counts is the interior openness, the readiness to accept salvation as a gift from him. The questioning, the searching and sometimes the even desperately searching man is more surely on the way to an encounter with Christ than is the religious specialist who masters theological information without living it.

To Whom Will Christ Gift Himself? Who are we like? Who am I like? Am I content with a dead religious knowledge and a fossilized religious practice—or does the desire live in me for Jesus Christ and his salvation? He will let me find him, he can gift himself to me only if I am open to him like the "Wise Men from the East."

Petitions

Jesus Christ, eternal Son of the Father and the image of his glory, we beseech you, have mercy on us.

Lead the peoples that sit in darkness and the shadow of death to your light. . . .
Arouse in Christians the seeking and questioning faith of the "Wise Men from the East". . . .
Send us as bearers of your light into the darkness of the world. . . .

For you are the King of kings, who enlighten the whole world with your light, that all might come and adore you, who live and reign forever and ever.

St. Raymond of Peñafort (January 7)

PATRON OF CANONISTS

Introduction

"The five Commandments of the Church," the precepts for marriage in the Church and for the baptism of children . . . the Church in her sphere also has laws and regulations which the Church's members are to observe. There also certainly exists in the Church the danger that Church laws and regulations can be considered more important than the human being whom they ought to serve. In the life and work of St. Raymond, one of the greatest canonists of the Middle Ages, canon law stood completely at the service of pastoral care.

Penitential Rite

Merciful and gracious is the Lord, generous and rich in favor. Lord, have mercy. . . .

As a father cares for his children, so does the Lord care for all those who fear him: Christ, have mercy. . . .

The Lord's protection lasts always and forever upon those who fear him: Lord, have mercy. . . .

Talk

Raymond of Peñafort died in 1275 at about one hundred years of age. He lived in a new period of enlightenment in the Church. It was a time of political and spiritual tension and struggle with the world of Islam, especially in the Saint's Spanish homeland.

Years of Education and Travel. After a basic education in theology and work as a teacher in Barcelona, his home town, Raymond went at the age of 35 to Bologna, Italy, in order to begin his study of canon law. He was soon accredited as a professor of canon law.

Then in 1218 a preacher of the newly founded Dominican Order made a great impression on professors and students in Bologna. A number of university men enrolled in the community of preachers. Raymond was also impressed but did not yet enter. He first entered the diocesan priesthood in his home city. Only some years afterward did he become a member of the Dominican Order.

Pastor and Canonist. St. Dominic's intention was to found a community of priests that would bring together study and pastoral care for the salvation of the faithful. Raymond laid his expertise in canon law in the service of his order's purpose. First in Spain and then in Rome (to where he transferred his residence at the insistence of the pope), he worked as a scholar for the care of souls. He completed a compilation of the then prevailing church laws and wrote a handbook for confessors.

Missionary leanings. Raymond spent the greater part of his long life in his Spanish homeland, which was on the border between the Christian and Islamic worlds. He concerned himself intensely (relative to the prevailing standards) with the questions arising from the encounter between Christianity and Islam. In order to be armed for the intellectual struggle, he asked his confrere, St. Thomas Aquinas, to write a special theological work for the encounter with the Muslims. He took part in the establishment of an order for ransom of prisoners. He challenged his confreres to undertake missions among the Muslim population. He saw to it that the Dominicans, first in Spain and then throughout Europe, should study Arabic so as to prepare themselves for service among the Muslims.

St. Raymond of Peñrafort (January 7)

A Long Life. A lifetime of around one hundred years was granted to St. Raymond of Peñafort. At the age of 35 he began the study of canon law. He entered the Dominicans at 47. He was 63 when he became master general of his order. Well into old age he worked tirelessly as pastor, mission propagator, and canonist. What I marvel at in this saint is the intellectual agility with which he took on the current problems of the Church, and also his pastorally oriented work in canon law. If his spirit lived in our ecclesiastical authority centers and offices, then canon law would not be a danger, but rather an aid for living faith in our time.

Petitions

Lord Jesus Christ, you have said that the sabbath is for man, rather than man for the sabbath.

We pray for all who work as authorities in the Church: that they not become fixated on ecclesiastical legal demands, but that they render service to the faith of human beings. [Silence] Christ, hear us. . . . We pray for all who hold responsibility in the Church: that they may be open to the questions and needs of our times and courageously seek the right answers. [Silence] Christ, hear us.

For you came not to be served, but to serve human beings. You who live and reign forever and ever.

St. Hilary (January 13)

A BISHOP FOR THE PERIOD OF TRANSITION

Introduction

When the pressure of external persecution or suppression upon the Church is lifted, differences of opinion within the Church become especially evident. This is true in our time; it was also true after the official recognition of the Church by Emperor Constantine. The controversy over Arianism soon dominated all of Church life. In this process, Bishop Hilary of Pointiers in France played a meaningful part.

Penitential Rite

Jesus Christ, you have told us: You are the salt of the earth: Lord, have mercy. . . .

You have told us: You are the light of the world: Christ, have mercy. . . .

You have told us: The one who keeps God's command will be great in the Kingdom of Heaven: Lord, have mercy. . . .

Talk

A Singular Path to Faith. Hilary was a landowner with much property in the area of the town of Poitiers. He was intellectually inclined and taught himself in his free time. He read and studied, which

St. Hilary (January 13)

was then a modern thing to do (and yet with only costly manuscripts available). As a matter of course he read the Bible, which in those days of outreaching Christianity was among the best-sellers. He was captivated by its reading and found himself challenged by the Christian message. After long inner struggle, he contacted the small congregation in Poitiers and had himself baptized at the age of thirty.

The Call to be Bishop. After his baptism, Hilary kept his previous lifestyle as a landed nobleman. His intellectual pursuits continued apace, only now he took intensive interest in the sacred Scriptures. Then, around 350, when the city's bishop died, the people elected Hilary to be his successor. He accepted the election without great enthusiasm, but with a keen awareness of the responsibilities of the office.

Theological Controversies. In that age, the Church was rocked by the theological struggles over Arianism. The problem centered around the theological question whether Jesus Christ was really the Son of God, or whether just a singular creature of the Father. Given the existing tie of the Church to the State and to the Empire, these internal church controversies took on great political significance.

In these discussions, Hilary took clear sides with the official teaching of the Church on the sameness of the nature of the Son of God with God the Father. For his trouble, he was banished to Asia Minor. There he also, within his limited possibilities, spoke up for his theological convictions and articulated them in his books; his theological adversaries then obtained his expulsion from Asia Minor. Three years later, he was able to return to his see city. Thereafter he upheld clearly the Church's traditional teaching in France and Northern Italy.

Man of Dialogue. In these controversies, Hilary ran up against even his friends of the same opinions, since they thought him entirely too ready to compromise. In his writings, he strove to stress the common bonds of the different theological positions, rather than elabbrate on the points of division. He could say of himself, ''I have not seen it as a transgression to converse with Arians or to enter their churches." In the politics of his land's ecclesiastical controversies, he brought about the excommunication only of the two principal Arian leaders; otherwise, he used his influence to leave all other bishops of Arian persuasion in office.

"Hilarius." Hilary—the Smiling One, the Friendly One. He was called forth out of the contemplative silence of his country living and thrust into the midst of the church controversies of his day. Did he, during these exciting years as bishop, always bring honor to his own name? The bishop was able to pass the last years of his life in peace and quiet until he died in 367.

We want to ask God that, in our period of transition, he endows the Church with men and women who will go with her as leaders on the path to a new age.

Petitions

God our Father, in all ages you are near to your Church in your Son, Jesus Christ.

> Give to the Church bishops and priests who will recognize the signs of the times and will boldly show the way into the future. . . .
> Grant that theologians may discuss their disputed questions with mutual attention and respect. . . .
> Grant that the mutual understanding among Christian Churches may grow. . . .

For you are the God of Unity and not division, who live and reign forever and ever.

St. Anthony (January 17)

RADICAL CHRISTIANITY

Introduction

Christians of past times reckoned greatly with demons and devils. Sacred Scripture speaks of them (for example, in today's Gospel). In accounts of the lives of the saints, attention is often paid to their struggle with the devil and with demons (as is especially true in the case of today's saint, the monastic father Anthony). Still, the Christians of the past did not regard demons and devils as spine-tingling entertainment material (as in the recent wave of films on demons), but rather as embodiments of evil against which each Christian must conduct a life-long battle. Wherever in Christian tradition there is talk of combat with demons, there is found always a radical Christian life without compromise.

Penitential Rite

Lord Jesus Christ, you withstood evil even unto death: Lord, have mercy. . . .

You have allowed no false compromise in the struggle against evil: Christ, have mercy. . . .

You have overcome evil with good: Lord, have mercy. . . .

Talk

Legend and Reality. Who was this Anthony, hermit and father of monks, also known as "Anthony with the pig"? He lived from about 250 until 350, reaching the age of 105. His extraordinary life was embellished from the beginning with an array of legends that portray the Saint in constant battle with demons and devils.

Under the garland of legends, however, the sober facts of his life stand amazingly clear. He came from a well-to-do family in Egypt. Upon the death of his parents, he inherited the family property. He was a little over twenty years old when he heard in the liturgy once again the scriptural words: "If you want to be perfect, go, sell what you have and give the money to the poor; in so doing, you will have treasure in heaven. Then come, follow me" (Mt 19:21). This time the words so impressed him that he proceeded to secure a life income for his younger sister, divided the remaining property among the poor, and went into solitude, to follow Jesus in a totally radical way.

Radical Christianity—Then. Anthony first lived near a village. Later he withdrew progressively further into the desert. In this uncompromising life of solitude, the Saint encountered himself and the depths of his heart. He gave himself over to a life of prayer and self-mastery, so as to terminate the evil in his own heart. It is this struggle with evil that figures in the legends that speak of his struggle with demons and of his temptations. Yet this life of uncompromising battle with himself did not turn Anthony into a desert saint avoiding contact with other human beings. During times of great need in the Egyptian Church, he used to come personally to the city so as to intervene in the events of the times. Many people came out to him in the desert, so as to take counsel with him. Above all, however, large groups of religiously concerned men joined him; they were seeking from him direction for a similar uncompromising Christian life in the desert. Because of this, he is venerated as the founder of monasticism in the Church.

Radical Christianity—Today. We cannot sell our property. Nor can we withdraw into the desert. But are we as ready as Anthony to let ourselves really hear Jesus Christ and his call in our everyday life? "Today, when you hear his voice, harden not your hearts. . ." (Ps. 95:7f): this text applies to us as well.

We too stand in battle against evil. Against evil in the form of a God-opposing life on the part of many of our fellow human beings (see the Gospel). And, after the example of St. Anthony, against evil in the form of our own failings and weaknesses.

For this multifront war against evil, we also require the weaponry of God in order to endure with success (Reading).

Petitions

Almighty God, at your command we pray for all the "saints," for all people inside and outside the Church:

> For all those who struggle with evil in the form of sickness and deprivation [silence].
> For all those who seriously work within themselves and drive out the evil in their own hearts. . . .
> For all those who help their fellow humans to form their lives in responsibility before you. . . .
> For all those who, in proportion to their powers, further goodness everywhere in the world. . . .

God and Father, endow us with your power, so that we may succeed in battling against evil for goodness. You who live and reign forever and ever.

St. Fabian (January 20)

CARETAKER OF CHRISTIAN BURIAL PLACES

Introduction

Have you ever taken part in a Mass celebrated in the Roman catacombs? There we become aware, as in no other place, that we are bound mysteriously in Jesus Christ to the dead faithful of past generations. In each Mass we call to mind this communion with the dead in the commemoration of the saints. On each memorial day of a particular saint, we call this deceased Christian at once out of the darkness of the past by the special mention of his or her name [Eucharistic Prayer III], so that through him or her we might be reminded of the life-giving power of our faith.

Penitential Rite

Lord, let your mercy come over me, that I may live.
Let my heart be pure, then I shall not be confounded.
Let your kindness comfort me, as you have promised (After Ps. 199:77,80,76).

Have mercy, Lord our God, have mercy. . . .

St. Fabian (January

Talk

Daily Service in the Church. Fabian, today's saint, became bishop of Rome in 236. It was a time in which the Church lay sheltered in the midst of vehement political infighting and enjoyed relative calm. But the life of this pope ended in his execution, as Emperor Decius began afresh in 250 to persecute the Christians.

Fabian performed his service as bishop (Reading) with the basic attitude of selfless love for his congregation in the routine of daily administrative and pastoral work. A short biography can only mention that he divided the city of Rome into seven pastoral sectors and cared in a special way for Christian cemeteries.

Christian Cemeteries. Why was it a concern of the early Church that the corpses of her dead members should be lain in special burial places? What attitudes lie behind the care for our dead, as is demonstrated by the adornment of the graves?

We acknowledge in faith that our deceased have entered into a new life—and that this life with God is no longer dependent upon the subsequent fate of the body that lies in the tomb. But we thankfully remember our dead, with whom we have shared perhaps many years of our lives. Because of this, we cherish particular articles that belonged to them, since these things remind us of them. How much more will we respectfully treat their dead bodies, that belonged much more to them than material possessions!

We also see the truth in the proverb: "Out of sight, out of mind." On that account we prepare a special grave for our deceased, when we give their bodies "over to the earth" (whether by burial or by cremation). We thus care for their graves and visit them repeatedly; the graves help us, as visible signs, not to forget our dead.

In the catacombs we can even today see the symbols with which the early Christians decorated their graves, with the purpose of giving witness to their faith in the Resurrection (a fish, an oil lamp, a dove . . .).

We now place a cross on the grave or else inscribe a text from Scripture, so as to testify to our faith in eternal life, given to us in Jesus Christ.

Christian Graves. Catholics and Protestants in many places have their own denominational cemeteries. In most cities there are also cemeteries that belong to the municipality. In these civil cemeteries we are, of course, along with our dead, as near to God as in and by a grave "in consecrated ground"—that is, a specially blessed Christian "God's acre." Yet we are especially called upon, through the style of tomb decoration and the care of the grave, to give witness of how strongly we are aware of the bond with our dead beyond all human recall in faith in Jesus Christ and in the resurrection of the dead.

Remembrance of the Dead in the Eucharistic Celebration. As Christians—similar to Pope Fabian in his time—we care for our Christian graves. We do so not merely to keep the memory of our loved ones alive. We believe that they live with us in Jesus Christ. We know, therefore, that in every Eucharistic celebration we are united not only with the saints, but with all "our departed brothers and sisters, and all who have left this world in your friendship" [Eucharistic Prayer III].

Petitions

> Lord Jesus Christ, in you we know we are united with our dead:
>
> Accept their lives, filled with joy and pain, greatness and weakness. . . .
> Give to our deceased relatives and friends completion with the Father. . . .
> Reward them for the good that they have done for us and for other human beings.

For you are the Resurrection and the Life forever.

St. Sebastian (January 20)

A SOLDIER AS PATRON SAINT

Introduction

Sebastian: How many churches bear his name! How often do we see his statue (portraying him tied to a column or a tree and pierced with arrows) in churches and chapels! How many fraternal organizations have him as their patron!

A soldier as protector and patron saint? Let us not be distracted by this combination. Earlier ages have understood Sebastian not in the first place as a professional soldier, but rather as a Christian who stood by his faith with all the consequences.

Penitential Rite

"Have no fear and be not perplexed." [Silence] Lord, have mercy. . . .

"Keep Christ the Lord holy in your hearts." [Silence] Christ, have mercy. . . .

"Lead a righteous life with Christ in the community." [Silence] Lord, have mercy. . . .

Talk

Sebastian ranks among the many popular saints about whose lives we know nothing exact. According to the legend, the Milanese was an officer in the imperial bodyguard. Under Emperor Diocletian, he was condemned to death by arrows around 303 on account of his Christian faith. Left for dead, he made a recovery, and rebuked the Emperor for his cruelty. Thereafter he is supposed to have been beaten to death.

The majority of us will never have to give witness to our faith through a bloody martyrdom. Yet we should all be witnesses ("martyrs") to Jesus Christ in our time. We should confess our faith before other human beings in a way as free of compromise as that of Sebastian [Gospel]. We can learn from the Reading how Christian witness should appear in our world.

"Be not Afraid." The Christian makes an impression upon his critical or aggressively questioning contemporaries, only if he meets them without anxiety, with trust in Jesus Christ. As Christians, we have something to offer even to people of our time, something that can be discerned: the Good News that each human being is very personally affirmed and loved by God, that God is steadfast in his love for us, even if we have failed and stand before the shambles of our lives, that God is preparing for us a future that reaches beyond death.

The healthy Christian self-awareness does not have to suffer shock when we find out that we are not greeted everywhere with open arms on account of our faith-convictions. Contradictions belong to the experience of Christian witnessing, as can be seen in today's Reading. We should not be surprised if people sneer at us or aggressively try to shut us up!

"Lead a Righteous Life." A convincing Christian life must arrive at an inner security in faith. The Christian impresses his contemporaries with his faith only when he or she is truly a lovable person, one to be taken seriously. Gloomy fanatics and weird eccentrics can hardly create enthusiasm for their belief. Only a Christian who responsibly shapes his life in his family and vocation, in Church and community, who in addition radiates goodness and friendliness, can bring others to a deeper reflection on the Good News. If, then, true joy in faith can be

St. Sebastian (January 20)

detected in one's life, he has an attracting and inviting effect on a questioning and seeking people.

"Speak Modestly and Respectfully." Moreover, nowadays, there is even greater need that the Christian be able to give an account of his faith. The "martyr" (witness) of Christ needs in our times a basic knowledge of his faith in order to be able to offer discussion and answers to inquiring people. This necessitates an effort for continuing religious education.

This brings us to the matter of appropriate tone in contacts with critical contemporaries. According to the Reading, we should "answer modestly and respectfully": which means, we should keep our own security in faith while taking the partners in dialog seriously in their varying points of view, and respecting their convictions. It also means that we should allow our own joy in faith to be seen, and conduct discussion and argument in a reasoning way.

Is not a "martyrdom" of this kind—namely, witnessing to the faith—something convincing even today for Jesus Christ and his message?

Petitions

Lord Jesus Christ, you have handed on to your Church the proclaiming of the Good News even in our time.

Grant joy in faith to all believers. . . .
Help them to give witness through their lives to your Good News. . . .
Grant them your Holy Spirit, that they might find the right word in discussions on faith. . . .

For you acknowledge before the Father only those who acknowledge you before men. You who live and reign forever and ever.

St. Agnes (January 21)

RISKING EVERYTHING FOR THE SAKE OF THE KINGDOM

Introduction

Historians cannot provide us with any precise information on the virgin and martyr Agnes. All that is certain is that a saint of this name was venerated in Rome after the fourth century. The name became accepted into the Roman Canon, and the cult of this legendary saint became widespread. The absence of historically authentic details need not bother the current holders of the name. They can learn quite well from the legend (and from many bearers of the name over the course of history) that Christian life is only possible if one risks all that he has [Gospel].

Penitential Rite

"Listen, my people, I am speaking; I, God, your God. Invoke me in your troubles and I will rescue you, and you shall honor me" (Ps. 50:7,15).

Have mercy, Lord our God, have mercy.

Talk

The Legend. Agnes "is said" (as already Pope Damasus, at the end of the fourth century, cautiously worded it) to have come from an eminent family; further, she is supposed to have died for her faith at the age of thirteen during the persecution by Diocletian, around 304–305. The various legendary traditions do not agree as to whether she perished at the stake or by the sword.

All in all, the pious tradition portrays in Agnes a human being who found Jesus Christ through faith and, filled with the joy that springs from faith, regarded everything else—a pleasant life, the bonds with relatives and friends, life itself—as nonessential.

Other Saints of This Name. The Church's calendar of saints (which is more extensive than the liturgical calendar) lists three more saints of this name: Agnes of Bohemia (died 1282); Agnes of Montepulciano (died 1317); and Agnes of Assisi (a sister of St. Clare). All three were nuns and were contemporaries of St. Francis and St. Dominic. They found in their time, in line with today's Gospel, "the treasure in the field" and gave everything to obtain that treasure.

All these saintly personalities ask us today whether we have a similar experience in our own lives.

Seek and Find the Pearl. Jesus Christ, the precious pearl, the treasure in the field. . . . We can discover him as the most precious thing in our lives if we are seeking him. A deeper relationship with Jesus Christ grows only where we are interiorly restless, where we raise questions and seek an answer, where we extend ourselves to him in prayer, in personal reflection, and in the shaping of our lives.

In a conscious religious life, then, we have our "experiences" through faith. And perhaps one fine day we feel how Jesus Christ influences our whole life, how we cannot imagine our life without him, how deep a joy we feel over the gift of faith.

To Go Forth and Tell All, Full of Joy. Yes, how is it with us regarding this joy in faith? Is our religion only a burden that we cheerlessly bear? A duty that we complainingly fulfill? A tradition, to which we remain unthinkingly true, without being inwardly moved by it?

True enough, joy in faith is not something that one can command oneself to feel. It is a gift. Yet perhaps we ought to prepare ourselves for this gift. To this end, we can very consciously peel apart false images of God (God, the threatening judge . . .), and allow sacred Scripture to expressly tell us what he really is (he has stored the pearl and the treasure in the field for us; he chooses the small, the weak, and the humble; he is always ready to forgive, even when we have disappointed him . . .). It may happen that, in encountering him (in personal prayer, in communal worship, in dedication to his work in our day . . .), joy in our communion with Jesus Christ can grow. It can bring us to the idea of risking everything, even the course and direction of our lives, for our faith.

Petitions

We pray to God who through grace gives men and women the courage to risk all for the sake of the Kingdom:

For the young people in our Church communities . . . Lord, have mercy. . . .
For all who campaign for social justice for the sake of Christ. . . .
For all who are burdened with doubts and difficulties of faith. . . .

God and Father, let everyone find the treasure in the field and go forth full of joy to win it. You who live and reign forever and ever.

St. Vincent (January 22)

"HUNTED, YET NOT OVERTAKEN"

Introduction

In the prayer following the Our Father, we say: "Deliver us, Lord, from any evil, and grant us peace in our day." Is this a realistic Christian prayer, given the many martyrs found in our calendar of saints? Given the contrary accounts of events in the New Testament? Given the teachings that we must draw from a nearly two thousand year history of Christianity?

Penitential Rite

Lord Jesus Christ, we long for quiet and security—and you have predicted hard trials for us for the sake of our faith: Lord, have mercy. . . .

We are fearful of unrest and insecurity—and we forget that you are our strength: Christ, have mercy. . . .

We are ashamed to give witness to you—and we do not really trust that God's Spirit will speak in us: Lord, have mercy. . . .

Talk

Understandable Expectations. Always and everywhere, people are seeking a "quiet little place": clarity and security in personal and public life; understandable and unassailed faith in the religious sphere; a Church that is stable, and that goes forth, by human standards, with a steady pace on the way into the future.

Contrary Experiences. But life is otherwise. Political developments or economic crises suddenly darken our view of the future. Sickness or a grave disappointment unexpectedly burden our personal way through life. Our quiet certainty in faith can be placed into question by an encounter with unbelievers or by a religion program on television, or the joy of faith can flee because of all the little irritations in one's own parish community. In many countries, money is lacking for the Church's planning for the future, and in other countries there is a lack of needed priestly vocations.

"See, I Have Told You All These Things Beforehand."
This discrepancy between our (often unexpressed) expectations and the hard realities of life makes us pause. Yet can we as Christians be surprised by these experiences of insecurity, opposition, and difficulties?

Can you recall now about which life experiences Paul was speaking about in today's Reading? For which Jesus prepared his disciples in today's Gospel? (Note: perhaps some verses could be repeated here.)

Every memorial day of a martyr (today is the memorial of the early Christian deacon Vincent, who died for the faith in 304 in Spain) reminds us that the Church always "bears the mortal sufferings of Jesus in her body" [Reading] and stands everywhere in the imitation of the Crucified.

Yes, in each Eucharist we encounter the Risen One, who bears the wounds of the Crucifixion. At the end of the Mass we always make the Sign of the Cross, in order to remind ourselves that, in our everyday Christian living, we have to live not in some quiet little place, but rather in a world full of trials and burdens.

In the Power of Christ. We must, as Christians, deal soberly with the reality of insecurity and danger to our personal lives, and to the work of the Church. We take on these frequently discouraging experi-

St. Vincent (January 22)

ences not trusting in our own strength (our "good nerves," our "broad shoulders," or our "thick skin"). We believe that the "abundance of power" that we need—lest we despair—"comes from God" [Reading] who must "strengthen our backs" (and our nerves).

And we believe that the Risen One meets with us in this holy meal under the sign of bread. In it he signifies to us in a mysterious and sacramental way that he is the power of our Christian life, that protects us from going to ruin under the burdens of our life.

In this sacramental encounter with Jesus Christ, let us be reminded by the memorial of the holy martyr Vincent that insecurity, peril, and even persecution and death are part of Christian life. Let us, however, say of the Risen One that he stays by us in this life. And let us pray to him (by adapting the prayer after the Our Father): Lord, if you do not yet deliver us from every evil and protect us from all anxiety, then at least do not let us lose courage in all assaults upon our life and our faith.

Petitions

God, you let the Church share in the passion of your Son:

Strengthen our brothers and sisters, who are persecuted on account of their faith. . . .
Give them the strength to preserve their faith even under oppression. . . .
Let us recognize the cross in all the insecurity and burdens of our life, which cross we should bear along with your Son. . . .

You who live and reign forever and ever.

St. Francis de Sales (January 24)

CHRISTIAN LIFE IN THE MIDST OF THE WORLD

Introduction

We have all asked ourselves at one time or another: how can we lead a more intensive religious life amid the demands and burdens of our daily life (in marriage and family, in society and work)? Is it at all possible? Or is a deeper life in communion with Jesus Christ something only for specially select people, perhaps for monks and nuns, who are not under the stress of life's daily struggles?

Religiously concerned Christians queried and complained about this even four hundred years ago. St. Francis de Sales, whose memorial we celebrate today, strove to give them an answer. His answer can be of further help to us.

Penitential Rite

"God, you are my God, I will trust in you. You will stand by me, you are my refuge. I will not fear you, for you are not only beside me, you are also within me, and I am in you" (Francis de Sales).

Have mercy, Lord our God, have mercy. . . .

St. Francis de Sales (January 24)

Talk

The Saint's Life. Francis de Sales was born in 1567, the child of noble parents in the area of the French-Swiss border. After studying law in various universities of France and Italy, he decided to become a priest at the age of 25. After his priestly ordination, he worked with great eagerness and success among the Calvinist population of his native region. He became bishop of Geneva in 1602 and labored untiringly in his diocese until his death in 1622.

The saint became a towering figure in the religious life of his time, because he extended himself to lead individual Christians—in a time-consuming one-on-one ministry—beyond all superficiality and mere religious performance into a deeper life in faith. He thus set a religious tone that in his time was not always understood. Even today it can bestir us to make corrections in our own religious life.

Joyful Love of God. Francis de Sales went through a deep religious crisis in his youth. He nearly died out of fear of a God who had, he was convinced, predetermined him to everlasting damnation. Yet he finally grasped that God loves human beings beyond all understanding. He found in Jesus Christ the one who gives his life for his friends [Gospel] and in whom we have trustworthy access to God [Reading]. This realization gave his religious life a positive basis, that a theologian of our time has summarized in the book title, "Joyful Love of God." Francis de Sales loved God from out of this joy and spread it among the people of his time in numerous pastoral letters.

On what basis is our religious life formed? On fear, or on an anxiety-ridden fulfillment of duty, or on joy in God and the grateful acceptance of his call?

Christian Life in the World. In the saint's day there existed a strong religious concern in France, above all among men and women of the higher social classes. Many sought direction whereby they could live out their faith in all their duties in family, society, vocation, and politics. The Bishop of Geneva offered them this direction.

He realized that the laity had to put their Christian living into effect in the world. He did not demand that they differentiate themselves in their outward lifestyle from their more shallow contemporaries. But he did stress in his pastoral letters that they should strive to ingrain interior attitudes in accordance with the demands of the Gospel. He emphasized primarily the virtues of goodness, friendliness, readiness to help, and fulfillment of duty.

The saint was of the firm conviction that a deeper life stemming from communion with Jesus Christ is possible only if a Christian, amid all the demands of his daily life, regularly takes time for reflection and prayer. One must also, he believed, give regular participation in Mass and in the sacrament of penance a solid place in one's life.

You, dear Christians, in the midst of your obligations to family and work, must always strive to become ever more like Jesus Christ. You cannot step away from everyday stress. Yet Francis de Sales makes even you aware that becoming like Christ is not possible without a minimum of religious reflection and regular prayer. Is there a good habit of prayer in your life? Have you learned from experience at what times in the course of the day you can best be still and personally can pray (whether at home or in a visit to church)? Is there in your life a regular sharing in the mass, including occasionally on weekdays? Do you examine your conscience regularly, and do you make over and over a renewed effort toward conversion in penitential services and in the sacrament of penance? A "Christian life in the midst of the world" is only possible if one bestires oneself to prayer and religious reflection without exaggerations and false accents.

Conversion of the Apostle Paul (January 25)

THREEFOLD CONVERSION

Introduction

Paul came to faith in Jesus Christ only in adulthood (as did most members of the early Church). His conversion must have been of great meaning for the young Church. The Acts of the Apostles recount this conversion event a total of three times (Acts 9:1–13;22:1–21;26:1–23).

Penitential Rite

Lord Jesus Christ, you call us to conversion in communion with you: Lord, have mercy. . . .
It is your will that we follow you in the community of the Church: Christ, have mercy. . . .

Talk

Saul is a pious and fervent Jew. He seeks to take Yahweh and his demands in all seriousness. Then Jesus reaches out to this religious zealot before the gates of Damascus. This encounter with the Risen One throws him off his track and gives a new direction to his life. Where does this change from Saul to Paul precisely occur?

Conversion to the Risen One. In his zeal for the traditional Jewish faith, Saul had to deal every day with convinced Christians. But, according to the version in Acts, he finds his way to faith only in the direct encounter with the Risen One. At the same time he understands that Jesus Christ is the mysterious center of the Church. Thus, from the moment of his conversion onward, he wants to know only Jesus Christ. Therefore he can call the Church the "mystical body of Christ" in his later writings.

We are not really Christians in a full sense if we take part in parish life only because we have good friends there or because it is a fine communications center for us. All of that should not be undervalued. But we first learn what it means to be a Christian when we realize that in Church we seek Jesus Christ first—when we come before the Risen One in all common prayer and worship and are touched by him. Do we know, along with Paul, that the Church is the "mystical body of Christ"? Can we say with Paul that, for us, "Christ is all in everything"?

Conversion to the Community. True, Saul—become—Paul is directed by the angel of God toward the community of believers. Paul, following his conversion, is not to labor as a "lone warrior." He is to join the community and proclaim the Good News in the communion of the Church. Paul seeks contact with the Church—even if some meet him at first with mistrust and reserve—because he knows that no one can exist as a Christian without the help and support of fellow believers.

For us too, "no man is an island" in faith. We stand with our Christian life upon the shoulders of our parents and relatives, of our religion teachers and pastors, upon the shoulders of the entire parish community, within which we received our religious upbringing in childhood. In our own time, we see daily how we can as adult Christians rely upon the support of fellow believers. Here and there we also notice that others need our witness of faith in order to persevere as Christians. Whence the question: do we live out our faith in Jesus Christ consciously enough within the communion of the Church? Is the life of the parish community our concern?

Conversion to Witnessing the Faith. In the three areas of Paul's conversion, it is emphasized that he is called by Jesus Christ to announce the Good News to all people. He is to cooperate in the basic task of the Church: to bring the message of Jesus Christ to the ends of the earth. Paul fulfilled this task so well that he is named the greatest missioner of all time.

And we? "Whatever abounds in the heart pours forth from the mouth," says a proverb. "How can one be a 'convert' if he does not preach on what his conviction is?" This fair question is asked by many free (evangelical) Protestant Churches. We are converted in the full sense only if we try to win others for Jesus Christ.

Petitions

Lord Jesus Christ, innermost mystery of the Church, hear our prayer.

We pray for all who persecute the Church.   [Silence]
We pray for all who have just recently found you and who now seek a place in our parishes.   [Silence]
We pray for all who bravely witness to their faith in our world.   [Silence]

For you are with us in the communion of the Church on our road through time. You who live and reign forever and ever.

Sts. Timothy and Titus (January 26)

PAUL'S CO-WORKERS

Introduction

"The young Alexander conquered India. All by himself? Caesar defeated the Gauls. Didn't he at least bring a cook along?" With this witty remark, Bertolt Brecht reminds us that the great people of history have always accomplished their deeds of renown in cooperation with many unknown collaborators. Similarly, Paul could only have performed his farflung missionary activity with the help of many co-workers. In their ranks Timothy and Titus hold a special place.

Penitential Rite

"Enkindle further the grace of God that is in you."   [Silence] Lord, have mercy. . . .

"God has given us the Spirit of power, of love, and of prudence."
    [Silence]   Christ, have mercy. . . .
"Do not be ashamed to confess the Lord."   [Silence]   Lord, have mercy . . . (after 2 Tim 1:6–8

Talk

Sparse Biographical Data. Timothy was the child of a mixed pagan-Jewish marriage in Lystra, Asia Minor (Acts 16:1–3). Paul took him as companion and aide on his missionary journeys and mentioned him often in his letters (1 Thess 1:1; 2 Cor 1:1 . . .). Upon assignment by the Apostle, he traveled alone to Thessalonica, Corinth, and Philippi. Along with Paul he carried the collection from the Pauline communities to Jerusalem (Acts 20:4).

Titus was a pagan Christian. He accompanied Paul to the Apostolic Council in Jerusalem (Gal 2:1)—and the Apostle refused to allow his coworker to be circumcised for the sake of false consideration for conservative Jewish Christians. He was known to the Corinth community as helper and confidant of their church's founder.

Addressees of Three New Testament Letters. Moreover, three New Testament letters bear their names, which appear as letters from Paul the Apostle. According to them, Timothy is bishop of Ephesus and Titus has the leadership of the communities of Crete. The letters intend to provide direction to both in the fulfillment of their pastoral responsibility (and are thus called "the Pastoral Letters"). They call them to faithfulness to the faith handed on to them, and to combat against threatening false teachings; they also take a position on concrete questions of community order.

"Pseudo Epigraphs." Perhaps you were surprised as I just said that both Letters to Timothy and the Letter to Titus were not written by Paul himself. Don't the introductory verses in the Second Letter to Timothy, in today's Reading, sound authentic?

True, they do. But that does not alter the fact that the author(s), following a widespread custom of that time, entered to some extent into the role of the famous (and already dead) Apostle Paul, in order to lend greater strength to their writings. And they took—still in accord with the widespread custom of their time—the two renowned disciples of Paul, Timothy and Titus (who perhaps were also no longer alive) as the specific addressees of their letters; they were understood as admonitions to all the Christian communities that existed in their region around the year 100. Moreover, their contemporaries knew of these "tricks" and did not take this literary device to be a fraud.

"What Is Left of Sacred Scripture?" What I have here outlined perhaps does not correspond to our image of the origin of the New Testament. Some people may be confused and wonder, "What are we to think of these falsifications?"

Now, only the name of the authors and the recipients of the letters are "falsified." The letters themselves (even if their author writes "under a false name") are witnesses of the problems and difficulties of the faith-life in the young Church around 100. And the Church guarantees that, as parts of the New Testament, they arose under the particular presence of the Holy Spirit. For that reason, they provide us (with all their time-bound conditioning—as is the case of all the books in the Bible) with indications for the present-day shaping of Christian community life.

Finally, tbe "recipients" of these letters make it obvious that Timothy and Titus, Paul's disciples, stood in the high regard of the early Church as followers of their master.

Petitions

Lord Jesus Christ, Head of your Church: we pray to you for our bishop_____and all bishops:

Give them the fullness of your grace. . . .
Give them an eye open to everything that especially affects and burdens their fellow Christians. . . .

Let them understand the signs of the signs of the times and go forth courageously with the Church on the road into the future. . . .

For you yourself lead your Church in the Holy Spirit through the pope and the bishops. You who live and reign forever and ever.

St. Angela Merici (January 27)

FAR AHEAD OF HER TIME

Introduction

Nuns dressing out of habit and living in open contact with other people: we have gradually adjusted ourselves to this in the postconciliar time. Still, for us it was a great innovation. Yet St. Angela Merici accomplished the very same thing: She lived 400 years ago and founded the community of Ursulines.

Penitential Rite

Lord Jesus Christ, we ought to live prudently and soberly—and yet we let ourselves repeatedly be carried away by our moods: Lord, have mercy. . . .

We ought to hold fast to love—and yet we hold ourselves to be more important than our fellow human beings: Christ, have mercy. . . .

We ought to serve one another and yet we prefer to be served: Lord, have mercy. . . .

Talk

Slow Discovery of a Vocation. Angela grew up as an orphan with her relatives. In her young years she once ran away, with the desire to become a hermit. Her uncle, however, brought her back and, as the least she could do, she joined the Third Order of St. Francis. At an age—when Angela was 22—in which other young girls of her times had either already entered the convent or were preparing their weddings, she noticed that many children of ordinary people grew up without religious instruction. Together with some friends, she began to gather neighborhood girls and provide them with regular and systematic religious instruction.

Soon people from the nearby city of Brescia began to notice her and to ask her to move there and to work in that city. In this way she found the place where her work could develop.

Total Education. Angela and her companions at first worked—using our terms—as catechists and parish helpers. They gave religious instruction, visited homes, and cared for the elderly and the sick in their houses. Yet the saint's scope grew wider and wider. She sought the total education of young girls, within the limits of her era. She thought in this connection primarily of poor girls.

"Cloister in the World." With these goals, Angela did not found an actual convent. She did bind her helpers together in a religious community and also gave them a rule. However, only twelve of them formed a residential community with her, while the majority remained with their families and taught the children of the poor there.

In all of this, the saint was far ahead of her time. The bishop of Verona did approve her rule and thus confirmed this uncustomary life-style for religious women. As long as Angela lived, her sisters could live and work as it seemed fit to them. However, soon after her death, the Ursulines, in order to avoid the threat of disbandment, had to submit to the laws of general Church law, had to wear a habit, and had to close themselves off in a cloister. They could no longer visit people in their houses and give religious instruction there. They had to build their own schools and boarding facilities for girls. In order to maintain them, they had to collect tuition, and thus could only accept children of moneyed families. So the Ursulines became—quite contrary to St. Angela's original intention—

the religious community living in cloister and running schools for privileged girls in appropriate residences.

Renewal According to the Saint's Mind. The saint had given to her sisters during her lifetime the command "to adapt yourselves to the times at hand, even if it means changing the rule." Along with all other religious communities, the Ursulines today are thinking upon the original idea of their foundress: cooperation in pastoral work, education and training ministry for the children of the lower classes. They are working to modify their lifestyle in line with their beginnings. Let us ask God that, through the intercession of St. Angela, he might help her sisters and all religious communities to recognize the needs of our times and to meet these needs with action.

Petitions

Lord Jesus Christ, You have a heart open to children.

Give goodness and understanding to all who work in the education of children and young people. . . .
Let us find the right ways in the Church to announce the Good News convincingly to today's youth. . . .
Lead those religious communities that work in education in their current renewal through your Holy Spirit. . . .

For you have given your Church the task to proclaim the Gospel to each new generation. You who live and reign forever and ever.

St. Thomas Aquinas (January 28)

"KNEELING THEOLOGY"

Introduction

Thomas Aquinas—the great medieval theologian. We know that he would always go before a cross or a tabernacle at the beginning of study, and would pray for enlightenment. In the face of death he uttered this prayer: "For love of you I have studied, stayed awake nights, and made great efforts. I have preached you and taught about you. Never have I spoken anything against you. I do not cling stubbornly to my opinions, but subject them to the judgment of the Holy Roman Church . . . ." In this prayer there speaks a pious and humble theologian, who sought his whole life long to penetrate the mystery of God and to take life from this mystery.

Penitential Prayer

"Give me, Lord, a watchful heart, that no trivial thought distracts from you; a noble heart, that no unworthy passion debases; a true and upright heart, that no lowly endeavor can lead only false paths; a strong heart, that no distress breaks, a free heart, that lets itself be overcome by no evil power" (Thomas Aquinas: cf. GL 7,6).

Have mercy, Lord our God, have mercy. . . .

Talk

Adventurous Way into the Cloister. At age 14, Thomas Aquinas (1226–1274) was sent to Naples for studies. There he came to know the growing Dominican Order and joined it, in opposition to his family. On the way to Paris (where he was to continue his theological studies) he was kidnapped by his brothers. They imprisoned him in the family castle so as to draw him away from his cloister thoughts. With the help of his Dominican brethren, he was able to escape. Accompanied by the general of the order, he undertook the journey to Paris with no trouble. He became a disciple of St. Albert the Great and completed his training in Cologne.

The Great Theologian. Thomas grasped the work of his great teacher and tried, with the help of Greek philosophy newly discovered in Europe, to lead his contemporaries to a deeper understanding of the mysteries of salvation. His great theological works became the foundation of theology for centuries. His manner and system of thinking (one talks of ''Scholastic theology'') became exemplary for many generations of theologians.

Thomas did not withdraw into a quiet scholar's cell. He lived in the thick of church life in his time. He represented the concerns of the Roman Church in several councils, wherein reunion with the Eastern Church was considered. He became prefect of studies for his order and wrote his great work *Summa contra gentiles* for his Spanish confreres, who sought dialogue with the Muslims.

The Great Man of Prayers. On all pressing academic and church tasks, Thomas remained true to the motto of his order: *Contemplata aliis tradere*—bring what one has gained in prayer to others. He is the great man of prayer from whom a whole series of beautiful prayers have come (as seen in various texts of this type).

The great theologian was a man of his time in his prayer: This is clear in his eucharistic piety. During his lifetime, the devotion to the Eucharist through the celebration of the Mass became widespread. He received the commission to compose texts for the newly introduced Feast of Corpus Christi. The most beautiful eucharistic hymns that he wrote are still to be found in hymnals today: "Tantum ergo" (GL 541–44), "Adoro te" (GL 546), "Your Savior, Your Master" (GL Appendix and no. 545). In the following antiphon for Corpus Christi he concisely summarized the mystery of the Eucharist: "O sacred banquet: in which Christ is consumed, in which we celebrate the memorial of his passion, our hearts are filled with grace, and we receive the pledge of our future glory" (GL 372,1; cf. also GL 374,5).

Thus did Thomas Aquinas as a praying theologian give witness to Jesus Christ through his teaching and life. Let us pray with his words for the theologians of our time, so that they can render the same service to our generation.

Petitions

Creator of the universe, true Font of light and wisdom, exalted Origin of all being: we pray to you for all those who seek to bring your Good News closer to people today:

Give them discernment for understanding and good memory for retention. . . .
Give them refinement and accuracy in discourse. . . .
Give them fullness and grace—fullness in their expression. . . .

Teach the beginning, lead the continuation, help toward the completion, through Christ, our Lord (from Thomas Aquinas).

St. John Bosco (January 31)

A SAINT'S EDUCATIONAL WISDOM

Introduction

Who today does not have difficulties with his or her growing children or grandchildren? Even experts with all their well-intentioned and soundly based advice in the press and on television very often evidently end up intellectualizing the problems. Perhaps John Bosco, the great educator of youth, today's saint, can give us encouragement once again not to give up despite the difficulties.

Ask yourself at the beginning of our common worship, when was the last time you had a quarrel with your own children or grandchildren. But also ask yourself honestly: what did I do wrong there?

Penitential Rite

"Be mindful of that which is true, noble and right." [Silence] Lord, have mercy. . . .

"Be mindful of what is pure, lovable, and proper." [Silence] Christ, have mercy. . . .

"Be mindful of everything that is virtuous and praiseworthy." [Silence] Lord, have mercy. . . .

Talk

John Bosco was born in 1815 in a northern Italian village. He grew up with practically no school education and entered later on the road to the priesthood against many obstacles. Soon after his priestly ordination he went to Turin, and found his life's work among the youth of that industrial city, abandoned to themselves and left uncared for.

Don Bosco—as everyone called him—acted for the benefit of these orphaned, wandering, and partly asocial youths. In doing so, he took new and uncustomary ways. He worked to give young people enjoyment through sports and games. He also set up homes for them, in which they were provided with a useful academic and trade education. He prayed with them as well and led them into a living religious life.

The saint ran into misunderstanding and resistance in "respectable" circles, including the Church. People shook their heads over him and tried to block him in his work. Nonetheless, Don Bosco followed through with great success. The number of youths grew. Many co-workers joined him. Most of the young people who grew up and were educated in his homes found a stable place in life. When he died in 1888, his collaborators were taking care of around 130,000 youngsters in 250 homes.

The Secret of His Success. What is the secret of this educational success? Much of the educational style of Don Bosco is historically conditioned and is not necessarily applicable to our situation. But his basic attitude toward young people is even today the foundation for any fruitful educational endeavor. The saint once expressed this attitude in this way: "Love and kindness . . . should lead me in all things." One of his biographers summarizes this educational wisdom as follows: "Trust the youngster, even when he does not deserve it, and then you make him trustworthy. And even when he is not lovable, love him and demonstrate this love to him, and then he will be lovable."

Patient Love. You, dear parents and grandparents, know how necessary this attitude is in dealing with young people. Yet you also know better than I how hard it is in everyday family life not to "lose your cool" and not to grow tired of trying. Which will work better over the long run: resignation, irritation, and endless scolding, or another try every time to deal with it all as Don Bosco did ("Love and kindness should lead me in everything")? Going further, contemporary educational work certainly demands a patience that comes from the conviction that even in one's own children every good word and every selfless deed somehow brings forth its hundredfold harvest.

Petitions

Lord, Heavenly Father:

Let young people find their way to a living faith amid the welter of opinions. . .
Let all downhearted, desparing, and dislocated youths find good people who will help them. . .
Give parents and educators love, understanding, and patience for young people. . .
Be close to parents who suffer because their children have lost the bond with the faith and the Church. . . .

Lord, send us all the Spirit of your patient love, which you have revealed in your Son, Jesus Christ. You, who live and reign forever and ever.

Presentation of the Lord (February 2)

JESUS CHRIST—LIGHT LIKE THE LIGHT OF A CANDLE

(N.B.: For the Introduction, the text provided in the Missal is to be used. The Penitential Rite is omitted if the liturgical celebration begins with the Blessing of Candles.)

Talk

The Symbol of a Candle. Candles are central to today's celebration. You have lit them at the beginning of the liturgy. They were blessed. We have heard God's Word with burning candles in our hands. They have made us aware of him who according to the Gospel is a "light that shines on the nations."

True, there are different kinds of lights. Let us today make clear through the *light symbol of the candle* that Jesus Christ is the *light* of the whole world (cf. John 8:12) and that we should all be the light of the world (cf. Matthew 5:14).

Jesus Christ—Light Like the Light of a Candle. Have you ever sat in complete darkness? Then you have experienced how we human beings find darkness to be dangerous and threatening, and how we feel insecure and abandoned. From this experience you can perhaps grasp that, in the Bible, the external darkness is a symbol of a much deeper peril and threat to men and women, namely, the threat of death and sin. That is the real darkness which imprisons man (cf. Matthew 4:16).

Have you ever noticed how everything changes if light shines in extreme darkness? The feelings of insecurity and anxiety go away. We take a deep breath and renew our courage. In the same way, a light in Jesus Christ shines on us in our deeper darkness (cf. Matthew 4:16). Wherever he becomes meaningful for our life, there we lose the anxiety and insecurity, we breathe again in deeper awareness, and we take on new courage.

The *light of a candle* is different from that of a neon tube and from that of an automobile headlight. We try to hide ourselves from the glare of an auto headlight. A neon light is cold and impersonal. But the light of a candle spreads warmth and coziness. A person feels more welcome and understood where there is a candle burning than around a neon light. In the area of a candle one can speak more easily on a personal matter because one feels somehow "at home." Jesus Christ will not act upon us like the glaring beam of a headlight or like the cold brightness of a neon light. He will shine into our lives like the light of a candle. With him we are cherished and welcome. He understands us, with him we are at home, with him we can talk about everything that bothers us.

The candle spreads its light freely, *providing that it consumes itself.* It is light and warmth, it creates an atmosphere of protection, providing that it sacrifices itself. Jesus Christ became for us the Light of the World according to the law of the candle. He expended himself for us his whole life long and sacrificed his life for us totally in death. Only with this price does he bring brightness and warmth, encouragement and joy into our lives.

We Light up Like the Light of a Candle.

The light of a candle is *living light.* It consumes everything flammable that comes into its reach. It wants to pass the flame along so that the light might be spread. Jesus Christ wants to pass on his light to us Christians, so that *we might be light for the world in accordance with his command and example.*

Wherever we find people in the darkness of their lives (in sickness and pain, in embitterment and disappointment), light should come into their lives through us. Their anxiety ought to diminish, and renewed courage for living should waken within them.

We should not shine into their lives like the pitiless light of an automobile headlight or the uncaring brightness of a neon light. We should be like the light of a candle for them. Everyone near us should feel "at home." Each one should feel accepted and understood. Each one should be able to speak out even on personal matters and difficulties.

Of course, we become this kind of light for our surroundings only by following the law of the candle. It requires our time, strength, and energy if we want to bring the love of Christ into the lives of other people, if we want to give proof through our lives of God's kindness and love for human beings.

Light—like the light of a candle! The candle in our hands is a symbol of Christ, *the Light* of the world. It is, at the same time, a sign *of our task to be the light of the world.* We take it home with us as a continual reminder of our responsibilities in life.

Petitions

Lord Jesus Christ, you have made our lives bright through your Incarnation, your life, your death, and your Resurrection:

Send us forth as bearers of your light into the world. . . .
Give heart through us to the downhearted and to the despondent. . . .
Rescue human beings through us from the darkness of hate and discord. . . .

Lord, give us the strength to be your light in this world. You who live and reign forever and ever.

St. Ansgar (February 3)

THE APOSTLE OF NORTHERN EUROPE

Introduction

There are today in Northern Europe (Denmark, Norway, Sweden, Finland, Iceland) only small Catholic congregations. We easily forget that these countries have been Christian for centuries. Missionary activity began in them shortly after the death of Charlemagne in the ninth century, starting in Germany. It is evident that politics played a large role in these first mission efforts. Yet in the end there were men of the Church who consolidated the implanting of the faith over and above any "political conversion." St. Ansgar belonged to the pioneer ranks of missioners in Northern Europe.

Penitential Rite

Lord Jesus Christ, you brought us the Good News: Lord, have mercy. . . .

You have called us to conversion: Christ, have mercy. . . .

You call all men and women to your service, to spread your message more widely: Lord, have mercy. . . .

Talk

Politics and Mission. In 826 the Danish Prince Harald came to Ingelheim near Mainz; his purpose was to gain the help of Louis the Pious in carrying out his claim to the throne of Denmark. Out of politi-

St. Ansgar (February 3) 51

cal considerations, he had himself and his whole retinue baptized in the cathedral of Mainz. The Emperor then looked for a missioner who would accompany the prince home and would do missionary work in Denmark.

The abbot of Corvey Abbey on the Wesel River suggested to the emperor one of his monks, the twenty-five-year-old Ansgar. He was born in Northern France and there entered the Abbey of Corbie; for some time he was teaching in Corvey (a foundation out of the French abbey). Ansgar declared himself ready, along with a companion, to accept the task. He traveled with the prince's entourage to Denmark; after a year he had to leave the country, since Harald was unable to carry through his claim to the throne.

Missionary in Success and Failure. Two years later (830) Ansgar went north again. He accepted an invitation from the king of Sweden and was able to build the country's first Christian Church near Stockholm. He left his fellow missioners behind there and sought to establish the Nordic missionary effort on a firm basis from Germany outwards. The Diocese of Hamburg was therefore established in 832, and Ansgar was named its first bishop.

In the years following, the new bishop labored with mixed success in the North. He did not allow himself to lose heart over failures and proceeded to lay the foundations for the further development of the Church in Denmark and Sweden.

Then in 845, organizational catastrophe struck: The Normans overran Hamburg and completely destroyed it. For the time being, rebuilding was not possible. It was necessary that the Diocese of Hamburg be united with the neighboring diocese of Bremen. Ansgar had to handle tensions within the Church over the matter, until the union was finally achieved. By the end of his life (he died in 865 in Bremen), the Northern Church was somewhat consolidated and could look hopefully to the future.

The Religious Profile of the Missioner. Who was this man, so active as a missioner in the political tensions of his time and in the ebb and flow of success and failure? We know his life almost exclusively from the biography written by Rimbert, his successor as bishop. According to this source, Ansgar had weak health. He was a monk by inner inclination and loved solitude and prayer. Yet he also knew that precisely because of this, Jesus Christ had called him to be a missioner and "a fisher of men" [see the Gospel]. Because of this, he never placed "his own comfort and love of solitude above the welfare of the flock entrusted to him; he wanted to be a father to the blind eye, to the lame foot, to the poor man."

Another main thought flows through this written biography. Ansgar longed for martyrdom. However, he died a natural death. His successor believed that "a man who consumed himself in the service of the Lord in the midst of so many hard bodily needs and spiritual torments will not fairly be denied the honor of martyrdom." His life and work were a "martyrdom," a witnessing for Jesus Christ.

Petitions

Lord Jesus Christ, you have sent forth your Church to proclaim the Good News even to the ends of the earth.

Bless the Christian Churches of Northern Europe. . . .
Help them to win men and women of today to your Good News. . . .
Strengthen the ties among Christian communities. . . .

For you walk with your Church on the road through time, until you come in glory.

St. Blase (February 3)

BLESSING THROATS WITH CANDLES

Introduction

St. Blase's Blessing? It falls into the category of all "sacramentals": holy water, special blessings for people, animals, and things. Since they are sometimes taken to be "magic," we stand aloof from them with some skepticism. Yet perhaps it would still be of value to examine once again the meaning of St. Blase's Blessing, in order to make meaningful use today of this sacramental.

Penitential Rite

Lord Jesus Christ, when people believe, they have no reason to fear evil: Lord, have mercy. . . .

When people believe, they have no need to fear natural dangers or human intrigues: Christ, have mercy. . . .

When people believe, they can help others in their need: Lord, have mercy. . . .

Talk

Once Again, Legend and Reality. Blase died a martyr's death in 316 as bishop of Sebaste in Armenia. While in prison, he is said to have saved the life of a boy who had swallowed a fishbone; in this way he came to be honored as the patron saint of throat-ailment victims. In addition, he is portrayed as having brought back to a poor woman a pig that a wolf had stolen. By way of thanks, the woman is reported as having brought meat, bread, and a candle to him. Blase then, according to the story, ritually connected the yearly Candlemas offering to a special blessing.

Both legends surely led up to the emergence of St. Blase's Blessing in the sixteenth century in the form in which we know it today. But what place does such a symbol have in our religious life?

Man is Oriented toward Symbols. We human beings are entities of body and soul. We have to express our inner experiences in bodily gestures and signs, if we want to communicate with other people. Since God takes us seriously as human beings, he wants to meet us even in the "outward signs" of the sacraments. Since we ourselves know about our body-soul nature, we try to make ourselves aware in the religious dimension of "unseen" realities of faith to a certain extent through outward signs.

It is in this context that we have to see the Blessing of the Throats. Burning candles held in the form of a cross are placed over us. The priest says, "Through the intercession of St. Blase, may the Lord protect you from all ailments of the throat and from other evils. In the Name of the Father, and of the Son, and of the Holy Spirit." He makes at the same time the sign of the cross over us, and we answer (as we cross ourselves), "Amen."

Call for Trust in God. In this outward sign (which is made up of things, gestures, and words), let us remember that we—according to the Gospel—are safe within God even in sickness and want.

The self-consuming candle and the sign of the cross remind us of the love of God, with which he gave himself fully over to us in Jesus Christ.

The candle's burning light is an indication of Jesus Christ, who brings light into our lives with all their darkness and distress.

Our faith conviction in the intercession of St. Blase is expressed

St. Blase (February 3)

insofar as we live beyond the frontier of death in community with men and women who, like ourselves, believed and hoped through all the trials in their lives and have achieved perfection in God.

The outward sign of the Blessing of the Throats calls upon us to trust in God's help in all the perils of our lives. And when we answer "Amen" to the blessing form, we assert that we want to count in faith on the help of God.

We realize, of course, that weariness and sickness, pain and hardship, will not be lacking to us. Knowing this, in the very Blessing of the Throats we make the sign of the cross and declare ourselves ready to accept and bear the cross in our lives.

Patience in Affliction. Receiving the Blessing of the Throats thus becomes a confession that God's love is sent to us in Jesus Christ, and that we, trusting in this love even in sickness and suffering, are not without the help of God. This "outward sign" gives us encouragement in the midst of life's pains to move forward in trust toward the full revelation of the glory of God.

Petitions

Lord and God, hear our prayer through the intercession of St. Blase.

Be near to those who suffer persecution for their personal convictions. . . .
Grant your Holy Spirit to our bishops. . . .
Be present to the sick in the dark hours of their pain. . . .
For you are near to us through Jesus Christ in all the distress of our everyday lives. You who live and reign forever and ever.

St. Agatha (February 5)

"GOD HAS CHOSEN THE WEAK IN THIS WORLD"

Introduction

We speak even today of "the weaker sex"—and by this we mean women. Even in our liberated society, woman is still a figure symbolic of weakness. Against this background we can understand why the early Christians took precisely this faith-strengthened martyrdom of women as an illustration of the Pauline sentence, ". . . and God has chosen the weak of this world, in order to bring shame upon the strong . . ." (Reading).

Penitential Rite

"God has chosen the foolish to bring shame upon the wise." [Silence] Lord, have mercy. . . .

"God has chosen the weak of this world, to bring shame upon the strong." [Silence] Christ, have mercy. . . .

"God has chosen what is nothing to overcome what is something." [Silence] Lord, have mercy. . . .

Talk

Symbolic Figure of Weakness. The graceful physical build of a woman has (whether rightly or wrongly is not the point here) over and over led to the thought that woman is "weaker" than man. Does this relate to the fact that people in earlier centuries entrusted little moral steadfastness to a woman under "temptations"? That she had no rights and no place in the public life totally run by men was self-evident for earlier generations.

In this environment a young woman—in this case, Agatha—was ordered by a court to renounce Christ and sacrifice to the gods of the State. She refused, in the face of the full power of the State. She remained firm in her confession of Jesus Christ and went in bonds to her death. She showed herself thereby as being braver than many men, who in the same situation denied their faith.

A Christian woman of this kind stands as a direct illustration for the New Testament conviction that God's power is effective in human weakness. The legend accordingly embellishes St. Agatha's life in order to illumine more clearly this basic law of grace. According to pious accounts of her life, the saint was brought into a brothel in order to be seduced into prostitution and thus into a lapse away from faith. She, however, stayed strong. She was inhumanly tortured at the court hearings; still, she did not betray her faith and went unbeaten to her death.

Basic Christian Theme. "God has chosen the weak of this world to bring shame upon the strong"—this is a Christian theme that is still current in our time. It is heard, for example, over and over again in poetry. Gertrud von Le Fort takes it up in *The Dialogue of the Carmelites:* a fearful Camelite nun finds the strength in God's grace to go to her death along with her sisters during the French Revolution. Georges Bernanos wrote his *Diary of a Country Priest:* a priest, sick and timid, suffering from the failure of his work, nevertheless gains support in the conviction that "everything is grace." Graham Greene sketches a priest in his novel, *The Power and the Glory,* who has given in to alcohol and who, in all weakness, serves the faithful in God's power during the Mexican persecution of Christians and loses his life thereby.

Basic Theme for Our Lives? "God has chosen the weak of this world to bring shame upon the strong"—is this the basic theme for our lives too?

Maybe I am healthy and strong. I feel competent for the demands of life. I don't hesitate when I demonstrate my religious conviction in public (family, neighborhood, workplace . . .). Do I however know in faith that God is present to me, that he lends me strength, and that my energy and the courage of my convictions are his gift?

It will go otherwise for many others. Maybe they are sick and weak and experience their daily responsibilities as a burden. They recognize the scarcely ideal sides of their own personalities and endure them with difficulty. They feel themselves, with all their faith and good will, to be all alone in an environment where others think differently, and they dare not open their mouths. Can this basic Christian theme of God's power in human weakness not encourage us still to test it with trust in God? It is not only the example of the early Christian martyr Agatha, it is also the witness of many ordinary Christians in our time that challenges us to trust in the power of God in our lives and in its demands.

Petitions

Let us pray for all who feel weak and powerless in the face of life and its demands:

For the sick and the handicapped.   [Silence]
For those excessively burdened in family life and in work. . . .
For Christians in overwhelming or hostile circumstances. . . .

For you, Lord Jesus Christ, want to be to them the power of God in human weakness. You who live and reign forever and ever.

St. Paul Miki and Companions (February 7)

THE CHURCH UNDER THE CROSS

Introduction

Paul Miki and Companions—a saint's feast that the reform of the calendar of saints has bestowed on us. Where is the homeland of these martyrs? What century did they live in, work in, suffer in?

What do we really know about the history of the universal Church? Are we interested in knowing what went on in past centuries of Church history and what is happening today in other countries? This memorial day—for the group of martyrs crucified on February 5, 1597, in Nagasaki, Japan—can widen our vision for the worldwide Church in this eucharistic celebration.

Penitential Rite

Jesus, accused by false witnesses, repudiated by the High Council, condemned to death: Lord, have mercy. . . .

Jesus, stripped of garments, nailed to the cross, counted among criminals: Christ, have mercy. . . .

Jesus, laid in the tomb, descended into the realm of the dead, risen in glory: Lord, have mercy. . . .

Talk

Japanese Missionary History. In 1542–1543 the Portuguese discovered Japan, while the Reformation upheavals occupied Europe. Francis Xavier, the great missionary, began to work in that country in 1549. Realizing that Japan's culture was highly developed, Xavier, along with his companions, avoided imparting Christianity with a European bias. At the same time, the missioners assimilated the Japanese mentality and culture well.

This missionary method was successful. Around 1580 there were some 160,000 Christians in Japan; for the most part, they belonged to the country's upper social levels. At this time, however, the tide changed for the young Christian communities. The faction that had seized control through bloody internal power struggles viewed Christians with mistrust. They saw in the nobles converted to Christianity an internal political danger to their ambitions for absolute power. They suspected the foreign missioners to be agents of the European powers having the purpose of setting up the conquest of the country. Similar to the persecution of John the Baptist, the first wave of persecution in Japan emerged from political motives. Missionaries were expelled or executed along with Japanese Christians; Paul Miki and his twenty-five Japanese and foreign companions were executed.

After a short period of peace, the persecutions resumed in 1614 with ever greater vehemence. Every Japanese under suspicion of being Christian had to tread under foot the cross and Christian images as a sign of their apostasy. Executions took place frequently. The persecutions reached their last high point in 1637–1638. In all, some thirty thousand Christians were put to death.

During the next two hundred years, Japan remained hermetically sealed off from the outside world. As European missioners entered Japan again after 1870 following the new opening of Japan to the outside world, they discovered the remnants of an underground Christianity that had preserved itself over this long time.

Japanese Christianity Today. Today Japan has more than one hundred million inhabitants. The Catholic Church has about 360,000 members, i.e., not quite 0.4 percent of the total population. Other Christian Churches and sects likewise do not have very great numbers of members.

This small group of Christians lives in a highly industrialized and urbanized country, in which there are economic and social problems similar to our own. The Church in Japan cannot in the foreseeable future count on mass conversions (just as she cannot count on a mass return to ecclesial life in our midst). She will remain a mission Church for the "little flock," which will depend upon the personal witness of each Christian in the midst of an overwhelmingly non-Christian environment. The Christians of Japan need the intercession and the example of Paul Miki and his companions and of all the other Japanese martyrs, in order to be able to give witness energetically to their faith with trust in Jesus Christ.

Petitions

Lord Jesus Christ, you sent your disciples forth to all nations to proclaim the Good News even to the ends of the earth. With confidence in the intercession of St. Paul Miki and his companions, we pray for the Christians in Japan.

> Grant your Holy Spirit to bishops and church leaders. . . .
> Give Christians the courage to give witness to their faith in their non-Christian surroundings. . . .
> Let them cooperate energetically in the solution of the social and political problems of their country. . . .
> Let them be prepared for encounter with the great religions of the Japanese past. . . .

Lord, let your Kingdom grow in Japan and everywhere in the world. You who live. . . .

St. Jerome Emiliani (February 8)

A ONE-MONTH IMPRISONMENT WITH RESULTS

Introduction

"Feel with all the pain in the world, but do not channel your energies toward where you are powerless, but rather toward your neighbor, whom you can help and love and to whom you can bring joy" (Hermann Hesse). Jerome Emiliani—a saint of brotherly love, who is not too familiar to us—lived and worked by this motto.

Penitential Rite

Lord Jesus Christ: You have announced the Good News to the poor out of your merciful kindness: Lord, have mercy. : . . .

You have taken merciful interest in the sick and have placed the power of your miracles in the service of your love: Christ, have mercy. . . .

You let children come to you in heartfelt love, even after the fatigue and trouble of the day: Lord, have mercy. . . .

Talk

On the Eve of the Reformation. Europe—on the eve of the Reformation. The intellectual climate was governed by classic humanism, while the practical coexistence of the European nations was governed more by instincts for power. Italy above all was racked repeatedly by new wars. Morals decayed, land areas were laid to waste, broad segments of the population were pauperized, and chaotic conditions reigned to some extent in authority, law, and hygiene. It was the time in which Albrecht Dürer engraved in wood the four horsemen of the Apocalypse—war, hunger, plague, and death—and thereby caught a distressing aspect of the then realities of life.

Within the Church, lamentable conditions prevailed widely. Yet the powers of reform were also stirring, as can be seen in the person of Jerome Emiliani.

Imprisonment with Results. The proud son of Venetian patricians, Jerome wanted to make a name for himself in the ceaseless troubles of war. As the commander of a small fortress, he fell into captivity in 1511. This put his high-flying plans into question. Alone in a dungeon, he began to reflect upon his life and experienced an interior conversion. From a fame-hungry noble, he was turned into a man who had found Jesus Christ and who realized that he was called to the service of selfless love in the many needs of his time.

After his release from prison, Jerome returned first to his existing task as leader of the fortress entrusted to him. Then he decided on his path, which he knew to be the call of Jesus Christ. He was ordained a priest in 1518, aged thirty-two. All his time and energy were now at the service of the poor and needy of his time.

He proceeded to dedicate himself above all to orphaned children, who at the time wandered around in gangs. He secured lodgings for them, gave them food, gave them religious instruction, and prepared them for methodical work.

In times when hunger and pestilence raged with great force, his care was extended to the abandoned sick and the forgotten dead. He cared for the sick by day and buried corpses by night [cf. Reading]. He himself caught an infection in 1528 that brought him to the brink of death. After he recuperated, he extended his activity beyond Venice. Like-minded men associated themselves with him. Together they started the Congregation of the Somaschi, named after their principal house in northern Italy. Continuing into the present time, they have concerned themselves with the operation and direction of homes for orphans and the poor, and of hospitals.

During 1537, Jerome cared for those sick with the plague, and thus caught a fatal infection. Before he died, he urgently admonished his colleagues one last time to imitate the Crucified in their lives; to help the poor, the abandoned, and the sick; and to live together in concord and love—a spiritual testament that is valid for us as well.

To Serve One's Neighbor. "Feel with all the pain in the world . . . and channel your energies . . . toward your neighbor, whom you can really help" (cf. above). I believe that this is what genuine Christian love of neighbor is all about. Not through grandiose sentiments on the weariness of life will pain and want be fought, but rather only if I apply myself toward helping the person in need, and set to work effectively for him, as Jerome Emiliani did.

Petitions

Jesus Christ, our Brother, we commend to you the many men and women who suffer need:

All who are tortured and persecuted . . .   [Silence]
All who hunger and suffer . . .
All who are alone and abandoned . . .
All who are ruined and no longer accepted by anyone. . . .

Lord, awaken us to see the needs of our brothers and sisters, and make us ready to help. You who live and reign forever and ever (after GL 29,4).

St. Scholastica (February 10)

SHE HAD THE GREATER LOVE

Introduction

Where in our area is the nearest contemplative convent of women? Where is there a foundation of Benedictine, Poor Clare, or Carmelite contemplative nuns? These strict communities of women, and the more familiar "active" communities (working in hospitals, children's homes, and parishes) are different branches of the same great tree of female religious community life, represented to us in an earlier form by St. Scholastica.

Penitential Rite

Lord Jesus Christ, your Word reveals to us the love of the Father: Lord, have mercy. . . .
Your Word gives us life: Christ, have mercy. . . .
Your Word shows us the way: Lord, have mercy. . . .

Talk

The Legend. The only thing we know for certain about Scholastica is that she was the sister of St. Benedict (and thus lived around the year 500). She is supposed to have lived as a consecrated religious in the area of Monte Cassino, the foundation of her brother. It is said that her brother had the custom of visiting her once a year, in order to converse with her on religious matters. At the last visit, Scholastica, according to the story, caused a sudden storm to come by prayer, which forced her brother to stay longer with her. The author of the legend accounts for her power by asserting that "she had the greater love." When Scholastica died shortly thereafter, Benedict had her buried in Monte Cassino in his own grave.

The Inspiration. The saint is representative of all those women who in these centuries have laid the foundations for the development of religious female communities in the Church.

This development was taken in the course of centuries in another direction than that of male religious life, owing to the prevailing place of women in society. While male religious would lead a contemplative life and would also generally take part in active public life, religious women remained limited more to the sphere within the convent.

A series of foundations of active female communities ran afoul of these notions of religious life for women. They had to give up their work among needy fellow human beings outside of their cloister and tried to continue their work from within the convent walls (e.g., the Salesian nuns, the Ursulines . . .). St. Vincent de Paul was the first to overturn these notions with his "Daughters of Charity."

Listening to His Words. Today in the Church, both the more contemplative and the more active forms of religious life are found. There was a time when it was thought that the contemplative communities were "stricter" than, for example, the communities active in charitable and social works. That led people in the past to pay excessive attention to external life-style. We should leave such comparisons behind. It is not easy to sort out in which circumstances of life it is harder or easier to imitate Jesus Christ. Besides, it is not the external life-style, but rather the inner attitude that determines whether or not the imitation of Christ is genuine. Whether Benedictine or Daughter of Charity, whether unmarried or amid family demands, each Christian must—in keeping with his life circumstances—sit at the Lord's feet and listen to his words [cf. the Gospel]. And even a nun can stand before Jesus Christ only if her life is sealed by selfless love for God and man (which also holds true for a wife and mother).

The Meaning of Contemplative Cloisters. What, then, is the task of contemplative cloisters in our time? Are they merely a relic of the past with their rules of strict enclosure and high walls? Even in the opinion of cloistered nuns themselves, a great deal must change in their rules of enclosure. However, they can unmistakenly remind the Church—which rightly, like Martha, is anxious over many things—that she remains Church and does not degenerate to a mere social welfare union, when she, like Mary, sits at the Lord's feet and concentrates on his Word.

Petitions

God and Father, you see in your Church different vocations that serve to build up the one Body of Christ.

> Make the convents of contemplative nuns to be places of recollection and prayer. . . .
> Let the Sisters in active works give witness to the faith in their labors. . . .
> Call young people to your service in religious life. . . .

This we pray through Christ, our Lord.

Our Lady of Lourdes (February 11)

"WHERE HEAVEN TOUCHES EARTH"

Introduction

Since February 11, 1858 (the date of the first apparition), Lourdes has steadily grown into the largest place of pilgrimage in the Catholic Church in modern times. Each year hundreds of thousands of people come from all parts of the earth to the little French town in the Pyrenees. Why do they come? Because there "heaven touches earth" and God is nowhere else so close to us (either in our residences or in our countries . . .) It is worth it for us to reflect a while on this point.

Penitential Rite

"Lord, where can I go from your spirit, or where can I flee from your face? O search me, God, and know my heart. O test me and know my thoughts. See that I follow not the wrong path and lead me in the path of life eternal" (Ps. 139:7, 23f).

Have mercy, Lord our God, have mercy. . . .

Talk

God is Everywhere Close to Us. Do we really live with the conviction that God is everywhere close to us in Jesus Christ—in Church as well as at home in our living room, in the corner tavern as well as at the office in New York or Toronto as well as in Lourdes? With this conviction, the author of Psalm 139 prays, "Where can I go from your spirit, where can I flee from your face? If I climb the heavens, you are there. If I lie in the grave, you are there. If I take the wings of the dawn and dwell at the sea's furthest end, even there your hand would lead me, your right hand would hold me fast" (Ps. 139:7ff). Paul speaks of the God "who is indeed not far from any of us: for in him we live and move and have our being" (Acts 17:27f).

God Reveals His Closeness in Certain Places. It is, therefore, not necessary to go to Lourdes (or enter a church) "to find God," if we "cannot find him" elsewhere. Everywhere God is the same distance away.

Yet God realizes that we human beings depend upon visible and tangible signs of his presence and love, if we want to live with him permanently. Knowing this, he gave himself to us in the tangible human form of his Son (who lived during a particular time in a particular country and left his traces in earthly history). He therefore comes to us in the visible form of the Church and in the outward signs of the sacraments.

God also lets us detect and experience his nearness at sites of apparitions—often through the appearance of Mary—so that we human beings can again and again be moved to count on his presence everywhere in our lives. He first lets "seers" experience his nearness (and Bernadette Soubirous gained from her encounter with Mary the strength to become a saint); then he lets everyone who comes to such a place of apparitions in faith and prayer to experience this nearness.

The True Miracle of Lourdes. The goal of all revelations from God is, according to the testimony of sacred Scripture, that human beings should again be able to live with the present God. They should rejoice anew over the love of God [Reading] and should seriously attempt to do whatever God requires of them [Gospel]. They should learn all over to take God as seriously as Mary did: she expressed the joy of her faith in the "Magnificat." In saying, "Behold the handmaid of the Lord; be it done to me according to your word," she gave herself over completely to God's will.

The true miracle of Lourdes, which has been occurring every day for over a hundred years, is not one for the physicians to determine—even as they investigate extraordinary healings of people who come to this site of grace. The "true miracle" occurs in secret everytime that people—whether healthy or sick, whether with hidden wounds of the soul or with a fully joyful faith as they come into the Pyrenean town—are strengthened in their certainty of faith and begin to live out more seriously the prayer in the Our Father: Father, your will be done. The effects of this miracle can then be observed in the healed sick who praise God's love in their healed lives; but also in the sick, who accept with greater awareness the cross of their sickness and carry it in union with Christ, and also in those people who place their trust in the closeness of God with new courage in the face of the hardships of their daily Christian lives.

Petitions

God of mystery, you are close to us and know what disturbs us. In union with Mary, the Mother of your Son and our Mother, we call on you:

> Be near to all who are sick and send them healing according to your will. . . .
> Help all who are tormented by hidden pain to bear their cross bravely, when no quick solution is forthcoming. . . .
> Strengthen in all believers the trust in your closeness and also the readiness to fulfill your will in life. . . .

For you invite us to entrust ourselves to you, as Mary entrusted herself to you. You who live and reign forever and ever.

Sts. Cyril and Methodius (February 14)

GOD HAS MADE ALL LANGUAGES FOR HIS PRAISE

Introduction

In our days a missionary epoch is ending, in which Europeans together with a European civilization transplanted a thoroughly Europeanized Christianity to other countries in the world. These countries now reject this form of missionizing and demand the right to their own way in faith, in liturgy, and in theology. As a consequence, our Church is faced in many countries by urgent questions of adaptation to languages, of forms of expression, of thought, and of a feeling for life on the part of various national groups.

How this problem of adaptation was resolved about 1100 years ago in southeastern Europe can be learned from the lives and work of Sts. Cyril and Methodius.

Penitential Rite

Jesus, Bread by which we live: Lord, have mercy . . .
Jesus, Light by which we see: Christ, have mercy . . .
Jesus, Way by which we walk: Lord, have mercy . . . (GL 765,2).

Talk

Around 850 there lived Slavic tribes in the region of present-day Czechoslovakia, Hungary, and Yugoslavia; these tribes had united into the greater Moravian kingdom. They were ready to accept Christianity, but not from Bavarian missioners: they feared that they might thus become a dependent province of the eastern Frankish kingdom. For that reason, they willingly accepted a group of Greek missionaries from Byzantium. Among them stood out the brothers Cyril and Methodius in a special way. Cyril was a highly educated Greek who had followed his older brother Methodius relatively late into monastic life.

Although they were Greeks by birth and education, both brothers spoke the Slavonic language from childhood on. While the Frankish missioners sought to introduce Latin as the liturgical language, the missioners from Byzantium relinquished the Greek liturgy and used the language of the people in their services. Cyril even fashioned a special alphabet for Slavonic, which in more developed form still exists today in Eastern Europe (e.g., in Russia).

This practice ran into the resistance of the Frankish Church. Narrow political interests adapted the argument that only those languages should be used in the liturgy that appeared on the inscription on the cross (thus, Hebrew, Greek, and Latin). However, Rome approved their practice.

Cyril died in 869 while visiting Rome. Methodius, however, worked another sixteen years as papal envoy for the upbuilding of the Slavic Church.

With their missionary method of linguistic adaptation, that tide of missioners safeguarded and further developed the language and the cultural heritage of the Slavic tribes. At the same time they built up a church united with Rome that developed its own liturgical traditions; the Slavic Eastern Churches and in the Catholic Church of Yugoslavia.

Cyril and Methodius were Greeks by birth and education. The Eastern Roman Empire, with its Greek language and culture, had at that time a thoroughly national self-awareness. Yet the two saints, along

Sts. Cyril and Methodius (February 14)

with their companions, kept themselves free from all national arrogance and narrowness. They were deeply imbued with the conviction that Christ had died for all men and had called all nations to salvation. In a truly Catholic—that is, embracing the whole world—perspective, they drew the conclusion that the liturgy could be celebrated in every language. Since they wanted the Light of Christ to shine everywhere without unnecessary covering, they struggled against all resistance for the Slavonic language in common worship. Pope John supported their point of view in 880 when he wrote, "The same God who made the three principal languages—namely, Hebrew, Greek, and Latin, also made all other languages for his praise and honor."

In the contemporary Church we have found again something of this Catholic latitude. We celebrate the Mass in the language of the people. With this, however, we are just at the beginning of the necessary adaptation of the liturgy and of religious living to the different nations. Let us pray on this feast of the great Slavic apostles that missioners all over the world, yet also the ecclesiastical authorities in Rome and elsewhere might serve in their spirit.

Petitions

Lord Jesus Christ, you are the Light for the gentiles, Salvation even to the ends of the earth. All nations in their own way are to praise with you the Father who is in heaven:

> Give to missioners throughout the world the readiness in their preaching to enter the cultures of different peoples . . .
> Give to those responsible for the universal Church in Rome and elsewhere a truly Catholic breadth of mind . . .
> Support the efforts for indigenous liturgies in young churches. . . .

We therefore pray to you, who live and reign as King of all ages and nations forever and ever.

The Seven Holy Founders of the Order of Servites (February 17)

DETOUR THROUGH THE DESERT?

Introduction

According to the Gospel account, Jesus of Nazareth withdrew into the desert before he began his public life (cf. Mt. 4:1–11). Paul also went into solitude right after his conversion, before he began his missionary activity (cf. Gal. 1:17f).

Something similar is reported to us concerning today's group of saints. Does the direct way to the service of our fellow human beings lead perhaps through the "desert"?

Penitential Rite

Lord Jesus Christ, you searched for silence and solitude in order to find yourself: Lord, have mercy . . .

You sought communion with your Father through prayer in the solitude of the desert: Christ, have mercy . . .

You left solitude to go out to men in communion with the Father: Lord, have mercy. . . .

Talk

Leading Merchants . . . Florence developed during the thirteenth century into a powerful trade center. Merchants set the tone within it, and were also the great travelers of their time. They went to

The Seven Holy Founders of the Servites (February 17)

other countries and brought new ideas back from their trips. They also brought new religious concepts along (it was after all, the time of the great Franciscan movement and of other groups that sought to live "according to the Gospel"). They wanted to put these concepts into action.

. . . go into the desert . . . Around 1230 seven leading merchants joined together in a pious society. They wanted to live consciously according to the Gospel in the midst of the demands of their occupations and to show concern for the needy of the city.

Some years later, these men disengaged themselves from business and family obligations, with the purpose of leading a life in common near the gates of their city, dedicated to prayer and charitable service. Soon they withdrew even more into solitude. They lived as hermits on Mount Senario, some twenty kilometers away from Florence. In the wilderness the community of the seven, along with their followers, became the Order of the Servites, the "Servants of the Blessed Virgin Mary." They wanted, in special relation with Mary, to contemplate the life, passion, and death of Jesus and imitate his life for the salvation of the world.

. . . and return to the midst of people. Yet the first members of the Order of Servites did not remain in the "desert." They settled in the area of Florence to labor for their fellow men in prayer and active love for neighbor.

Our Way to Our Neighbor. For the founders of the Servites, the way through solitude on Mount Senario was the direct way to the service of their fellow men—similar to Paul and to Jesus of Nazareth.

Perhaps one can say that only a man who has come to know himself can truly be among other human beings; only a man who has come to know God in his own contemplation can serve other people.

We do not have the time to withdraw into silence for some years with the aim of preparing ourselves for everyday demands. Yet each one of us can set aside a few minutes daily to know oneself and to turn consciously to God. Each one of us can take a weekend once in a while in order to have time for deeper religious recollection. And perhaps we will thereby experience how this bit of "desert" in our life is the direct way to a deeper bond with our fellow human beings.

Petitions

Lord Jesus Christ, you call your Church to conversion. We pray to you:

> Let everyone who feels the stress of their work find time for personal prayer . . .
> Give all who are in service to their neighbor the inspiration for personal reflection and prayer . . .
> Help all the sick to feel your presence in the loneliness of their sickbeds. . . .

Lord, hear us by the intercession of your Mother and ours, the Virgin Mary. You who live and reign forever and ever.

St. Peter Damian (February 21)

INTERIOR RENEWAL

Introduction

During recent years in the Catholic Church, in the wake of the Second Vatican Council, we have abrogated a number of obsolete forms of expression and have introduced many new ones. Our parish has seen some changes as well: the renovated church, the parish council. . . .

Yet in the great reforms in the history of the Church, external changes were never the primary concern. It was first and foremost a matter of interior renewal in the Spirit of Jesus Christ. During the time of St. Peter Damian as well, this interior renewal was the goal.

Have we perhaps in recent years sometimes overlooked to some extent this interior renewal in the Spirit of Jesus Christ?

Penitential Rite

Lord Jesus Christ, you are the vine, we are the branches, Lord, have mercy. . . .

You grant us fellowship with you: Christ, have mercy. . . .

You call us in our failure to greater faithfulness: Lord, have mercy. . . .

Talk

Around the year 1050, a bleak period of Church history was gradually ending. The Church had become a pawn of political powers. This led to serious abuses. For example, ecclesiastical offices and blessings became pieces of merchandise traded for payment. Many priests lived in forbidden marriage. Many monasteries experienced a sad low point of religious life. Yet at the same time forces were at work in many saints that in the coming decades would help the breakthrough of the so-called Gregorian Church Reform.

Among these saints was the Italian Peter Damian. Born in 1007, he joined a community of hermits at the age of 28 after his basic education. Soon he labored from his solitude in letters and other writings for the reform of the Church. The popes of his time paid him attention and entrusted special tasks to him. In 1057 he became bishop of Ostia and a cardinal, and had to leave his beloved hermitage. The pope allowed him in 1063 to resign his bishopric and to return into solitude. Yet even in the years following he had to travel time and again by mandate of the pope and to conduct special assignments. He died on February 22, 1072, while on one of these trips.

How did this saint work for the reform of the Church? He was in the middle of ecclesiastical political struggles of his time and worked hard for external reforms. He took clear sides with the pope and his ideas for reform. In sharp controversies he sometimes displayed a harshness that, by our standards, crossed over the lines of mutual respect and Christian love of neighbor. In this he was just a man of his time as well as the prisoner of his own fiery temperament.

At the same time, however, the often combative seeker of reform was deeply certain that the reform of the Church begins with the religious renewal of the individual Christian. In his many writings, the conviction is often expressed: the more a Christian works on his own sanctification and on his own conversion, the more he brings about the best of the whole Body of Christ, the Church.

Therefore, he who in public would frequently "correct, reprove, and admonish'' [Reading], who struggled for the accomplishment of external Church reform through many homilies and many more letters, sought out solitude. For him, a hermit's life was the way to ever more profound growth in communion with Jesus Christ, the true vine from whom we the branches draw our life [Gospel]. Since Peter Damian realized that the renewal of the Church was not possible without Christ, he worked in solitude for his own renewal, so much so that he ran up against the limits of his own character.

Peter Damian was a hermit. Yet from his solitude he wrote almost as much for popes, bishops, priests, and laity as he did for hermits and monks. He demanded of all of them without exception that they start with their own renewal in faith. Is that not the message that this day's saint calls out to us?—that the contemporary renewal of the Church begins even in the twentieth century with an eager life of prayer and with serious personal effort toward selflessness in the imitation of Jesus Christ.

Petitions

Our Lord Jesus Christ is the Head of the Church; from him comes all sanctification and to him every authentic reform leads. We therefore call upon him:

Grant us fervor for our own conversion. . . .
Make us witnesses of selfless service in your imitation. . . .
Give us the courage to stand up for the faith and the Church in public. . . .

Lord, our God, let us not remain fixated on externals, but rather convert your people to yourself. Through Christ, our Lord.

Chair of Peter (February 22)

THE POPE: TEACHER IN THE CHURCH

Introduction

In recent years, the discussion among theologians on the meaning of the "papal teaching office" and the manner of its exercise has gone on without interruption. The feast of the Chair of Peter can give us the occasion to tell ourselves what images we associate with the special teaching responsibility of the bishop of Rome (and thus the successor of the apostle Peter).

Penitential Rite

"When I think: 'I have lost my foothold,' your mercy, Lord, holds me up. When care increases in my heart your consolation calms my soul. The Lord will be a stronghold, my God will be the rock where I take refuge" (Ps. 94:18f,22).

Have mercy, Lord our God, have mercy.

Talk

The Feast. In these February days the Romans used to solemnly memorialize their dead. They would prepare food and make a chair ready for their use. The Christians spontaneously adopted this practice,

Chair of Peter (February 22)

and at their gatherings would set an empty chair for Peter (and for other martyrs on other occasions).

Later, from this custom arose a particular memorial day of Peter assuming community leadership. The chair—we speak yet today of a "teaching chair"—became a symbol of Peter's special mandate, to lead and to strengthen his fellow disciples and Christians in faith (cf. Lk. 22:32).

This feast, at first glance curious, recalls to us the "papal teaching office" and raises also the question of its proper understanding. The following reflections can perhaps aid us in this.

Task within the Church. First, the following word of Jesus applies both to Peter and to every pope: "Nor must you allow yourselves to be called teachers, for you have only one Teacher, the Christ" (Mt. 23:10). That means that even the pope is first a "learner." He must listen to Jesus Christ and let himself be led by him.

Jesus Christ takes the pope seriously in his human reality. The teaching task of the pope thus begins with the pope seeking to know what Jesus Christ teaches his Church. To this end the pope needs—like every other Christian—study, reflection, discussion with others, and of course a prayerful encounter with the Lord of the Church.

Only when the pope has "learned" Jesus Christ in this way—in contact too with bishops and with theological specialists—can he responsibly speak and officially instruct the Church with trust in the presence of the Holy Spirit.

Teaching Office and Pastoral Office. Accordingly, the teaching task of the pope is clearly aimed at Christian ways of living and not primarily at developing a theology invulnerable to attack. Certainly we must be united in the Church on central faith convictions. But beyond this "iron presence" of truths of faith (that God has gifted himself to us in Jesus Christ, that he has called us into his community, that he is on pilgrimage with the Church through time in the Holy Spirit and leads us to fulfillment in eternity . . .), we tend to think today that there are many wider areas of discussion, of necessary deeper clarification and explanation, than earlier generations suspected.

It is not the task of the pope to intervene continually in these discussions. True to the mandate of strengthening his brethren in faith (cf. Lk. 22:32), it will be his concern to help them not to lose trust in Christ and the joy of faith amid all open questions and unresolved theological problems. As teacher of the Church he will recall the promises of Christ in his statements, who walks on the way with the Church even to the end of time. He will warn about dangers and problems, but he will much more call to faith in Him who at every high wave and gusty wind is there in the ship of the Church and who gives her ultimate security.

Petitions

God, in your providence you selected Peter as the leader of the apostles.

> Protect and bless your servant, Pope _____, whom you have called to be successor to St. Peter. . . .
> Give him the strength to be an effective sign of unity in the Church. . . .
> Help him so that he may, through his addresses and writings, strengthen trust in Jesus Christ and in his presence. . . .

You who live and reign forever and ever.

St. Polycarp of Smyrna (February 23)

A FOLLOWER OF THE APOSTLES

Introduction

In recent years, a number of early Christian saints were taken off the liturgical calendar of feasts, because little was really known about their lives and works.

It is a different matter with St. Polycarp, bishop of Smyrna (in modern Asia Minor) who lived around 70–160 after Christ. We know a fair amount about his life and works. A letter from St. Ignatius of Antioch to the Smyrna community, a letter by our saint to a neighboring community, and the report of his martyrdom all give us information on him and point him out to us as a true follower of the apostles.

Penitential Rite

Lord Jesus Christ, you have entrusted your Good News to us human beings so that we might transmit it with no dilution: Lord, have mercy. . . .

You placed your disciples into a community that must always strive anew for union: Christ, have mercy. . . .

You have called your Church into imitation of you: Lord, have mercy. . . .

Talk

Symbol of Tradition. Around the year 150 after Christ, Polycarp was a worthy graybeard over eighty years old. He was one of the few who still knew of the primitive Church from his own experience. Understandably, people regarded his opinion highly in the internal Church disputes of the time, and saw in him a true witness of the doctrine and practice of the early Church. Decades later, the early Christian writer Irenaeus testified to the correct faith of the Roman Church by asserting that Polycarp had also taught the same things, "as he had learned them from the apostles and had handed them on to the Church."

In the Midst of Church Disputes. As guarantor of Tradition, Polycarp went with his community on the road into a new age. During his long life, the conviction arose in the young Church that, for the sake of fidelity to Christ and for the unity of doctrine, the leadership of the community had to be centralized in the hands of the bishop. The bishop became more and more the one primarily responsible for preaching and for the celebration of the Eucharist (for which the "preachers" and "teachers" were authorized beforehand). As with all innovations, there was resistance. The opponents of this development refused to participate in the bishop's worship and held their particular assemblies elsewhere. Polycarp had to carry this cross of disunity in his community his whole life long. He sought unperturbed the unity of his community, but he could not forestall some defections.

A Church Leader Able to Compromise. During the bishop's time, contrasts between the eastern and western Churches began already to make themselves felt. They were inflamed by the question of the date for the Christian Easter celebration. Polycarp upheld the prevailing practice of the East, which tended to invoke the apostle John—thus, always the fourteenth of Nisan—while the western Church invoked

St. Polycarp of Smyrna (February 23)

Peter and each time celebrated the feast on the following Sunday. Polycarp traveled to Rome on this matter, so as to come to an agreement with Pope Anicetus. They did not succeed in setting a common date, but both Church leaders had a sufficiently Catholic outlook, that they could acknowledge the different traditions and find no occasion for a split between the Churches.

Witness in Death. Polycarp was eighty-six years old when he was forced to pay with his life for his faith in Jesus Christ. Popular desires were boiling over looking forward to the public games so favored by the Romans, and they were looking for a sacrifice. Polycarp knew of the danger and moved in concealment around the land. Then a servant betrayed his hiding place. He was arrested and brought to public trial. The stirred-up crowd demanded his death with the word, "He is the teacher of all Asia! He is the father of the Christians, the scorner of our gods! It is his fault that they do not offer sacrifice or adore!" The bishop was publicly executed and became like unto Jesus Christ in death.

Who was St. Polycarp of Smyrna? What does he have to say to us? Let us answer that after his example in the petitions.

Petitions

Lord, heavenly Father, you reveal to us in your saints what it means to imitate your Son. With trust in the intercession of St. Polycarp we pray:

For the Church in the changes of our days: help her to remain true to the Good News amidst all her efforts of timely renewal. . . .
For our communities: Let them not collapse over efforts to adapt the Church to our times. . . .
For the various Christian Churches: grant that, in the Holy Spirit, they may be mindful above all of what we have in common. . . .

For you guide your Church yet in our time and you give her the power to work for your kingdom. You, who live and reign forever and ever.

St. Casimir (March 4)

RESPONSIBILITY OF CHRISTIANS TO THE WORLD

Introduction

The postconciliar development has given us parish councils and other committees in which Christian laypeople share more than ever in the leadership of their communities. There are committed Christians who look upon this development with concern. They do so, not so much out of worry for the priest's position of authority, as they do because they wonder if thereby too much Christian energy is tied up in internal Church tasks, with too little remaining for Christian commitment in state and society.

Penitential Rite

"Who is he who longs for life and many days, to enjoy his prosperity? Then keep your tongues from evil and your lips from speaking deceit. Turn aside from evil and do good; seek and strive after peace" (Ps. 34:13–15).

Have mercy, Lord our God, have mercy. . . .

Talk

King as Example. In a more hierarchical age, it was only the crowned heads that counted even in the political sphere (although the day-by-day work was done by others). It should therefore be no surprise

St. Casimir (March 4)

that the Church, in her calendar of saints (which even after the most recent reform is not yet fully adapted to our times), offers kings, emperors, and other high nobility as models of Christian responsibility in the world.

Among these we find Casimir of Poland (1458–1484), a king's son and co-regent. His father gave him an early share in all affairs of state and even made him his deputy. The ambitious plan of his parents—to secure the Kingdom of Hungary for him—fell through. He himself was stricken with tuberculosis and died at the age of twenty-six.

In the short span of his public career, the young prince made an enduring impression upon his contemporaries. They praised him for his sense of justice and for his concern for the country's security in the struggle against banditry. An admirer wrote of him, "He either should never have been born or he should have lived forever."

Casimir's piety was nothing unusual. According to the testimony of witnesses in his canonization process—which started shortly after his death—he used by choice the hours of the night or of early morning for silent prayer. From this conscious encounter with God he drew the power for practical love for his fellow human beings that influenced his political activity.

Responsibility to the World Today. Casimir of Poland reminds me of Dag Hammarskjöld, the Secretary General of the United Nations, whose deep and hidden piety became known only after his sudden death. In our era, he served people in the political dimension out of a framework of faith.

His name reminds many of our current politicians (on local, national, and global levels), the ones who know they are called by Jesus Christ, to work for a more human world in the power politics of our age. They know that politics can be dirty business. They are aware that they can give in to corruption and just line their own pockets—but they are vigilant enough over themselves to watch out for this danger. They have the ability to compromise, because in shared human life it is always a question of the art of the possible—even when know-it-alls accuse them of betraying their principles. They are ready to "get their hands dirty" in politics, as Jesus Christ got his hands dirty in the service of humanity. They get involved as Christians in the political field, because they are convinced that one can certainly change the world without Christ—but can improve it only with him.

Gratitude toward Politicans. Maybe I have drawn here just an ideal picture of a Christian politician. Even among them there are weeds among the grain. We should ask ourselves: are we ready, in proportion to our capabilities, to involve ourselves in politics? Do we thank our politicians for their nerve-wearying involvement? Do we pray for all who, conscious of their responsibility, take part in political life?

Petitions

Lord of Lords, it is your will that people live in peace with one another:

Teach politicians how they may lessen tensions and avoid new wars. . . .
Give success to movements for disarmament. . . .
Be near to all who, in the councils of our cities and states, work for politics that will serve human beings. . . .

Lord, let us not become accomplices when hate and enmity pit people against one another. Help us cherish peace, since you have made peace with us. You who live and reign forever and ever (after GL 31,2).

Sts. Perpetua and Felicity (March 7)

JOY IN FAITH UNTO DEATH

Introduction

Christian fathers and mothers of our day have their worries over their growing children when they break out of the well-ordered life of their parents and join radical groups or religious sects. Can we imagine that around 200 pagan parents had similar worries over their children, because their young people were joining the forbidden sect of Christians? This was the situation for the parents of St. Perpetua and her companions.

Penitential Rite

"If God is for us, then who can be against us?" [Silence] Lord, have mercy. . . .

"What can separate us from the love of Christ?" [Silence] Christ, have mercy. . . .

"We overcome all things through him who has loved us." [Silence] Lord, have mercy. . . .

Talk

A Group of Young Adults. Perpetua, a young woman from a good home (married, with a small son), and Felicity (married young and now pregnant) had become catechumens in the despised Christian community. Along with other young people of differing social class, they took instructions for baptism.

Then a decree of the emperor was promulgated that forbade, under severe punishment, that anyone should become Jewish or Christian. The group of young religious seekers was arrested.

Perpetua's parents were shocked. Her father tried to move her to renounce the faith by talking about her little son, but without success. The young men and women sought after baptism in prison. It was administered to them at the first opportunity.

Joy in Faith Unto Death. The new Christians in prison stared at death. We know from personal notes of Perpetua what her attitude was as she proceeded toward death. The captives suffered under gruesome prison conditions (a dark subterranean cubicle; oppressive heat from overcrowding; sly extortion attempts by the soldiers; Perpetua grieved that she was separated from her small son . . .). Yet at the same time they were filled with joy over their communion with Christ.

After being sentenced "to the beasts" (they were to be thrown to wild starved animals in the circus for the "amusement of the people"), they "went down again joyfully into the dungeon" (so Perpetua wrote). They prayed that Felicity might give birth before the execution day, so that she might be able to die with the others for Christ. (It was forbidden under Roman law to execute pregnant women.) When birth pangs came, Felicity moaned and cried out with them; the jailer asked her then how she would take it when thrown to the wild beasts. She answered, "What I am now suffering, *I* am suffering; in the arena there will be Another in me, and *He* will suffer for me."

A Question for Us. When we now hear quotations from the accounts of the martyrdom of Perpetua and Felicity, the critical question certainly occurs to us whether later history writers idealized them. Or else we suspect that these youths had really manipulated each other.

Yet let us ask ourselves the question: what is there of joy in faith in my own life? Judging from Romans 8, Paul was so filled with the certainty of communion with Jesus Christ that he could say, "For I am certain that neither death nor life . . . neither past nor future can separate us from the love of God . . ." (v. 38f). Out of this same conviction he called upon the Christians in Philippi; always and everywhere to rejoice (Phil. 4:4f). Perpetua and Felicity, along with their companions, made it their goal to hold fast to this joy while in prison and in the face of death. Is this joy alive in our everyday Christian living? Do we feel something of it in dark hours, in illness, and disappointment? Can we also rejoice as we are united in suffering with Jesus Christ? Let us give a like response to these questions, and let us ask God to strengthen joy in faith within us.

Petitions

God our Father, hear our prayer:

Be close to Christians who are persecuted because of their faith. . . .
Let all those feel your presence who face death in incurable illness. . . .
Give to all believers deep joy in confessing you and in your Good News. . . .

For in Jesus Christ you have given us reason for confidence and joy. You who live and reign forever and ever.

St. John of God (March 8)

LATE VOCATION

Introduction

According to our widespread impressions, the good Christian grows up in a respectable family. As a boy he serves on the altar and as a girl she at least belongs to a children's group. He is loyal to the Church even through the storms of youth, and is a reliable member of the parish community his whole life long.

This need not, however, be the case. Jesus called the malicious tax collector Levi into the circle of his disciples. And St. John of God found his way to his religious calling in life only after straying a long time.

Penitential Rite

"I was hungry, and you gave me something to eat."   [Silence] Lord, have mercy. . . .

"I was homeless and you took me in." [Silence]   Christ, have mercy. . . .

"I was sick, and you visited me." [Silence]   Lord, have mercy. . . .

Talk

A Not Commendable Early Life.   John (he lived from 1495 to 1550) ran away from home when he was eight. His mother died from grief over his departure. Kindly people took him into their family and

St. John of God (March 8) 93

brought him up as their own child. Later on, when they wanted him to wed the daughter in the house, he ran away again and entered the military. Grown up in Spain he fought as a Portuguese against Frenchmen and Turks. In the rough environment of soldiers' life he slid down a steep path. He barely escaped imprisonment and execution by firing squad under his own superiors.

Slowly, religious desire awoke within him. After his release from the army, he made a pilgrimage to Compostela, the most famous Spanish place of pilgrimage. He went to Africa in order to help imprisoned Christians. He came back to Spain and sold small holy pictures in Gibraltar. Soon he established himself in Granada as a merchant of religious articles. He was forty-two years old.

Conversion to the Service of the Sick. One day John was so moved by a sermon that he gave away all his property and closed his shop. Since he then went running through the city screaming and beating his breast, he was put away in a madhouse. After being released, he came to understand while on pilgrimage that it was his task to give help to the destitute sick.

He began his service to the sick with empty hands. At night he went into the forest to gather wood which he sold during the day to provide food and medicine for his sick ones. With the income from this business he was able to rent a house and accept the sick into it. Then he went about begging for those in his care.

His self-abnegating dedication to the sick made its mark. People in Granada gave him the name "John of God," because in him they saw God's kindness and love for humanity. Soon he had no need to beg, since people brought to him whatever was necessary. His example caused young people to join him, and serve the sick also. He united them into a community without yet founding an order (the transformation into the order of the Brothers of Mercy did not occur until thirty-six years after the saint's death).

Help for All. John brought those in his care from the streets of Granada (similar to Mother Teresa today in India). Without distinction he admitted into his hospitals everyone who needed help. On that account, he was accused before the bishop of harboring vagabonds and prostitutes, and of tolerating abuses in his houses. John answered "If I took in only righteous people, my halls would rapidly become empty, and how could I work then for the salvation of sinners?" He remained available from then on for everyone who needed his help.

John caught the germ of his fatal illness as he tried to rescue a young man who came close to drowning in a flooding river. He thus loved his brethren unto death and crossed from death to life (1 Jn 3:11).

Conversion to Love—For Us. Whether young or old, it is never too late for us to have a serious conversion toward service to our fellow men. How might it appear in the circumstances of our lives?

Petitions

Lord Jesus Christ, you took the sick unto yourself. We pray:

Be present to all who, without much ado, serve the sick and the needy in family and neighborhood. . . .
Bless the Sisters and nurses in our hospitals and nursing homes. . . .
Give strength to all who take interest in the mentally retarded and in the terminally ill. . . .

For that which we do for our least brethren, we do it for you. You who live and reign forever and ever.

St. Frances of Rome (March 9)

FORTY YEARS MARRIED

Introduction

In the Catholic Church's calendar of saints there are but few wives and mothers. Frances of Rome (1384–1440) is among them. If we look at her life, we come to know an energetic wife and mother who, like every wife and mother, would cope with the difficulties and problems of her life and her time. Yet we detect traits in her that today are strange and unfathomable to us.

Penitential Rite

"Is not this the sort of fast that pleases me: to break unjust fetters, to let the oppressed go free, to share your bread with the hungry, and shelter the homeless poor, to clothe the man you see to be naked, and not turn from your own kin?" (Is. 58:6ff, Reading for Friday after Ash Wednesday).

Have mercy, Lord our God, have mercy. . . .

Talk

Women's Destiny. The noble wife and mother Frances of Rome shared in the destiny of many women. She lived in painful and unsettled times. The popes were in Avignon. During her lifetime Rome was conquered and plundered several times by hostile armies. Her own house was for the most part destroyed. Her husband, a leader of the papal party, became gravely wounded and had to leave the city for quite a while. Of her six children, five died as infants or as small children; her only daughter-in-law did not bear children for her first several years of marriage.

Frances did not just fill in for her husband in these trials and burdens. Seeing the overwhelming need in Rome, she helped where she could, only to draw reproaches from her family. She founded a hospital and won others over to support her charitable efforts.

Unusual Forces of Piety. Frances of Rome was considered as being a wife and mother who stood with both feet on the ground of reality. Yet other traits of hers (or should we more cautiously say, traits appearing in accounts of her life) seem strange to us. At the age of eleven she took on hard penances (fasting, scourging . . .); at thirteen, she wanted to enter a convent, but was forced by her father into marriage (at her age!). The longing for religious life stayed alive within her during her long marital years and was acted out in the founding of a community of pious women which she herself joined after the death of her husband. She usually slept only two hours and would spend nights in prayer. She related that, during the last twenty-three years of her life, she continually saw her guardian angel at her side. She described this angel in detail and could read and write in his radiance even at night. . . .

Appropriate Piety Today. I realize that in our day we cannot imitate the life of St. Frances of Rome in the hardships that she imposed upon herself. We will also not be expecting to see our guardian angel in the form of a child next to us on a daily basis. Yet the character of this holy housewife and mother makes this clear: serious Christian life, in the necessary practical sense for mastering each day, is in effect only if faith is of some value to us and if we are ready to pay the necessary price (in these forms—interest, improvement, time, disadvantages); and if we live in trusting relation to God (regular prayer, occasional religious reflection during the tasks of the day).

How is it with me? How could my Lenten resolution be stated this year? Have I read the bishop's Lenten pastoral letter at least once and given thought to his suggestions?

Petitions (or else Thanksgiving)

Lord, if I lift my eyes to you, I often see only the spots of oatmeal on the kitchen ceiling and the new crack in the plaster.

I would like to perform notable deeds—yet must iron white shirts and bake little pastries for the children's party.

And yet, how much communion with you have I already experienced at the ironing board! And I can touch genuine love in the dough for small pastries!

Actually, I need no visions in order to sense your presence. Thank you, Lord! Thank you for not demanding of me anything I cannot do or desire or be. Help me pray, serve, love, to be the best of my ability. Amen. (Taken from Carr and Sorley, *Lord, Bless This Chaos.*)

St. Patrick (March 17)

IRISH CATHOLICISM

Introduction

Who in modern times has done most for the extension of the Catholic Church? I believe that one can hazard the answer: Irish Catholics. Through their mass emigration they have laid the foundations for the development of strong Catholic communities in New Zealand and Australia, among the whites of South Africa, and in great measure in the United States and in England itself. What kind of a Catholic country is this, in which—according to reliable inquiries in 1975—the majority of Catholics take part regularly in Sunday Mass?

Penitential Rite

O Lord, God great and to be feared, we have sinned, we have done wrong, we have acted wickedly, we have betrayed your commandments and your ordinances and turned away from them. Integrity, Lord is yours. To the Lord our God mercy and pardon belong (from Dan. 9:5,7,9, Reading for Monday of the second week of Lent).

Have mercy, Lord our God, have mercy. . . .

Talk

A Long and Painful History. Ireland was Christianized in the fifth century (a good three hundred years before Boniface brought about the thorough Christianization of Germany). In the early Middle

St. Patrick (March 17)

Ages, a flourishing Christian life prevailed on the Emerald Isle. It soon became called "the Isle of Saints."

It was with the Reformation in England that the centuries-long time of suffering of Irish Catholics began. The English overlords sought to impose the Reformation upon them by any means possible, even by bloody persecution and economic reprisals. Yet the Irish remained true to their hereditary faith, even when it caused them to suffer many disadvantages. In the centuries that followed, the mass emigration went on, because there was greater religious freedom and better economic opportunities in the English colonies.

The greater part of the island gained its independence (virtually as a "Catholic state") only in this century. Only Northern Ireland, with its heavily mixed population, stayed with England. The troubles there, frequently recurring and verging on civil war, for years have had their roots in the oppression of Catholics by the ruling Protestant upper class in past centuries.

St. Patrick. At the outset of Ireland's Christian history stands the figure of St. Patrick, still vital to the worldwide Irish Catholicism of our day. He was born in England and was carried off as a child to Ireland. After his successful escape, he became a priest in his homeland, then returned to Ireland in 432 as a missioner. There he became the driving force in the missionizing of the country and in the development of ecclesiastical organization. He died as archbishop of the island in 461.

These sober facts became wildly embellished by legend. Unbelievable claims were made especially with regard to the saint's prayer life. As a shepherd boy, he allegedly always prayed a hundred times both day and night. As missionary bishop, he supposedly: prayed the whole psaltery every day along with a great amount of other prayers and hymns; made the sign of the cross a hundred times at each prayer time; accompanied his prayer every day with three hundred genuflections; and sat during the night in a tub of cold water, so as not to fall asleep at prayer. . . .

Living Piety. True enough, this staggering load of prayer is legend and is not historically verified. A piety becomes evident through these legends that gives primary attention to the external fulfillment of certain rites and sees salvation in the repetition of prayers and devotions. This can allow the concern for interior sharing to get short shrift.

A kind of piety that runs this danger is attributed to the strongly traditionalist Irish Catholicism (in Ireland and England, in America and Australia). Greater problems remain for congregations of Irish influence everywhere, when they try to break out of their isolationism—understandable from historical perspective—toward an environment with different beliefs (which Irish Catholics for centuries have experienced as a hostile environment) and to begin a genuine dialog. The memorial day of Patrick, the Irish national saint, is a good occasion to make ourselves one in prayer with our fellow Irish Christians.

Petitions

Lord God, you will that every nation find itself at home in your Church and serve you.

> Open up the congregations of Irish influence throughout the world to the demands of our age. . . .
> Awaken in them deep piety, whether expressed in traditional forms or in new ways . . .
> Grant to people in Northern Ireland greater understanding of one another and the readiness to forgive and to begin anew. . . .

You who live and reign forever and ever.

St. Cyril of Jerusalem (March 18)

PASTOR AND CATECHIST

Introduction

The breakthrough occurring with Vatican Council II has made us aware that old and familiar worship forms evolved considerably during the course of Church history and can therefore be changed. If we know more about the worship customs of the past, we would be astounded to learn that the Council brought back into use various rites that had disappeared over the course of centuries. As an example, Cyril of Jerusalem gave a sermon in 348 with specific instructions for a worthy communion in the hand.

Penitential Rite

> Lord Jesus Christ, you call us to conversion: Lord, have mercy. . . .
> You come to us in the eucharistic meal: Christ, have mercy. . . .
> You send us back into our everyday life: Lord, have mercy. . . .

Talk

Bishop in Troubled Times. It is a reality that is still observable in our time: as long as the Church is under external pressure, the existing differences of opinion and the tensions barely reach the surface; however, as soon as the external pressure is lifted, it becomes evident that there are theological opinion differences vehemently discussed within the community of believers (as well as human and all-too-human rivalries), which suddenly are dragged out to public attention. As a comparison, it is enough for us to look at the different situations of the Church in western and in eastern Europe today.

The situation was similar in the decades after the public recognition of Christianity in 313. They were full of long and enduring controversies over church politics and theology. It is difficult for us today to gauge how much they were aggravated by personal rivalries between individual bishops.

Cyril (313–387) stood, as bishop of his home city, in the middle of these controversies. He spent eighteen of his thirty-eight years as bishop in exile. He himself matured into an understanding minister of souls during the years of his persecution. In his concern for the unity of the Church in Jerusalem, he came under suspicion of having secret sympathies with his theological opponents!

His Call as Catechist. Cyril must have been a good speaker and religion teacher. What his contemporaries praise about him are things we can verify in twenty-four catecheses (we would call them sermons) that the future bishop delivered in 348 to baptismal candidates. They display his clear and image-filled style with which he would directly speak to his audience. At the same time, these writings contain useful information on the liturgical usages of that period.

Worthy Communion in the Hand. Cyril gave this typical instruction to his baptismal candidates and new Christians: "When you go up to communion, you should not stretch your hand out flat nor spread your fingers. Rather, you should lay your left hand under the right, making at that time a throne to receive the King. Take the Body of Christ up with your empty hand and answer, 'Amen.' Keep your eyes holy during contact with the holy Body and be careful to lose nothing thereof. If someone gave you grains of gold, would you not take the greatest care to lose none of them? Will you therefore not take still greater care that not even the smallest crumb fall away of that which is far more precious than gold and jewels?''

This text shows that our postconciliar communion in the hand is no new invention. In the time of St. Cyril, communion in the mouth was obviously unknown. In addition, these ancient ecclesiastical instructions demand of us to handle reverently the consecrated Host, the sacramental Body of Christ.

Let us then ask ourselves the question (whether we receive Holy Communion in the hand or have it placed in our mouths): Do I approach Holy Communion with reverence and recollection? Am I deeply aware that Jesus Christ comes to me under the sign of bread? Do I bring to the blessed Bread the attention and reverence that I bring to Jesus Christ in faith?

Petitions

Lord Jesus Christ, hear our prayer.

We pray for the young men and women who are confronting their faith in preparation and conferences for marriage. [Silence]   Christ, hear us. . . .
We pray for those parents who are hearing the Good News anew in preparing for their children's baptism. [Silence]   Christ, hear us. . . .
We pray for the parents of our First Communion children, who are being led to reflection on their own faith in meetings for parents.   [Silence]   Christ, hear us. . . .

Lord, let catechetical work in our community be fruitful. You who live and reign forever and ever.

St. Joseph (March 19)

JOSEPH THE JUST

Introduction

The image of the great son, behind whom the father withdraws, holds true in a special way for the father-son relationship in the family of Nazareth. Matthew and Luke (they alone mention the foster-father Joseph) decided to write in the first chapters of their Gospels primarily about the Messiah, in whom the Old Testament hopes and promises were fulfilled. Joseph was of interest to them only for his connection with Jesus and for the way in which he cooperated in the fulfillment of Old Testament prophecies. Joseph is portrayed above all as a "just man," a model for all his namesakes and for every Christian.

Penitential Rite

> "Lord, do not reprove me in your anger: punish me not in your rage.
> Have mercy on me, Lord, I have no strength;
> Lord, heal me, my body is racked;
> Return, Lord, rescue my soul;
> Save me in your merciful love" (Ps. 6:2f,5).

> Have mercy, Lord our God, have mercy. . . .

Talk

Through Joseph, Son of David. According to the Old Testament promises, the Messiah was to come from the line of David. Since no inheritance in Israel passed through the female line, Jesus of Nazareth could have a connection with the ancient Israelite royal house only through his foster father Joseph. For this reason today's Gospel features Joseph's geneology, since he was the legal father of Jesus and had acknowledged him as his child in ritually giving him his name (which God had revealed to him). This is, then, the unshakable place granted to Joseph in the history of salvation: as Mary's husband and as Jesus' legal father he attests to the fulfillment of the Old Testament prophecy, that the lordship of David would last forever in one of his descendants (Reading).

God Chooses the Poor. Joseph (and his family), as "descendants of David," did not belong to the "better circles" in Israel. Their home town of Nazareth was unimportant and did not even enjoy a good name (cf. Jn. 1:46). Carpentry was a little-respected trade. "Is he not the carpenter's son?" (Mt. 13:55). "Is this not Jesus, the son of Joseph, whose father and mother we know?" (Jn. 6:42). These questions came forth later from people of his home village, and they imply that the whole family suffered disdain.

Still, it becomes clear in Joseph's work what is presented as the basis of God's action in Mary's Canticle: "He has cast down the mighty from their thrones, and has lifted up the lowly."

Joseph the Just. As one of the "humble" in the land who received from God a special task in the history of salvation, Joseph was also a devout man who lived completely from the Covenant with Yahweh.

His righteousness (i.e., faithfulness to the demands of God's Covenant) is evident in, for example, the way in which, in today's Gospel, he was going to release his bride. Joseph was confronted with a puzzle by Mary's pregnancy. In all his feeling and thought, he could no longer go through with the marriage to her. Yet, out of compassionate love, he wanted to create no scandal out of the matter. He wanted to divorce Mary in the quietest way possible (i.e., simply in the presence of two witnesses who had to cosign the letter of divorce).

It is certainly in this scene that Joseph's fundamental righteousness is manifest. Even though the Bible puts no *fiat* into his mouth (as Luke did with Mary), he is still a man who submits completely to the will of God and then unquestioningly fulfills God's tasks, even when he himself does not grasp their meaning: "When Joseph awoke, he did what the angel of the Lord had commanded him, and took her as his wife" [Gospel]. That is also his attitude with which he goes with the Child and his Mother to Egypt (Mt. 2:14f) and returns again to Israel (Mt. 2:21ff).

Joseph was a devout man who without question fulfilled God's command in his situation. He lived, even before the coming of Jesus of Nazareth, in complete accordance with the petition in the Our Father, "Thy will be done!" He encourages us to make this petition from the Lord's Prayer our life program.

Petitions

God our Father, with confidence in the intercession of St. Joseph, Patron Saint of the universal Church, we pray to you:

Lead the Church in our times along the ways that you have marked out for her. . . .
Give her the courage to progress on these ways, even though they are new and unfamiliar. . . .
Help her to serve all people in caring and humble love, like Joseph. . . .

God our Father, strengthen us all with your grace, so that we, like Joseph, may affirm your will, now and in the hour of our death. You who live and reign forever and ever.

St. Turibius of Mongrovejo (March 23)

A SOUTH AMERICAN BISHOP

Introduction

Turibius of Mongrovejo—an unknown name in our calendar of saints. The memorial of this South American saint can widen our vision in the eucharistic celebration to the fact that the Church lives not only in our community but also throughout the world. Let us feel ourselves today bound in a special way with the Christians of Latin America, as we pray in the eucharistic prayer, "Remember your Church throughout the world and make us grow in love" (Eucharistic Prayer no. 2).

Penitential Rite

"Cease to do evil. Learn to do good." [Silence] Lord, have mercy. . . .
"Search for justice, help the oppressed." [Silence] Christ, have mercy. . . .
"Be just to the orphan, plead for the widow." [Silence] Lord, have mercy. . . .
(Is. 1:16f., Reading for Tuesday of the second week of Lent).

Talk

Exploitation of and Care for the Oppressed. The Spanish soldiers, officials, and merchants committed some unimaginable cruelties during the conquest of Central America in the sixteenth century. There were indeed even priests and missioners who sought during those times to spread Christianity by means of fire and sword.

There were also, however, idealistic priests and religious of Spanish origin who took the Indians under their protection against their European brethren and used all their leverage at the royal court in their homeland to secure a more humane and Christian policy. Reinhold Schneider has memorialized them in his play, "Las Casas Before Charles V."

Turibius of Mongrovejo. Around 1580—only a few decades after the Spaniards and therefore Christianity set foot in the Americas—there was a flourishing Catholic life in the Spanish colonies. Lima was the political and religious hub. Insofar as Indians had contact with Spaniards, they were Christian. Yet many natives fled from the rapacious and murderous conquerors into the wilderness and were not reached by the established pastors in the cities.

In 1579 Turibius of Mongrovejo, a Spanish layman and jurist, was named archbishop of Lima. He immediately learned the Indians' language (and sought throughout his life to have priests required to learn the indigenous language). Following his great model, the reforming bishop St. Charles Borromeo, he renewed his diocese in the spirit of the Council of Trent. Undeterred by any toil or hardship, he traveled the entire length of the territory entrusted to him three times during his twenty-five-year rule. He summoned a council to Lima and worked with his fellow bishops to apply the decisions of the Council of Trent to South American circumstances.

His great concern was the ministry to the Indians. He worked to alleviate their material want and to secure mission work among them.

St. Turibius of Mongrovejo (March 23)

To that end he established new mission stations and parishes. He forbade (in agreement with the pope and the Spanish king) order priests to administer city parishes, so as to pressure them to found mission stations among the still pagan Indians in deep forests and in the mountains.

It is quite understandable that this fruitful activity of the pastorally zealous bishop met with passion and cross, with resistance among his fellow Spaniards and with calumnies at the royal court—none of which should surprise us now in Passiontide. Yet this experience of communion with Jesus Christ did not discourage him. He proceeded on his way as servant of all, especially of the poorest of the poor in his diocese, the Indians.

The Latin American Church Today. Today Latin America is the largest Catholic continent. Yet the Church carries a burden in the past and the present of the faith in these countries: crass social contradictions (in which the Church has often been aligned with the rich), unbelievable shortage of priests, religious ignorance among believers. . . . Yet there are also positive signs: living faith in small groups (the so-called Base Communities), an alert sensitivity for social justice, growing awareness of responsibility among laity. . . . Let us offer the Latin American Church to God in our petitions.

Petitions

God our Father, in fellowship with St. Turibius of Mongrovejo and all saints of the Latin American Church, we pray to you:

Help pastors in Latin America in their efforts toward a deepening awareness of the faith. . . .
Awaken in all Latin American Christians a sense of responsibility for the Church's life and work. . . .
Support them in their struggle for social justice. . . .

For it is by your will that the Church is a sign of salvation among human beings. You who live and reign forever and ever.

Annunciation of the Lord (March 25)

THE INCARNATION

Introduction

The official name of today's feast, in the middle of Passiontide, is no longer the "Annunciation of Mary," but rather the "Annunciation of the Lord." Nine months before Christmas, the Christmas mystery of God becoming man comes before our eyes in the thoroughly different light of Lent and Passiontide. Let us then celebrate the Eucharist in fellowship with Jesus Christ, who in dark hours looked for his Father's will [Reading]. Let us also celebrate in fellowship with Mary, who declared her *fiat* to the enfleshment of God in the hour of her calling [Gospel] and likewise withstood the times of darkness.

Penitential Rite

Lord Jesus Christ, become man for our salvation: Lord, have mercy. . . .

Lord Jesus Christ, man with us in both dark and joyful hours: Christ, have mercy. . . .

Lord Jesus Christ, dead on the cross and risen from the dead: Lord, have mercy. . . .

Annunciation of the Lord (March 25)

Talk

Incarnation on Christmas Day and Today. "And the Word was made flesh, and dwelt among us" (Jn. 1:14). This truth is the authentic core of the Christmas mystery. When John speaks of God becoming "flesh," he means that God accepts weak, endangered human life in its height and in its depth.

Yet we, as modern people, are tempted to dilute and domesticate this truth. The birth in the manger, the poverty in the shed, the flight into Egypt, even the massacre of the infants in Bethlehem—all signs of the hard realities of the world into which God came—turn into merely charming stories for us, that displace the reality of the Christmas message.

The Feast of the Annunciation of the Lord (or, of the beginning birth of Christ), in the midst of Passiontide, opens our eyes more clearly to what it means for God to become one of us in Jesus Christ. He truly shares in our life. Not only does he enter the world in material poverty; not only does he belong to the rejects and the unaccepted; not only must he fear for his life from the cradle onward. He must also work hard in order to earn a living. He lives for his ideal (the coming Kingdom of God)—and thereby runs up against misunderstanding, good-natured teasing, hate-filled rejection, and cold hostility. He is spared no human reality, even to the point of fearing death on the Mount of Olives, and of despairing on the cross of God's remoteness. He came to know the sadism of his torturers and his enemies' pitiless pleasure at his suffering. He genuinely experienced in his own body what it means to be a man (and to fall into the hands of men).

"And the Word became flesh and dwelt among us." This means (beyond all Christmas cheer) that God goes with us into the darkest hours of our lives and shares our most bitter degradations. And the result? A God of this kind understands us completely in our anxieties and needs, in our worries and problems.

And Mary? Even though Mary is not the central focus of today's feast, she shares nonetheless in the process of the Incarnation. She opened to Jesus the door to this world by her "yes" in the power of God's grace. By answering, "Be it done unto me according to your word," she placed herself at the disposal of the same will of the Father that ruled over the life of her Son as well. In her affirmation, repeated daily, of this will, she shared in the same experiences of Jesus and thus became the Mother of Sorrows, to whom nothing human is alien. She too understands with her whole heart.

Ourselves under God's Will. "See, I come to fulfill your will." This motto from the Reading holds true for the life of Jesus Christ. This program led into a life of trouble and conflict, that only after the cross ended in the joy of resurrection. Mary took on the same program by declaring, "Behold the handmaid of the Lord; be it done unto me according to your word" [Gospel]. She shared in the life, death, and resurrection of her Son. If we declare in the Our Father the same program ("Thy will be done") for ourselves in imitation of God's incarnate Son, then we too—with trust in his help—will share in the same destiny.

Petitions

Let us pray to Jesus Christ, who has shared in our human life in its height and its depth:

> For those who are discouraged and despairing. [Silence] For those who are disappointed and misunderstood. . . .
> For those persecuted and denied of their rights. . . .
> For the sick and the dying. . . .

Lord Jesus Christ, be near to all who carry the cross in their lives, and help them to bear it in union with yourself, so that their way of the cross might become for them the way to resurrection. You who live and reign forever and ever.

St. Francis of Paula (April 2)

SILENCE FOR GOD'S SAKE

Introduction

"People talk practically without interruption. One may find it quaint that a person may try to spend a whole day or certain hours without speaking. Yet if one believes that one's word has meaning, one will try to keep times for silence." How do we view this thought of Jörg Zink? On the memorial day of the holy hermit Francis of Paula—who withdrew into solitude at the age of sixteen and sought to be silent for the remaining fifty-five years of his life—we can reflect a bit on our own attitude toward silence.

Penitential Rite

Lord Jesus Christ, you went into the desert for forty days in order to pray: Lord, have mercy. . . .

You withdrew to a place set apart early every morning and prayed there: Christ, have mercy. . . .

You went apart from your disciples on the Mount of Olives and communed in solitude with your Father: Lord, have mercy. . . .

Talk

What is a Hermit? What is a hermit? A rich recluse who can afford a little cottage in the woods away from traffic noise and air pollution (and, of course, with a color TV and a car), and who also carries on some praiseworthy pious hobby? A modern refugee from civilization, with a religious twist, who wants to go "back to nature," who lives in a simple cabin in the forest and favors a meatless diet and natural healing aids?

The great hermits of Christian history were people who were driven to probe the question of the meaning of life and thereby the question of God. They wanted to go into the ground of their life and took a life with God very seriously. They recognized the danger of failing to hear or see God in the swirl of multiple external stimuli; and in the noise of their own inner disquiet.

So as not to fail to hear or see God, the hermit retreats from "the tumult of the world." He settles in an environment that has little change or outside contact and purposely leads a simple or undemanding life.

Within this external remoteness he experiences even more intensely the noise and uproar of thoughts and ideas within himself. He sees that his life's work is to bring his inner disquiet more and more into peace through recollection, so as to hear God's still, small voice more closely.

Silence as the Way to the Essential. The religiously motivated hermit (as St. Francis of Paula) has little in common with romantic characters that crop up in popular novels or plays. He leads a life of inner and outer silence for God's sake.

He therefore stands in contrast with current-day life-styles and attitudes. Today's average human being is after many different experiences: He wants change, new stimuli, excitement, trips. He relies on hectic activity and ever-new sensory thrills, because he thinks that joy and fulfillment in life depend on how much he experiences.

The hermit takes the opposite approach. In his opinion, man touches intensely what is essential in life if he shields himself as much as possible from outside experiences and stimuli, and holds himself in silence before God.

Create Silence! Silence—outer and inner isolation as a way to God and as a provision for a vital religious life. Do I have the courage for it?

A suggestion: every day set aside a ten-minute period, either early morning or evening. Sit in a quiet corner of your room. Light only a candle. Leave the radio and television off. Breathe deeply a few times—and then for once be with yourself for these ten minutes.

You will soon feel how restless you are, how driven you feel toward external activity. Restrain this restlessness (without getting impatient with yourself) and try to direct yourself inwardly toward God amid all the noise of your own thoughts and ideas—and to converse with God in prayer.

It may be that by maintaining faithfully this ten-minute desert, you may notice after a time that your very life is becoming more genuine—and happier.

Petitions

I ask, Lord, that my judgment be merciful, my decisions provident, and my answers thought out. I want to make peace and lend strength with my words. I will achieve this only when my word comes forth out of silence. Lord, I will be silent so that I may learn to tell the difference between your word and mine. For I want to speak with your mouth and not with my own. Amen (from a prayer by Jörg Zink).

St. Isidore of Seville (April 4)

THE LAST FATHER OF THE CHURCH

Introduction

"He gave alms generously, was thoughtful in his hospitality, warmhearted, true to his word, just in his judgments, zealous in preaching, friendly in admonishment, skilled at winning souls for God, careful in explaining the Scriptures, wise in counsel, modest in clothing, moderate at meals, ready to lay down his life for virtue, and excelling in every form of kindness." With these words a biographer portrayed St. Isidore of Seville. To what extent has each one of us—in proportion to our life circumstances and everyday responsibilities—merited praise like this?

Penitential Rite

"God of hosts, bring us back; let your face shine on us and we shall be saved.

And we shall never forsake you again: give us life that we may call upon your name" (Ps. 80:20,19).

Have mercy, Lord our God, have mercy. . . .

Talk

A Model for Life. The words below have been handed on to us from the "last father of the Church," Isidore of Seville (556–636), as they appear in his writings on monasticism: "In his life the abbot has to

St. Isidore of Seville (April 4)

be a perfect model of obedience, convinced that he may lay down no rule that he himself has not already carried out. He must inspire each individual and admonish each one according to personality and necessity." With these words the great scholar, church politician, monk, and educator set a goal for a new generation of priests, a goal that is valid for anyone responsible for leadership of other people (in the family, in church, in society . . .). Isidore worked to put this ideal into effect in his highly active life.

Monk and Bishop. Isidore was brought up by his brother Leander, whom he later succeeded as abbot and bishop. He took advantage of a wide-ranging education that prepared him for his own extensive literary accomplishments.

Amid the transitions of his time (it was the age in which the European tribal migrations were coming to an end, and relationships within Europe were starting to consolidate again), he strove with all his might to order and organize church life anew. With this goal, his first concern was life in the monasteries. He summarized carefully the many rules and regulations that had accumulated over a period of time and simplified them. For him, monastic life (understood to be an especially serious life) called for renunciation, strict poverty, perseverance, and faithfulness in a life decision once laid down, liturgical prayer, reading, and work.

Isidore published a new Latin Bible which became used throughout Spain. As bishop (beginning in 601) he organized his diocese with such success that ecclesiastical authority throughout the whole country adapted itself to the new realities by using his model. He established a training center for future priests in Seville, which gained influence far beyond his diocese.

Church Politician. His sense of law and order shows itself in his compilation of laws which he drew together for the Visigoths in Spain. It became the foundation of civil order for several centuries.

Less fortunate, when seen with hindsight, were Isidore's stated goals for cooperation between Church and State. Adhering to the practice of his era, he linked the official power of the highest civil authorities with the power of the bishop. His whole policy was directed toward the fundamental union of ecclesiastical and civil power. It was very much his belief that the royal court should become a center of church authority. He did not foresee the danger of the unreliable involvement of the State in the affairs of the Church, which the medieval Church (to give one example) battled violently against.

In all his efforts on behalf of the Church and his country, in all his pastoral work, the motto of his life was: demand from others only what you demand from yourself. Perhaps this was the secret of his success. And perhaps we can make our commitment to family, Church, and society more effective by applying this motto to ourselves.

Petitions

Lord Jesus Christ, on this memorial day of the holy bishop Isidore, we pray for our bishop and for all bishops:

Fill them with your Holy Spirit and grant them anew every day the power of faith, hope, and love. . . .
Grant that they may lead their dioceses for your glory and for the salvation of the faithful. . . .
Send them wise, trustworthy, and unselfish co-workers. . . .
Bless their efforts for the training of future priests and pastors. . . .

For you lead the Church through the successors of the apostles. You who live and reign forever and ever.

St. Vincent Ferrer (April 5)

ON THE WRONG SIDE?

Introduction

A contemporary biographical account of the late medieval penitential preacher, Vincent Ferrer (1350–1419), states that his greatest accomplishment was to persuade women of high social class to give up their outlandish hairdos. His genuinely sanctifying life, however, shows more clearly in that, in a turbulent time, he did not lose faith in the Church and was ready to make a painful change of commitment for the sake of her unity.

Penitential Prayer

"But who can detect all his own errors? From hidden faults acquit me. Then shall I be blameless, clean from grave sin, O Lord, my rescuer, my rock!" (Ps. 19:13,14b,15b).

Have mercy, Lord our God, have mercy. . .

Talk

Times of Confusion. In the fourteenth century, great saints worked tirelessly for the return of the pope from the Avignon exile. They eventually succeeded. In short order, however, events led to the great western schism. Beginning in 1379, there was one pope in Rome and another pope in Avignon. Each one claimed to be the rightful successor of Peter. Both sought the recognition of European countries, and both were supported by great saints.

Vincent Ferrer, a Spaniard, was on the side of the Avignon pope. The Dominican friar had acquired a good name as a theologian and preacher in his own country. Ordinary people revered him because of his austere way of life and his great love for the poor.

At the age of forty, Vincent left his country as part of the retinue of the future Avignon pope, Benedict XIII. On different trips, he came to see the discouraging conditions in different parts of the Church. At the same time, his love for the Church grew along with his commitment to serve her.

The Great Penitential Preacher. His papal patron called him to Avignon as confessor to the court. Yet he did not stay there long. He felt driven to call people everywhere to penance and conversion, since he was certain that the end of the world was at hand.

For this reason, he undertook at fifty years of age a preaching tour that took him through much of Europe. He spoke out whether welcome or not; he counseled, blamed, admonished, and patiently instructed (Reading), in order to help his contemporaries to be ready and awake to await the Lord coming again [Gospel]. Through powerfully worded talks, he aroused his audiences and stirred them to religious renewal. Many joined him in his preaching journeys. Others displayed their readiness for conversion by public flagellations. Vincent often had to intervene to control his ecstatic listeners and to warn them against fanatic foolishness.

Between Parties in Church Politics. In all his pastoral and political activity, the renowned preacher remained on the side of the Avignon pope until the later years of his life. He first became unsure when a third pope set up residence in Pisa. When the Council of Constance demanded of all three popes that they renounce their claims and make room for a newly elected pope, Vincent left Avignon and used all his moral authority in Spain and southern France in support of the council's decision. Even though it came hard for him to break his ties with Benedict XIII in Avignon, he placed the well-being of the universal Church above his personal loyalties and had the courage, in his old age, to carry out a change of opinion.

Faithfulness to the Church in Hard Times. Vincent Ferrer—a committed Christian within the Church, who in a confused time took clear sides with firm resolve; who, however, always asked what the welfare of the Church demanded here and now; who sought an answer to this question from Jesus Christ and had the courage to make a course correction when in Christ it was necessary. I think he can be a model for us in our time of change, where we deal not with different popes, but with being "liberal" or "conservative."

Petitions

Lord Jesus Christ, we pray for all who find it hard to stay true to you in your Church:

For all who worry that the Church might corrupt the faith by the changes in our day. [Silence]
For all who fear that the Church might betray the Good News out of excessive concern for new approaches. . . .
For all who strive to bring out the common elements that bind all groups in the Church together in you. . . .

Lord, help us all, in faithfulness to you, to bear up under the Church's difficulties and to proclaim the Gospel in our time. You who live and reign forever and ever.

St. John Baptist de la Salle (April 7)

EDUCATIONAL REFORM IN THE SEVENTEENTH CENTURY

Introduction

Our present-day school system is mainly in the hands of the State. Schools under religious direction are in the minority. Yet in earlier centuries the Church alone ran schools, and pathfinding educational reforms were achieved by churchmen. An early advocate for modern education was St. John Baptist de la Salle, in France around 1700.

Penitential Rite

"Unless you convert and become like little children, you shall not enter the Kingdom of Heaven." [Silence] Lord, have mercy. . . .

"Whoever humbles himself as this little child shall be the greatest in the Kingdom of Heaven." [Silence] Christ, have mercy. . . .

"And whoever shall accept such a child in my name will also accept me." [Silence] Lord, have mercy. . . .

Talk

The Privilege of an Education. In the France of Louis XIV, the "Sun King," there were schools enough for the sons and daughters of the upper classes. Many religious congregations were dedicated to the education of the children of nobles and of gentry. However, children and youth from the common folk (whether of the city or of the country) had no access to these schools.

Education for the Common People. John Baptist de la Salle (1651–1719) came from a rich noble family. He attended the right schools and pursued a university education. As a newly ordained priest he became aware of the lack of schools for the common people, a lack due basically to political reasons. He turned away from other attractive ecclesiastical careers and made it his life's work to promote schooling for the lower social classes.

The saint did not take up this work alone. He gathered around himself a group of teachers, with whom he established the "Society of Brothers of Christian Schools." Together with his confreres he founded elementary schools on the outskirts of towns and in open country. He set up teachers' academies in order to train his own confreres as well as laymen for service in basic schools. He was the first to organize schools in a system of classes, so familiar to us. He substituted the vernacular for Latin as the language of instruction, and forbade the beating of pupils with a rod. No tuition charge was made of the pupils.

These pedagogical innovations did not always attract favorable attention to John. Churchmen mistrusted him, and teachers in established schools (that charged tuition and lived from it) gave him difficulties. Inner conflicts as well endangered the existence of the young religious community. Yet gradually the saint's work consolidated. The number of brothers grew, men who accepted his pedagogical concepts and developed them further. When John died on Good Friday, 1719, the community of the Brothers of the Christian Schools was well launched into a future which, continuing in our day, has accomplished immeasurable good for Christian education in parochial and boarding schools.

Religious Education Today. In St. John Baptist de la Salle's time, the religious education of youth was assumed by a Christian school system. Today academic education and education for a conscious life of faith do not necessarily happen together. Private Catholic schools do not alter this situation greatly. The Christian family and the parish today more than ever before must provide religious education for youth and must strive to lead the upcoming generation into an aware faith.

Are we sufficiently aware of this task in our families and parishes? What is being done for the living transmission of faith in the family (in common prayer and in religious conversations with the youngsters)? How do we relate to the efforts in our parish to intensify instruction for First Communion and Confirmation by forming small groups? Are we ready to participate and make our own contribution to the transmission of faith in our parish?

Petitions

Lord Jesus Christ, we are to pass on to coming generations what we have learned in faith.

We pray for those children who are making their first holy communion during these days. [Silence] Christ, hear us. . . .
We pray for the fathers and mothers who have shared in the instruction of their children. [Silence] Christ, have mercy. . . .
We pray for our children's teachers, who give witness of their faith in their entire teaching. [Silence] Christ, hear us. . . .

Lord, let us all be strong in faith. You who live and reign forever and ever.

St. Stanislaus (April 11)

IN DEFENSE OF HUMAN RIGHTS

Introduction

According to tradition, Bishop Stanislaus of Krakow was murdered and quartered in 1079 in a church in his see city by soldiers of the (Christian!) king of Poland. The king is spoken of as himself having taken part in this brutal act. Stanislaus thus became the sacrifice of an incompetent and despotic ruler, who aroused the resistance of his subjects and clung to power with brute force—something that can still happen in our time.

Penitential Rite

"My soul gives thanks to the Lord, and all my being, bless his holy name, who redeems your life from the grave, who crowns you with love and compassion, who fills your life with good things, renewing your youth like an eagle's" (Ps. 103:1,4,5).

Have mercy, Lord our God, have mercy. . . .

Talk

The Conflict Then. The fatal conflict in Bishop Stanislaus' life is quickly recounted. Boleslaus the Clever became king of Poland when he was fifteen or sixteen. Out of his family background he carried in himself the seed of spiritual sickness, which he acted out in a lack of mental balance, in a tendency toward gruesomeness, and in often uncontrolled behavior.

His rule became a torment for the whole country and brought out the resistance of responsible people. Bishop Stanislaus had ties with this group or was himself outright a leading figure among them. Whether the king in his mistrust only suspected an attempt to overthrow him, or whether steps to that end had actually been taken, he in any event tried to strengthen his claim by naked force and had the bishop murdered at the altar in a church.

The Conflict Today. Even today there are despotic rulers who arrange purges because of mistrust. And there are also men and women aware of their responsibilities who alone and in groups resist arbitrary and violent power and who therefore get pushed out of the way. We can think of Stalin, of Hitler, of many known (and unknown) dictators in the so-called Third World. We will spontaneously recall men and women (whether of Christian inspiration or not) who out of a sense of responsibiliy move to the defense of a whole nation; churchmen who pay for their courage with death; priests and ordinary faithful who land in political prisons; civil rights activists and dissidents in many countries. . . .

Martyrs? Stanislaus became venerated by the Church as a witness of faith, as a Christian who paid with his life for his faithfulness to Jesus' Christ. He was not murdered by enemies of Christianity who were rejecting Christian teaching. He was killed by the king: in his rule by might, the king saw himself threatened by a churchman who had committed himself in Jesus Christ to people oppressed and deprived of their rights. In today's terms, he paid with his life for his commitment, motivated by his Christianity, to human rights and to the welfare of the entire nation.

We can therefore name this Polish bishop the patron and exemplar of all those who, in our present-day conditions and often with awesome commitment, defend the rights of the individual against attacks of the State both east and west. Among them are groups united by their Christianity who know they are sent for this task by Jesus Chrust (cf. Gospel), Dom Helder Camara and the Scholl brothers (who gave up their lives during the Nazi terror) are symbolic figures of these groups.

Yet there are also many organizations and individual militants not of Christian inspiration who share the same goal. Think of "Amnesty International," of many Russian dissidents—or of various groups of socialist persuasion. If the Church venerates Stanislaus (who dedicated himself to human rights) as a martyr, we must also see the bond with all those who—without sharing our religious conviction—risk their lives (their property, their careers), like Jesus Christ, for those who are oppressed and deprived of their rights.

Petitions

Let us pray for all those who dedicate their lives for human rights:

For Christians, that they not become weary of laboring for freedom and justice. . . . Christ, hear us. . . . .
For international organizations, that they may constantly awaken the world's conscience by their actions. . . .
For all who want to change conditions by the use of violence, that they might follow the nonviolent way of Jesus Christ. . . . .

Lord Jesus Christ, you will that we dedicate ourselves even in the political sphere to the dignity of our fellow human beings. Give us the courage and strength for this even in difficult and dangerous circumstances. You who live and reign forever and ever.

St. Martin I (April 13)

A POPE IN THE POLITICAL ARENA

Introduction

We call the pope "vicar of Christ on earth." Are we aware that we thus see him in imitation of the crucified Redeemer, who lived entirely for a religious reason—and thereby became involved in politics? Pope Martin I shared in this lot of Jesus Christ in his own way.

Penitential Rite

Jesus, betrayed by Judas, abandoned by your disciples, denied by Peter: Lord, have mercy. . . .

Jesus, deprived of freedom, beaten with whips, crowned with thorns and mocked: Christ, have mercy. . . .

Jesus, accused by false witnesses, thrown out by the Sanhedrin, condemned to death: Lord, have mercy . . . (Gl 166).

Talk

Politics and Theology. Around 650, Byzantium was the unchallenged political center of the Mediterranean area. Italy belonged to the Eastern Roman Empire, but the emperor had his difficulties in maintaining his rule there.

Within the Church—which then was an integral component of soci-

St. Martin I (April 13)

ety—there arose once again vehement theological controversies on the right understanding of the mysteries of Jesus Christ, known as the monothelite controversy. This intrachurch issue became compounded with rigid political interests and led to great turmoil.

A Pope in the Political Arena. The emperor in Byzantium used all political means of power to support those bishops, resident mostly in the Eastern Empire, who held the teaching of only one will in Jesus Christ. The Western Church (Italy, Spain, France) held the theological opinion that there must be two centers of will in Jesus, in keeping with his two natures as God and man.

During these controversies, Pope Martin I was elected in 649 in Rome. He took office without gaining the approval of the Eastern Roman emperor. The emperor was enraged by this and commanded his Italian deputy to jail the pope. The deputy (obviously counting on the support of the Western Church) rebelled against the emperor and was able to hold his ground in Italy for three years.

After the final suppression of the rebellion, the captured pope was transported to Byzantium and there was sentenced to death on grounds of high treason (he was accused of complicity with the rebellious imperial officials). At the behest of church circles, his sentence was commuted to deportation to the island of Crimea, where he died shortly thereafter. It was his particular grief that, soon after his arrest in Rome, a new pope was chosen and his community forsook him.

The Christian in the Political Arena. During Pope Martin I's time, theological conflicts still held so much public interest that they had influence on politics. Discussions among our theologians certainly create waves in the Church, but they do not excite our secularized society.

It is different, however, when Christians today try to live out the implications of their faith. That means that even now they can find themselves in the political arena. Christians in an atheistic country try to live their faith while keeping a low profile—and they are seen as an element menacing the State. They struggle against the discrimination against certain groups in our society and get accused of revolutionary agitation. They dedicate themselves in a Christian country to social justice—and they get labeled as Marxists. They call for peace and for fair balance in the social and racial tensions of our time—and suddenly find themselves in the crossfire. They bear up under unjustified suspicions, economic disadvantages, persecution, and imprisonment.

The Christian in the political arena! May we ask ourselves, when might something similar happen to us? After all, it happened that way to Jesus Christ. He wanted to bring men and women to God. He was dedicated to the poor and the needy because he knew they were especially beloved to God. People feared that he would disturb the carefully established political peace. He was accused of preaching sedition and political revolution. And he came to ruin—by human standards—in the political arena, as did Pope Martin I and as do many Christians today. Yet for Jesus this way was the way to resurrection—which we believe is also true for all those who imitate him.

Petitions

Lord Jesus Christ, you lived and worked in faithfulness to your Father's command—and you became involved in the political arena.

Be near to those who try to live out their faith in atheistic countries. . . .
Give courage to all who are dedicated to social justice. . . .
Support all who fight discrimination against certain classes in our society. . . .

Lord, be close to all who follow you on the way of dedication to humanity, on the way of the cross. You who live and reign forever and ever.

St. Anselm (April 21)

FAITH SEEKING UNDERSTANDING

Introduction

"Lord, I do not seek to penetrate your heights; my understanding can in no way reach you. I only ask to grasp somehow your truth, which my heart believes and loves. For I do not try to understand in order to believe; rather I believe, that I may understand." Do we think like the great theologian Anselm, from whom this quote comes? Do we try, through continuing religious education, to penetrate more deeply into the mystery of our faith, even though we know that we can never totally exhaust the reality of God?

Penitential Rite

"The waves of death rose about me; the torrents of destruction assailed me.

In my anguish I called to the Lord; I cried to my God for help.

He brought me forth into freedom, he saved me because he loved me" (Ps. 18:5,7,17).

Have mercy, Lord our God, have mercy. . . .

Talk

Lifelong Calling. At the age of twenty-three, Anselm (1033–1109) left his northern Italian home after vehement quarrels with his father. Restless, he wandered throughout Europe for some years.

Then he became a monk in western France. In 1093 he became archbishop of Canterbury and thus leader of the English Church. Sharp disagreements with the king brought on his exile two times. Only the last three years of his life passed on a calmer course.

In every period of his life, the great love of this monk and bishop was theology. For him, his faith in Jesus Christ is the most normal thing in the world, set as it is against the background of the Christian-influenced Middle Ages. His writings display deep piety. In his theological works, he does not content himself with repeating traditional formulations and with citing biblical passages. He uses his intellect to understand articles of faith more deeply and at least to find the traces of the mystery of God in Jesus Christ.

An Ever New Task in the Church. What Anselm attempted in his time is the Church's task time and again. Since human ideas and thought develop and change, in the Church it is not enough merely to repeat "what we've always said" in theology, in religious instruction, and in preaching. Each generation must strive to grasp in terms of its own thought and questioning what earlier generations have grasped and expressed in their own terms.

The Church, therefore, needs theologians and pastors (and so do we, for our living faith) who are rooted in faith and try to determine—with an ear to the problems of our time—how they can proclaim the Good News to people of our time clearly, credibly, and impressively. Of course, these theologians sometimes spoil familiar religious notions that we think are essential to our faith even though they are not. However, when we open ourselves to their reflections and arguments, we perhaps see how they can lead us to a deeper understanding of Jesus Christ. For instance: if we today consider no longer as a thing that earlier generations called "sanctifying grace," but rather speak of "divine life" or "communion with God," then we are surely closer to the Word in the Reading: "May Christ live in your hearts through faith."

St. Anselm (April 21)

Ever a New Task for the Individual. Faith looking for understanding: this is a lifelong program for each individual Christian. Anyone who relies only on his religious instruction in school, or who clings to obsolete religious notions, will soon lose joy in faith. Contemporary people are used to raising questions in every area of life and forming their own opinions. They should also have the interest in the area of religion to examine all of it in depth.

This does not happen, however, without investing time and mental effort. Listening to a Sunday homily is not enough. Reading the diocesan newspaper or some other religious weekly helps a bit more. Attending a preaching series, a seminar, or something similar, are also further steps on the way of faith looking for understanding.

Petitions

Lord Jesus Christ, your Church will proclaim the Good News until the end of time. We pray for all who help in this task:

For scholars and professors of theology, Christ hear us. . . .
For pastors and teachers of Christian doctrine. . . .
For all the faithful caught in hard religious controversy. . . .

Lord, be near to your Church in the Holy Spirit, so that she might uncover new ways of thinking in faith wherever it is necessary. You who live and reign forever and ever.

St. George (April 23)

SOLDIER OF CHRIST

Introduction

George, a Roman officer, probably was executed in 303 under Emperor Diocletian, for his religious convictions. In legend he appears as the hero who gloriously conquers the dragon in battle. In this role he became a much-revered popular saint, patron of soldiers and patron of Scouts. As a soldierly symbolic figure of Christian life, he reminds all of us of the basics of our following Christ.

Penitential Rite

"Rejoice, my brothers and sisters, when you are beset by all sorts of temptations." [Silence] Lord, have mercy. . . .
"You know that the testing of your faith makes for perseverance." [Silence] Christ, have mercy. . . .
"Whoever remains steadfast will receive the crown of life." [Silence] Lord, have mercy. . . .

Talk

Symbolic Figure of Christian Life? It is understandably hard for us to compare living in imitation of Christ with living like soldiers. Yet, maybe we can look at certain ideal images of military life on this memorial day of St. George and consider how they hold true for each Christian life as well.

The soldier of Christ pledges his allegiance in his baptismal promises to Jesus Christ. He pledges to be loyal to Jesus Christ and promises to dedicate himself actively to the concerns of the people of Jesus Christ and to the service of the Church in today's world. This dedication is concerned not only with the defense of the faith, but also especially with an assertive, outreaching witness to the Good News.

Honor and Distinction. A soldier repeatedly was told that it was an honor and a distinction to belong to a given army. He was told that he should be proud to be able to carry the emperor's cloak. Dishonorable discharge awaited unworthy soldiers.

I don't know how many soldiers today look upon their job as a special honor and distinction. The Christian, nonetheless, sees his call to faith in the imitation of Christ as a special privilege. For him, faith is not in the first place an oppressive burden, but rather a gift that ever astonishes him. Without being overbearing, he is proud to belong to the army of Jesus Christ.

Life on Trial. The soldier does not live in safe circumstances. He puts aside comforts and accepts hard living conditions. He knows that stress is part of his job. He must risk his life. By many standards, this way of life is a school of authentic manhood: Under these conditions, a man emerges for what he really is.

Here is not the place to decide whether the army is really the true school of the country. Yet when this idea is elevated to the level of faith, it bears a striking similarity to this passage from the Reading: "Rejoice, my brethren, when you are beset by all kinds temptations, for you know that the testing of your faith makes for perseverance." The thought he is expressing here is that faith grows more in a life confronted by uncertainty of faith and by attacks on belief than it does in a life of secure religious surroundings. In situations of external and internal religious controversy, it becomes clearer that my faith is more alive than in times of quiet certainty of belief.

If this is true, will we not really pray that God lead us into testing and uncertainty of faith in order to strengthen our belief? Yet if such situations arrive, if sickness and death make us doubt God's goodness, if the external situation of the Church discourages us, if we cannot see our way clear with all our human optimism, we will then pray that we might come closer in fellowship with Christ and all the saints even in this testing of faith and thus "remain steadfast in temptation" [Reading].

Petitions

God our Father, together with St. George we pray for all who today live tested and uncertain in faith.

> For young people confused by conflicts of opinions around them [Silence].
> For adults who are troubled by the internal and external situation of the Church. . . .
> For the sick and the aged, for whom the face of God is obscured by their experience of great pain. . . .

Lord, stay near to these and to all in their temptations, so that their faith might grow and be fulfilled. You who live and reign forever and ever.

St. Fidelis of Sigmaringen (April 24)

FOR THE ONE CHURCH

Introduction

Among the Christian Churches today there exists a climate of openness and of searching for mutual understanding. We consider ourselves in the Catholic Church to be on the laborious path toward unity in faith together with other Christian denominations. This ecumenical climate has not always been there. At the start of the Thirty Years' War, during the era of the Counter Reformation, Catholics and Protestants went around splitting open each other's heads. Fidelis of Sigmaringen was a victim of a hostility among Christian communions that for us today is barely imaginable.

Penitential Rite

Lord Jesus Christ, you recognize our longing for the unity of the Church: Lord, have mercy. . . . .

You know how little power we have to achieve this unity: Christ, have mercy. . . .

You alone open the door to the unity of Christian Churches: Lord, have mercy. . . .

Talk

Time of the Counter Reformation. By 1600 the new faith of the Reformation had spread over nearly all of Europe (aided not only by religious concerns, but also with the involvement of strong political considerations). The Catholic Church had undergone inner renewal in the aftermath of the Council of Trent and had launched the Counter Reformation in order to win back lost areas. It was again supported in this quest by interested political forces. The agents of this renewal of Catholic faith were above all the newly established orders of the Jesuits and the Capuchins. It was not unusual that in areas that were to be won back for the Catholic Church, it came often to hand-to-hand combat among the Protestant population, the troops of the Catholic sovereign, and the Catholic preachers.

Martyr for the One Church. During this turbulent time lived Markus Roy (1578–1622) from Sigmaringen in Swabia, Germany. He studied philosophy and law and finished his studies with his doctorate. He worked first as a lawyer. Then he was deeply moved, at the age of 34, by the fearless dedication of Capuchins during an epidemic of the plague in his home area, to the point where he entered the order and was ordained a priest. He took Fidelis as his name in the order.

Father Fidelis worked mostly in Switzerland and in western Austria. In 1622 he accepted the assignment to work in the canton of Grisons among the Calvinist inhabitants for the purpose of winning them back to the Catholic Church. As he was preaching in one village at the people's invitation, a riot instigated by some townspeople ended with the death of the preacher, on April 24, 1622.

Ecumenism Today. Dedication to the one Church during the time of St. Fidelis of Sigmaringen showed itself in heroic dedication to winning back Protestants to the Catholic Church. Behind the great struggles of the Counter Reformation, there were certainly political

St. Fidelis of Sigmaringen (April 24)

reasons as well. Yet the missionaries of the re-Catholicization of large areas of Europe were more moved by the ideal of saving souls. Fidelis, for one, was thinking of Calvinists when he prayed, "Have mercy, most gracious Father of mercies, on our poor world and lead back to the truth those who have strayed from the faith. Let not so many who are made in your likeness perish. . . ." For him, all those who did not confess the Catholic Church were lost for eternity

We realize today, in the Church of the Second Vatican Council, that every human being who follows his own conscience with sincere awareness is on the path to fulfillment in Jesus Christ. We therefore consider non-Catholic Christians (and non-Christians) to be people of good will, who seek to follow Jesus Christ according to their best conscience. We're even ready to learn from them. And we know that we find unity with other believers in Christ only if we talk out and patiently clarify our divergent views on faith with respect for one another. Our ecumenical efforts will be marked, even in the external modes of contacts among confessions, more by the spirit that is expressed in this prayer by St. Fidelis of Sigmaringen (which we use here instead of the Petitions):

> Most loving Jesus, safeguard me lest I ever, even if a man hate and persecute me, despise, scorn, or degrade him, or turn away from him. Let me never bear hatred toward him or even any bitter feeling; and do not let me ever despair of his correction for as long as he yet lives (Fidelis of Sigmaringen).

St. Mark (April 25)

THE FIRST EVANGELIST

Introduction

Vehement arguments have come about in recent years concerning the "truth" of the Gospels, those four New Testament books that are intended to lead people to belief in the Risen One, as they present the mystery of him with the aid of remembrances of his earthly life. The oldest Gospel is attributed to Mark, the saint for today.

Penitential Rite

"God brings down the proud, but lifts up the lowly." [Silence]   Lord, have mercy. . . .
"Cast all your worries upon the Lord, and he will care for you." [Silence]   Christ, have mercy. . . .
"God will place you on solid ground."   [Silence]   Lord, have mercy. . . .

Talk

John Mark.   According to the Acts of the Apostles, John Mark was the son of the Mary in whose house the first Christian community gathered in Jerusalem (Acts 12:12). He accompanied Barnabas and Paul on their first missionary journey, but retuurned disenheartened early to

Jerusalem (Acts 13:13). This caused a grave quarrel between the two missioners as they were getting ready for the second missionary journey (Acts 15:36–41). Mark is mentioned later among Paul's companions (Phlm. 1:23; Col. 4:10; 2 Tim. 4:11). Tradition has it that he later founded a Christian community in Alexandria, Egypt, and died there a martyr.

We can leave aside the question whether this John Mark was really the author of the oldest Gospel or not, a point which is still unsettled among Biblical scholars. It is more important that we take a clear look at what the Gospel of Mark (just as the other three Gospels) intends to tell us.

The Situation of the Gospels. The oldest writings of the New Testament are the early Letters of the Apostle Paul. In them, the missionary to the gentiles tries to lead people to faith in the Risen One, without expressly recounting the earthly life of Jesus. Since he wanted to lead people to the Risen One who was present then and there in the Church community, he was able to dispense with memories of Jesus' earthly life.

Mark also wanted to lead people through his Gospel to faith in the Risen One present here and now. But he tries to shed light on the mystery of the Risen One by describing the deeds and words of the earthly Jesus, who in fact is the Risen One.

Mark was convinced that Jesus of Nazareth, who wandered through the towns and villages of Palestine, was one and the same person as the Risen One, revealed himself after death on a cross to his disciples and now was present in the Church. Thus he could make known to the Christians of the young Church what Jesus Christ meant to them by telling about his earthly life. At the same time, he modified the stories of Jesus' earthly life in such a way as to allow Christians (or Jews and pagans through missionary efforts) to see more clearly the mystery of the Risen One. Toward this end, he was able to take liberties with the historical remembrances.

The Gospel's Message for Us. If the purpose of Mark's Gospel (as of all the Gospels) is to lead us to faith in the Risen One and not primarily to satisfy historical curiosity, we do not fulfill this purpose if we merely ask: what really happened then in Palestine? We have to ask, who is the Risen One whom the Church confesses, and what meaning does he have for our lives?

Let's take an example—the story of the storm on the lake (Mk. 4:35–41), let us allow ourselves to be asked by Jesus amidst all the present-day problems of the Church, "Why are you afraid? Do you have no faith?" Then let us remember that the Risen One here and now travels with the Church—he is along in the boat!—and that he is stronger than any buffeting wind or treacherous wave that may threaten the existence of the Church and our faith.

If we listen to the Gospel in this way, then we will also understand why the priest, after announcing the Gospel, says, "May the Word of the Gospel strengthen our faith." And we, strengthened in our faith in Jesus Christ, can answer, "Praise to you, Oh Christ!"

Petitions

Lord Jesus Christ, you travel along with us in the ship of the Church. We pray:

Strengthen the faith of insecure Christians. . . .
Awaken hope in all who are discouraged. . . .
Light the fire of your love in all who think only of themselves. . . .

You who live and reign forever and ever.

St. Peter Chanel (April 28)

PATRON SAINT OF THE SOUTH SEA ISLANDS

Introduction

I don't know if our travel agents include the small South Sea islands of Wallis and Futuna in their tour packages. If you were to go there today, you would discover not only the enchantment of the South Sea, you would also find a Catholic population. On these islands the life of St. Peter Chanel came to an end on April 28, 1841.

Penitential Rite

Lord Jesus Christ, even in our day you offer the Good News of God to men and women: Lord, have mercy. . . .

You demand from us also conversion and faith: Christ, have mercy. . . .

You call people even today to your following, to make of them fishers of men: Lord, have mercy. . . .

Talk

Missionary Awakening in France. Shortly after the upheavals of the French Revolution and the convulsions of the Napoleonic period, a new religious life bestirred itself in France. Because of it, the

French Church opened itself in a special way to worldwide missions. Among the laity, tbe foundation was laid for the later "Pontifical Society for the Propagation of the Faith." Newly founded religious communities and associations of diocesan priests sent forth missionaries to lands outside of Europe.

Missionary Assignment in the South Seas. The newly established Society of Marists had accepted the responsibility for spreading the faith in the South Seas island kingdom. Among the first missionaries that made their way to the distant mission territory in 1836 was Pierre-Louis-Marie Chanel. After some failed attempts at setting up a mission, he settled on the islands of Wallis and Futuna with some confreres.

Peter Chanel started his work on Futuna. As a European, he came to this South Sea folk with a very different mentality than theirs. Their language, morality, and customs had not yet been studied. The missioners could not draw help from any book in order to learn their language and to understand the meaning of particular rituals. He could only fall back upon himself. He progressed laboriously in learning their tongue and mentality. It is understandable that, after eighteen months, he could only report, "Twenty baptisms—four adults, the rest children, and all while in danger of death—that is the entire harvest that I have reaped in eighteen months."

Yet more and more the missioner impressed the island's dwellers by his life-style and by his selfless service to the sick. He gained friends and followers. This aroused the resistance of the chief, fearful for his power, who was worried that his own son might become Christian. Some aides to the king went to the missioner to ask for medicine; they struck him dead as he bent over to look for it in his hut.

No Revenge. In the nineteenth century with its colonial ways of thinking, the missionaries in the South Seas lay under the special protection of the French state. When the French military commander in Tahiti heard of Peter Chanel's murder, he mobilized his men for a retaliatory strike on Futuna. However the bishop and the martyr's surviving confreres opposed this action—they wanted no bloodshed. They required only that the body be returned to them. This refusal of violence so moved the people of Futuna that they requested another priest and made a mass conversion to Christianity. Soon everyone was Catholic; the faith is still living today on the islands.

Our Bond with the Young Churches. The memorial of this martyred missioner of the last century can remind us that today's young Churches need workers along with prayer and material support. They cannot yet solve all their problems purely by their own resources. They still need men and women from Europe and America who will help them prevail over their problems. Let us ask God that he grant young people from our country the readiness to serve as twentieth-century missioners to the Christians of the Third World in the spirit of Peter Chanel.

Petitions

Lord our God, hear our prayer:

Social upheaval and political unrest make the Church's task difficult in many developing countries: grant Christians courage and trust in God in these situations. . . .
The young Churches need workers from America and Europe: call young people from our country to serve the Church worldwide. . . .
The Church in the South Sea islands must find its way to sustain itself: Grant that your Holy Spirit may help it toward this end. . . .

For you will that your glory be praised throughout all the earth. You who live and reign forever and ever.

St. Catherine of Siena (April 29)

DOCTOR OF THE CHURCH

Introduction

Catherine of Siena, an extraordinary woman of the late middle ages (1347–1380), died when she was thirty-three. She never studied theology—yet the Church honors her as a doctor of the Church. She was an ordinary girl of bourgeois background—and had massive influence on the church politics of her time. She had totally dedicated followers—yet ran into fierce criticism and rejection. She was an example of how God's power works through human weakness: the weakness of official social standing, the weakness of physical and spiritual illness—and the weakness of a poorly balanced character.

Penitential Rite

"If we say, there is no sin in us, then we are deceiving ourselves, and the truth is not in us."   [Silence]   Lord, have mercy. . . .

"If we confess our sin, then God is faithful and kind: he forgives us our sins and purifies us from every injustice."   [Silence]   Christ, have mercy. . . .

"If we say, we have not sinned, then we make God into a liar, and his Word is not in us."   [Silence]   Lord, have mercy. . . .

St. Catherine of Siena (April 29)   147

Talk

A Divided World. Around 1350, the growing cities and the leading families were battling one another even to the point of bloodshed. Since 1309, the pope had resided in Avignon and was falling more and more under the influence of the royal French court. The Church—the greatest financial power of the time—was losing credibility. Still, in this divided world, there was a new religious awakening: many believers discovered Jesus Christ anew; they engaged in a vital life of prayer—and their renewed love of Christ drove them to dedicate themselves with all their strength to the renewal of the Church.

Bound to Christ. Catherine lived during these times. She grew up in a family of many children. Following the death of her most beloved sister, she decided at age fifteen to join the Third Order of St. Dominic: Its female members in Siena led a life in common. The young woman lived a very secluded life and grew during these years into a deep union with Christ. Her many letters and her book on the way to mystical union with God (written toward the end of her life) give evidence of her profound religious life. These were the basis for declaring her a doctor of the Church.

Tirelessly Active for the Renewal of the Church. However, Catherine did not stay in obscurity. Her love for Christ made her give up solitude and drove her to serve other people with all her might and to labor for church renewal. She traveled greatly during the final ten years of her life. During the terrible plague year of 1374 she cared devotedly for the sick in her home city. In 1376 she went with twenty followers to Avignon to persuade the pope to return to Rome (after previously urging him through letters to do so)—and she succeeded. She intervened in the warlike conflicts of her region and sought to reconcile the combatants with one another.

Her reform efforts soon collapsed again, however. A schism developed as a consequence of the papal election of 1378. Now Christendom was divided even more deeply, since both Avignon and Rome had a pope, each with his own followers. Once again Catherine tried to reconcile opposing factions in the Church, but her health could stand no more. She collapsed at St. Peter's in Rome in the spring of 1380 and died in her sickbed after several hard weeks. .

Dedication in Faith for the Church and the World Today. From out of her deep union with Christ, Catherine of Siena had an influence on her contemporary public affairs beyond all her personal limits and weaknesses. How can we, with all our own limits and weaknesses, work on behalf of Christ in our world? Some ideas: parish social service, activity in a political party, letters to the media and to authorities in Church and world. . . .

Petitions

God our Father, you accept us into your service. We pray:

Give to all who actively serve Church and world a living faith in the Risen One. . . .
Bless the work of all women who, quiet and unrecognized, do good works in our communities. . . .
Strengthen the influence of women in religious and secular circles. . . .

For you have entrusted the care of the Church and the world to us. You who live and reign forever and ever.

St. Pius V (April 30)

THE POPE OF THE TRIDENTINE MISSAL

Introduction

In many church groups, strong arguments go on over the "old" and the "new" Mass, over the Latin Tridentine Mass and the post-Vatican II Eucharist in the vernacular. But do all parties in the discussion realize that the rites of the so-called "old Mass" were first made obligatory some four hundred years ago by Pope Pius V for the Western Latin Church (not for the Eastern Catholic Churches)? Do they realize that before that point there was a great variety of different rites?

Penitential Rite

"Simon, son of John, do you love me?" [Silence] Lord, have mercy. . . .

"Simon, son of John, do you love me?" [Silence] Christ, have mercy. . . .

"Simon, son of John, do you love me?" [Silence] Lord, have mercy. . . .

Talk

Servant of Christ in His Time. The Gospel dwells on love for Christ as the condition for Peter being called to become the first pope. Judging from the Reading, the apostle (as well as the pope) is the servant of Jesus Christ and of the faithful. When Michele Ghislieri was chosen pope in 1566, his contemporaries could hardly believe that the above mentioned conditions for the most important responsibility in the Church were met by the new Pope Pius v. Bishop and Dominican friar, he was feared as an unrelenting grand inquisitor, known to be harsh toward himself, but who also proceeded against straying elements in the Church with great severity. Pius v himself well realized what his reputation was, when he remarked shortly after his election, "With God's help I hope to rule in such a way that the sadness will be greater at my death than it was at my election."

The Great Reformer. As pope, Pius v knew himself to be obliged by the Council of Trent—which had ended in 1563—and he energetically sought to implement its decisions. In his lifestyle he differentiated himself clearly from his splendor-loving predecessors on the chair of Peter. He led an ascetic life and insisted upon the same from the papal court and from the Roman clergy. He appointed worthy men to the College of Cardinals and thus fashioned for himself a circle of capable co-workers. He achieved a reform of the Curia. He obligated bishops once again to reside in their dioceses. He promoted theological studies and had the famous Roman Catechism compiled, which attempted to summarize Catholic doctrine for religious instruction.

In all his labors for reform, Pius remained himself and a man of his era. He could be quite authoritarian. He did not let up on petty rules or harsh penalties. Yet the faithful in Rome also realized that it was love for Christ and the Church that motivated him in all his strictness and inflexibility. It happened that the sadness at his death on May 1, 1572, was indeed greater than that at the time of his election as pope.

And the Missal of Pius v? Among the major reform measures of this great pope was the publication of an obligatory missal for the entire western Latin Church. This reform did not question whether other rites would make the eucharistic celebration invalid. It simply dealt with the practical question of what was necessary for the vitality of the faith

St. Pius V (April 30)   151

in those times. Pius v reckoned, along with many others, that standardization of the liturgy (including the keeping of Latin as its language) would strengthen the Church in conflict with Protestants.

The Second Vatican Council, starting with same pastoral concerns, came to the conclusion that the introduction of the vernacular, the revision of rituals, and a greater freedom in the shaping of the eucharistic liturgy were necessary to promote living faith in the Church.

Why should we think that Pius v's liturgical reform was more the work of the Holy Spirit than the Second Vatican Council's liturgical reform? Whatever strengthened the faith of Christians in 1570 is not necessarily effective in 1980. We act in the spirit of Pius v only if we rely in our time upon the Second Vatican Council.

Petitions

Merciful Father, we humbly pray for your entire holy Church.

Fill her with truth and peace. . . .
Cleanse her where she is defiled. . . .
Protect her from error . . . .
Lift her spirits when lack of faith depresses her . . . .
Supply her with whatever she needs. . . .
Strengthen and enable her as she walks in your way . . . .

Through Christ, our Lord.

(After "Gotteslob," 27.1)

St. Joseph the Worker (May 1)

LIFE AND WORK

Introduction

May 1—for most of the world, Workers' Day. Is it a holiday that makes us rejoice in our human work? Is it a memorial day that reminds us of our duty to earn our bread? Whether blue-collar or white-collar, whether on the production line or in the office, whether as employee or employer, do we live to work or do we work to live?

Penitential Rite

Lord Jesus Christ, son of the carpenter, you became like us in the burden and the joy of our labor: Lord, have mercy. . . .

You bore the heavy burden of the duty to earn your bread: Christ, have mercy. . . .

You have experienced how meaningful work gladdens human beings: Lord, have mercy. . . .

Talk

Work as a Burden. No one will deny that professional work is to a large extent a tiring burden for men and women. Whether working with heads or hands, people feel it in the same way. The practice of a profession demands self-discipline and effort. To go on living, one must invest much strength and energy in one's work. The job tires one out and saps one's health. "You will toil for your food all the days of your life. . . . You will earn your bread by the sweat of your brow . . ." (Gen 3:17,19): This applies both to the laborer and to the chief executive officer.

Work as Joy. Work, however, is not just a burden. Many people find meaningful professional work to be a perpetual source of joy. Even many assembly-line workers speak with pride of the machines produced by their shop.

Obviously, not every occupation or workplace offers this experience of joy in the same way. A great and unresolved task of current economic and social politics is precisely to set up modern working conditions in such a way that everyone, as far as possible, can enjoy their professional work. To have work is so basic to human happiness that, even when unemployment is covered by insurance and material needs are provided for, the unemployed individual is still discontent because he has no meaningful work.

We understand this human experience more deeply when we see it in the light of the Biblical story of creation. According to the Reading, man's likeness to God is found in that he, along with God is to rule and shape the earth. He is to realize himself as man, insofar as he accepts responsibility for the world and for his neighbor, modifies creation according to his needs and capabilities, and enjoys himself in working contact with his life's world. Work for man is not just a burden and a curse (as the same Book of Genesis brings out), it is also joy and happiness for him.

Life and Work. Work is both a joy and a burden. We see our occupation, our domestic work, and our devotion in church in a double perspective. There are times in which the element of joy pervades our activity. There are also times—days, and even weeks—in which we stumble under the duty to earn our bread and under the demands of particular commitments.

Yet in both sets of experiences we know by our faith in Jesus Christ, who has shared in our life, that both the joy and the burden of work belong to human life. We are reminded by the example of Jesus, the carpenter's son, and of St. Joseph, that even physical work has its value in God's eyes, be it the work even of a handyman or a garbage collector.

Above all, let us say over again, along with the Reading, that celebration is part of man's likeness to God. Just as God rested on the seventh day, so does man have a right to rest from his work, to a pleasurable vacation. He should be like unto God not only in work but also in rest, and therefore happy.

Petitions

Creator of the world, grant us by the intercession of St. Joseph:

That we might put up with the fatigue and monotony of work . . .
That everyone who works receive fair pay . . .
That people might see the success of their work . . .
That we serve our neighbor in everything we do . . . .

Then we, like Joseph, will give glory to you by our lives. You who live and reign forever and ever (after GL 784.8).

St. Athanasius (May 2)

HIS STRENGTH WAS ALSO HIS WEAKNESS

Introduction

"He talked and talked, he admonished, he resorted to force. When attacked, he defended himself. If he was stronger, his foe was in for a bad time. A man without fear has the weakness of not moderating his strength and often strikes too hard. Because he himself was always being assaulted, he also lashed out and struck hard." This is how one of his contemporaries saw Athanasius, bishop and doctor of the Church (295–373).

Penitential Rite

Lord Jesus Christ, we believe that you come from God: Lord, have mercy. . . .

Our love for God means that we keep his commandments: Christ, have mercy. . . .

By faith in you we can overcome evil in ourselves: Lord, have mercy. . . .

Talk

Person and Cause. Even today in the Church, many people harm the good cause that they work for by regrettable character traits and an unattractive attitude. Obstinacy and personal vanity, unapproachable behavior or uncontrolled outbursts of sarcasm by theologians and pastors sometimes arouse hostility against the positions they uphold.

It is the same way now as it was 1,600 years ago, when the great Egyptian bishop Athanasius provoked the whole world against himself and his worthy cause by his stormy zeal. To be sure, the situation then was made more complicated by the fact that the controversies within the Church and the high-level politics of the Eastern Roman Empire were entangled.

The Struggle for Orthodoxy. During the decades following the Council of Nicaea, this faith-saying was widespread in the Church: "Jesus Christ is true God and true man." This phrase came to occupy a central place in the Church's life. On the other hand, this involved tough theological controversies; on the other side, patient dialog and compromise with the Arians (who would not accept this declaration) in order to preserve church unity.

In Athanasius' diocese, the heresy of Arius had already entrenched itself. The conflict was thus especially vehement there, and the bishop aggravated the contrasts by his hard and turbulent character. His contemporary, quoted above, faulted him for lacking any trace of mildness or gentleness. A present-day biographer notes that: "For his whole life long, it came hard for him to distinguish between a person and the person's opinions."

Accordingly, his long term as bishop (forty-five years!) was a period of enduring conflicts. Athanasius had to flee his see city at different times when strong opposition made itself felt. A large group of bishops wanted him deposed on the grounds that he acted violently and unlawfully in his diocese. He was packed into exile several times by the Byzantine emperor. All told, he spent twenty of his years as bishop outside of his diocese in exile or in flight.

His Meaning. For all his unfortunate traits and his sometimes imprudent and tactless behavior and appearance, Athanasius nevertheless was, in his time, a "pillar of the Church," as later generations called him. His unflinching dedication helped bring about the establishment of the creed of the Nicene Council in the Church. He fought for the Church's independence from the state's supervision (a situation that had developed after the Constantinian peace). Above all, he was pastor for the ordinary people. He stayed untiringly in contact with the faithful. He knew how to speak to them through his preaching and how to strengthen faith within them. He held a positive attitude toward the newly emerged monastic movement in Egypt (ordinary people who, owing to religious sentiment, went into the desert in order to live entirely for God). In his writings he recommended this new form of Christian living.

We can summarize in the petitions what Athanasius can mean for the Church today.

Petitions

Lord Jesus Christ, your Church carries the Good News in earthen vessels. Look upon her human weakness and hear our prayer.

For theologians: Let them search, with all their personal limitations, open and unprejudiced for your truth. . . .
For pastors: Let their efforts, despite their human weaknesses, be fruitful for their congregations. . . .
For all of us: Help us to respect dissenters in controversy, even when we cannot share their opinion. . . .

For your power is fulfilled in human weakness. You who live and reign forever and ever.

St. Philip (May 3)

ON THE PATH OF FAITH

Introduction

We may be trying for years to live a conscious Christian life—and suddenly, in listening to a homily, in reading an article, or in personal prayer, we understand an article of faith in a whole new light. In such moments we experience how we are on a journey in faith and that we can enter ever more deeply into the mystery of God in Jesus Christ. This experience is no cause for unrest. According to John's Gospel, the Apostle Philip had to be told by Jesus in the upper room at the last supper that, up until that time, with all his enthusiasm for Jesus of Nazareth, he did not yet realize the true mystery of his Master.

Penitential Rite

Lord Jesus Christ, you died for our sins: Lord, have mercy. . . .
You were raised up as the Scripture had said: Christ, have mercy. . . .
You appeared to Peter and then the Twelve: Lord, have mercy. . . .

Talk

The Zealous Disciple. Philip, as did Andrew and Peter, came from Bethsaida. Shortly after his calling he was able to speak for the little circle of disciples: "We have found him, about whom Moses, in

St. Philip (May 3)

the law, and the prophets have written: Jesus of Nazareth, Joseph's son'' (Jn. 1:45). In his enthusiasm for his master, he spoke to Nathaniel and led him to Jesus.

According to Jn. 6:5–7, Jesus put Philip to the test by asking him where they could get bread for so many people. Philip did not pass this test of faith. He immediately began to talk seriously and decided that to take care of everyone would be rather expensive. He did not expect Jesus himself to provide food for the large crowd.

According to Jn. 12:20–23, his enthusiasm for Jesus of Nazareth is still lively: he acts as a mediator to introduce gentiles to Jesus. Yet toward the end of his time spent with Jesus, it becomes clear just how imperfect his knowledge of Jesus is. Shortly after his calling, Philip was able to declare that he had found the promised Messiah. At the last supper it was evident that he had not progressed much beyond that in his long association with Jesus. He saw Jesus of Nazareth only as the great prophet. Jesus had to tell him, "Philip, after I have been with you all this time, you still do not know me? Whoever has seen me has seen the Father . . ." (Gospel).

Our Journey in Faith. An apostle who for Jesus Christ would catch fire; who lived a long time in fellowship with him and dedicated himself along with Jesus to proclaim the Kingdom of God; who, however, at first stayed on the surface of his faith and walked a long journey before he recognized the love of God in his Master.

Should we wonder that the same happens to us? From childhood onward we meet Jesus Christ in the fellowship of the Church. We have caught fire for our faith. We are enthusiastic for the cause. We take part in the parish's social life and join the organizations. We come regularly to worship services and try to be interiorly present. Yet do we perhaps remain on the surface? Do we consider Jesus Christ to be just a great example for a responsible way of life? Is the Church to our mind just an organization of people who spread the ideas of Jesus more or less successfully?

If that is the case, then Jesus Christ is saying to us now, "After I have been with you all this time, you still do not know me?" We approach the true mystery of Jesus Christ only if we recognize God himself in him, offering himself in love for us to the very end; if we understand that the Risen One is journeying with us here and now; if we live with the certitude that the Church fulfills her mandate not with human power, but with the power of Jesus Christ.

Have we recognized this mystery of Jesus Christ? Do we live by it? If we have to admit to ourselves that we still have a long way to go, we still have no reason to despair: Christ goes with us on our path to complete faith. By the power of the Spirit, we recognize in Jesus the face of God, who loves to the end.

Petitions

Father in heaven, you reveal yourself in your son, Jesus Christ. We pray:

Be close to all who ask themselves about the meaning of their lives. . . .
Bring all those to a deeper faith who are complacent with a superficial religious life. . . .
Grant new firmness of faith to all who are tormented by doubt. . . .

For you have promised us through your Son to give us all that we ask for. You who live and reign forever and ever.

Sts. Nereus, Achilleus, and Pancratius (May 12)

HISTORY LIVED BY MEN

Introduction

We know little about the lives of the martyrs Nereus and Achilleus. They probably suffered martyrdom around 304 during the persecution by Diocletian. According to a tombstone inscription they were soldiers who had converted to Christianity. The data on St. Pancratius are uncertain: he is supposed to have been beheaded for his faith during the same persecution at age fourteen. This is all that a biography in a missal can tell us about these three Roman martyrs of early times. How is it that they have a place in the Church's universal liturgical calendar?

Penitential Rite

Lord Jesus Christ, our rescue comes from your Father and our God: Lord, have mercy. . . .

Through you he rescues us from great trouble: Christ, have mercy. . . .

Honor and praise be to him through you: Lord, have mercy. . . .

Talk

The Church as Lived by Human Beings. I cannot tell you why Sts. Nereus, Achilleus, and Pancratius came to find a place in the universal liturgical calendar. Are their graves in Rome particularly well-known? Is there a special devotion towards them in the Eternal City? However that may be, these three unknown saints from early times remind me of realities of faith that nowadays often receive too little attention.

We look back upon a *Church* history of two thousand years. During this long time, there were both periods of enthusiasm and epochs of shame. For now, we need not dwell further on this. What is important is the realization that we are really looking at a history of *Christians*. Throughout the centuries the institution of the Church has lived from people and in people who attempted to practice the faith in their daily lives. The Church was present in Rome at the beginning of the fourth century through men like Nereus, Achilleus, and Pancratius. She is present in our time and through people like ourselves. The Church is not an abstract reality. She is only present when made so by people living in her.

The Lesson of History. In these times we look more readily into the future than into the past. In our fast-paced world, this is easily understandable, yet we can still learn something from history as well.

We live in an age of great changes. Developments in the Church's sphere cause us sometimes to wonder with concern if the Church does not have her future already behind her. Christians here and there fear for her survival. For me, the memorial of these Roman martyrs of the early centuries is a reminder that the Church has been wending her way through time with great effort for nearly two thousand years and, with God's help, has always found a path into the future.

How did she look at the time of today's saints? The Church had consolidated herself internally in the ebb and flow of three centuries, in the swing between persecution and calm. Then the Roman state (at the peak of its worldwide power) under the Emperor Diocletian struck ruthlessly. The result was the bloodiest persecution of Christians in the early centuries. When Nereus, Achilleus, and Pancratius were executed for their faith, the future of the Church looked bleak indeed. And yet, a few years later, Constantine established peace with the Christians and thus opened up to the Church new possibilities for her life and mission.

God Still Offers a Path into the Future. Many times in the course of her history, the Church—in the opinion of both hostile and benevolent observers—stood at the edge of her own grave. How often has her demise been predicted? How often did she have to walk her path into the future under threats of destruction?

I feel that, by looking at her history, our confidence can grow that the Church even today still has her future ahead of her. If we put forth the effort to live as Church and "to await rescue by God" [cf. Reading], then God in his Spirit will be with us and will walk with us through all trials on the path into the future [cf. Reading and Gospel].

Petitions

Lord Jesus Christ, you assemble your Church from all nations and races and peoples and tongues—and also from all centuries.

> Make us all realize that the Church is alive only where Christians live their faith. . . .
> Be near to those Christians who have lost heart because of outside pressure and persecution. . . .
> Grant your Holy Spirit to all who must declare their faith to other people. . . .

For you walk with your Church in the Holy Spirit and enable her to recognize the good and do it. You who live and reign forever and ever.

St. Matthias (May 14)

THE REPLACEMENT

Introduction

Pilgrimages on foot, lasting days, still take place from Rhineland parishes toward the "only tomb of an apostle on German soil," at the abbey church of St. Matthias in Trier. Tradition has it that St. Helena had brought the apostle's mortal remains to Trier. Whether the tradition is factual or not, his memorial can remind us that we are supposed to be apostles of Jesus Christ in our time.

Penitential Rite

"You have not chosen me; rather, I have chosen you." [Silence] Lord, have mercy. . . .

"I have appointed you to go out and bring forth fruit." [Silence] Christ, have mercy. . . .

"This I command you: love one another." [Silence] Lord, have mercy. . . .

Talk

Of the life and work of the apostle Matthias, we only know what today's Reading tells us. His apostolic activity became lost in the shadows of history. We can reflect on the context of the Reading in order to understand more deeply what form apostolic service took at the dawn of the Church, and what meaning it has for the Church today.

Apostolic Service Then. After the betrayal by Judas, the college of twelve had to be completed by the special election of another apostle. Why? Well, the young Church did not consider the apostles to be mere functionaries responsible for proclaiming the Good News. They were to live out the Good News as a group and thus be the kernel of the Church. And since the Church understood herself to be in continuity with the twelve tribes of God's people of the Old Testament, she placed great importance on the count of twelve apostles.

For a replacement of the betrayer Judas, only a disciple who had shared experiences with Jesus during his earthly life could be considered. He had to have been present "beginning with the baptism by John up to the day when he was taken up away from us." The young Church could not imagine as an apostle anyone who had not known Jesus during his earthly life.

Matthias, the replacement, was to be "a witness with the other apostles of his resurrection." He was not only to tell of Jesus' past earthly life and help keep alive the memory of this great prophet. He was to give witness that Jesus of Nazareth lives and is mysteriously present in the Church.

Apostolic Service Today. The whole Church makes up the following of the first apostles, and everyone baptized should be a witness to Jesus' resurrection.

We Christians, as Church (and as members in her), must first live out our faith in Jesus Christ before we can talk convincingly about him to questioning and searching souls. We have to live as Church in order to be able to give witness to Christ.

It is not necessary for us to be witness of Jesus' earthly life. That was required only of the original apostles. Yet even we can give witness to Jesus Christ only if we have experienced life with the Risen One through conscious faith; only if we have learned to know and love him in prayer and religious study.

When we gather as Church, we remember not merely the long-past earthly life of Jesus. When we speak of Jesus, we are not just talking about the way things were. We witness much more to the fact that he, the Risen One, is mysteriously present among us, that he lives and uses his power in our time.

We Are All "Replacements." The special election of Matthias became necessary when Judas turned out to be unfaithful to his vocation. For nearly two thousand years special elections have been needed time and time again, because new generations have had to carry on the witness to the Resurrection. Today, all of us are replacements for past generations of believers with the mandate to be witnesses of the Good News.

Petitions

Lord Jesus Christ, it is your will that your Church bring forth fruit, fruit that will endure.

> We pray for all who, through their commitment in our communities, give witness to your resurrection. [Silence]
> We pray for all missionaries who work in the service of young churches in foreign lands. [Silence]
> We pray for the Church's younger generation that finds it hard in these times to grow into the Church's faith. [Silence]

For we are your friends when we do what you have commanded. You who live and reign forever and ever.

St. John I (May 18)

CONDEMNED TO FAILURE

Introduction

"In the veneration of the saints, John is often included in the category of churchmen who conquered only through their suffering." This is the conclusion of one brief evaluation of this pope who died in 526 in Ravenna after a reign of only three years. In tradition, John is portrayed as a hero, while his opponent Theoderic the Great is described as a fierce persecutor of Catholics. In reality, the conflict between the Roman bishop and the king of the Ostrogoths in Ravenna took a different form.

Penitential Rite

"For as the heavens are high above the earth so strong is God's love for those who fear him. As far as the east is from the west so far does he remove our sins. As a father has compassion on his sons, the Lord has pity on those who fear him" (Ps. 103:11–13).

Have mercy, Lord our God, have mercy. . . .

Talk

Balance of Interests. In the decades before the reign of Pope John I, the Arian Ostrogoths were the dominant power in Italy. The Roman Church was in schism with the Eastern Roman Empire (once again, due to a theological controversy). The Catholic pope and the Arian king both stressed their independence from Byzantium and supported each other because of their common concerns. Theoderic the Great was accordingly in favor of peaceful coexistence between his Arian Goths and the established Catholic population of Rome.

Conflicting Interests. Then, in 519, the schism between Rome and Byzantium was overcome—and Rome began to consider the relations with the Catholic Eastern Roman emperor to be more important than those with the Germanic Arian king in Ravenna. At the same time, the proud Gothic prince saw himself as outflanked by the Byzantine emperor. Sympathy and friendship for Byzantium could seem like treason to Theoderic.

In addition, Byzantium was attempting by force to convert to Catholicism the Arian Ostrogoths that lived within its territory. Theoderic declared himself the protector and advocate of the ethnic and religious minorities in the Eastern Roman Empire. He forced the pope to travel to Byzantium, making him responsible for campaigning for the rights of persecuted Ostrogoths.

We do not know for certain whether and for how long the pope carried out this imposed task. Fearing reprisals against Catholics within Ostrogoth territory, the emperor made some concessions within his own realm. Understandably, he dealt with the pope very politely (since he could display the pope at the head of his chariots in his quarrels with Theoderic).

Is it any wonder that the Ostrogoth king was distrustful toward Pope John, and arrested him in Ravenna right after his return to Italy? Was it coincidence or the consequence of his detention that the pope died a few days later? At any rate, the remains were allowed to be carried back to Rome and interred in St. Peter's Basilica.

Martyr? Posterity came to see Pope John I as a martyr. Maybe this is wrong, if we consider only the circumstances of his death. Yet maybe it is right, if we look at the life and work of this pope as a witness to faith through suffering.

St. John I (May 18)

As a servant of the Church, John wanted to do what was best for her (Gospel). He saw himself faced with conditions that doomed him to failure. The situation was stronger than his good will. He could no longer risk the unity of the Catholic Church by relying too heavily on Theoderic—he had to deal with the real balance of power in Italy. As many popes since then—right up to our own time—he displayed his faith by trusting in the help of God as he tried to do everything humanly possible. That he nonetheless had little success can surprise no one in a Church that stands under the cross of Christ.

Petitions

Lord Jesus Christ, Head of your Church:

Be close in the Holy Spirit to diplomats representing the Vatican. . . .
Enlighten bishops' conferences when they take positions on basic political questions.
Guard the Church from mistaken ties with people of power in economics, society, and politics. . . .

For you yourself safeguard the future of the Church on her path through time. You who live and reign forever and ever.

St. Bernardine of Siena (May 20)

A GREAT PREACHER

Introduction

In our time, we do not put up with long sermons. People had different standards, however, during the time of St. Bernardine of Siena (1380–1444): he sometimes preached as long as five hours. Yet it was not the length of his homilies that was remarkable, but rather their astonishing success. His biographer put it this way: he knew how to lead people home to God. Contemporary chronicles described his preaching journeys this way: it was as if spring were coming into the world. What do we know of the life of this preacher, whose words went directly to the hearts of his listeners?

Penitential Rite

Lord Jesus Christ, you are the cornerstone on which everything depends: Lord, have mercy. . . .

Through you alone comes our redemption: Christ, have mercy. . . .

By your power sickness and death are overcome: Lord, have mercy. . . .

Talk

Experiences as a Youth. A student from wealthy and prestigious background. A favorite of his fellow students by reason of his generous sharing of his resources with them. A twenty-year-old student

St. Bernardine of Siena (May 20)   171

who did not flee from the plague in Siena but stayed to care for the sick. A young man who himself caught the plague and narrowly avoided death. This was the young Bernardine of Siena.

This close brush with death motivated the convalescent to give his fortune away to the poor and to enter the Franciscans at age 22. He thereby made a break—similar to his order's founder, Francis—with his past life and gave himself over fully to the imitation of Christ in religious life.

A "Late Vocation." After his ordination to the priesthood, Bernardine lived and worked for several years in an isolated mountain monastery. His gift of preaching did not yet become evident. At the age of 37, he had to replace a confrere who had fallen sick. Thus began his emergence as a powerfully effective preacher all over Italy. He spoke before ordinary people, before the ruling classes in town and country, before professors of the renowned University of Bologna.

Bernardine saw himself as responsible to God alone. Since he was dependent on no one, he could speak the truth freely to sick and poor, to the powerful and the humble. He wanted his listeners to put his words into action, and he succeeded. "Adulterers began a new life, public sinners returned to the Church, paupers and orphans found shelter, wars and feuds were ended, order and peace descended on towns and villages," reads one account of his life.

The Cross in His Life. In the course of his labors, Bernardine twice endured great disappointments. He was the victim of false accusations under two successive popes. The popes believed the charges, had the preacher arrested and forbade him to preach. It would have been an easy matter for the great preacher to whip up the masses in favor of himself and against the popes. Still, he observed the prohibition and went back into solitude. We do not know what this silence cost him personally. His contemporaries simply tell us that, after the years of silence, he was able to reach even embittered souls because he himself had suffered through and worked out everything that could lead to embitterment.

Last Fruitful Years. The older the saint became, the greater became his effect and influence on all classes in Italy. He was called upon from all over to preach especially in large towns and to reconcile warring factions. In 1444 he was invited to Naples, the great port city, where he had long desired to preach. On the way there, however, he fell sick and died.

We have looked at the outer circumstances of the life of St. Bernardine of Siena. Perhaps this has helped us to see that he backed his words in preaching with the deeds of his own life. He did not merely proclaim that our redemption comes from Jesus Christ alone. He dedicated his own life to imitating Christ and thus gave witness to Christ as the cornerstone on which all things depend [Reading].

Petitions

Lord our God, you will that the Good News be proclaimed to people of today.

Enlighten the Church's theologians in their search for correct understanding of your revelation. . . .
Give to pastors a feel for people's questions in our time. . . .
Let everyone responsible for preaching find the words that will touch the hearts of other human beings. . . .

For you have promised the Holy Spirit to your Church, that she might testify to the Good News by his power. You who live and reign forever and ever.

St. Bede the Venerable (May 25)

AUTHOR AND TEACHER

Introduction

In 597 Rome began systematic mission work among the Anglo-Saxons. A hundred years later England had flourishing cloisters with great libraries and scholarly activity. The scholar Venerable Bede (672–735) and the missioner Boniface (675–754) are perhaps the best-known figures attesting to the vitality of that young church.

Penitential Rite

"God knows of what we are made, he remembers that we are dust.
But the love of the Lord is everlasting upon those who hold him in fear.
His justice reaches out to children's children when they keep his covenant in truth, when they keep his will in their mind" (Ps. 103:15,17f.).

Talk

Life in a Small Territory. At age seven, Bede was entrusted to a local Benedictine monastery for his upbringing and education. He tells of himself: "I spent the whole rest of my life in this cloister and dedicated myself completely to the study of Scripture. And while I lived in observance of the rule and sang the office day after day in choir, my special joy was always study, teaching and writing."

Nationwide Influence. Bede's life was not filled with outward events and changes. From the privacy of his cloister cell he served his era—and helped to shape it.

Bede started out in small ways. He first wrote instruction books in spelling, grammar, and poetry for his students, in the cloister's school.

His special interest soon came to dwell on the history of his own monastery, the history of the Christianization of England, and the lives of the great figures of the young English church. In this ambitious work, he acted in a clearly modern way: He sought to distinguish between facts and pious edifying tales so as to compile a "history of England as it truly was."

As professor of theology in the monastic theological academy, he occupied himself above all with sacred Scripture. Like the other great scholars of his epoch (e.g., his predecessor Isidore in Seville and his successor Rhabanus Maurus in Fulda), he saw his principal task to be the handing on to his students of the treasures of Christian antiquity.

Bede did not thereby entomb himself in his study. He critically observed developments in the Anglo-Saxon church and called attention to dangerous developments in his letters. He concluded, for example, that the people were becoming negligent in receiving the sacraments and demanded of a bishop that he encourage the daily reception of Holy Communion, as was understood to be normal in the Roman Church.

Saintly Teacher and Scholar. If Bede was called "venerable" shortly after his death, if the Church has venerated him as a saint for centuries, she admires in him not only the range of his profane and theological knowledge. She honors in him the way in which he proceeded with this knowledge.

For Bede, all reality (worldly and religious) is a revelation of the depths of God (Reading). Even in profane events he saw the traces of God. Since for him his scholarly work was always also an encounter with the mysterious God, his study was embedded in prayer, in which he asked God to open his eyes to God's wonders in this world.

As a teacher, he knew that it was not enough to marshal astounding knowledge about God and pass it on in lovely words. Only the one who does the Heavenly Father's will can enter the Kingdom of Heaven [Gospel]. His scholarly work with the Bible and with church history shaped his life. It made his life, teaching and writing believable.

Is all our knowledge, religious and profane, a way to the mysterious God? Does our religious knowledge shape our lives? Does our life make our word believable?

Petitions

God of mystery, only in the power of your Holy Spirit can we approach your mystery awed and humbled.

Illumine teachers and students of theology. . . .
Be close to preachers and their listeners. . . .
Teach the Church to reflect on her past so as to learn for her future. . . .

Lord, let us know by your Spirit what comes from you. You who live and reign forever and ever.

St. Gregory VII (May 25)

FOR THE INDEPENDENCE OF THE CHURCH

Introduction

In the course of history, the Church has slipped time and again into an unhealthy dependence upon state authority and has had to extricate herself with some trouble. In the struggle over lay investiture during the high Middle Ages, the problem revolved around independence from political patronage. On the Church's side, Pope Gregory VII played a decisive role.

Penitential Rite

Lord Jesus Christ, you have gained the Church by your blood: Lord, have mercy. . . .

We are entrusted to you and to your grace: Christ, have mercy. . . .

You guide the Church by the Holy Spirit, whom you send to your leaders: Lord, have mercy. . . .

Talk

The Situation. The Church had shown herself to be a considerable power and promoter of order in the first centuries of German history. Understandably, German kings and emperors tried to avail themselves of the Church to achieve their political goal of unifying the empire and of securing a lasting peace. Understandably as well, the Church gladly took on the royal and imperial support in her missionary activity on the borders of the empire.

This development led quickly to an unhealthy mingling of religion and politics. Inasmuch as bishops had become secular princes as well in most cases, the custom had spread so widely that the emperor, independently of the pope, filled the episcopal positions with an eye more toward the political rather than the ecclesial and pastoral qualifications. Since one could live well as bishop and secular prince, the custom also crept in of buying a bishopric with an appropriate sum of money. One would then be set up well for the rest of his life.

That resulted in many unworthy men seated in episcopal chairs and in many abuses throughout the entire Church that cried out for energetic reform. The reform movement that swept the Church in the eleventh century recognized that the renewal of the Church depended upon competent and church-conscious bishops. This had to push the reform movement into conflict with the German king and emperor, who had political reasons for packing the bishopric with men loyal to himself.

The Conflict with Henry IV. This conflict came to a head under Pope Gregory VII. From 1049 onwards, this northern Italian Benedictine monk was the central figure of the reform movement as the right-hand man of several popes. He himself was elected pope in 1073. He immediately sought a compromise in the question of new appointments to vacant episcopal sees (the investiture quarrel). However, since King Henry IV refused to discuss the matter, he placed him under excommunication. That practically meant the deposing of the German king by the pope. This unprecedented action by the pope caused so much political pressure on the king, that he had to submit to the pope. What followed was the march to Canossa. Gregory received Henry and lifted the excommunication from him, hoping for a compromise in the quarrel-ridden question.

It soon became evident, however, that King Henry was not really going to come around. Gregory laid a second ban on him, and this time the king answered with war. At the end of 1081 he stood outside of Rome with a large army and conquered it in 1084. The pope was able to take refuge in the Castel Sant'Angelo until the Normans came to his aid. However, the liberators so embittered the Roman population by reckless plundering that Gregory had to leave Rome with them. On May 25, 1085, he died in exile alone, forsaken, and physically broken.

Later Success and Continuing Task. The reform policy of Gregory VII ended with short-term failure. He wanted the best thing; and yet he left a Christianity behind that was internally divided without having come nearer to a solution for the controversy over lay investiture. A compromise was first found a good forty years afterwards, which would guarantee to the Church the necessary independence for her in the medieval world. For that age, the problem of the right relationship between Church and state was solved, just as we must solve it with lively feelings for the necessary independence of the Church in our time.

Petitions

Lord Jesus Christ, you said to your disciples: Give to Caesar what belongs to Caesar, and give to God what belongs to God. Hear our prayer:

> For the Church in totalitarian countries: give her the freedom she needs for fulfilling her mission. . . .
> For the Church in free countries: let her work responsibly for the solution of the great problems of our age. . . .
> For the Church in our country: guard her from mistaken dependence upon political powers and parties. . . .

For you are the Lord of the Church and of nations, who live and reign forever and ever.

St. Mary Magdalene of Pazzi (May 25)

CONCERNED WITH THE LORD'S BUSINESS

Introduction

> It falls alone to those who pray
> to stay the sword over our heads
> and by a holy life to wrest
> this world from condemning powers.

These lines were written in the last phase of World War II by the poet Reinheld Schneider. Unless the power of prayer is a reality for us, we will not understand that the Carmelite Mary Magdalene of Pazzi (1566–1607) is counted among the great personalities of the Catholic reform in the period following the Council of Trent.

Penitential Rite

> "O Lord, hear my voice when I call; have mercy and answer.
> Hide not your face; dismiss not your servant in anger" (Ps. 27:7,9).
> Have mercy, Lord our God, have mercy. . . .

Talk

Contemplative Life in Community. When Paul speaks in the Reading of "the Lord's affairs," it is clear that he is referring to the whole world created by God and redeemed by Jesus Christ. Because of this, both the married and the unmarried must work with God for creation. Thus even contemplative nuns cannot merely be there for Christ; they must be concerned along with Christ for the salvation of the whole world.

All nuns living in strict locked cloisters realize this. They also believe that they have a special contribution to make for the world's redemption through a serious life of prayer. We can all learn from them—represented as they are by today's saint—what it means to live consciously with Jesus Christ.

"Love is Not Loved." Mary Magdalene of Pazzi became a Carmelite at age 16 in her native Florence. She took her contemplative life in the cloister seriously. In her deep life of prayer, often accompanied by extraordinary spiritual conditions such as ecstasy, she recognized ever more clearly God's boundless love for human beings and for all of creation.

At the same time she clearsightedly realized that people (and, above all, even Christians) hardly concerned themselves with the love of God. She lamented many times that "Love is not loved." She took as her life's program the task of showing her love for Jesus Christ in a consistent life of abnegation and suffering. Her hard life-style—living only on bread and water on weekdays, sleeping only for five hours, going barefoot even in winter—was shaped by this commitment. It is in the light of this practice that we must understand the saying that came out of her years-long final illness: "Suffering, not death"—a saying that we would not apply to our lives without further examination.

Still, Mary Magdalene of Pazzi did not content herself with hidden penances behind cloister walls. She wrote letters to the pope and other church officials and demanded of them in God's name to carry forth church reform in the post-Tridentine era.

Concerned with the Lord's Business. The holy Carmelite from Florence took God with complete seriousness in her prayer. She learned to know the loving God ever better in the quiet hours of meditation. She came into intimacy with God, as brothers and sisters, as parents and children came into intimacy with each other [cf. Gospel]. She entrusted herself to God, as the Mother of Jesus had entrusted herself to God. She held fast to God even during the long stretches in her life in which she felt nothing of God's presence when she prayed. She responded to God's love with a radical personal Christian life (as seen, of course, against the background of her time and its concepts of piety). She felt compelled to act upon the conditions of her era in proportion to her possibilities.

Do Jesus Christ and his teachings likewise stand in the center of our lives? In a serious prayer life, in line with our life circumstances? In the attempt to integrate the love of God into our personal ways of life? In the purpose of becoming responsible for world and Church (again, in line with our circumstances) and thereby witnessing the love of God to everyone?

Petitions

Lord Jesus Christ, you died out of love for us men:

Strengthen the faith of Christians so that they may recognize you as the true Life. . . .
Build up their hope in the coming Glory. . . .
Teach them to understand the mystery of your love. . . .
Help them to display this love in their lives. . . .

For you come to redeem the whole world. You who live and reign forever and ever.

St. Philip Neri (May 26)

A COMICAL ODDBALL?

Introduction

An Italian people's saint—with four letters. Many have already answered this question by finding it in the crossword puzzle of a diocesan paper or church magazine.

St. Philip Neri is the one we mean. He must have been a man of great humor, given as he was to making jokes anytime anywhere. At the same time, he was loved and respected by both the great and the humble in Rome.

Was he a comical oddball, as one might suspect upon hearing of some of his capers? What is the secret of his life?

Talk

The Seeker. Philip Neri was born in 1515 in the mercantile city of Florence. His father was a notary, and Philip received an early, proper education from the Dominicans. When he was eighteen, he was sent by his father to a rich uncle in the area of Rome, with the purpose of later taking over his business. After three years the young man gave up the inheritance and along with it an assured bourgeois livelihood. He went into Rome, in order to live poor and penniless in deliberate imitation of Jesus Christ.

In Rome he earned a meager living as a tutor. At the same time he

St. Philip Neri (May 26)

studied philosophy and theology on his own. More than that, however, he took on social responsibilities. He cared for Rome's poor and did regular service in a hospital.

Apostolate of the Street. Philip Neri decided one day to terminate his studies. He sold his books and gave the proceeds to the poor. He later said about himself, "I never studied much, because I was busy with prayer and other spiritual exercises."

From that point onward he spent his time in the apostolate of the street. He mingled with passersby and got involved with street rowdies, young merchants, small shopkeeprs, and impoverished artists with his quick-witted phrases in cheerful and sometimes coarse conversation. He would then wait for a favorable moment to bring up religious matters and lead his listeners on to a Christian life.

While the young man spent his days moving around the streets of Rome, he spent his nights with God. He prayed for hours on end in the environs of Rome or withdrew into the catacombs. Sometimes he would visit a church, pray there, and then sleep a few hours in the foyer.

"Place for Prayer"—the Oratory. At age thirty-six, Philip was finally ordained a priest at the urging of his confessor. Even as a priest he remained a street missioner. His pastoral work, however, began to center more and more on the confessional, in which he often spent up to fifteen hours a day. He had the gift of finding the right word for each penitent and of leading each one to a lasting improvement in life.

Beyond that, he developed a pastoral undertaking that he had already begun as a layman: he invited people with whom he conversed on the street to come and visit him. People came around for religious lectures, for spiritual conversations, and for common prayer outside of church services. More and more interested people showed up. After his priestly ordination, there were primarily many of his penitents who came regularly to these gatherings. It was not long before they needed more room. A loft was converted into an oratory and assembly hall. With this association, the religious foundation itself came to be called "The Oratory."

Out of this circle of laity there proceeded a strong force for renewal of church life. Soon other priests joined Philip Neri and shared the operations with him. The priestly society of the Oratorians was developed and is still working in cities in Europe and America.

Moved by Christ. What is the innermost secret of Philip Neri, this popular shepherd of souls? He discovered Jesus Christ in his young years. He summarized this experience by saying, "If you wish for something apart from Christ, you do not know what you are wishing for. If you long for something apart from Christ, you do not know what you are longing for. If you work apart from Christ, you do not know what you are doing." His deep communion with Christ revealed itself in special graces of prayer and in visions. Yet he was skeptical about any prayer activity removed from living. His union with Jesus Christ motivated him to active dedication to his neighbor whether in human aid or in pastoral work. He also led all who trusted in him to an active love for neighbor.

There is still something else that can be understood only as a result of his deep union with Christ: his evident and sometimes hilarious effort to behave in ridiculous fashion. That sprang not only from his natural flair for comedy. By acting this way, he deflected any exaggerated veneration of himself. He also wanted to be like Jesus Christ in this respect, that he too was misunderstood and laughed at.

Philip Neri, a "comical oddball"? A man who found Jesus Christ, who was a cheerful human being in communion with Christ, who helped everyone experience the goodness of Jesus Christ [cf. Reading], who showed his love for Jesus Christ sometimes in unusual ways, to the point of becoming a clown for him.

St. Augustine of Canterbury (May 27)

WITHDRAW INTO ISOLATION?

Introduction

Are we aware that in our own country we live within mission territory? In our midst live many Muslims, Buddhists, Hindus, and other non-Christians, working in a wide variety of positions or doing career studies here. Among our own acquaintances we see many baptized, both Catholic and Protestant, who have never found the true approach to Jesus Christ or who have lost their faith without noticing it over the years. What can we do to bring Jesus Christ close to them?

Penitential Rite

"Serve the Lord with awe and trembling, pay him your homage lest he be angry and you perish; for suddenly his anger will blaze" (Ps. 2:11f).

Have mercy, Lord our God, have mercy. . . .

Talk

An Old Christian Country. The south of England is ancient Roman territory. With the Romans, Christianity also came early to the British Isles, and flourishing congregations developed. In the turmoil of the tribal migrations, this Roman province was conquered by pagan Anglo-Saxons. Yet evidently the new rulers gave religious freedom to the Christian Celtic population, for around 600 there were Christian communities with bishops and theologians in the south of England.

Yet these communities had withdrawn into religious isolation. There was little religious contact between the subjugated Celts and the Germanic masters. The political differences were so great that the Christians did not even think to extend the faith to the intruders.

Mission from Outside. The start of missionary activity to the Anglo-Saxon ruling class came from outside. The Germanic tribal kings would marry Christian princesses from the continent, and these would bring the faith with them. This prepared the soil for systematic missionary work, which the great Pope Gregory initiated in 591. He sent a group of forty monks from a Roman monastery to England, under the direction of Augustine, later archbishop of Canterbury. Soon after the arrival of this missionary group, King Ethelbert of Kent had himself baptized along with about ten thousand of his followers.

The Roman missioners maintained close contact with the pope during their labors. He in turn counseled them with pastoral instructions that have become famous: They were to adapt the forms of church life and liturgy to the customs of the new converts and were not to impose an alien form of Christianity upon them.

After an encouraging start, the work of the foreign missioners faltered, because the old established Christian communities refused to share in the missionary effort. Rejection of the hostile intruders, as well as mistrust for the missioners who catered to their enemies was stronger than the impulse to spread the Good News.

Withdraw into Isolation? History shows that the above-mentioned difficulties in old England were soon overcome (a hundred years later, English missioners were the ones who spread the faith to what is now Germany). Yet it is still worthwhile to compare the situation of the old English Church with our own.

We live as a Christian community in a Christian country (whether in Europe or America). There are groups of people among us who have no clear idea about Jesus Christ. Think of journalists and media people, groups of workers and academicians, many adolescents and young adults. They do not always wear velvet gloves in dealing with us Christians. Often enough they tell us what they think in a harsh and inconsiderate manner.

How do we react to these, our contemporaries? Sometimes we fear them. Instinctively we reject them. Some church circles want to have nothing to do with them. Yet do we not, as the community of Christians, have the mandate to bring Jesus Christ close even to them? Ought we not be the ones to approach them, begin the conversation with them, be missioners to them with the means at our disposal? If they are to meet Jesus Christ, then we ought not to isolate ourselves. We, then, ought to present our faith in an attractive and convincing way even to them.

Petitions

God and Father, it is your will that the Good News be proclaimed to all people:

Awaken in all our shallow contemporaries a readiness to ask themselves deeper questions about their lives. . . .
Break down the defensive resistance of all who think they have dismissed Christian faith for good. . . .
Heal the bitterness of those disillusioned by the Church and by externals of her life. . . .

Lord, give us the courage to witness to the Good News before all groups and classes of our society. You who live and reign forever and ever.

Visitation (May 31)

"HE WHOM YOU, O VIRGIN, BROUGHT TO ELIZABETH"

Introduction

The Visitation of Mary to Elizabeth—the believing Church has meditated on this scene over and over, beginning with the evangelist Luke and continuing right up until our time. Some concentrated mostly on the encounter of the two women; others, mostly on the encounter of the two unborn children. Luke presents Mary as the great believer. A meditation of the Rosary—"He whom you, O Virgin, brought to Elizabeth" (in the sense of today's Reading)—makes us think more of the helping love that moved Mary to visit her relative.

Penitential Rite

"Your love must be sincere. Detest what is evil, cling to what is good." [Silence] Lord, have mercy. . . .

"Love one another with the affection of brothers. Anticipate each other in showing respect." [Silence] Christ, have mercy. . . .

"Do not grow slack but be fervent in spirit; he whom you serve is the Lord." [Silence] Lord, have mercy. . . .

Visitation (May 31)

Talk

Mary in Prayer. There are innumerable artistic representations of the Annunciation to Mary. I believe all the artists have depicted Mary in line with a hymn verse: "Mary was alone, deep in prayer . . ." We too can only imagine this momentous encounter of Mary with God in an atmosphere of silence and prayer. In it Mary hears God's call; in it she declares herself ready to collaborate in the Redemption, and entrusts herself totally to God; in it she also conceives/receives Jesus Christ, and not only in the physical sense.

Like Mary, we too need times of silence and prayer. For "God lowers his anchor only into a quiet soul," as one prayerbook puts it. We can hear God's call only if we truly listen; we can seriously give ourselves over and make ourselves available to him only if our answer comes from the depths of our own hearts; only in this way can we really receive Jesus Christ.

Mary with Elizabeth. Yet Mary did not remain "alone, deep in prayer." As a result of her encounter with God, she "set out, proceeding in haste into the hill country to a town of Judah, where she entered Zechariah's house and greeted Elizabeth . . . and remained with Elizabeth about three months . . ." [Gospel].

The piety of the faithful has always seen as the motive for this visit the readiness of Mary to be on hand for the final weeks of Elizabeth's pregnancy (even though Luke does not say so). I believe it thereby touches upon something essential. When one meets God, one's joy over this experience comes out not only in a prayer of Thanksgiving (as Mary does in her Canticle). When one discovers Jesus Christ in the encounter with God (and in him "conceives" God's love), one will also go out and do everything to spread this love of God throughout one's own life and make it available to others. The person will try in this way to bring

Jesus Christ to his neighbors, as Mary brought Jesus out of helping love to Elizabeth.

To Bring Jesus Christ to People. What form does this bearing of Jesus Christ into our lives take? What it basically involves is underscored by the Reading with amazing clarity: "Your love must be sincere . . . anticipate each other in showing respect . . . , look on the needs of the saints as your own; be generous in offering hospitality. . . ." Each of these verses bears repetition again and again.

How should this love be practically manifested in our own lives? That is something for us to resolve with zeal and imagination. Each one of us in his own little world (family, neighborhood, acquaintances, workplace . . .), and it is there that he ought to make Christ present. Moreover, each one has his own talent and capability which he can apply for this purpose (the gift of listening, of expressing consoling words; the capacity to cheer up others by one's own humor; practical help with the little tricks of modern technology; material help, when needed . . .). Each one must become in his or her own way a bearer of Christ into his or her own world.

Petitions

Almighty and loving God, your Church, like Mary, should bear your Son Jesus Christ to human beings in the service of humble love:

Open our eyes to worldwide needs in our time. . . .
Touch our hearts and make us restless with our narrow, settled world. . . .
Stir us up to go forth like Mary to our neighbors in need. . . .
Let us help others in a way that will not debase or embitter them. . . .

For you will that the witness of our love lead other people to you. You who live and reign forever and ever.

Feast of the Sacred Heart (Friday following the Second Sunday after Pentecost)

REDEMPTION THROUGH LOVE

Introduction

In the past there was a certain amount of kitsch in connection with devotion to the Sacred Heart. Think, for example, of the maudlin pictures or the treacly hymns. Yet these excesses do not alter the reality that, in the symbol of the Heart of Jesus, central truths of our faith come to light. Thus, the open Sacred Heart is a sign for us that God has redeemed us by love. In connection with the Reading (Year C, Rom. 5:5–11), let us reflect on this truth—and entrust ourselves right from the start, as sinners in need of redemption, to the love revealed in the exposed Sacred Heart of Jesus.

Penitential Rite

Lord Jesus Christ, full of goodness and love, patient and full of mercy: Lord, have mercy. . . .

Lord Jesus Christ, laden with disgrace, beaten for our misdeeds, pierced by a lance: Christ have mercy. . . .

Lord Jesus Christ, our resurrection and life, our peace and reconciliation: Lord, have mercy . . . (Gl 768,2).

Talk

We Live Dependent on Others. There are people who will not accept things from anyone, who do not want to owe anybody anything. It is a matter of pride for them to live completely by their own power. But does that work? Do such self-made people give the impression of being mature individuals, or do they seem more like caricatures of humanity?

We human beings cannot live without our fellow men. This is true not only because we live in a society with divisions of labor and could not survive without the services of others. Beyond that, we are always in need of being loved and affirmed by other human beings.

We have grown up and have thereby developed as persons, because our parents, our siblings, our teachers, our relatives, and our acquaintances have loved and affirmed us. We still experience now how an encouraging glance, a gesture of sympathy and love gladden us and reinvigorate us.

What Love Can Do. The importance of the love that is given to us can be seen clearly in the following example. There is a person whom life has treated badly. He is inwardly embittered and imprisoned inside himself. He does not give himself any credit, he lives in perpetual anxiety that people will exploit him, he keeps up his defenses against his environment all the time.

Now, a loving person gives to this individual his attention and trust. What happens? Maybe this trust is abused for a long time, and finds no echo. The kind person, who wants the best thing for the other, is pained that his love is thrown back at him, that he has to endure one disappointment after another. He is tempted to give up and let others try, because it all seems like a waste of time and effort. Yet he perseveres, trusts him again, offers his love to him again.

Slowly, a change starts to show in the one given love. Since he is experiencing that another accepts and affirms him without exploiting him, he loses his fear of people. He tempers his aggressions toward the world around himself and opens himself to others. He develops the ability to go out of himself and give trust and love to other people. The power of selfless love has made a new person out of him.

Loved by God. This transforming brotherly love is a sign of the redeeming love of God, which transforms us much more deeply than any human kindness. Brotherly love is unable to remove all anxiety and self-centeredness from us. For we live with the lasting fear of losing this love (when, for example, the other discovers our less noble sides that up until now we have been able to conceal from him).

In Jesus Christ God has definitively revealed his love for us. He has plainly said yes to us and has held fast to this yes right up to the last breath. He has loved us, even unto death on a cross, even though he knows us better than we know ourselves. We can no longer disappoint him.

Should not this love, of which the open Sacred Heart is a symbol, free us from all anxiety? Free us from all self-centeredness? Make new persons of us, who by trusting this love, trust life and become capable of passing love and trust along?

With Paul let us declare before the exposed Heart of Jesus, through which "the love of God has been poured out in our hearts" (Reading): "If God is for us, who can be against us? . . . I am certain . . ." that nothing in the world "will be able to separate us from the love of God that comes to us in Christ Jesus, our Lord" (Rom. 8:31–39). And with John let us say, "Beloved, if God has loved us so, we must have the same love for one another" (1 Jn. 4:11).

Immaculate Heart of Mary (Saturday following the Second Sunday after Pentecost)

"SHE HAS A HEART FOR US"

Introduction

Devotional forms come and go in the Church. The feast of the Immaculate Heart of Mary was instituted in 1944. A monthly Immaculate Heart Saturday was observed, parallel to Sacred Heart Friday. There were hymns and prayers to the Immaculate Heart. In the new *Gotteslob*, none of this is to be found. Nonetheless, let us try to understand during this eucharistic liturgy what it can mean to put emphasis on Mary's heart in our devotion to her.

Penitential Rite

Lord Jesus Christ, you are full of love for sinners and sit with them at table: Lord, have mercy. . . .

You will not break the bent reed nor snuff out the smouldering wick; Christ, have mercy. . . .

You love your own and have loved them to the end: Lord, have mercy . . . (Gl 781,7).

Talk

A Man with Heart. The difference between a robot and a human being is found, among other things, in that the person has a heart. Here we do not mean the biological heart, which takes care of circulating blood through the body. Rather here we mean that the healthy person, when encountering other people (and even things), does not react coldly and impersonally (as a machine would), but rather somehow "with a heart": the other person does not leave him cold; emotions come into play; he behaves in either a friendly or a hostile way, but at least his whole character (including his feelings) come into play.

"A person with heart," in this context means: a person with genuine interest, who can become enthusiastic, who can demonstrate his love and his joy, and who is therefore vulnerable and capable of compassion.

Mary—a Person with Heart on Earth. In this sense, Mary was certainly a person with heart during her earthly life. Her relation to God was not drab fulfillment of duty or mere reasonable assertion of specific articles of faith. She has her heart in her faith. According to the Gospel of Luke, she exalted God with joy in her Canticle. According to folk piety, which has passed down both the "Seven Joys" and the "Seven Sorrows" of Mary, she also suffered in her communion with God over the darknesses on her path with Jesus Christ.

We can also imagine how Mary was warm-hearted in her contact with other people. She rejoiced with them, suffered with them, showed them her interest and love. She was a human being among human beings.

Mary—a Person with Heart in Heaven. Our faith tells us that Mary entered into communion with God as a complete human being. Her joy in God does not rest alone in the pure vision of God (as a purely intellectual theology presented it in the past); she rejoices in God with her whole heart. The total communion with God penetrates her whole human reality; it lets her sing—to our way of understanding—her Canticle with full joy even now.

Mary is bound to us in her Son even in her fulfillment with God. Her heart is involved in her interest in us. She does not have the interst of an objective camera in the struggling Church, nor that of an aloof reporter. She is concerned for us like a warm-hearted mother. Her heart beats for us, she rejoices with us, she wants to show us her love.

We—Persons with Heart. Mary is a person with heart in her relation with God and in her ties to men and women. Of course, we can only grope our way into the mystery of Mary's fulfillment with God with inadequate human words and images. Yet these attempts may also make it clear that Mary, while with God, is still fully human, and her heart has a place in her communion with us.

From Mary we can also learn: our own heart must be involved in our faith in God: in joy and pain that we experience in our personal history with God; in our personal prayer and in liturgical celebrations. And our heart must be involved in our contact with other people; they ought to discern that we love them, that we rejoice with them—and sometimes even suffer with them and because of them.

Petitions

Lord Jesus Christ, you have a heart for us men. Hear our prayer:

Fill all servants of the Church with kindness and understanding for people today. . .
Grant that something of your kindness and benevolence toward humanity may be felt in all administrative offices of the Church. . . .
Let us celebrate liturgy in such a way that our hearts are in it. . . .

Grant us these requests through Mary's intercession, who, as your Mother and ours, has a heart for us. You who live and reign forever and ever.

St. Justin (June 1)

WITNESS FOR CHRIST IN A PHILOSOPHER'S ROBE

Introduction

"You certainly love good discussions, but in no way are you close to action or reality." This statement, by his own account, moved the young intellectual Justin in the second Christian century to involve himself seriously with the Good News of Jesus Christ and finally to be baptized. Today on the feast of this early Christian saint, this thought can become for us a stimulus for a personal examination of conscience.

Penitential Rite

"Out of the depths I cry to you, O Lord, Lord, hear my voice!
If you, O Lord, should mark our guilt, Lord, who would survive?
But with you is found forgiveness: for this we revere you" (Ps. 130:1,3f).

Have mercy, Lord our God, have mercy. . . .

Talk

Seeker of Truth. Justin, as a young Palestinian intellectual, found himself to be very much in the mainstream of the available world views of his age. He studied, as he himself later recounted, under the

Stoics and the Pythagoreans, under the disciples of Aristotle and the followers of Plato. Yet their answers to his questions on the meaning of life did not satisfy him. Eventually, with the aid of a Christian, he encountered Jesus Christ—and discovered the "wisdom of the cross" (Reading).

Preacher of Truth. He had discovered what he termed "the only reliable and useful philosophy," and he wanted to spread it among non-Christians of his day. In order to be a light to his age [Gospel], he held forth as a Christian in the style of then-current philosophers. Still a Christian layman, he traveled through the Roman Empire as a wandering preacher in a philosopher's robe. In town public squares, he joined in conversation with people of the most varied social backgrounds, in order to win them over to faith in Jesus Christ.

After a long period of wandering, Justin eventually came to Rome. There he established residence and founded his own school of philosphy, which gained a good name for itself. His main objective was intellectual exchange with pagan world views, and he published his thoughts in various writings.

As a known intellectual member of Christianity, Justin was drawn inevitably into conflict with the pagan state. He was accused of godlessness by his philosophical opponents and was executed in Rome in A.D. 166.

Early Christian Eucharistic Celebration. Justin is an example of the Christian who adapts to his time in order to bring Jesus Christ closer to his contemporaries in an understandable way. He could well be the patron saint of all those who try out new forms of catechesis, preaching, liturgy, and sacred music, in order to win over people in our time to the Good News.

We are also indebted to this early Christian martyr for an accurate description of the Sunday eucharistic liturgy of his age. Here are some excerpts, which will help us see that the basic elements of our eucharistic liturgy have changed very little.

St. Justin (June 1)

"And on the day named after the sun, everyone assembles . . . for a common celebration, and then the memoirs of the apostles or the writings of the prophets are read [liturgy of the Word]. . . . When the reader has completed his service, the presider gives a talk in which he sternly admonishes them to observe these beautiful teachings [homily]. Next, we all stand up and offer prayers [intercessions]. Now, after the prayers are completed, . . bread is set out as well as wine with water, and the presider offers up prayers and thanksgivings as best he can [offertory, Eucharistic prayer] . . . The people affirm this by saying "Amen" [before the Our Father]. Then that is distributed to all present, over which the thanksgiving was uttered [communion] . . . Afterwards, those who have more than others make an offering, as much as they choose. The collected offerings are handed over to the presider, who uses them to help orphans and widows . . . [collection]."

Petitions

Let us pray:

> For courage and imagination for all who witness to the Good News of Jesus Christ in the press and on television . . . Lord, have mercy. . . .
> For patience and perseverance for all who try new approaches in religious education. . . .
> For openness to God's ways in our time for all who bear responsibility in the Church. . . .

For you, O God, desire that your Church be a Light that shines in the darkness of our time. You who live and reign forever and ever.

Sts. Marcellinus and Peter (June 2)

MARTYRDOM IN LIFE

Introduction

Marcellinus and Peter—we used to mention their names during every eucharistic celebration, prior to Vatican Council II. They occur in the Roman Canon in the prayer for sinners shortly before the doxology (and can be omitted at the priest's option). They are believed to have been a priest and an exorcist and to have suffered martyrdom around 303. Their relics are venerated in Seligenstadt am Main in Germany. As is virtually usual among early Christian martyrs, no further details are known about their lives. We may take their names as symbolic of all unnamed witnesses for Christ, who have endured life and death in a Christian way, in the sense of today's Reading; with them we enter into our eucharistic celebration before God.

Penitential Rite

Jesus Christ, sacrificial Lamb for sinners: Lord, have mercy . . . .
You, our peace and our reconciliation: Christ, have mercy . . . .
You, our resurrection and our life: Lord, have mercy . . . (GL 768,2).

Sts. Marcellinus and Peter (June 2)

Talk

Martyrs of Everyday Living. A pope once named missioners to the Eskimos in northern Canada "martyrs of the cold." By that he meant that they had offered their lives for Christ in the many weeks and months of their lives and work under the most extreme climactic conditions. They were thus similar to actual martyrs executed for their religious convictions.

"Martyrs of everyday living" could justifiably be the category for all those who cling to their faith under extreme living conditions and thus dedicate their lives to Christ. In light of the description given in today's Reading, Paul was one of these. Yet there are also many unknown servants of God in our age, in whose lives neither television nor the popular press are interested; in future generations there will be as little to tell about them as there is about Sts. Marcellinus and Peter, the saints for today.

We can think of people who fulfill their roles in life with great steadfastness, even though they are bothered, on account of unclear consciences, by the anxiety of whether they have done everything right. There are mothers of families who nearly collapse under the weight of work at home and on the job (which they hold, because they need the money). There are the sleepless nights by the sickbeds of old mothers, whom people will not shunt aside into a nursing home despite pressures on the job. Examples like these can be easily multiplied.

How many "ministers of God" live out today their faith in Jesus Christ under similar burdens with patience, kindness, and "sincere love, . . . always rejoicing . . ." and enriching many! How much encouragement comes forth from a woman, who is nearly swamped with work in her family, but who nevertheless displays an inner peace that clearly comes from her faith in Jesus Christ! How many people carry the burden of a chronic illness or of advancing old age, with courage and trust in God that put a healthy person to shame!

Whether Honored or Dishonored. We can think of those Christians who unerringly follow the way of faith "whether honored or dishonored, spoken of well or ill, . . . called impostors, yet . . . truthful." The compass of their lives is directed toward Jesus Christ. They follow this compass in their family life, in their service to the community, and in their involvement with the world around them. They are gladdened by recognition, yet they are not discouraged by a lack of praise. They are pained if someone attributes the wrong motives to them and attacks them, but they do not give up and withdraw on that account.

"With the Power of God." We can call to mind all ministers of God who endure this situation as well as others like them. We can also think of people who live exemplary lives without consciously believing in Jesus Christ. Let us remember during this eucharistic celebration that Jesus Christ died for all human beings in order to give them strength for this life. Let us request, in communion with him and with all the unknown everyday saints (whether still journeying through this life or already completely in God's presence), that God strengthen them with his grace over and over, so they can show themselves forth in their life circumstances as ministers of God in all things.

Petitions

Let us pray:

> For all those who must acquire self-mastery in anxiety and inner unrest. (Silence).
> For all who run the danger of collapsing under external pressures . . . .
> For all who must suffer from slander and vicious gossip . . . .

God our Father, give all people the power to control their lives so as to become joyful and bring joy to others. You who live and reign forever and ever.

St. Charles Lwanga and Companions (June 3)

THE UGANDA MARTYRS

Introduction

Idi Amin, the deposed dictator of Uganda, was for many people the example of a lawless tyrant who wielded his power ruthlessly in a different place each day. If that was possible in present-day Uganda (and not only there, and not only in Africa!), it is no surprise that, a hundred years ago, the young missionary Church in Uganda suffered under a lawless king; under his rule, Christians had to yield up their lives in witness of their faith.

Penitential Rite

Lord Jesus Christ, you have said:
Blest are the lowly; they shall inherit the land: Lord, have mercy . . . .
Blest are those persecuted for holiness' sake; the reign of God is theirs: Christ, have mercy . . . .
Blest are you when they insult you and persecute you and utter every kind of slander against you because of me; your reward in heaven is great: Lord, have mercy . . . (cf. Mt 5:5, 10, 11f).

Talk

Mission in the Last Century. The origins of the great modern missionary history in the last century were strongly connected with the colonial ideas of that time. European missiónners considered themselves to be not only messengers of Christ, but also the exponents of European civilization or even agents of their countries, which wanted to establish spheres of influence in the non-European continents.

For their part, the young nations—for example, in Africa—wanted to gain a share in European civilization. They were grateful for schools and medical aid and gladly accepted technical assistance.

The new ideas and perspectives that the missioners brought to these territories naturally disturbed the prevailing power structures and had to arouse the opposition of all those whose place in society was threatened (tribal chiefs, medicine men . . .). This readily led to outbreaks of hatred toward foreigners, which became directed also toward those natives who had accepted the faith.

The Uganda Martyrs. In the East African country of Uganda, the first Christian missioners arrived in the seventies of the last century. They soon had to leave the country. Yet a small community, remaining true to the faith, had formed at the royal court. There belonged to it trusted servants of the king and boys from leading families, who served as pages.

In 1885 a persecution was unleashed, directed equally against the country's Anglican and Catholic Christians. Intrigues, plans for revolt within the royal court, and mistrust toward all foreigners all entered into these events. In the course of a year and a half, twenty-two Ugandan Catholics met violent deaths.

Among those killed were thirteen young men from the royal court. Charles Lwanga was the leader of this group. Together with fifteen others (of whom three were later arbitrarily spared) he was condemned to death by the king. They were immediately led off onto a two-day march to the place of execution. There they still had to wait six more

St. Charles Lwanga and Companions (June 3)

days, until preparations were completed. During this interval, relatives and parents pleaded with the young men to renounce the faith, but had no success. On June 3, 1886, they were put to death at the stake.

The Church in Africa. On October 18, 1964, during the Council, the twenty-two Ugandan Martyrs were canonized. This solemn act duly underscored that the Church in Africa makes her own irreplaceable contribution to the life of the universal Church.

A glance at church statistics for recent years shows that the number of Catholics in Africa has increased the most. Our black fellow Christians will now become more and more aware of their own cultural and historical worth and will try to express the message of Jesus Christ in African forms.

To this end, they require not only models from their own ranks (like the Ugandan Martyrs), and not only our mission donations and supply of church workers; before all these things, they need our prayer.

Petitions

Lord our God, look upon the Christians of Africa, who live our their faith amid many tensions and difficulties and give witness to your Good News.

Accompany the local African Churches on their way toward self-sufficiency . . . .
Help them in their efforts to set the Good News into African forms, that it might become more understandable to Africans . . . .
Be near to those African Christians who undergo hardships for their faith . . . .

For you call all men and women into your Kingdom. You who live and reign forever and ever.

St. Boniface (June 5)

APOSTLE OF GERMANY

Introduction

In the crypt of the cathedral of Fulda (Germany) is located the tomb of St. Boniface. In front of it sits a tombstone from the Baroque period with this image: Boniface, with his bishop's miter and crosier, is lifting up the cover of his coffin; he is climbing out in order to look around to see what has become in Germany of the faith in Jesus Christ, for which he labored and died twelve hundred years ago.

What meaning does this Anglo-Saxon monk and bishop have for the Church and the faith in Germany?

Talk

The Situation in Germany. Around 700, the religious situation in Germany was in flux. In the territories that had belonged to the Roman Empire along the Rhine and the Danube rivers, Christianity had established an early foothold and had spread. Christian communities were also to be found to the north and west of these areas. However, Christianity was not yet really rooted in the Germanic tribes of that region.

In this border territory—a political struggle existed over whether it belonged to the Frankish kingdom—missionary monks from Scotland and England had long since been working. They had left the monasteries in their own countries and were active as wandering missioners, since they wanted to be homeless as Jesus of Nazareth had been during his public life.

Bond with Rome. Winfred (his original name) belonged to this class of itinerant missioners. He was an Anglo-Saxon by birth and received his education in English monasteries. He himself became a Benedictine; after priestly ordination at thirty, he became a teacher in his home monastery. His confreres also elected him to be abbot.

Still, at age forty, Winfred left his cloister in order to work as an itinerant missioner on the continent. His first missionary attempt among the Frisians (in present-day Holland) failed. He returned to his homeland, only to leave it for good in 718. On this second missionary expedition Winfred first sought out support from the Frankish authorities. Above all, however, he made contact with the pope. He made a pilgrimage to Rome, in order to receive an official mandate for his missionary work and to become invested with specific authority. In order to highlight his tie with the pope, he assumed the name of a local Roman saint, Boniface. This bond with Rome had great importance for the remaining work of spreading the Gospel.

Missioner among the Heathens. Boniface then went to work together with St. Willibrord in Friesland. However, he split off from him in 721 and began to work on his own in Hesse and Thuringia. He made himself known to the neglected Christian communities and penetrated into heathen territory. While doing this, he followed closely the normal pattern of his time in accepting the support of the authorities of the Frankish kingdom. Through his activity (aided as he was by many missioners from his home country), the dominance of paganism was broken.

Organizer. From about 725 onwards, the specific mission to pagans receded more and more into the background of Boniface's life in favor of the work of setting up a firm organization for the Church in Germany. The first step was the establishment of new dioceses in Hesse and Thuringia. In 732 he received from the pope the right and the responsibility for ordaining bishops for the entire mission area east of the Rhine. He was named papal legate for Germany in 738 and established a new arrangement of dioceses for all of Bavaria, Hesse, and Thuringia. In the following years his cooperation with civil authorities brought about reform and new organization for the Church among the Frankish tribes (in present-day France). Boniface gave the whole reform effort a good foundation by establishing many monasteries and convents begun with monks and nuns from England.

Target of Hostility. During the years of this tireless development activity, Boniface drew down the rejection and even, to some measure, the hate and enmity of the local established Frankish clergy. The priests and bishops were mistrustful of the foreign Anglo-Saxons and sought to roll back their influence. Boniface gradually was pushed aside along with his collaborators, while his reform work continued to be fruitful.

Martyrdom. Did this development play a part in the fact that Boniface, in his old age, once again dedicated himself to real missionary work among the heathens and returned to work again in Friesland? Here he met his life's end on June 5, 754, under the swords of plundering heathens. His grave is located in his favorite foundation, the monastery at Fulda.

Apostle in Paul's Image. These are the outward elements of the life and work of the Apostle to the Germans. If we inquire as to his inner character, Winfred/Boniface could answer of himself what Paul in today's Reading says about his own missionary service. He knew he had been chosen by God (Gospel). He proclaimed the Gospel with trust in God and under great hardship. He did not aim to tell people only what they wanted to hear and made no material profit from his missionary service. His work was penetrated with concern for people—and he dedicated his life to preaching the faith.

St. Norbert of Xanten (June 6)

PLAYBOY, PREACHER OF PENANCE, PRINCE OF THE CHURCH

Introduction

"If anyone comes to me without turning his back on his father and mother, his wife and his children, his brothers and sisters, indeed his very self, he cannot be my follower" [Gospel]. How many people throughout the history of the Church have been so moved by these words of Jesus, that they shifted the course of their lives and set out in an entirely new direction! Norbert of Xanten (1082–1134) was one of these.

Petitions

Lord Jesus Christ, we neglect one another and forget our neighbors in their need: Lord, have mercy . . . .

We do not try hard enough to understand and bear with one another: Christ, have mercy . . . .

We are often filled with bitterness and resentment toward one another and speak evil of each other: Lord, have mercy . . . (After GL 7,2).

Talk

High-living Cleric. As a late-born son of a noble family in the Lower Rhine, Norbert was destined in a way for an ecclesiastical career. While still young in years, he was made a canon in Xanten.

The young cleric led a life corresponding to his background in nobility. He was rich, given to luxury, and had the reputation of being an untroubled epicure who knew how to savor the comforts of life. He established contacts with the imperial court and became a partisan of the emperor in the current quarrels between the pope and the emperor. When the emperor offered him a bishopric for his loyal service, Norbert turned it down on the grounds that he was already rich enough and did not need the additional income of a bishop's chair!

Penitential Preacher. In 1115—Norbert was just thirty years old—the life of this worldly cleric reached the point of a genuine conversion. He came into contact with circles that were working for the renewal of the Church. He retired to the monastery at Siegburg near Cologne. He sought to be ordained a priest as soon as possible. Then he sold off his possessions and renounced his ecclesiastical incomes. He went around the country barefoot and clothed in a penitential robe, and succeeded in reaching both the great and the lowly by his preaching. His greatest aim was to make peace.

At the same time, Norbert worked for the religious reform of the clerical state. Above all, he addressed priests and clerics who lived in community at cathedrals and other main churches, and tried to interest them in a pastoral life in poverty and penance. When he had little success in this, he founded his own community of priests who would combine pastoral service with life in a cloister: the Order of Premonstratensians (whose name was taken from the place of the first foundation).

Bishop of Magdeburg. The newly founded order spread and grew rapidly, but Norbert did not tie himself down to any one foundation. He continued to be a wandering preacher, moving from place to place and calling people to penance, until he was named to be bishop of Magdeburg in 1126. This time he accepted the episcopal office out of a sense of pastoral responsibility. In his attempts to bring about a fundamental renewal of his diocese, he ran afoul of factions hostile to reform

St. Norbert of Xanten (June 6) 211

and nearly lost his life during an uprising. As bishop of Magdeburg, he also had considerable influence on the politics of the whole empire, and on the church controversies of that period. During a journey to Italy, which he undertook in the emperor's company, he caught an infectious disease and died from it on June 6, 1134.

Our Conversion. We are not Norbert of Xanten. Our lives have proceeded on other paths. We may be used to these paths. Do we nonetheless need a new conversion—to a more committed life with Christ, to a more conscious dedication to the Church and to the world today? "Give me the courage to know myself, / make me ready to do new things. / Shake me out of my old ruts; / then, my Lord, things will go well" (GL 165,3).

Petitions

Lord, we pray for our priests:

Teach them to make known your message that our hunger for truth and life might be satisfied . . . .
Give them the courage not to flatter anyone, even when many hold the Gospel of the Cross to be nonsense . . . .
Let them feel your mysterious presence, so that they may be capable of strengthening the faith of their brethren . . . .

For you have called them to be servants of the faith in the midst of your communities. You who live and reign forever and ever.

(After GL 27,4)

St. Ephrem (June 9)

TEACHER, WRITER, AND POET IN A RESTLESS TIME

Introduction

In an explanation of the penitential sermon of Jonah in Nineveh, St. Ephrem (306–373) wrote: "As sensible people, the inhabitants of Nineveh knew of God and of men; they knew that men behaved humanly but that God behaved mercifully. They saw that the prophet was strict, but they wisely judged that God was kind. . . . They granted that the prophet was right, but they attributed kindness to God. . . ." God, whose nonhumanity (his differentiation from human beings) rests on his kindness and on his readiness to forgive! At the beginning of this eucharistic celebration we turn to him as men and women in need of conversion.

Petitions

"Lord, let your ears be attentive to the voice of my pleading.
My soul is waiting for the Lord, I count on his word.
Because with the Lord there is mercy, and fullness of redemption"
(after Ps. 130:2,5,7).

Have mercy, Lord our God, have mercy. . . .

Talk

Unsettled Times. Ephrem lived in the region of present-day Turkey. At that time his home area was a frontier zone between the Roman sphere of influence and the expanding Persian kingdom. His home town of Nisibis was besieged at different times and finally conquered by the Persians. Toward the end of his life the unstable political conditions forced him to move to Edessa, further westward.

Ephrem grew up in a Christian family and community. He lived through the last persecution of Christians in antiquity under Emperor Julian the Apostate. In his writings are reflected the struggles of Christianity with the Persian religion of Mani, with the different forms of astrological superstitions, and with Gnosticism. The intrachurch controversy over Arianism is also evident in his theological work.

Teacher and Writer. During this time of external troubles and sharp intellectual controversies, Ephrem was active as a theological teacher and writer. In his writings he used Syrian, the language of his home area. His theology was developed entirely from the Bible. He wrote not merely against pagan influences and against superstitions embellished with Christianity in his age, but he also presented the faith in a positive manner, to make it clear and desirable.

"Harp of the Holy Spirit." Ephrem's work took on a special accent owing to his poetic gifts. He reacted to the then current religious controversies by composing Christian folk hymns of notable poetic worth; in them he attempted to bring truths of Christian faith to the minds of ordinary people. His poems proved to be a good way to bring Christian thought to the song-loving people of his homeland. They were gladly sung by everyone, found a place in the liturgy, and are still used today in the liturgy of the Syrian Church (for example, among Lebanese Catholics). They earned their composer the descriptive title of "harp of the Holy Spirit."

Songs and Preaching. In his attempts to clothe articles of Christian faith in song form, Ephrem was following early Christian practice. The young Church had from the beginning not contented herself with the hymnal of the Old Testament, the Psaltery. Many songs arose that embodied Christian belief. A sample of them is found in the New Testament writings (and also became part of the Christian heritage of hymns in *Gotteslob*—see its table of contents, p. 13).

Evidently out of fear of heresies that propagated their doctrines in hymns, the Church in the post-Apostolic period examined new texts very critically and made the Book of Psalms the official songbook of the Church. Ephrem is the first we know of to make a new attempt at proclaiming the faith through attractive songs.

For us, the Christian treasury of hymns is something taken for granted. It ought also to be taken for granted that our hymnals also contain new songs written in our time. Many Christians respond better to a pleasant melody and to a lyric with clear thought than they do to a long homily. Which new hymns have already become an accepted part of our worship?

Petitions

Lord Jesus Christ, in the eucharistic celebration you speak to us in the prayers and songs. We call upon you:

For the Christian songmakers of our age.   [Silence]
For the members of youth choirs and instrumental groups who contribute their talents to our worship services . . . .
For the editors of official church books of worship . . . .

For you want to declare the Good News not only to our heads, but above all to our hearts. You who live and reign forever and ever.

St. Barnabas (June 11)

FRIEND AND CO-WORKER OF PAUL

Introduction

Have you ever wondered how Paul succeeded in gaining access to Christian communities after his conversion? We can imagine how they met the new convert with suspicion. Was this conversion perhaps just a trick to undermine the community in order to be able to destroy it more easily?

Judging from the account in the Acts of the Apostles, this mistrust did in fact exist among the Christians of Jerusalem. In this situation Paul found an advocate who trusted him and argued for him before the leading people of the Christian community (cf. Acts 9:27): Barnabas, "a Levite, who came from Cyprus" (Acts 4:36).

Talk

Respected Member of the Community. Barnabas is mentioned relatively often in Acts, at least in comparison with other figures of the first generation of Christians. When and how he became a Christian is not known. Acts 4:36 mentions that he sold off a parcel of land and gave the proceeds over to the community. He must have earned a respected place, as further information about him indicates.

Missioner to the Gentiles with Paul. Barnabas is spoken of as an apostle in Acts, even though he does not belong to the circle of the twelve original apostles. This leads people to see him as the most important missioner of the young Church before and at the same time as Paul. Even before Paul, he had dedicated himself to work among the Gentiles.

Banished disciples of Jesus had come together in community in Antioch and had received an influx of interested pagans. Barnabas apparently went to Antioch with a mandate from the first community in Jerusalem to see that everything was in order. He recognized in the conversion of pagans the work of God and encouraged the Christians to continue in the direction they were going.

Because he needed help with the community and mission work, he sought out Paul (who had stayed rather withdrawn after his conversion and had returned to his homeland) and won him over for work in Antioch [cf. Reading]. Together with Paul he brought the proceeds from a collection to Jerusalem (Acts 11:30).

Barnabas and Paul undertook together the first great missionary journey that led them into cities of Asia Minor with Jewish communities of the diaspora (Acts 13–14). Despite the resistance of Jews that led even to ill-treatment and expulsion, they were able to found small yet lasting communities in many cities.

Intrachurch Controversies. In the great controversy between Jewish and pagan Christians—which led to the Council of Jerusalem—Barnabas stood with Paul on the side of the "progressives." They did not want to force the newly converted pagan Christians to observe the Mosaic Law. Both met with the people from Judaea and were sent as representatives of the Antiochian community to Jerusalem. They were able to present their case in such a way that a reasonable compromise was made which made possible the coexistence of the two different ways.

Human Frailties. The last thing that Acts reports on Barnabas, this "excellent man, filled with the Holy Spirit and faith" (Acts 11:24), reveals that these first Christians were and remained human beings like

St. Barnabas (June 11)

ourselves. Shortly after the Council of Jerusalem, a "bitter quarrel" arose between Paul and Barnabas, which—at least for some time—resulted in the separation of the two missionaries (Acts 15:36–41). The fight came up because Barnabas wanted to take Mark along on the second missionary journey, while Paul had not yet forgiven the young man for leaving them in the lurch on the first missionary journey. He therefore refused to have him along. The two could not resolve their difference, and so each one went on his own mission journey. A later reconciliation and further work together could possibly have occurred, but is mentioned nowhere in Scripture.

We have no further documentation on the subsequent life of the young Church's great missioner to the gentiles, who was originally named Joseph but later received the surname Barnabas, "Son of consulation," from the apostles. Nonetheless, along with Paul and many unnamed missioners of the early times, he set the pattern for the worldwide expansion of Christianity.

Petitions

Lord Jesus Christ, you have given your Church the task of making known the Good News to all nations till the end of time. Hear our prayer:

> Take away from the Church any mistrust of new forms of piety and of church life . . . .
> Grant that she may have the necessary critical approach to her own traditions while being ever true to you . . . .
> Strengthen the bonds between older national churches and mission churches in underdeveloped countries . . . .

Lord, bring all men together to confess your name. You who live and reign forever and ever.

St. Anthony of Padua (June 13)

THE SAINT WITH THE CHILD JESUS ON HIS ARM

Introduction

Anthony of Padua: "responsible" for lost articles. Known to most of us as a tasteless plaster statue, with a book in one hand and the Child Jesus on his arm. Many recognize the offering box with the legend, "St. Anthony's bread—for the poor of the parish." Who is the man and the Christian hidden behind this special "responsibility"?

Penitential Rite

Lord Jesus Christ, you bring the Good News to the poor: Lord, have mercy . . . .
You heal all who are downhearted: Christ, have mercy . . . .
You decree the release of prisoners and the unfettering of those in chains: Lord, have mercy . . . .

Talk

A Withdrawn Life. Anthony was born in Lisbon in 1195. He became an Augustinian at the age of fifteen. When he was twenty-five, he left his rich cloister and joined the mendicant Franciscan brethren, whom he had met at the gates of his monastery. On his way through

St. Anthony of Padua (June 13)

Morocco—where he wanted to labor as a missioner—he was forced to head for northern Italy; there he spent some time in a Franciscan hermitage. Ordained a priest in 1222, he was chosen to give the thanksgiving after the ritual. His superiors then and there recognized his speaking talent and assigned him to preaching activity.

Preacher to the Dissatisfied. During the saint's lifetime, tendencies became evident in Christianity that took a critical attitude toward the Church, which was in need of reform. Demands arose for restoring Christian life in accordance with the Gospel. Alongside justified criticism and honorable efforts, ideas emerged that led to separation from the Church for the groups known as the Cathars and the Waldensians.

Francis of Assisi responded to the great religious trends of his time not only through the life-style of his brotherhood, he also sent his brethren as preachers into dangerous areas. Anthony was the leader of these Franciscan preachers. He was well-versed in the Bible and could thus argue with his listeners on their favorite ground. His style of preaching allowed him to make a winning impression. He never held forth with threats or condemnations. When speaking, he directed himself not only to the understanding but also to the hearts of his listeners. He worked with great success for the unity and renewal of the Church.

Anthony of Padua. After untiring activity as a wandering preacher, Anthony came to Padua in 1231 to give the homilies for Lent. It was the last station for his pastoral care. He died during that same year at the age of thirty-six.

The saint, however, had turned the city around in a lasting way by his preaching. Ancient enmities were set aside. Property acquired dishonestly was returned. The city authorities instituted a debtors' law that kept needy people from at least going to debtors' prison.

To us the saint is known as Anthony of Padua. Why this zealous pastoral worker and preacher has become responsible in popular piety for lost things, I do not know. Bible (book) and Infant Jesus indicate a man who is familiar with the Bible and who through it finds Jesus Christ in his personal piety. The special poorboxes in churches remind us of his dedication to justice between the rich and the poor.

Anthony of Padua—on his feast day, he places the question before us whether we, in all our religious activity, have found Jesus Christ and are clinging to him; whether we are ready for the sake of the love of Jesus Christ to work for justice between rich and poor; in our personal world and in the larger world of nations and continents.

Petitions

Let us pray to the Lord of the harvest, that he give growth and well-being to his Church:

> For everyone who suffers because of the all-too-human element in the Church: Christ, hear us, Christ, graciously hear us.
> For preachers who try to proclaim the Good News clearly to human hearts . . . .
> For all who work for justice between the rich and the poor . . . .

Lord Jesus Christ, accompany your Church on her way through time, so that she might be a witness to your love. You who live and reign forever and ever.

St. Romuald (June 19)

"LET ME BE FORMED INTO THE PATTERN OF HIS DEATH"

Introduction

"When I read the lives of the saints, I feel it in my bone and marrow; and when I see what I do, I want to die of shame and sadness." These words are attributed to St. Romuald (952–1027). His life appears strange to us at first. Only if we break through the external forms of his radical imitation of Christ and manage to look at the true core of his believing life, do we feel the radicalness of faith "in bone and marrow" and become ashamed of our own mediocrity as Christians.

Penitential Rite

"I have come to rate all as loss in the light of the surpassing knowledge of my Lord Jesus Christ." [Silence] Lord, have mercy . . . .

"I wish to know Christ; let me be formed into the pattern of his death." [Silence] Christ, have mercy . . . .

"I give no thought to what lies behind but push on to what is ahead." [Silence] Lord, have mercy . . . .

Talk

Life Events. At age twenty, Romuald was a witness of his own nobleman father striking a relative dead in a fight. He went in his father's stead to a monastery in order to do penance for the deed through forty days of strict asceticism. During this experiment of temporary monastic life, he decided definitively to become a monk.

In the following years (and decades) of his life, Romuald joined several monastic communities in Italy. Still, the life-style was not strict enough for him anywhere. He finally established several foundations himself and gathered disciples around himself in order to put into practice his ideal of strict ascetic life. Only toward the end of his life did he accomplish the founding of the hermit colony at Camaldoli, which became the center of the religious order of Camaldolese monks.

This strict ascetic, who was always in search of solitude, tried once in the course of his life to be a missioner. He wanted to emulate his former disciple, St. Bruno of Querfurt, who had met his death in the missions to the Prussians. Nonetheless, he had to curtail soon his missionary journey because of his advanced age and his stricken health.

"Let Me Be Formed into the Pattern of His Death."

These life scenes—taken together with his hard ascetic life-style—of St. Romuald reveal something of the radicalness of a saint who, completely within the religious style of his time, wanted to become like Jesus Christ in his death for the salvation of the world. He renounced a comfortable life, he fasted, he did without sleep, he whipped himself, all in order to die with Jesus in the midst of his own life. He called for more obedience in monastic life (by this he meant subordination to the will of the abbot), in order to die to his own ideas and to let himself be led like Jesus Christ entirely by the will of the Father. He lived with the longing to become like Jesus even by the violent death of martyrdom. He wanted to be formed into the pattern of his death for the salvation of the world in his own life and death.

Let Us Be Formed into the Pattern of His Love.

Perhaps in the times of St. Romuald the death of Jesus was seen in a somewhat isolated fashion, and people tried to become like him in ways that for us seem somehow violent. We suggest that the sentence from the Reading (Phil 3:8–14) be expanded in this fashion: "Let me be formed into the pattern of his own love unto death." Our Christian goal in life consists in integrating into our life and death the selfless love with which Jesus Christ has first loved us.

This love in the community of life with Jesus Christ demands from us a strictness with ourselves. It is not accomplished without material renunciation, by which we want to help others. It demands that in our daily life we think and behave more in consideration of our neighbors than of our own interests and needs. It will only succeed if we prepare ourselves through a personal training program for the real thing: if our practice in selflessness also yields voluntary sacrifices and renunciations.

How do we feel about this serious desire to become like Jesus Christ, of which the Reading and the Gospel speak? And was it a living desire in St. Romuald's life? Can we match his radicalness, or must we "die from shame and sadness"?

Petitions

Lord Jesus Christ, you have taken us up in your grace, and you want us to push on to what is ahead:

Awaken in all Christians the longing for a genuinely holy life . . . .
Be close to those from whom genuine love in everyday life demands hard sacrifices . . . .
Bless the prayer and work of religious in today's world and Church . . . .

For you have called us in your love, and you will that we be formed more and more into the pattern of this love in our lives. You who live and reign forever and ever.

St. Aloysius Gonzaga (June 21)

PATRON OF YOUTH

Introduction

We know his picture from the banner of youth organizations. "Flower of purity . . ." begins one song that exalts him as "patron of youth." Certainly no other saint in the course of time has become so sugar-coated in picture and word as has Aloysius Gonzaga. Insofar as we see him in legendary tales and plaster statues, he does not come across as a model for our times. Let us look at his real life (without the choir robe and the lily in hand), so as to see what he really can say to today's youth.

Penitential Rite

Lord Jesus Christ, you call upon men and women to follow you: Lord, have mercy . . . .
You send them forth as your messengers: Christ, have mercy . . . .
You give them the spirit to confess you: Lord, have mercy . . . (GL 495,7).

Talk

An Ambitious Family. The northern Italian clan of Gonzaga held only a small domain. Its members would either enter into the emperor's service and become ruthless warriors, or would go into an ecclesiastical career, reaching even to the college of cardinals.

Aloysius was born in 1568 as his parents' eldest son. This meant that the path of a hereditary prince lay before him. As a page in various princely courts, he learned everything that was proper education for his rank: courtly conduct and appearance, use of arms and horses, classical and modern languages. At the same time he lived in an environment in which all religious norms were kept in their externals, yet in which little of Christian living otherwise prevailed.

An Independent Young Man. In this milieu Aloysius went his own way between the ages of ten and fifteen. He did not conform. He remained independent and protested through his life-style against the superficial religiosity of his surroundings. Is it any wonder that his religiously motivated individuation sometimes took on provocative forms?

Aloysius displayed the same independence in his decision to become a Jesuit. That meant that he had to renounce officially his inheritance rights, which he did at the age of eighteen. Only after a long conflict did he gain the consent of his father; the latter could not come to terms with a son as Jesuit, since the Jesuits made a vow to accept no ecclesiastical posts of honor.

With Both Feet on the Ground. The young noble, starting his novitiate at age eighteen, stood with both feet on the ground of reality. When his father brought down trouble on the family by his love for gambling, it was the fourteen-year-old son who acted as mediator with the relatives. While studying theology, he had to leave school for a while to smooth out a quarrel within his own family. His brother, who had succeeded his deceased father as head of the family, had eloped with the daughter of a respected family and was living with her. In addition, he was entangled in a property-line dispute with a neighboring prince. Aloysius came on as an arbitrator. He succeeded in reconciling the parties to the conflict and convinced his brother officially to marry the woman of his choice.

Aloysius stood with both feet on the ground in still another sense. As part of their training, young Jesuits would carry out a practicum in hospitals and in religious instructions for children from Rome's streets. Thus it was normally provided that the theology students should not unlearn their contact with real life. When the plague broke out in Rome in 1590–1591, it was a matter of course for young Jesuits to offer themselves in care for those stricken with the plague. While doing this, Aloysius became infected and died after a lingering illness on June 21, 1591. Aware of his approaching death, he consoled his mother beforehand with a letter on the impending loss of her oldest son.

Model for Youth. When we look at Aloysius' life in its reality, there is nothing of the lily and the bowed head. Here was a young man who, in his particular surroundings, made his own way very deliberately. He remained true to his ideal and shaped his life according to his faith. He stood in the middle of life and knew how to handle his problems. All this makes him a model for young Christians even in our day.

Petitions

God our Father, we pray for the youth of the Church:

Guard them against our contemporary dangers to faith . . . .
Awaken in them the readiness to deal seriously with questions of faith . . . .
Give them the strength to practice their belief in practical love for neighbor . . . .

For you grant us the grace of faith, hope, and love. You who live and reign forever and ever.

St. Paulinus of Nola (June 22)

"SELL WHAT YOU HAVE . . ."

Introduction

A while back, the media were full of discussion on the topic of midlife crisis: people in their best years become dissatisfied with their lives, change course, switch jobs, and try out something new, in order to find their way to a meaningful life. In the lives of many saints we observe something similar: they begin at a mature adult age to live a consciously Christian life and thus alter their whole life-style. Paulinus of Nola (353–431) was one of these saints.

Penitential Rite

"Sell what you have and give alms." [Silence] Lord, have mercy . . . .

"Get purses for yourselves that do not wear out." [Silence] Christ, have mercy . . . .

"Prepare a never-failing treasure with the Lord which no thief comes near nor any moth destroys." [Silence] Lord, have mercy . . . .

Talk

Respectable Environment. Paulinus grew up in the area of Bordeaux, the son of a Roman official family in the best conditions. In line with the prevailing custom of the time, the boy was not yet baptized, even though his parents were Christians. He received an excellent education. Good contacts with the imperial court in Trier led to his becoming governor of the Italian province of Campania already at age twenty-six.

Yet Paulinus unexpectedly gave up his government post very soon and withdrew with his young wife to his agricultural estates in order to "privatize," i.e., to give himself over to study, music, and poetry. In the tranquillity of these years his decision ripened to receive baptism at last and to lead a deliberate Christian life.

As a Christian on the Way. Paulinus was thirty-six years old when he accepted baptism along with his brother in 389. Soon after this conscious "yes" to Christian faith, he began to sell off his great holdings and to put the proceeds to use along the lines of Christian charity. He wanted to be poor like Christ and to help the poor in Christian love. His worldly acquaintances had no comprehension for this kind of extravagance.

Paulinus soon settled with his wife in her Spanish region. The murder of his brother and the early death of his only child strengthened him for taking with complete awareness the path of poverty and renunciation. On the occasion of his priestly ordination, he donated to the church in Barcelona a part of his still remaining property. Even as a priest he lived intentionally in solitude and did not exercise pastoral ministry.

Around 395 Paulinus moved to Nola in the Italian province of Campania. There, as governor in his younger years, he had formed a special tie with the tomb of the martyr Felix. At a mature age he settled in the neighborhood of the tomb with a purpose: separated from his wife—who lived a short distance away with the same spiritual ideals as he—he set out to lead a monastic life with like-minded men. He used his revenues for the construction of a church and for various pilgrimage facilities.

The last phase of his life began when Campania was hit by the storms of the tribal migrations. Paulinus was elected bishop of Nola in 409. He had to witness how the Visigoths conquered and destroyed his see city, and for a short while was imprisoned as a hostage. Until his death in 431 he had to concentrate on the rebuilding of his diocese, and had to try to adapt to the new conditions along with his community. We can infer how he carried out this task by the fact that his memory was kept alive and that the people soon venerated him as a saint.

A Consistent Life. This saint came out of a well-to-do background. He made a conscious decision to be baptized, and acted in a manner consistent with this decision. He broke with his earlier lifestyle: he sought in faith to imitate Jesus Christ in his own way, in line with his era and culture.

We have been baptized while we were still infants. Where have we had a crisis, which led or is leading us to live with a more aware faith—and, where necessary, to break with our past way of life (pleasures, spending of time, commitment in the parish community, political responsibility)?

Petitions

Lord Jesus Christ, your Word holds true even now: "Sell what you have and give the money to the poor."

> Help the Church so that she might work with dedication for everyone trapped on the dark side of life . . . .
> Guard her from unwise reliance upon material wealth and political power . . . .
> Give Christians the willingness to share their wealth with the poorest of the poor . . . .

For this way we prepare for ourselves a never-failing treasure in heaven, which no thief comes near nor any moth destroys. You who live and reign forever and ever.

Sts. John Fisher and Thomas More (June 22)

GENTLEMEN

Thomas—as family man and politician, patron of Catholic youth groups. Perhaps you have heard his famous prayer for a sense of humor. Maybe you also know that he put his thoughts down on the ideal Christian state in his book *Utopia*. During the Church's conflict with Henry VIII of England, he went with dignity to his death, as did his friend Cardinal John Fisher.

Penitential Rite

Lord Jesus Christ, it is you who tell us: Do not fear those who deprive the body of life but cannot destroy the soul: Lord, have mercy . . . .

Do not be afraid, for before God you are worth more than an entire flock of sparrows: Christ, have mercy . . . .

Do not be afraid, for whoever acknowledges me before men I will acknowledge before my father in heaven: Lord, have mercy . . . .

Talk

Contemporary Historical Background. Henry VIII, king of England, was a headstrong, moody ruler. At first he took a stand in writing against Martin Luther and the Reformation on the European continent. Soon after, however, for political and private reasons (regarding divorce and remarriage) he forced the separation of the English Church from Rome. In the midst of all this, he tried to make use of the renowned Bishop John Fisher of Rochester, and of his own chancellor, Thomas More.

The Two Saints. The bishop, committed in the Church, and the politically active father of a family were good friends. John Fisher became bishop at age thirty-five. He distinguished himself from many of his fellow bishops by his broad education, by his unpretentious and modest life-style, and by his effective love for the poor. With various publications, he took part in the controversies of his time for the reform of the Church, in both her head and her members.

In his young years Thomas More thought of becoming a priest. He decided, however, to follow the path of politics. In his personal life, the highly educated and powerful politician was remarkably modest. He led a conscious Christian life together with his family; daily holy Mass was its centerpiece as well as regular evening devotions with the entire household. This led to active charity for the poor and needy of London.

Poised in Death. The conflict between the king and the befriended saint broke out when, as Henry VIII, he tried to make himself the highest authority of the English Church, and demanded a loyalty oath for his reordering of church structures.

Bishop John Fisher openly opposed the king—and from that point onward, his life was no longer secure. He was imprisoned, and treacherous attempts were made to poison and to shoot him. Finally he was condemned to death. He went to it with dignity and inner resignation. When, on the day of his execution, he was awakened early, he requested, "Please, allow me to sleep a little while longer." And, in fact, he slept for another two hours!

Thomas More submitted his resignation as chancellor in 1532, since he could not go along with the king's church policies. He lost his income and became impoverished along with his family. When he did not make the required oath, he was thrown into prison and condemned to death. Only a few days after Bishop John Fisher, he was put to death on July 6, 1535. He too went to his death inwardly peaceful. When someone had to help him go up to the execution platform, he was able to jokingly remark, "I will come back down by myself."

Life in Faith. The bishop and the father of a family. Two trained scholars and all-around involved men. Even then they followed their consciences, although harsh consequences resulted. The power for such living and dying was given to them in their divergent life circumstances and tasks by their faith in Jesus Christ and in his and our Father, who acknowledges us if only we acknowledge him.

Can these two saints, in our very different life circumstances, be examples for us?

Petitions

Lord Jesus Christ, you have said to your disciples: Give to Caesar what is Caesar's, and give to God what is God's.

Strengthen politicians in their quest for a world more worthy of human beings . . . .
Give to people of the Church, when considering cooperation with other social powers, the gift of discernment of spirits . . . .
Be near to all who are persecuted on account of their personal convictions . . . .

For you want us to meet you in your coming, and thereby to give witness to your Good News in word and deed. You who live and reign forever and ever.

St. John the Baptist (June 24)

GOD'S INSTRUMENT

Introduction

John the Baptist becomes known to us in the New Testament almost without personal appearance. He came from a family of Jewish priests, gathered disciples around himself, baptized in the Jordan, aroused the resentment of King Herod, and finally was executed. The Bible speaks more extensively on his significance in the history of God among men. It portrays him as an instrument of God and thus points him out as a model for our Christian living.

Penitential Rite

"Happy the man who fears the Lord, who takes delight in all his commands.
He is light in the darkness for the upright: he is generous, merciful and just" (Ps 112:1,4).
Have mercy, Lord our God, have mercy . . . .

Talk

Child of Promise. The New Testament envelopes the birth of John in a garland of marvelous events. Elizabeth and Zachary were childless and at an age where, by normal human expectations, they would no longer be able to have children (Lk 1:7). The birth was announced by an angel. Zachary's disbelief was castigated: the father received his power of speech back only at the child's birth.

In a similar marvel-filled way, the births of great people in the Old Testament were recounted. Isaac was born of an aged and infertile mother (Gen 17:21). The same held true for Jacob and the children of Jacob and Rachel. Through this literary form the Bible underscores that these children—in our present case, John—are, in a special way, God's gifts and are supposed to lead his people along on the way of salvation (cf. Lk 1:79).

Man in the Desert. John lived, according to the Gospel, "in the desert until the day when he made his public appearance in Israel." For the Bible, this is no mere mention of location.

The Old Testament people of the Covenant came out of the desert. There they had their deepest religious experience and sealed the Covenant with Yahweh. In the hindsight of later generations, this first period of the Covenant was seen ever more clearly. It was the time of the first love (cf. Jer 2:2), of a living relationship with God, in comparison with which all the rest of Israel's religious history represented nothing but a decline.

"To live in the desert" means, for the person steeped in the Bible, to live in a living relationship with God, to renew oneself with faith in Yahweh, to recover the first great love of Israel for its God of the Covenant. In this sense, John also is a "man of the desert": a man of living faith and of unconditional fidelity to Yahweh and his commands.

Pointing the Way. Chosen by God and faithful to him, John accepted his life's task. He was indeed the "greatest man born of woman" (Mt 11:11), yet he was the "forerunner." He lived for the acceptance by the people of the one who came after him. He accepted that he should decrease while Jesus of Nazareth should increase. He fulfilled his life's task, even when he was disturbed by doubt whether

Jesus of Nazareth were truly the one for whom he was to prepare the way (cf. Mt 11:1–6).

Instrument Like John. What the Bible says of John the Baptist holds for each one of us. Each Christian is an instrument of God in this world. Each one of us must cherish the "first love" of a living relationship with God. We are all "forerunners of Christ." Through us Jesus Christ will come to other people. We prepare, by our devotion, ways in the world for him and his grace. And yet we also, in the midst of our efforts, sometimes have the questioning doubt whether Jesus Christ really is the one on whom it all finally depends.

John made his way as instrument for the salvation of the world with trust that Yahweh had made him his servant and had given him the needed strength [Reading]. At the end of his life, he did not see the success of his labors as forerunner. Yet he was indeed the forerunner of Jesus.

Should we not then begin each day afresh, with trust in this help, to prepare ways for Jesus to human beings—even when we sometimes see very little success, and when it is often wearisome?

Petitions

Let us call on God with trust in the intercession of St. John the Baptist:

For the spirit of conversion in all Christian churches . . . . Lord, have mercy . . . .
For the readiness to share by all those who live on the bright side of life . . . .
For humility and modesty in all who work in our communities . . . .

God our Father, give your Church the power to prepare the way for your Son into the hearts of men and women, and to lead them to him. You who live and reign forever and ever.

St. Cyril of Alexandria (June 27)

THEOLOGICAL SQUABBLING OR DEFENSE OF THE FAITH?

Introduction

"For the time will come when people will not tolerate sound doctrine, . . . and will wander off to fables. . . ." How many theological conflicts were unleashed at the first opportunity under cover of this scriptural test? Cyril of Alexandria (died 444) is, with all his zeal for the true doctrine of the Church, more of an example of how one should not invoke the above-quoted text from today's Reading.

Penitential Rite

Lord Jesus Christ, we take ourselves too seriously—and listen too little to others. [Silence] Lord, have mercy . . . .
We ourselves talk too loud and too long—and do not allow others to say a word. [Silence] Christ, have mercy . . . .
We attribute noble motives to ourselves—and suspect others of having unworthy motives. [Silence] Lord, have mercy . . . .

Talk

An Abrasive Character. "At last, at last is this evil man dead. His departure brings joy to us survivors, but he must have brought grief to the dead." This sentence comes from the pen of what is obviously not a friend of the bishop of Alexandria. Yet it must have been that way: the famous "defender of orthodoxy" was an abrasive character who engaged in local and worldwide politics very much in a shirtsleeve fashion. At times he lived with his whole see city in strife. He was involved in a pogrom against Jews. He controlled the entire wheat trade in Egypt, in order to consolidate his position. He employed dubious means of diplomacy in order to gain the support of the Roman pope, and knew how to make himself appreciated at the imperial court in Constantinople through large gifts (read: graft).

Bad Climate for Theological Controversies. It is understandable that this churchman did not exactly take an objective position in the then current theological controversy (which was burdened still by old rivalries between Alexandria in Egypt and Antioch in Asia Minor).

In Cyril's time, the question still revolved around the correct understanding of the mysterious divine and human reality of Jesus Christ. New to the controversy was that it now involved the Virgin Mary. The question was whether the ancient title of "Mother of God" could rightly be given to her. Cyril held fast to the title along with his Alexandrian theology professors—clearly, stemming from the background of their particular way of theologizing. Bishop Nestorius of Constantinople went along with the theologians of Antioch who criticized the title.

Now Cyril was not the kind of man who could empathize with the whole theological thought of his opponents. In the sense of today's Reading, he saw "the sound doctrine" imperiled (i.e., his own conviction)—and battled for the tradition of the Fathers with all (except theological) means. With his dedication he surely rendered a service for the preservation of the faith in the full divine and human reality of Jesus Christ. Yet the way and method in which he did this poisoned the atmosphere and divided the Eastern Church (without resolving and building upon the prevalent theological question).

Cyril brought into the whole discussion one further unwholesome element. He emphasized authority rigidly and unbendingly, and presented it as demanding specifically that its opinion be accepted, and laying no value on substantive discussion and shared seeking for truth.

Theological Controversy Today. The Church survived the crises of the Council of Chalcedon, just as she has overcome other crises by the power of Jesus Christ. These often enough have had their roots in the personal weaknesses of her theologians and pastors than in a menace from outside. Yet history is also there that the Church might learn from it.

We must therefore ask ourselves whether, in discussions in today's Church (in the university, in parish groups, in the family), we listen enough to one another and attempt to understand one another; whether we strive for objectivity and consciously set aside prestige considerations; and whether we follow ways in controversy that are proper for "sound doctrine" (thus: no insinuations, no half-truths, no defamations . . .).

Petitions

God of mystery, you have given to the Church your Holy Spirit, so that she might understand the Good News ever more deeply. We pray:

> For theologians of the different schools of thought, that they may always try to communicate with one another . . . .
> For bishops and theologians, that they might carry out their service to the truth of the faith in trust-filled cooperation . . . .
> For progressive and conservative theologians, that they might try to learn from one another and mutually encourage one another . . . .

For your Church can only be a light for our time when she enters ever more deeply into your mystery. You who live and reign forever and ever.

St. Irenaeus (June 28)

"FATHER OF CATHOLIC DOGMATIC THEOLOGY"

Introduction

The acknowledged originator of Christian theology was not an academic theologian who lived only for theological scholarship. He was Bishop Irenaeus (died 203), who, in an age of external menace and internal controversy, led the small Christian community of immigrants in Lyon in France. His theological writings were of immediate service to the faith of his community and to the endangered unity of the whole Church. He was a pastor, ecclesiastical politician, and theologian all in one. During his lifetime he brought honor upon his name Irenaeus—man of peace.

Penitential Rite

"I called to the Lord in my distress; he answered and freed me.
The Lord is at my side; I do not fear.
What can man do against me?
It is better to take refuge in the Lord than to trust in men" (Ps 118:5,6,8)

Have mercy, Lord our God, have mercy . . . .

Talk

Bishop for a Community of Foreigners. Irenaeus was born in Asia Minor. In his youth he made the acquaintance of St. Polycarp, who had personal memories of the apostles. As a Christian Greek, he acquired a broad education in the secular and religious knowledge of his time.

In his adult years Irenaeus was an elder for a small congregation of merchants in Lyon, made up of immigrants from Asia Minor. In the year 177, he lived through the horror of a sudden persecution of Christians, which claimed forty-eight congregation members as victims. He himself escaped death only because, in the name of his bishop, he was in Rome handling a minor procedure against heretics from Asia Minor.

After the horror of the persecution, Irenaeus took over the leadership of the shrunken and intimidated community in Lyon. During all menacing new persecutions, various new foundations in France came out of his see city in the years of his episcopacy.

Originator of Christian Theology. Beyond the limits of his diocese (and his age), Irenaeus became renowned for the first (as far as we know) complete presentation of the Christian body of faith. He wrote by his own account out of pastoral concern. He wanted to provide the faithful with a reliable presentation of Christian faith. He wanted to bring heretics (who were mainly Gnostics) back to Jesus Christ, "who out of boundless love became what we are, in order to bring us to perfection into what he is" (Irenaeus).

Irenaeus further influenced the Church and theology beyond his death by his theological works. He himself withdrew so much behind his writings that the last years of his life are lost in oblivion. It can no longer be said for certain whether his life ended in martyrdom or not.

A Man of Peace. Through his literary activity, Irenaeus was effective in the Church of his age as an advocate of unity and of reasonable compromise. As an elder, he worked for readiness for compromise in

Rome in the year 177, and for a "solution by way of negotiation." In 190, the question arose as to the uniform date of Easter between the western and the eastern Church. Pope Victor considered the idea of abandoning ecclesial community with the congregations of Asia Minor (thus, of "excommunicating" them). Irenaeus thereupon pleaded with the pope "in the name of the Gallic brethren subject to him not to cut off entire Churches of God that held firmly to old traditional practices," but rather "to work for peace, unity, and love." Judging from contemporary sources, his intervention (upon which today's Reading and Gospel have a bearing) was successful: the parties to the conflict soon reached a complete understanding.

Irenaeus was a bishop for whom the unity of the Church was a central concern. He was ready to compromise for the sake of unity and to allow diversity within unity. Perhaps it is precisely this side of his work that is especially exemplary for bishops and theologians, for priests and laity in the Church of today.

Petitions

Lord Jesus Christ, you prayed: Let all be one, as you, Father, are in me and I in you. We pray to you for the unity of your Church in our community and beyond its limits.

Break down the walls that separate us . . . .
Strengthen what unites us . . . .
Help us seek out ways to one another . . . .

Lord Jesus Christ, hasten the day in which your faithful, united in love, can praise and glorify you. You who live and reign forever and ever (Gl 28,3).

The Holy Apostles Peter and Paul (June 29)

PETER—"CHRISTIAN WITH US"

Introduction

The straight facts of the life of the apostle Peter (to whom we give primary attention in the entire liturgy of today's double feast) are quickly recounted. He was a fisherman by trade (cf. Mk 1:16) and married (cf. Mk 1:30). He joined the circle of Jesus' disciples (cf. Mk 1:16–18), and therefore left his family, at least for some time. In the early Church he played a central role [cf. Reading]. According to the common tradition, he was later executed in Rome. Where the Bible speaks about more than these straight facts about Peter, it features either his special role in the young Church or else says things about him that are true for each one of us. As the first pope, Peter is also "a Christian with us" (Augustine).

Penitential Rite

"O God, you are my God, for you I long; for you my soul is thirsting.
My body pines for you like a dry, weary land without water.
For your love is better than life, my lips will speak your praise" (Ps 63:1,2,4).   [Silence]
Have mercy, Lord our God, have Mercy . . . .

Talk

Called. How is Peter, in the view of the New Testament, "a Christian with us"? The fisherman from Lake Genesareth one day met Jesus of Nazareth. He heard his call, left his existing place of residence, his fishing business, and his family, in order to live together with Jesus and to cooperate in proclaiming the Good News. He saw his remaining life as an answer to this call by Jesus. He gave this answer even unto persecution and death.

Growing Faith. How did this answer appear in the concrete? Today's Gospel passage speaks of Peter's messianic confession. Peter evidently went through an unfolding of his faith, until he grasped more deeply what there was about Jesus of Nazareth and his message of salvation through the cross (cf. Mt 16:21–23).

The Gospel of John has Peter saying, "Lord, to whom shall we go? You have the words of eternal life. We have come to believe; we are convinced that you are God's holy one" (Jn 6:68f). Yet even this devout confidence of Peter was weak and prone to temptation. True, he set out into the midst of the lake at Jesus' word and cast out his net (cf. Lk 5:5), and he also let himself be called by Jesus out fom the safety of the boat (cf. Mt 14:28ff). However, his faith then became weak in the storm of life (cf. Mt 14:30). Indeed, he became so weak that he denied his Lord (cf. Mt 26:66–72). Yet it was precisely this man, to whom "nothing human was alien," for whom Jesus prayed, that his faith might not waver (cf. Lk 22:31ff), upon whom he built his Church (cf. Mt 16:18), to whom he gives the task of feeding his flock (cf. Jn 21:15–17) and of strengthening his brethren (cf. Lk 22:32).

Taking Up the Cross. Peter not only shared in the life and work of his Master, he also suffered his fate. He resisted the cross and could not at first understand the teaching of the suffering Messiah (cf. Mt 16:21–23). Yet his commitment to Jesus of Nazareth led him "off against (his) will" (Jn 21:18). Acts pictures how the cross belonged to his life's work. From tradition we learn that he ended up on the cross like his Lord. He exposed himself to the cross because it was impossible for him to keep silence over what he had seen and heard (Acts 4:20). Yes, he even rejoiced that he was allowed to suffer insult for the sake of Jesus (cf. Acts 5:41). And he endured everything, like his fellow apostle Paul, in him who was the source of his strength (cf. Phil 4:13).

We Ourselves. Peter—"a Christian with us." The first pope stands before us as one who has taken on the risk of faith with us and exactly like us. He realized this risk in his own life through failure and constant renewal. For him, faith was never a definite possession.

Peter thus stands before us as one who, precisely in his humanity in which God's power reaches perfection (cf. 2 Cor 12:9), is given the mandate to strengthen us in our faith.

If Peter is "a Christian with us," then we also, in our weak faith, must be a "rock" [Gospel] with him and try, with trust in the power of Jesus, to strengthen the faith of our fellow Christians along with him.

Petitions

Lord Jesus Christ, you are the true rock of the Church. Hear our prayer:

Enlighten and strengthen our Holy Father, Pope_____ . . . .
Give the Church worthy bishops and priests at all times . . . .
Enlighten all the baptized and all of humanity by the light of your Good News . . . .
Increase our faith and strengthen our hope . . . .

Lord Jesus Christ, let your power take effect in the human weakness of the Church, so that men and women may find you. You who live and reign forever and ever.

First Martyrs of the Church of Rome (June 30)

OUTSIDERS AS SCAPEGOATS

Introduction

Along with Peter and Paul (yesterday's saints), other Christians were also put to death during the reign of Emperor Nero. Today's feast is meant to bring to mind this first generation of martyrs in Rome. It makes us aware (as does every martyr feast) that the Church has lived with the cross since her very beginnings. How could it be otherwise, since the Church lives from the celebration of the Eucharist, with Jesus as the center, who for love of us died on the cross . . . .

Penitential Rite

Jesus Christ, grieved to death on the Mount of Olives, covered with bloody sweat, given over to the will of the Father: Lord, have mercy . . . .

Jesus Christ, tortured by thirst, given gall and vinegar to drink, thrust into abandonment: Christ, have mercy . . . .

Jesus Christ, laid in the tomb, descended into the realm of the dead, risen to glory: Lord, have mercy . . . .

Talk

What Tacitus Was Able to Report.
The Roman historian Tacitus wrote an account of the first Roman wave of persecution against Christians. In order to squelch the rumor around the world that he himself had set the city of Rome afire (a devastating fire had occurred), "Nero shifted the blame upon others and laid the most refined punishments upon those hated for their crimes, whom the people called Christians . . . . They were held responsible not just for arson, but for all-around hatred of humanity."

This witness of Tacitus is first of all interesting because it is the first time outside of the New Testament that an account is given that Jesus was put to death under Pontius Pilate. He also describes the gruesome way in which the Romans then dealt with "criminals" (sewn into animal skins, they were torn to pieces by dogs; nailed to crosses, they were turned into living torches . . .). Yet it is also worth considering about all how, according to him, the persecution against the Christians arose.

Christians as Outsiders.
We cannot suppose that the first Christians could really have been convicted of capital crimes. Obviously, they could not be convicted of the arson either. Their "all-around hatred of humanity" rested on the fact that they were simply different from their surroundings. They did not share in the normal social concerns. They had a different life-style, they refused before anything else to acknowledge and adore other gods beside the God who had revealed himself in Jesus Christ. That had to render them suspicious to their neighbors and unleash hostile feelings all around them.

Emperor Nero detected this mistrust easily, directed as it was toward everything unusual and strange, and which had especially built up against Christians. Through clever manipulation he was quite able to let it develop into open hatred for foreigners and thus draw the hostility away from himself. He was then able to liquidate Christians with public support.

Without a doubt, this element of mistrust toward everything foreign has had its effect in all the persecutions against Christians over the centuries. Whether in ancient Rome, in the medieval German east, in China at the beginning of the modern age, or in African countries in the last century: Christians have been persecuted not only on account of their faith, they have also been attacked because they were different from the people around them.

Christians and Their Hatred of Foreigners. Yet the coin has to be turned over. For, often enough, Christians have taken the place of Nero's public and have persecuted and liquidated the outsiders in their own society as scapegoats.

Could crimes be really attributed to Jews in the Christian Middle Ages, when they were driven out of the cities and their residential areas were burnt down? Perhaps many "heretics" were in fact only different in their thought and feelings when compared to the normal cross section; yet the Christian society was able to use them as scapegoats, to draw the blame away from others.

And how are things today? How much mistrust exists now against people who are different from us? People like immigrants, nonconformists, artists? How ready are we to attribute bad motives and questionable behavior to them? And how readily does mistrust turn into active hate?

Are we ourselves truly free—or must we also be on guard against ourselves?

Petitions

Let us pray to God, Father of all men and women:

For those in our society who are of different races and nationalities. (Silence)

For all those who hold political and social views different from our own . . . .
For Christians who are in the minority in their countries and are mistrusted as such . . . .

For it is your will that we, as your children, love one another as brothers and sisters. You who live and reign forever and ever.

St. Thomas (July 3)

"BLEST ARE THEY WHO HAVE NOT SEEN AND HAVE BELIEVED"

Introduction

Every age has its own way of faith. In certain eras, faith is just taken for granted. Christians then resembled Peter in his proud confession, "You are the Messiah, the Son of the living God" (Mt 16:16). We men and women of today find ourselves with our faith more like the apostle Thomas, who came only through doubt and questioning to the humble prayer, "My Lord and my God" [Gospel].

Penitential Rite

"To you, O Lord, I call, my rock. Do not turn in silence from me.
Hear the voice of my pleading as I call for help, as I lift up my hands in prayer to your holy place.
The Lord is my strength and my shield; in him my heart trusts" (after Ps 28:1,2,7).

Have mercy, Lord our God, have mercy.

Talk

"Blest Are They Who Have Not Seen and Have Believed." At the end of the first century by our calendar (around the time that the Gospel of John was composed), the small Christian communities were in a situation similar to our own: they had not known

Jesus Christ during his earthly life, and the Risen One had not revealed himself to them personally in particular apparitions. In their faith they were (as we are) dependent upon the witness of the apostles, which is passed onward in the Church. It is not always easy to trust in the Risen One by pure faith. The author of the Gospel of John must have heard this statement of Thomas over and over in his own time: "I'll never believe it without probing the nailprints in his hands, without putting my finger in the nailmarks and my hand into his side."

John gave to his contemporaries (and to us) in the tale of doubting Thomas an answer to this critical objection. For him, faith is ignited not by meeting the earthly Jesus, but by meeting the Risen One. For him, man comes into faith in the Risen One because God gives him the grace of faith. In this gift of the grace of faith man is clearly called "to believe without seeing," insofar as he relies on the faith of the Church and makes his way through life with trust in Jesus.

"How Can We Know the Way?" The problems of the young Church (like ours) were not resolved by the demand to believe without seeing. Because of this, John has Thomas saying at another point, "Lord, we do not know where you are going. How can we know the way?" (Jn 14:5). To this came Jesus' answer: "I am the way, and the truth, and the life" (Jn 14:6). This means: man comes to belief and to living communion with Jesus Christ, if he tries to live like Jesus of Nazareth; or, concretely, if he seeks out communion with God and a communion of service with his fellow human beings.

"Let Us Go Along to Die with Him." There is still a third word that the Gospel of John places on Thomas' lips. As Jesus went back into the area controlled by the Jews (and thus placed his life in danger) in order to raise Lazarus from the dead, Thomas said, "Let us go along, to die with him" (Jn 11:16). At first, this sounds like resignation. Yet therein lay the readiness of the disciple to remain faithful to the mandate of the Father in imitation of the Master, even to the point of offering up his life for him.

Thomas and We. Thomas—our model of faith. We have not sought out the age in which we live as Christians. Doubts about faith and attacks on faith in our times are not the result of trivial games with the basic questions of life. We must accept them as our lot and try to believe through them.

Our faith still starts from the fact that "the Father draws us" (as John expresses it in his Gospel)—and that we pray for the gift of faith. It will grow when we try to live like Jesus Christ, who lived totally for God—and who was ready during his whole life to wash the feet of his fellow human beings, i.e., to give of himself completely for them. Our faith will be perfected when we are prepared to dedicate ourselves like Jesus Christ for God and neighbor even to the end.

Petitions

Lord Jesus Christ, you have called men and women to go with you to the Father:

> Be the Word that they hear and follow . . . .
> Be the light that shines on them . . . .
> Be the power that fills them . . . .
> Be the support that does not fail them . . . .

Grant us this by the intercession of the apostle Thomas. You who live and reign forever and ever (after Gl 6,4).

St. Elizabeth of Portugal (July 4)

CHRISTIAN LIFE IN A DIFFICULT MARRIAGE

Introduction

Love as active and charitable love for neighbor: a bright example of this is Elizabeth of Portugal (or rather, Queen Isabel)—a relative of St. Elizabeth of Hungary. Yet it must have been substantially more difficult for her to treat fairly everyone in the circle of her family with love and not to lose her faith in the goodness of other people for she lived her life under difficult conditions.

Penitential Rite

Lord Jesus Christ, you blessed children and lifted up the downhearted: Lord, have mercy . . . .

You were full of love for sinners and sat with them at table: Christ, have mercy . . . .

You loved your own, and loved them till the end: Lord, have mercy . . . .

Talk

A Woman in the Labyrinth of Political Interests.
Elizabeth (or Isabel) came out of the highest noble circles. Her father was sovereign (or future sovereign) over part of Spain. Yet that did not

St. Elizabeth of Portugal (july 4)

guarantee her a carefree and sheltered youth. Since the kingdom was rocked for years by battles between the reigning king and the heir to the throne, she grew up as a "peace pawn" living with her grandfather. This is supposed to have curbed her father's quest for adventure.

Soon after her grandfather's death (and her return to her parents' house), Isabel was given in marriage to King Dionysius of Portugal for political reasons. Whether political calculation disappeared from the marriage, is not the question here. At any rate, difficult years began for the young queen with her wedding day.

A Difficult Marriage. King Dionysius was no model husband for Isabel. He was never true to his wife and had a series of mistresses one after another. At the same time, he harassed her with jealous mistrust, turning her life into a hell. For her part, Isabel strove to bring her husband around through consistent gentleness and patience. Out of her awareness of duty she was even willing to bring up her husband's illegitimate children along with her own. Still, her kindness had little effect. Her husband did not improve, and she bore throughout her life the cross of her marriage.

The tension reached its peak when the king blamed Isabel for having instigated their son against the father. The enraged husband, deeply wounded as a father by the conflict with his son, banished his wife and confiscated all her properties. Yet, when it threatened to all come to open battle, Isabel succeeded in halting the forces already mobilized for combat and brought about a reconciliation between father and son.

Active Charity. In addition to her concerns within her own family (where conflicts were forever flaring up), Isabel was also a kind mother to her country. In following the Gospel, she had a heart for every suffering and needy person. The spirit of her selfless love was expressed by her in these lines: "I would sooner die myself of hunger rather than deny my help to the poor, who would otherwise despair. God will surely help me in the future; now, however, I will distribute available food to the hungry poor."

Patroness of All Wives and Mothers. The marital and familial lot of Isabel of Portugal repeats itself beyond counting even today. Wives, who suffer the unfaithfulness of their husbands; who are persecuted by the unfounded morbid jealousy of their spouses; who put up with humiliation after humiliation by their husbands (nor can it be forgotten that the roles are sometimes reversed). Mothers, who get dragged into conflicts between fathers and children and who are accused of taking sides unfairly . . . .

I know: it is difficult in such situations to carry on in the hope of better times and to dwell on forgiveness, reconciliation, and concord. I feel for wives and mothers who become discouraged under these burdens. Yet I admire (and support) all those others who, after the example of St. Elizabeth, continue to work for peace and understanding within all their families.

Petitions

Let us pray for all married people that have become burdens to one another: Lord Jesus Christ:

Let them know what they have done wrong . . . .
Help them to forgive one another . . . .
Let them always find a way that leads to each other . . . .
Let their love grow through crisis and become more mature . . . .

Lord, give to all married people the power of your patience and love, so that their communion of love might become more of an image of your love for us men. You who live and reign forever and ever.

St. Anthony Mary Zaccaria (July 5)

IN THE SPIRIT OF THE APOSTLE PAUL

Introduction

"Religion is more a matter of living than of academic controversy." In keeping with this statement of Erasmus of Rotterdam, St. Anthony Mary Zaccaria, during the time of Martin Luther, tried to work in Milan for the renewal of the Church. In his own life and work, and in the work of the male and female religious congregations founded by him, he placed greater importance on personal example of Christian life than on any necessary pastoral activity. "Religion is more a matter of living than of academic controversy" (or of religious knowledge, or of fascinating conversation about religious questions . . .). Is this an authentic motto for our lives as well?

Penitential Rite

"In you, O Lord, I take refuge.
Let me never be put to shame.
In your justice, set me free, hear me and speedily rescue me.
Be a rock of refuge for me, a mighty stronghold to save me, for you are my refuge" (Ps 31:2,3,5b).

Have mercy, Lord our God, have mercy . . . .

Talk

Open to the Demands of the Times. With hindsight, the Church of the Reformation period can be accurately assessed. The papacy displayed great splendor. The Church still exercised great power in public affairs. Yet it was also a time of unwholesome conditions that unleashed the cry for a "reform of the Church in her head and her members," and led to a splitting of faith in Germany.

In this period of external ecclesiastical splendor and internal religious misery, Anthony Mary Zaccaria (1502–1539) lived and worked. After successfully completing medical studies, he went on with his theological education. At the same time, he gave catechetical instructions and introductions to the Bible for lay people interested in religion in his home city.

After priestly ordination in 1528, the young man, possessed of a spirit of enterprise and a will to win, expanded his apostolate. True to his conviction that "religion is more than academic controversy," he began the reform of the Church first in his own person. He declined a well-endowed church office; he distanced himself demonstratively from the widespread enthusiasm among clerics for contemporary literature and art; he led a simple life, and dedicated himself to pastoral work with the devotion of a Paul the apostle. In a letter written in 1531 he wrote, "Up, up, brethren! If a certain indecision has been with us up until now, let us cast it out along with negligence and run like madmen not only to God but also to our neighbors. . . ."

He at first dedicated himself to the spiritually elite of his time. After founding the "Clerks Regular of St. Paul" in 1533, he worked along with his brothers in parish missions for the religious renewal of his people.

New Pastoral Approaches. In his broad pastoral work in the spirit and after the example of St. Paul the apostle, the saint took new and unusual ways. He preached in the squares of Milan (he had moved there). He walked through the city streets (in order to do personal penance and to move others to conversion) with a cross on his shoulder, a rope around his neck, and bare feet. His confreres worked at times in hospitals or as fishmongers, in order to move the population to conversion through these and other similarly despised occupations.

Anthony Mary sought however to pour the newly awakened religious feeling into solid forms. He encouraged the "perpetual prayer" in parish churches. He introduced the practice of ringing the bells at three o'clock on Fridays as a remembrance of the hour of Jesus' death. He invited people to frequent reception of Holy Communion, and gathered Christian couples into a special organization.

Reform of the Church Today. This saint, who "ran after God and neighbor like a madman," died at the age of thirty-six. In his intercessory prayers he stays close to us in our efforts for the renewal of the Church in our day. Even today, following his example, it is necessary that we begin the reform with our own selves and, at the same time, take the steps necessary now for the Church in our commitment to her.

Petitions

Let us pray to God, our almighty Father:

For the authorities in Christian Churches, that they might be open to the questions and demands of our age . . . [Silence]
For pastors and co-workers in our congregations, that they might let themselves be led by courage and trust in God in their daily problems . . . .
For Christians amid the controversies of our times, that they might give witness to the Good News in a missionary spirit . . . .

Lord our God, be near to your Church and lead her in our age. You who live and reign forever and ever.

St. Maria Goretti (July 6)

THE RESULT OF DEFICIENT CLARIFICATION—OR MORE?

Introduction

"Brutal crime of passion! A youth assaults eleven-year-old neighbor girl and stabs her with fourteen critical wounds!" These could have been the headlines from Nettuno (near Rome, Italy) under the date of July 6, 1902. A day later, the report would have come that Maria Goretti died of her wounds. . . . In a few sentences, there is the newsworthy part of the death of this Italian village girl. What made it so meaningful as to result in the canonization of Maria Goretti forty-eight years later?

Penitential Rite

"I trust in you, Lord, I say: 'You are my God.' My life is in your hands, deliver me from the hands of those who hate me. Let your face shine on your servant. Save me in your love" (Ps 31:15–17).

Have mercy, Lord our God, have mercy . . . .

Talk

The Result of Deficient Clarification? Was not Maria Goretti's anxiety over sin exaggerated? Should she not have known that merely enduring a rape (with all its traumatic effects) is still no sin?

St. Maria Goretti (July 6)

Would not things have been different if the eleven-year-old girl had been able to speak openly with her mother about sexual matters? After all, Alessandro Serenelli, who lived with the Goretti family, had already approached Maria several times . . . .

Was not the prudish public of the turn of the century liable for the fact that the half-grown youth "from asocial circumstances" (his father was a drunkard) could not release his sexual energy in some other way, and that it all led to the repeatedly attempted rape?

Or More. We would have to answer these and similar questions in the affirmative. Yet that does not alter the fact that Maria Goretti lived then with her family and wanted to live out her Christian life in line with the ideals of that time. As far as the sixth commandment was involved in those days, consciences were especially acute. For the eleven-year-old girl in her desperate resistance against the unruly neighbor boy, it meant not only the defense of her own honor, but also of the honor of God.

Her whole religious foundation, through which she wanted to live in imitation of Jesus Christ, was made more clearly manifest by her love for her enemy and by her readiness to forgive (her mother also displayed this virtue twenty-six years later, when her daughter's murderer begged for her forgiveness). When she was asked shortly before her death whether she forgave Alessandro Serenelli, Maria answered, "Of course I forgive him. I will pray from heaven for his conversion. For Jesus' sake, who forgave the repentant thief, I want to see him beside me in paradise."

Model for Youth? In this Christian foundation of love for neighbor, which does not exclude even an enemy, Maria Goretti is right away a model for every Christian today.

With responsibility to Jesus Christ and in communion with him, young people even today are trying to shape their lives against the background of our sexual climate. How can we aid them in this?

We make the effort even with children to speak openly and without prudery on sexual questions. We encourage them to tell us if anyone molests them. And, out of Christian responsibility, we will tell a girl that, if it ever comes up, it is better to allow herself to be raped that to endanger her life unnecessarily.

Yet we will also make young people aware that they have to account to Jesus Christ for the use of their sexual powers. We will discuss with them what the meaning and purpose of their sexual structures and capacities are in the sight of God.

Amid the many questions that have to be raised and answered in this context, one comes up over and over concerning the meaning of the perspective provided by today's Reading: man as a body-soul unity is God's creation, and as such (as a "temple of God") must be accountable for his sexuality before God.

Petitions

Let us pray to God, our merciful Father:

For children and youth who are sexually abused   [Silence]
For girls and women who are trapped in the web of prostitution . . . .
For young people whose sexual values are corrupted by malicious exploiters . . . .

Lord, forgive all whose lives are ruined by the misuse of human sexuality. You who live and reign forever and ever.

St. Benedict (July 11)

FATHER OF THE WEST, PATRON SAINT OF EUROPE

Introduction

Monks transmitted the civilization and culture of the Mediterranean area to the Germanic tribes. They cultivated wide areas of Europe and educated youth for a period of centuries. Monks still live today by the basic principles of the rule drawn up by Benedict of Nursia (died 547 in Montecassino, Italy). In it he gave to western monasticism (the Benedictines, Cistercians, and Trappists, and many other communities that developed out of them) a basic law that has kept its usefulness even into our own times.

Penitential Rite

"I love the Lord for he has heard the cry of my appeal. How gracious is the Lord, and just; our God has compassion. The Lord protects the simple hearts; I was helpless so he saved me" (Ps 116:1,5,6).

Have mercy, Lord our God, have mercy . . . .

Talk

The Saint. We know of Benedict's life only from the account given by Pope Gregory the Great. He intended to present Benedict in his biography as a charismatic personality, who influenced his contemporaries by his extraordinary holiness. Accordingly, Gregory was more interested in edifying anecdotes than he was in straight facts.

Yet we do know this much about Benedict: He came from Nursia (in Umbria) and studied in Rome. He was not at home in the crumbling metropolis and withdrew into the solitude of Subiaco. In his attempt to organize the monasticism existing there, he ran into difficulties. Finally, the great monastic father settled in Montecassino. There he succeeded in founding a community like the one he envisioned. From there his rule spread over the course of the following centuries over all of Europe and became the dominant monastic rule in the western Church.

By it, Benedict understood his monastic community as a group of Christians who wanted to live out the Gospel with special seriousness. The fundamentals of his rule are thus valid for all Christians. They can also serve as inspirations for us. Let us now hear some passages from the Rule of St. Benedict—and apply them to our own lives.

Of the Good Zeal that the Monks Should Have (Chap. 72).

"The monks should use this zeal with flaming love: they ought to anticipate each other with respect. They should bear with others' physical or spiritual offenses patiently . . . . Let no one seek something for himself, but rather whatever is of advantage for another. They should manifest brotherly love to one another with a pure intention, they should render worship to God in love, they should submit to their abbot with sincere and humble devotion, and they should put nothing before Christ, who desires to lead all of us to eternal life."

Of Sick Brethren (Chap. 36).

"You should be concerned for the sick before all and above all. Serve them as you would serve Christ himself. He himself has said, 'I was sick, and you visited me.' . . . For their part, the sick must consider that people serve them out of love for God. They should also not cause resentment in the brothers who serve them by immoderate demands . . . ."

Qualities of the Abbot (Chap. 2). "The one who accepts the dignity of abbot must teach his disciples by a double lesson, that is, he must point out all that is good and holy more by deed than by word. He should teach by his instructions the commands of the Lord to the disciples who can grasp them; he should inculcate in the slow-witted and the narrow-minded the divine precepts by his example . . . ." He should "adapt his conduct to the situation, insofar as he lets prevail sometimes strictness, sometimes gentleness, and as he shows sometimes the sternness of the Master, sometimes the loving-kindness of the Father . . . . He should be aware how difficult and trying is the charge that he has received, namely to lead souls and to adapt himself to the characters of many others . . . ."

Petitions

Lord our God, you are a help to the upright and a shield for the just:

Grant that mutual respect and readiness to help grow among men and women . . . .
Grant that consideration for the sick and the weak not disappear from our performance-oriented society . . . .
Give to all who are responsible for leading or bringing up others the awareness that they can best teach others through good example . . . .

For from your mouth comes knowledge and understanding. You who live and reign forever and ever.

St. Henry and Bl. Kunigunde (July 13)

QUEEN AND EMPRESS

Introduction

In the calendar of the saints there are few married couples. Henry and Kunigunde are an exception. The Church attests that this couple, on the imperial throne and on the floor of the world political stage around the year 1000, lived exemplary lives and fulfilled their tasks conscious of their responsibilities. What went on in the life of this couple, especially in the life of the Empress Kunigunde?

Penitential Rite

Lord Jesus Christ, you lowered yourself in order to serve everyone; Lord, have mercy . . . .

You gave yourself over with all your strength to your life's task: Christ, have mercy . . . .

You call us to the same readiness for service: Lord, have mercy . . . .

Talk

Legend. We may remember some tales from old legends of saints that a subsequent piety entwined around the saintly imperial couple: that Henry and Kunigunde had a marriage like that of Joseph (i.e., had no sexual intercourse); that Henry mistrusted his wife's fidelity and would let himself be convinced of her innocence only by ordeal (walking with bare feet over red-hot iron plates) . . . .

Reality. The reality of their lives was prosaic. Kunigunde came out of a noble family in Luxembourg. She became wedded to Henry, who at that time was duke of Bavaria. Her husband was in poor health for his whole life.

Kunigunde lived with her husband in unsettled times. After the death of Emperor Otto III, the twenty-nine-year-old Henry succeeded in securing the imperial throne for himself with shrewdness and energy. This did not happen without military conflict. As emperor, he headed a defensive war against the Slavic tribes that were pressing into the empire from the east. His greatest concern, however, was for peace within the empire.

Completely within the practice of his time, Henry relied in his politics on the cultural and political power of the Church. He strengthened the organization of the Church within the empire and promoted mission activity on the imperial borders. He founded dioceses and monasteries. The best known is the founding of the diocese of Bamberg and the construction of its cathedral, where the graves of Henry and Kunigunde are found.

At the Side of Her Husband. It is indicative of the place of women in those days that we have to speak about Henry in order to describe the life of Kunigunde. Very much in line with the ideas of her time, she shared in the life of her husband, who determined policies in virtue of being emperor. Nonetheless, Kunigunde did not merely stand in his shadow. She was an authentic partner for him (and in this their marriage did not completely conform to the prevailing pattern). She was versed in political matters and took a lively part in the affairs of government. In many questions she was a prudent counselor to her husband. After his death she conducted government business further until his successor was elected.

Holiness on the Imperial Throne. Henry and Kunigunde were canonized in 1200, at the time of the great unfolding of the power of the medieval Church. It could be that that era saw their holiness embodied in the fact that (unlike the then emperor and kings) they actively advocated and promoted the interests of the Church. It was not merely a political calculation that motivated their concern for the Church; Kunigunde showed this after her busband's death. She established the convent of Kaufungen near Kassel in Germany and lived there as a simple sister for fiteen years until her death. That was only possible because Christ was a lifelong reality for her.

This religious foundation showed itself well, in the sense of today's Gospel, in her life and work as empress, insofar as she developed her gifts of character and dedicated herself actively in work for the empire. Her imitation of Christ can also be seen in that she bore undismayed the illness of her husband, the cross of childlessness, and the burdens and cares of her office. More and more, in the sense of today's Reading, she became like Christ in sincere mercy, in mutual forbearance, and in readiness for ever-new forgiveness. In brief: in her life, everything was done more and more in living union with Jesus Christ.

Petitions

God, you have given us talents with particular abilities so that we might dedicate them where we have found our life responsibilities.

Help everyone to face with courage the demands of their lives . . . .
Give married people patience with one another when either one is sick . . . .
Let Church and State cooperate effectively in our country . . . .
For you will that your Kingdom should take shape in our world through our action. You who live and reign forever and ever.

St. Camillus de Lellis (July 14)

A "MOTHER TERESA" OF THE SIXTEENTH CENTURY

Introduction

"How can God's love survive in a man who has enough of this world's goods yet closes his heart to his brother when he sees him in need?" [Reading]. Mother Teresa of Calcutta answers with her life this passage and others like it from the Bible, inasmuch as she serves the hopeless sick and the dying. Camillus de Lellis gave a similiar answer in the sixteenth century. The Romans named him and his confreres the "Brothers of Happy Death."

Penitential Rite

"You will live in my love if you keep my commandments." [Silence] Lord, have mercy . . . .

"This is my commandment: love one another as I have loved you." [Silence] Christ, have mercy . . . .

"There is no greater love than this: to lay down one's life for one's friends." [Silence] Lord, have mercy . . . .

Talk

A Disorderly Youth. Camillus grew up in an officer's family. His father was often away from home. His mother died while he was a child. He had little liking for school and preferred to indulge in his passion for gambling, which often got him in trouble as time went on.

His father ended up taking the son along in the company of soldiers in which he was serving. Camillus became wounded in his left ankle; it remained an open, irritating wound lasting the rest of his life.

While he was sick, he became acquainted for the first time with the hospitals of that age, which were hardly to be compared with our hospitals. The filth and the stink were indescribable, and the workers were untrained. People with minor illnesses would often take employment as hospital workers in order to earn a little money. Camillus became thus employed, but was soon fired for fighting, insubordination, and gambling.

The failed hospital worker tried once again to be a soldier. In tough situations he vowed at different times to become a Franciscan, but would soon forget again his good intentions.

In Permanent Service to the Sick. Around the age of thirty, Camillus found his permanent calling in the service of the abandoned sick. He settled in Rome at a hospital as a worker. He discovered Jesus Christ even in the most wretched and ungrateful of the sick, and thus served them with devoted love. He gradually gained mastery as well over his less than ideal character traits.

With his readiness for tireless dedication in kindness and friendliness, he found himself in conflict with the other workers, who considered his example to be an open reproach. On the other hand, his example moved many to join him and to give over their entire lives to the service of the sick. Thus there arose under Camillus' leadership the "Society of Hospitallers," the Order of Camillans, who make a special vow even today that they will serve even people with contagious disease. As a distinctive symbol they chose to wear a large red cross on their garments, which later the founder of the International Red Cross adopted.

The Camillans saw their work blessed in many Italian cities. They established their own hospitals or labored in other hospices. Their special concern was for the totally abandoned and the dying. They themselves came to know death over and over as whole groups of the brothers became infected by the epidemic of that time and died in the exercise of their service. Yet over and over they found new men who were prepared like Camillus to help the poorest of the poor and to take on the most menial of chores in their service to the sick. When the founder died on July 14, 1614, the order had been consolidated. In the succeeding centuries they contributed substantially to the development of the modern hospital system.

Our Answer. "How can God's love survive in a man who has enough of this world's goods yet closes his heart to his brother when he sees him in need?" [Reading]. What would our answer be to this challenging passage of the Bible? In our time of social insurance and the most modern clinics? In our time of lonely old people in their big-city tenements? The immigrant who lives in wretched conditions . . . ?

Petitions

Lord Jesus Christ, you came in a special way to the sick and the needy. We pray:

Be present to the sick in our hospitals and clinics . . . .
Grant that old people in our community may not become lonely in their homes . . . .
Open our eyes to the need in our surroundings and give us the strength to help by action . . . .

For we fulfill the law of love only when we approach all the needy as you approach them. You who live and reign forever and ever.

St. Bonaventure (July 15)

THE SECOND FOUNDER OF THE FRANCISCAN ORDER

Introduction

A marriage thrives over a long term not only from the tempestuous enthusiasm of first love: the official wedding, the joint household, the children all help toward keeping at least a part of the original enthusiasm for each other alive over the years. If this is true for marriage, it is also true for any group in the Church (and in society): if such a group is to last, its original enthusiasm must be preserved in stable forms, and—for once, to use words only recently become common—charism needs institution. St. Bonaventure realized that and, as long-term general superior of the Franciscans, drew the conclusions.

Penitential Rite

"Your word, O Lord, for ever stands firm in the heavens. Your justice is eternal justice and your law is truth. Give life to my soul that I may praise you" (Ps 119:89,142,175).

Have mercy, Lord our God, have mercy . . . .

Talk

Humble Servant of All. In the person of Francis, something new emerged in the Church of the late Middle Ages. The saint from Assisi wanted to live the Gospel unconditionally with his companions. He did not want to wrap the spirit of the Gospel in human organizational forms. He bound his followers only to the Bible—and his life caught fire.

When Bonaventure (1218–1276) became minister general of the Order in 1256, there were about 30,000 Franciscans, even though the community was little more than fifty years old. However, the followers of Francis were seriously divided among themselves. There were some who, like Francis, wanted to take the Gospel literally and who rejected any more specific organization for the community. There were others who had adjusted their life-style to the contemplative (and "established") monasteries. There was above all also the Church, the pastoral needs of the cities, the necessity of a basic education for Franciscan brothers engaged in preaching—all points of view that Francis had not assimilated.

The balanced, clear-thinking, and theologically well-educated Bonaventure (next to Thomas Aquinas, he was the greatest theologian of the Middle Ages) sought to be, as general superior, the servant of all in his divided Order. His service consisted not in the inspiring word that moved masses, but rather in the dry work of organizing the community. In this, he strove to take a middle way between undemanding enthusiasm on the one hand and deadly overinstitutionalization on the other. In this way he brought a needed stability to the Franciscan Order and enabled it to handle well the many tasks of pastoral ministry. On this account, he is justifiably called the "second founder of the Franciscans."

Theologian and Mystic. This man, who was general superior of his community for nearly twenty years, who worked actively in the councils of his time and, in his last years, as a cardinal was at the service of the pope, was a theologian by inner inclination. The works of his that have come down to us fill nine thick volumes.

Theology for him, however, was by no means some sort of interesting intellectual game. In his theological efforts, he reflected on his own relation to God (and on God's relation to himself). He saw, as the goal of his scholarly work, that a person should live consciously from communion with God. To his mind, theology completed its task only if the person bended his knee before God and attained "to the fullness of God himself" [Reading].

In his theological and pastoral work, Bonaventure was convinced that he was but God's instrument, as can be seen by this quote: "A person can understand the words of a homily only if the Holy Spirit speaks to his heart. We preachers and teachers produce only external noise and yet achieve nothing, unless he works within hearts by his grace."—This is a thought which, as a pastoral worker and preacher, I can only echo.

Petitions

Lord Jesus Christ:

> Bring to the Church your Kingdom of glory . . . .
> Let the faithful grow by your grace in power and strength . . . .
> Grant that everyone might be firmly rooted and planted in love . . . .
> Grant that we all might understand your love, which surpasses all understanding, ever more deeply . . . .

For you desire that the fullness of God fill us all totally. You who live and reign forever and ever.

Our Lady of Mount Carmel (July 16)

"FEAST OF THE SCAPULAR"

Introduction

Scapular (originally an article of clothing specially blessed and worn by the faithful—today, a religious article made of cloth and carried in the pocket or wallet), Miraculous Medal, St. Christopher Medal in cars, holy water. . . . . What attitude do we as "enlightened Christians" of the twentieth century take with these forms of piety? Do we simply turn up our noses at their "superstitions of past generations" (and of "primitive believers" today)—and reject them out of hand?

Penitential Rite

Lord Jesus Christ, you became man through the Virgin Mary: Lord, have mercy . . . .

You meet with men in the visible form of the Church: Christ, have mercy . . . .

You have put bread and wine, water and oil in the service of your work of salvation through the sacraments: Lord, have mercy . . . .

Talk

Superstition? Without question, the danger has recurred time and again in the Church that Christians would veer off into superstition with the "outward signs of salvation." They have assumed that the mere possession of a medal was a guarantee of God's protection. They have taken a novena in honor of a saint as a ticket into heaven (even when they made no effort to live as the saint did, free from distorted exaggerations). And they have also time and again misunderstood the giving of absolution in the sacrament of reconciliation as a guarantee for peace with God (without spending much thought on a firm conversion in their own lives). There were and are many superstititions infecting the sacraments and sacramentals. The point of origin of such abuses is that one would like to "do business with God" (or else ward him off), without investing one's own heart.

Dependent upon Outward Signs. Given all this, are sacramentals (and even sacraments) therefore to be rejected root and branch? As human beings made up of body and soul, we are dependent upon outward signs, whether or not we like it.

This is clearly true in our interpersonal relations. I can give a gift without putting my heart into it. But when I want to show another person my fondness for him or her, I have to make use of outward signs—a kiss, an embrace, a card, a bouquet of flowers, a little gift. I can erect monuments to my parents and provide for the care of their graves without bothering to think much about them. But if I want to keep alive their memory, I can make use of a picture for this purpose kept in the home, a watch used for a long time by my father, or a visit to their grave. Examples could easily be multiplied.

This certainly holds true with our communion with God. It is even more "unseen" than our communion with human beings. On that account, Christ intends to meet with us under the visible signs of the sacraments. Under the sign of a meal we are to understand that he is in communion with us and that he is the nourishment of our lives. Under the sign of absolution we experience that God is making peace with us again. . . . .

The faithful have developed further outward signs beyond the sacraments in the sacramentals, which remind us of God's love and care: the crucifixes in our homes and churches; blessings upon people and animals; medals and scapulars that remind us of the concerned intercession of Mary in the life and suffering of the Church and of each individual Christian . . . .

True Piety. Granted, these signs for believing Christians, considered in themselves, are not guarantees that automatically work. The eucharistic celebration leads me into deeper communion with God only if I make the effort to live by this communion. The crucifix at home will be meaningful for my life only if it reminds me of Jesus Christ and if it encourages me to live like Jesus Christ. The scapular—as well as the Miraculous Medal—leads me further to God only if I honestly try to live after the example of Mary. Seen in this way, these outward signs can be powerful aids on our life's road toward God.

Petitions

God and Father, you meet with us in your Son become man, Jesus Christ:

> Protect the faithful from superstitious reception of the sacraments . . . .
> Let them realize in their use of sacramentals that your love strives to be seen and grasped in all outward signs . . . .
> Grant that your Church may be the visible sign of your love in the world . . . .

Grant us this through Mary's intercession. You who live and reign forever and ever.

St. Lawrence of Brindisi (July 21)

THE CAPUCHINS AND THE COUNTER REFORMATION

Introduction

In every liturgy of the Word, you hear passages from sacred Scripture. How familiar have the Biblical stories and accounts from the Old Testament and the New Testament become to you in the course of a year? To what extent have they become second nature to you? The Capuchin priest Lawrence of Brindisi (1554–1619) could claim that he could write down accurately from memory the Bible in its original languages (namely, Hebrew and Greek). We don't have to go that far. Yet let us open ourselves at the beginning of the liturgy of the Word to Jesus Christ, who wants to speak to us in the Reading and the Gospel.

Penitential Rite

"Those on the path are the ones to whom, as soon as they hear the word, Satan comes to carry off what was sown in them." [Silence] Lord, have mercy . . . .

"Similarly, those sown on rocky ground are people who on listening to the word accept it joyfully at the outset. Being rootless, they last only a while. When some pressure or persecution overtakes them, because of the word, they falter." [Silence] Christ, have mercy . . . .

"Those sown among thorns are another class. They have listened to the word, but anxieties over life's demands, and the desires for wealth and cravings of other sorts come to choke it off; it bears no yield.'' [Silence] Lord, have mercy . . . .

Talk

A Leading Figure of His Age. Lawrence lived in the period of the Counter Reformation. His life and work were decisively shaped by it.

The young Capuchin gained a thorough knowledge of sacred Scripture and learned to use it in scholarly work and in popular preaching. At the age of forty-two, he took over the direction of his religious order. As a known preacher and wandering missioner, he was active in the diplomatic sector. Even in this political activity (peace missions, work toward forming a European alliance for repelling the Turkish encroachment in eastern Europe), he saw a service for the rescue of the menaced Church.

Winning Back Protestants. The special pastoral concern of St. Lawrence of Brindisi was by any means to win back Protestants for the one true Church. In doing so, he also took part in theological argument between the separate Christian factions. Yet he did not publish his scholarly contribution after all, perhaps because he was too deeply convinced of what he once said to Maximilian of Bavaria (when he called upon the saint to work in Germany): "The weapons by which the faith will be defended are the holy conduct of its preachers and teachers, and sufferings and persecutions borne patiently. Not by the sword will hearts be won, but by persuasion."

True to this thought, Lawrence lived as a humble priest and religious. True to this thought, he conducted a dialogue with Italian Jews and (during an eight-month missionary journey) with German Protestants. In the spirit of his conviction he put up with mockery, scorn, and abuse, confronted often by these things in his many pastoral undertakings. In all things he completed, with never-diminishing zeal, the task

God had given him: to proclaim the one Jesus Christ to a divided Christianity [Reading].

The Capuchins and the Counter Reformation. Lawrence of Brindisi brought, by his activity, the first Capuchins to Germany, which then had become almost totally lost to the Catholic Church. These confreres of his continued the work of church renewal and of winning back Protestants in his spirit. While the Jesuits upheld the cause of Catholic faith more among intellectuals (in schools and universities, in royal courts and in international politics), the Capuchins were more "men of the people," who served the faith through a deliberately simple life and popular preaching. In a very short time, they had two hundred foundations on German soil. Wide areas of Austria, southern and western Germany, Switzerland, and Holland, thanks to the tireless pastoral labors of the confreres of St. Lawrence of Brindisi, stayed Catholic or were won back for the Catholic Church.

Petitions

God our Father, even in our time you sow the seed of your word. We pray to you:

> For the Church of Jesus Christ: that she might look more in her life to your grace than to political power plays . . . .
> For the servants of the Church: that she might proclaim the Gospel by the witness of their lives . . . .
> For Christians in dialogue with people who think differently: that they might succeed in leading seekers and doubters through persuasion to Christ . . . .

Lord, let the abundance of your power become effective in the human weakness of the Church. You who live and reign forever and ever.

St. Mary Magdalene (July 22)

CALLED BY HER NAME BY THE RISEN ONE

Introduction

Mary Magdalene, Mary of Bethany (the sister of Lazarus), and the great sinner mentioned in Lk 7, were seen as the same person in the western veneration of saints. The New Testament specialists, the exegetes, distinguish among these three women. Today we can separate the figure of Mary Magdalene from any bond with the other two personages, insofar as we concentrate on what the Gospels tell us about this woman.

Penitential Rite

Lord Jesus Christ, you are the one who sets us free from evil: Lord, have mercy . . . .

You are the one who calls us by our names: Christ, have mercy . . . .

You are the one who sends us with the message of your resurrection to our brothers and sisters: Lord, have mercy . . . .

Talk

Renewed by Jesus. In Lk 8:1–3 there is expressly mentioned, among the women who accompanied Jesus and whom he had "cured of evil spirits and maladies," Mary of Magdala, "from whom seven devils had gone out." Who was this Mary of Magdala? We know nothing of her earlier life. What is meant by the demons that were cast out from her? Was she mentally ill? Did she have other weaknesses? Did she have a dubious life-style? To these questions we find no answer.

More importantly: by Jesus' action, she became a new person. Like the other women in Jesus' circle, she suffered heavily before meeting him. In the encounter with him her life became free from the tormenting burden of the past.

Her Answer: Service. Mary Magdalene experienced in her encounter with Jesus that God freed man in him from the path of evil (in one's own heart, in the form of sickness . . .). Her answer was that she was joining Jesus of Nazareth and was dedicating her feminine abilities and her resources to him and to his activity of proclaiming the Word. She thus belonged as a woman to the circle of disciples that wanted to reach further into the mystery of Jesus. And she stayed loyal to her Master even unto death and beyond death. She is the first woman named as being among those who witnessed the crucifixion from a distance (Mk 15:40), when all the disciples had cowardly fled. Together with another woman named Mary, she held out until the evening of the execution in order to determine where the body of Jesus would be laid after being taken down from the cross (Mk 15:47).

Messenger of the Resurrection. According to Mk 16:2, Mary Magdalene was one of the women who came to the grave on Easter morning in order to anoint Jesus' corpse. After discovering the empty grave and meeting up with the angel, she fled away from the grave in a great state of agitation (Mk 16:8).

According to John the Evangelist [see the Gospel], Jesus revealed himself to Mary at the open tomb and gave her the responsibility of witnessing to his Resurrection before the (up until then, disbelieving) disciples. She went forth and announced to the disciples: "I have seen the Lord," and reported to them what he had told her.

St. Mary Magdalene (July 22)

Mary—Rabboni. The deepest mystery in Mary's life comes in the Gospel's description of her encounter with the Risen One. Mary is confused and troubled. She is unable by herself to recognize the Lord. Then Jesus calls her by her name. Once the Risen One approaches her and speaks to her, she is able to see him as the Master.

Our Calling. Without our encounter with Jesus, we also would be people possessed by evil spirits. We would be imprisoned in our selfishness and could hardly defend ourselves against evil, present in the hearts of each one of us. Jesus has come to us through faith. He has called us by our names, each one of us personally. He has opened our eyes to his mysterious reality. Let us acknowledge him, as Mary Magdalene did. Let us seek his presence and put all our possibilities and capabilities at his service. Let us become, like her, messengers of his Resurrection for doubters, for those who no longer believe, and for those who do not yet believe.

Petitions

Lord Jesus Christ, you are concerned for the sick and the weak and you gift them with new love in their encounter with you.

> Give to all who are plagued with physical pain patience in their suffering . . . .
> Take away from all the mentally ill the anxieties over their lives and problems . . . .
> Guard from discouragement all those who look back upon a botched life . . . .

For you give man a new beginning by which sickness and guilt are overcome. You who live and reign forever and ever.

St. Bridget of Sweden (July 23)

NOBLE LADY AND PROPHET

Introduction

Even after the International Year of Woman, women in high politics are still rare exceptions. So far all democratic equalization and all emancipation have changed nothing.

That makes it all the more surprising that there were women already in the so-called "dark Middle Ages" who attained political influence not only through men who accommodated them but also by their own dedication.

One of these female political figures was Bridget of Sweden—in the opinion of many, an extraordinary woman of the late Middle Ages.

Penitential Rite

Lord Jesus Christ, you sanctified the family by your earthly life: Lord, have mercy . . . .

You put the will of your Father ahead of your ties to your family: Christ, have mercy . . . .

You have called human beings to conversion: Lord, have mercy . . . .

Talk

Prosperous Life. Bridget, born in 1303 on a Swedish estate, married a nobleman. She gave life to eight children. As a young wife and mother, she enjoyed a comfortable house and drew upon available prosperity.

At the Royal Court. Bridget was thirty-two years old when this bucolic idyll came to an end. The king, a relative of her husband's family, entrusted an office to her at the royal court. Even though it came hard to her to break up her own household and to send off her children for education in different monasteries, she nonetheless took on the new post out of Christian responsibility to her people. She strove over the next several years to influence the character-weak king for the welfare of the whole country, and to correct moral abuses at the king's own court. Still, she had little success. She left the royal court along with her husband and undertook a pilgrimage to Santiago in Spain.

Prophet at the Royal Court. During this pilgrimage her husband died. After his death, Bridget—forty-two years old—moved definitively into another life direction. Concerned with her religion since her youth, she lived from then on for the cause of Jesus Christ, which she perceived as being extremely endangered in her time. She made it her life's task, in the fashion of the Old Testament prophets, to act against social injustices in society and against abuses in the Church.

Dressed in a shabby penitential robe, she returned to the royal court in Sweden. There she fought with sharp and angry words against the lust for luxury at the court and the oppression of the poor in the country. In all this she did not spare the authorities of the Church.

Bridget ran into resistance. She was suspected of being a witch and was reproached on the grounds that a woman was to keep silence in

Church. Her admonitions bore little fruit. Civil war came to Sweden and the king was deposed.

In Rome. In 1349 the saint left her country and settled forever in Rome. She dedicated herself to beggars and pilgrims in the impoverished city. However, she considered that her major task was to work for the return of the pope from Avignon and for the inner renewal of the Church. In this as well she had little success. (The pope, for example, returned to Rome only after her death in 1373.)

In the Power of Jesus Christ. Bridget was an extraordinary woman, who fervently dedicated herself, for the sake of Jesus Christ, to the cause of God and of humanity in her time. Yet, for all her dedication, she saw little result: she had worries over her grown children, some of whom took the downward path; she had little success at the Swedish royal court; her plans for a convent were realized only after her death; she saw little progress in the renewal of the Church. She had every reason to become discouraged. Yet, from her deep union with Jesus Christ (the Gospel uses the metaphor of the vine and branches) she could encourage herself and us with the words, "Know that the friends of God will be crowned for every word and deed that they say and do for the sake of God and for the betterment of souls, and for every hour of trouble that they have borne for God's sake—whether they have converted many or few."

Petitions

Lord our God, you have called men and women to be followers of your Son, that they might proclaim the Good News to all people.

> Be near to all women who are politically active out of Christian responsibility.
> Grant that we might listen in the Church to all the voices of women and consider their contributions thoroughly . . . .

Give to the Christian Churches in Sweden committed men and women who will proclaim you in public . . . .

For you are Lord of our time also, you who live and reign forever and ever.

St. James (July 25)

"WE CAN"?

Introduction

The (legendary) grave of the apostle St. James the Greater, at Compostella in Spain, was the most heavily frequented Christian place of pilgrimage in the Middle Ages after Jerusalem and Rome. According to the account in the synoptic Gospels, James was called into discipleship out of the fishing boat of his father along with his brother John. Both belonged, along with Simon Peter, to Jesus' most intimate circle of friends. His apostolic work terminated in the year 44, when King Herod had him put to death. As a disciple of Jesus he had, judging by the account in today's Gospel, a long way to go before he could admit with Paul in today's Reading, "We possess a treasure in earthen vessels . . . ."

Penitential Rite

Jesus Christ, splendor of the Father, archetype of creation, Son of the Virgin: Lord, have mercy . . . .

Jesus Christ, friend of the poor, salvation of the sick, rescue of sinners: Christ, have mercy . . . .

Jesus Christ, brother of men and women, hope of the earth, Lord of life: Lord, have mercy . . . (GL 564).

Talk

Intimate Friend of Jesus. James belonged to the closest circle of the disciples of Jesus. Their Master led Simon, John, and James more deeply into his mystery than he did the other apostles. They were witnesses of the reviving of Jairus' daughter (cf. Mk 5:37). They were present at the transfiguration (cf. Mk 9:2). Jesus explained to them (along with Andrew) the mysteries of the end times (cf. Mk 13:3). And, finally, he took only Peter, James, and John with him as he went to pray in Gethsemani.

What Did He Learn? What a contrast all that is with the scene (also described in Mk) in today's Gospel! James gets his mother to step forward—he, then is a coward. He sees in Jesus a political messiah, who has lucrative and prestigious posts to assign—he does not yet know much about the basic law of service. He believes that he can earn this special place in Jesus' Kingdom—he does not yet correctly understand that Jesus is proclaiming the coming Kingdom as a gift. And, finally, he is confident, along with his brother John, that he can prevail over the unavoidable hardships on the way toward this goal by his own strength—he is thus evidently not aware of his own limitations. When one takes the whole situation into consideration, one can readily ask, what did James really learn by being with Jesus?

The Contrast in the Reading. In the Reading, Paul seems to be somewhat ahead of James. He knows that Jesus is not a political messiah and that his Kingdom begins with his death and Resurrection (v. 14). Participation in this Kingdom is a gift and not human merit—for it is God who raises us up (v. 14). The call to this Kingdom is the call to proclaim "...so that the grace bestowed in abundance may bring greater glory to God because they who give thanks are many" (v. 15) while carrying the cross (vv. 8–12). Paul, missioner to the Gentiles, came to know the hard reality of this carrying of the cross in his work for Christ (vv. 8–12). In this he experienced himself as an "earthen vessel" (v. 7) and therefore placed all his trust in God: "...its surpassing power comes from God and not from us" (v. 7).

A Lifelong Learning Process. Gospel and Reading today show the beginning and end of authentic imitation of Christ. Paul had certainly started off the same way as James. James, in his later life, could have written the same sentences as Paul. Both apostles finished this learning process in faith.

We are still pursuing this learning process. We dream of a Church in power and glory and do not want to hear much of a weak and modest Church. We look for praise and recognition (and sometimes even personal advantage) in our work for the community and forget that Jesus came to serve. We think that we can and must earn Heaven for ourselves because it depends on our human performance; we do not consider that God has given us everything and will enrich us over and over. Often enough we trust entirely too much in our own ability and strength and cling too little to Christ amid the burdens of our Christian life.

Where do I personally stand in this learning process? What learning steps are especially important for me?

Petitions

Let us pray for the Church, built on the foundation of the apostles:

> For humility and modesty in all church leaders. . . .
> Lord, have mercy. . . .
> For the spirit of service in all community workers. . . .
> For realistic awareness of one's own limitations in all who presume themselves to be secure in faith. . . .
> For trust in God's mercy by all who know themselves to be sinners. . . .

Lord, let the power of your grace become visible in the Church. You who live and reign forever and ever.

Sts. Joachim and Ann (July 26)

LEGEND OF THE MIRACULOUS BIRTH OF MARY

Introduction

As a matter of course, Jesus of Nazareth had grandparents on his mother's side. Yet nowhere in Scripture are their names mentioned (in the two genealogies provided in Mt and Lk, only Joseph's forebears are listed). A writing emerges for the first time in the second century—the so-called Proto-Gospel of James—that tells in edifying prose of the miraculous birth of Mary. In it we find the names of Joachim and Ann. The special concern of the legend is, following the New Testament data, to show that Mary has a special place in the history of God with man.

Penitential Rite

"I cry to you, O Lord.
I have said: 'You are my refuge, all I have left in the land of the living.'
Listen then to my cry.
Bring my soul out of this prison and then I shall praise your name" (Ps 142:6,7a,8a).   (Silence)

Have mercy, Lord our God, have mercy . . . .

Talk

A Couple's Heartbreak. The legend portrays Joachim and Ann as bound to each other by love. They were God-fearing and wealthy. For the longest time they had no children (like the parents of Samuel and of John the Baptist). Their neighbors accordingly suspected that all was not right with their piety (since childlessness was considered to be a punishment for personal sins).

Joachim and Ann were deeply saddened by all this. They began to converse with God over their childlessness. Joachim withdrew for forty days into the desert, to do penance with God through fasting and prayer. Ann lamented her childlessness (as did Samuel's mother) before Yahweh.

God's Intervention. By message from God, Joachim and Ann received the promise of offspring. Both were overjoyed and went forth to meet each other. The scene of the spouse's reunion is described with feeling: "And lo, Joachim came leading his flocks, and Ann stood at the door and saw him coming. She ran to him and clung to his neck, saying, 'Now I know that the Lord God has richly blessed me. For now the widow is no longer a widow, and I, childless, am to bear a child.' "

The pregnancy began with the spouses's coming together, and after nine months Mary was born. The legend of Mary's birth came to a close: "And so, just as she herself was miraculously born of a barren woman, she also was, through an incomparable miracle in which she remained a virgin, to bring into the world the Son of the Most High . . . the Savior of all nations."

All in all: the major concern of this legend is clearly the statement that Mary was chosen by God in a special way, and has a particular role in the history of salvation. Joachim and Ann are simply background figures.

Joachim and Ann. Yet the pair do not fade into the background. They are portrayed as holy people in the Old Testament sense. Joachim constantly brings double his portion of gifts to the Temple. Each dwells

Sts. Joachim and Ann (July 26)

with Yahweh as a matter of course. God is evidently pleased with their piety.

And yet, he does test their faithfulness (as he also tested the piety of Job). The fate of childlessness (which they had to take as a sign of divine punishment) burdened them, but it did not shake their trust in God. They wrestled with God, just as the patient one in the Old Testament did. God finally gave them an answer, showing that he had heard their prayer.

Their faith in God is also manifest in that they gave their three-year-old daughter over to the Temple (in fulfillment of the vow Ann had made before the birth) and allowed her to live in the Temple. They gave back generously to God what God had sent them as a gift, without wishing to cling to it for themselves.

Joachim and Ann: faithful to God even in trials of faith, they take their proper place in the history of salvation (namely, to be the parents of Mary) and place themselves completely at God's disposal through their child. They are a standard for all who bear their names.

Petitions

Father in Heaven:

Bless the love of married couples . . . .
Strengthen the spirit of faith, hope, and love in our families . . . .
Give to parents and children the ability to speak with each other even on religious questions . . . .
Let the readiness grow in young Christians to dedicate themselves completely to your Kingdom . . . .
You who live and reign forever and ever.

St. Martha (July 29)

THE BELIEVING AND SERVING WOMAN

Introduction

Mary and Martha—they belonged, together with their brother Lazarus, to those whom Jesus loved (cf. Jn 10:3,5). They did not move with him around the country like the women of Galilee who belonged to his circle of disciples. Rather, they lived in the area of Jerusalem and had him many times as a guest in their home. This is the historical reality that we can discern behind the Gospel stories, which have the purpose of presenting a truth of faith and of showing Martha and Mary to be models of Christian life.

Penitential Rite

"The Lord builds up Jerusalem and brings back Israel's exiles, he heals the broken-hearted, he binds up all their wounds.

The Lord raises the lowly; he humbles the wicked to the dust" (Ps 147:2,3,6).

Have mercy, Lord our God, have mercy. . . .

St. Martha (July 29)

Talk

Faith in the Risen One. In the scene described by Luke (to which we will later return), Martha stands, to our way of thinking, somewhat in the shadow of her sister Mary. Yet the Gospel of John portrays her in the story of Lazarus' raising as the great model of the believing Church (first Gospel option).

Martha, even in her grief over her dead brother, is still full of trust for Jesus: "Even now, I am sure that God will give you whatever you ask of him." As Jesus tells her that her brother will live, she declares, "I know he will rise again in the resurrection on the last day." She finally lets Jesus lead her further in a decisive step. At the end comes her declaration of faith in Jesus Christ (and not just in an article of faith): "Yes, Lord, I have come to believe that you are the Messiah, the Son of God: he who is to come into the world."

Christian faith involves in the first place not "objects," but a person. The Christian believes not in the first place in "something" (the creation of the world by God, original sin, the Church, the Resurrection. . .); he trusts in the first place in Jesus Christ. He lets himself be moved by him, he lives in communion with him (and, in this framework, he holds as true whatever Jesus Christ reveals in the community of the Church). Are we sufficiently aware of this? We do not believe—to speak with some subtlety—in "the resurrection on the last day." We entrust ourselves in faith to him who is himself "the Resurrection and the Life," and we trust (like Martha) that we come with him into life that will not perish.

Mary and Martha. Luke does not intend to disparage Martha in his story (in the second Gospel option for today). After all, this passage is preceded by the parable of the good Samaritan, in which the outwardly pious priest and Levite clearly come off badly. Yet it is the evangelist's purpose to point out that both factors belong to Christian life: listening to Jesus Christ (in prayer, liturgy, in reflecting on his Word in the Bible. . .) and active service to people who need our help.

In all this, Luke is convinced that listening to Jesus is a requirement for Christian service to people in need. He knows that there is no true piety without love of neighbor (as seen in the tale of the good Samaritan). Yet he also underscores that there is no Christian love of neighbor without listening to Jesus Christ.

Has this reality yet become part of our way of thinking? If we take it seriously, then we will always be looking for moments and hours in which we sit at the Lord's feet and listen to his Word, so as to serve him more actively in our fellow human beings, and to be available to all those who wait precisely for us as their good Samaritans.

Petitions

Lord Jesus Christ, you are the Resurrection and the Life. Listen to our prayer:

Awaken in all Christians joy in the liturgy and in personal prayer. . . .
Strengthen the unity of the Church, so that she might become a living sign of that life that has come into the world with you. . . .
Be near to all who, without saying if or but, help people who need their support. . . .
Grant to all who do us good in our lives, a share in your eternal life. . . .

For whoever listens to you and loves his brothers and sisters, comes from death to life in you. You who live and reign forever and ever.

St. Peter Chrysologus (July 30)

TO PROCLAIM THE UNFATHOMABLE RICHNESS OF CHRIST

Introduction

"If one takes his pleasure with the devil, he may not celebrate feasts with Christ." Thus did Bishop Peter Chrysologus (his name means "the one with the golden words") thunder against the abuses of new year's celebrations in the fifth century. For our situation, we can apply it this way: if one does not live with Jesus Christ on an everyday basis, one may not celebrate the Eucharist with him. Where have we need of conversion to him who "has come to take on our weakness and to give us his power" (Peter Chrysologus)?

Penitential Rite

Lord Jesus Christ, teacher with divine authority: Lord, have mercy . . . .

Royal victor over death and sin: Christ, have mercy . . . .

Son of Man, enthroned on the right of the Father: Lord, have mercy . . . .

Talk

Bishop of the Imperial City. By 420, the once mighty Roman Empire, west and east, had crumbled. For a long time, Rome had no longer been the residence of the western Roman emperor. After a period in Milan, the imperial court had transferred to Ravenna, which offered better defense possibilities as capital amid the uncertainties of the increasing migrations of the tribes.

Around 420 (or some years later) Peter Chrysologus became bishop of Ravenna. He saw his city's ascendance. He was able to dedicate churches that were built at the expense of the imperial court (some of which are still standing today). He fulfilled his service as bishop according to the ideal that he himself described in this way: "The bishop ought to work well with the civil government, offer respect to old people, kindness and amiability to young people, love to brethren, affection to children; in everything, he must show himself to be a free servant in Christ."

"Man with the Golden Words." His contemporaries gave this bishop (whose activity is little known) the honorific surname "Chrysologus," the one with the golden words. Bishop Peter must have reached the people of his day with his homilies. A portion of his "spiritual talks" have come down to us. They reveal his vivid style (yet also his preference for borrowed Greek words). He could use words concisely and impressively. He considered it important to preach never longer than a quarter of an hour. On hot summer days he showed some understanding for his hearers by dispensing with the homily.

To Proclaim the Unfathomable Richness of Christ. In the homilies of the bishop of Ravenna that have reached us, we see reflected the theological controversies and the pastoral problems of his day (Arianism, Nestorianism...questions of Christian conduct of life...). They give evidence of the Church's efforts of that time "to proclaim the unfathomable riches of Christ" [Reading], which show themselves in a correct understanding of the mystery of Jesus Christ, and in a responsible Christian life.

The Church still has this task today: to live and to talk in such a way that people come to know "God's manifold wisdom," revealed in Jesus Christ [Reading]. In this, it is not just a matter for "pagans" (a long way from us in third-world countries, or among immigrants here). It is now also a matter for zealous and less zealous Christians.

Have we grasped the mystery of Christ when we have learned by heart the old venerable formulas of faith (the Creed, catechism questions and answers, old prayers...)? Do we already live by faith if we are able to converse in current theological discussions? Can we bring closer people who are alienated and critical by employing hallowed formulas of the past? I believe that we ourselves grow in the faith and then live it and speak for it convincingly before others, only when we make it our business to penetrate more deeply into the very mystery of God in Jesus Christ.

Let us try a test: "In Christ and through faith in him we can speak freely to God, drawing near him with confidence" [Reading]. What do these words mean? Basically, they are saying that God is a God of love, whom we can trust. Christian faith does not lead to anxiety before God, Christian faith calls us to trust. Do we really live in this knowledge? Do we manifest it with enthusiasm to others?

Petitions

Let us pray to our Lord Jesus Christ, "who has taken humanity for us, so as to safeguard the divine for us" (Peter Chrysologus):

For the leaders of Christian Churches... (Silence).
For preachers and religion teachers....
For zealous and less-than-zealous Christians....

Lord Jesus Christ, grant that we may come to know the wisdom of God ever more deeply and live by it ever more convincingly. You who live and reign forever and ever.

St. Ignatius of Loyola (July 31)

GOD ABOVE ALL

Introduction

Many of you have already made a retreat. If it was an authentic retreat (and not just a day of recollection), you attempted through prayer and reflection to see again more clearly what God wants of you in your life circumstances. Ignatius of Loyola stands at the beginning of the retreat movement. At the age of thirty he came to know in the solitude of Spanish mountains what God expected of him. He set down his religious experiences in the *Spiritual Exercises,* which in the following centuries has helped many people to discover Christ at deeper levels and to pattern their lives decisively after his example.

Penitential Rite

"Whether you eat or drink—whatever you do—you should do all for the glory of God." [Silence] Lord, have mercy. . . .

"Give no offense to Jew nor Greek or to the church of God." [Silence] Christ, have mercy. . . .

"Imitate me as I imitate Christ." [Silence] Lord, have mercy. . . .

Talk

Cannonball with Long-lasting Effects. On Pentecost Sunday, 1521, the Spanish nobleman Iñigo de Loyola (he later changed his name to Ignatius) was hit by a cannonball, which put his military career to a sudden end and forced him into a convalescence lasting several months. His companions later said of him that he had been "wanton in gambling, wenching, brawling, and armed fighting." Now thirty years old, in the boredom of his recovery period in his home castle he could find for reading only a life of Jesus from the Middle Ages and the Lives of the Saints. He was stirred by what he read, even though he would never have picked them up while he was healthy. He decided that he would imitate the saints of the past and would follow Christ radically.

Ignatius began his new life by wandering through Spain as a beggar. Then he went as a pilgrim to the Holy Land. Finally, after much reflection, he became convinced that he should spend some time in studies so as to be better able to help people. He passed the next ten years of his life on a school bench and in the university.

During his studies in Paris he found his first companions. On August 15, 1534, the students promised to live lives of poverty and celibacy, to serve God, and to minister to souls. The little band wanted first to go to the Holy Land. When this plan fell through, they went in 1538 to Rome (after Ignatius had been ordained a priest at age forty-six) and placed themselves at the service of the pope. There their community became the ecclesiastial order of the Society of Jesus, and it gained papal approval in 1540.

Ignatius still had sixteen years as general superior of the young congregation to build it up into a special corps for the Church, fullfilling his own vision. The company accomplished great things for the renewal of the Church in the next centuries. The Jesuits from the beginning were admired and attacked, challenged and suppressed. Yet in the spirit of their founder, for whom God came above all things, they placed themselves over and over in the service of the Church and addressed the needs of their time.

God Above All. For Ignatius, God is at the center of human life. A person should be completely open to the plan of God in his life. Therefore, nothing earthly (people, things, honor. . .) can be more important than God and his will. One must then be ready even to accept the cross and suffering if they are bound up with the mandate from God. In this freedom for God's will, the person can ask in each decision-making situation—that would fit better with God's will, and make his choice without improper consideration of earthly ties. He will then pray in the Our Father not only: Father, your will be done; he will let his life be shaped by the demands recognized as being of God's will, even when it is to his disadvantage or is tied up with hardships.

Ignatius himself lived with this attitude. He directed his Jesuits to seek the will of God in this freedom for God. In the exercises, as Ignatius understood them, there is the concern for this freedom for God and for the readiness to shape one's life completely according to God's will. A prayer that is attributed to Ignatius expresses this attitude well:

Eternal Word, only Son of God,
teach me true greatheartedness.
Teach me to serve you as you deserve:
to give without counting,
to fight without noticing my wounds,
to work without seeking rest,
to dedicate myself, without expecting any other reward except the awareness
of having fullfilled your holy will (cf. Gl5,3).

St. Alphonsus Mary de Liguori (August 1)

CHRIST, THE LAW OF OUR LIFE

Introduction

It used to be that "the Church" (Rome, bishops, moral theologians, confessors) told us exactly what we had to do and to allow in our concrete lives. Today the emphasis, even in church documents, is more on individual responsibility and personal decisions of conscience. Many people are confused by this development and ask worriedly, "What, then, is really a sin?" Let us reflect, on this feast of St. Alphonsus Mary de Liguori, on why we in the Church of today lay more stress on the spirit of personal and individually responsible decision.

Penitential Rite

"If salt goes flat, how can you restore its flavor?" (Silence) Lord, have mercy....
"Men do not light a lamp and then put it under a bushel basket." (Silence) Christ, have mercy....
"I have come to fulfill the law and the prophets." (Silence) Lord, have mercy....

Talk

Alphonsus Mary de Liguori, a native of Naples, was able to earn two doctorates by the age of seventeen; by twenty, he had a flourishing law practice. At twenty-seven, he decided to enter into the Church's service as a priest. He was soon working with a group of like-minded people for the religious instruction and charitable care of the city poor. During a convalescence in the country (he had exhausted himself in his work) he came to see the shocking pastoral need of the simple shepherds and mountain peasants. To meet this need, he founded the Congregation of Redemptorists in 1732.

In the following decades, as a tireless priest zealous for souls, he stood at the head of his brethren in extraordinary pastoral work. At sixty-six, he was made bishop of a small diocese in the area of Naples. Thirteen years later the pope accepted the resignation of the gout-afflicted cleric; he spent the last twelve years of his life as a sick man in the company of his confreres.

His Moral Theology. As a pastor, Alphonsus also took up the pen as occasion demanded. He became famous above all for his moral theology, which was intended to help his priests in the confessional give advice to the faithful in concrete questions of conscience. Therein he dealt with many practical cases and gave very concrete answers to many individual questions.

This type of moral theology influenced the entire life of the Church in the ensuing decades. However, it also led to the result that many pastors thought that they were obliged to give to the faithful always and everywhere specific advice down to the last detail for their Christian conduct of life—and many of the faithful would only anxiously ask for "counsel" (or "norms") and could no longer find the courage to make a personal and responsible decision.

Current Approaches. Contemporary moral theology makes it clearer (before dealing with any specific questions) that the authentic "law" for the Christian is Jesus Christ himself, who summed up the foundation of Christian living in the great commandment of love for God and love for neighbor. In every life situation, the aim of the Christian is to apply this love with which Jesus Christ has first loved us.

Now, life in the concrete is much more complicated than many well-intentioned books. Even the best pastoral counselor can never completely put himself in the situation of the person being advised. Accordingly, we are more careful nowadays with "norms" and "advice."

When it is a matter of personal Christian conduct of life, today we prefer to seek clear answers with this approach. As believing Christians, we think out a matter first for ourselves, then also with each other (in the universal Church, in a synod, within the family, during individual confession . . .); we ask how the great commandment of love for God and neighbor ought to be applied to the specific situation. In this, we will give special attention to the opinion of the Church (her traditions, official statements . . .) and the opinion of specialists (moral theologians, pastoral workers . . .). But after this exchange of different points of view, I will then have the courage to make a decision on my own responsibility that, by my honest conviction, is what Jesus Christ would decide to do in this situation. And I can be certain in this that he accepts my decision, if I have an informed conscience.

Petitions

Lord Jesus Christ, you lead your Church and individual Christians in the Holy Spirit, so that they might know what is right and do it in their lives:

Enlighten moral theologians in their studies . . .
Be near to pastors in the confessional and in the counseling room . . .
Strengthen individual Christians in hard personal decisions . . .
Give them the strength to carry out decisions they have made . . . .

For it is your will that your love be active in every human life. You who live and reign forever and ever.

St. Eusebius (August 2)

FAITH OVERCOMING THIS WORLD

Introduction

Eusebius of Vercelli (died 371) is one of the many bishops of the fourth century who, in the course of the theological controversies of their time, were forced into exile. He, like many of his fellow bishops, did not allow himself to be embittered over the pains of exile. After years of degrading treatment, he was still ready to make peace with his opponents in theology and church politics. He had the strength after his return to his diocese to work there again, where years before he was made to stop. His life is a sign of how faith "that Jesus is the Son of God" conquers the "world" (Reading).

Penitential Rite

"Love the Lord, all you saints.
"He guards his faithful but the Lord will repay to the full those who act with pride.
"Be strong, let your heart take courage, all who hope in the Lord" (Ps 31:24ff).

Have mercy, Lord our God, have mercy . . . .

St. Eusebius (August 2)

Talk

A Bitter Experience. Many who once set out to change the world found themselves instead changed by the world. They did not hold up against the grinding resistance of life and collapsed under the very pressures that they had wanted to contain. They ended up becoming a dreary piece of the world they had rejected, every bit as embittered, tired, resigned, loveless, and selfish as all the others.

Many who started out idealistically to renew the Church and to live with new vigor in the spirit of Jesus Christ finished up by matching the mediocrity they sought to leave behind. They have slid back, perhaps even betrayed their ideals; at any rate, they have lost the vigor of a great beginning, and even as Christians are tired, resigned, and sometimes embittered.

We all know of such cases. These experiences are perhaps not unknown to us in our own lives. We ask ourselves why does it happen that so much idealism collapses in upon itself, that so much good will vanishes without success.

The Only Power. The First Letter of John (from which the Reading is taken) does not equate "world" with God's good creation. "World" exists where people are guided by their selfishness, where people live by their attachment not to God but to themselves. "World" exists where hate and strife, thanklessness and lovelessness, recklessness and complacency prevail. This "world" obviously develops a terrible undertow. It threatens to negate all idealism and to infect with its germs everyone who comes into contact with it. The result is then that even the most ideal person does not overcome this "world," but is altered by it.

This "world" crops up in private encounters with our fellow human beings, in politics and society, and even in church life. At some time we too will cave in to it—if we, in our idealism, trust only in our own power.

The Reading points out clearly to us the power by which we can overcome and change this world. "And the power that has conquered the world is this faith of ours. Who, then, is conqueror of the world? The one who believes that Jesus is the Son of God." What does this mean?

Victory by the Power of Faith. In faith we know: that God has irreversibly affirmed the world; that he loves each individual person; that he accompanies his Church in the Holy Spirit. This knowledge in faith gives us the courage to believe with him in the goodness of the world, of individual men and women, and of the Church, and to further this goodness by our service.

In Jesus Christ we know that selflessness and readiness to help, dedication to justice and love for peace, a life according to the Sermon on the Mount (Gospel), lead us not to personal ruin but through death into resurrection. That gives us courage to live after the example of Jesus without reservation, and not to become downhearted when we run into opposition, disappointment, cross, and suffering on that account.

Jesus Christ himself is the power in the Holy Spirit by which we can live by his example and overcome evil in the world, in individuals, and in the Church, and in faith to conquer the "world."

Petitions

Let us pray in union with all saints who were persecuted for their faith:

For statesmen and politicians who become weary in their dedication to peace . . . Lord, have mercy . . .
For bishops and priests who react with nervous irritation to the stress of their daily service . . .
For workers in social service who become discouraged in the face of unmistakable physical and spiritual need . . . .

Almighty God, give us the power of faith, by which alone we can overcome all temptation to give up. You who live and reign forever and ever.

St. John Mary Vianney (August 4)

HE HAD COMPASSION FOR THEM

Introduction

"The Cure of Ars": his limited intellectual capacity, his battle with the devil, his extraordinarily fruitful ministry in the confessional are well-known. He is a phenomenon for our enlightened age, in whom theologians and psychologists even today are "sinking their teeth." The deepest mystery of his pastoral success is rooted in the fact that he loved people as did Jesus Christ and in his love suffered with them. He proved himself to be a faithful follower of the Good Shepherd, Jesus Christ.

Penitential Rite

Lord Jesus Christ, you have compassion for all people who are tired and exhausted like sheep who have no shepherd: Lord, have mercy . . . .

You proclaim to them the Gospel of your Kingdom and heal their sickness and suffering: Christ, have mercy . . . .

You give us the mandate as your followers to heal sickness and suffering and to drive out unclean spirits: Lord, have mercy . . . .

Talk

A Simple External Life. John Mary Vianney (1786–1859) grew up during the disorders of the French Revolution. After Napoleon's seizure of power, a holy priest helped him against many obstacles on his path to the priesthood. In 1815 he was ordained a priest. After some years of service as curate under his fatherly friend, he went in 1819 to the godforsaken village of Ars in the area of Lyon. There he lived for the next forty years after the example of Jesus Christ in the love that shows compassion to people. For him, these forty years were a way of the cross. For his community and for many thousands who came to Ars for the Sacrament of Reconciliation, they were the source of religious renewal.

Suffering in the Dechristianized Community. The young pastor of Ars loved the people of his village. He saw them threatened by hell in their religious indifference. He dedicated himself to them, nothing was too much for him, only his warnings and pleadings fell on deaf ears. How he must have suffered over his parishioners! In his anxiety he constantly asked himself if he were at fault. He asked repeatedly to be replaced—and yet stayed on in his village. He repeatedly moved away secretly—and still would come back.

Suffering under Overwhelming Demands. If the Cure of Ars suffered during the early years on account of his imagined lack of success, later he wore himself down in tireless pastoral service to his people. His fame spread beyond his parish. People came from a distance to Ars, in order to confess to Father Vianney. Soon thousands and ten thousands were making their way to Ars each year. For the sickly pastor, beset with anxieties in his own conscience, this stream of humanity meant a huge burden. He spent hour after hour in the confessional and listened with evenhanded patience to people's small sins and great offenses. There was hardly time left over for sleep and relaxation

St. John Mary Vianney (August 4)

or for a minimum of private life. His life belonged completely to the people who sought his counsel—and his goodness.

Voluntary Suffering Out of Love. In his compassion for people, Father Vianney lived a strict ascetic life, in order to open people's hearts for the grace of God through vicarious suffering. He contented himself with a minimum of food. He would sleep for only a few hours on a hard and uncomfortable bed, and disciplined himself with a whip regularly.

Model Pastor. This priest, zealous for souls, was canonized in 1925 and was set before pastors in a special way as a model in 1929. We pastoral workers must always ask ourselves to what extent are we, along with the pastor of Ars, like Jesus Christ in his compassion for people. How ready are we to suffer as well in our care for people in our parishes?

Yet perhaps now and then you can remember that your pastors, in their service for the congregation, can go through some bad hours in which they feel the cross of Christ: hours when they achieve nothing; hours when too much is demanded of them. Perhaps you will then pray for your pastors, that they might not become discouraged under this cross and give up.

Petitions

Lord Jesus Christ, you have compassion on people. We pray for our pastors:

Give them understanding of people today and their problems . . .
Be close to them in hours of loneliness and failure . . .
Let their service not degenerate into mere routine in the times when too much is demanded of them . . . .

For you chose them to proclaim the Gospel of your Kingdom, and to heal sickness and suffering. You who live and reign forever and ever.

Dedication of the Basilica of St. Mary Major in Rome (August 5)

MARY, ARCHETYPE OF THE CHURCH

Introduction

Besides the ancient church of St. Mary Major in Rome (one of the four principal churches of the city), tens of thousands of Catholic, Protestant, and Orthodox houses of worship throughout the world bear the name of Mary. As the patroness of many church buildings, Mary makes us aware of what it means for the Church to be built from the "living stones" of believing Christians. For, according to Luke's presentation in the Gospel, Mary is the archetype of the Church, and in the Book of Revelation she and the Church in the form of the great woman of the end times are basically identical.

Penitential Rite

"The Lord is just in all his ways and loving in all his deeds.
He is close to all who call him, who call on him from their hearts.
The Lord protects all who love him; but the wicked he will utterly destroy" (Ps 145:17,18,20).

Have mercy, Lord our God, have mercy . . . .

Talk

"God's Tent among Men." We call our church buildings "the house of God among men." This description came into being as the Church started to conserve the eucharistic species in houses of worship and to venerate them with reverence. From that time onward, the tabernacle (the "tent") has been the central point of our Catholic churches.

This should certainly not allow us to forget that the true "house of God among men" is the fellowship of living Christians who live out their faith in people's midst. All our tabernacle-oriented piety in stone and wood church buildings (personal prayer, eucharistic liturgy) should enable us to be living tabernacles of God in our world.

Now, God began his special habitation among human beings by becoming flesh through the Virgin Mary. By her faith (Gospel) in which she was ready to accept God's mandate, she herself became the first home of Jesus Christ among men by the grace of God. Insofar as she served her Son in faith, hope, and love, she is the archetype and model for the whole Church. For we can be houses of God among men only if God prepares us by his grace and we go forth in faith, hope, and love.

"Prepared Like a Bride." Again and again the relation of the Church to Jesus Christ is compared in Scripture to the attitude of a bride. A bride thinks, by common account, mainly of her fiance. A girl in love cannot withhold herself from seeing her friend. A young woman who really loves a man wants to anticipate his every wish and to fulfill him.

This image is often used of Mary. She lived in constant thought of Jesus Christ. She wanted to be with him always. She anticipated his every wish and fulfilled him with her life. ("Blest are they who hear the Word of God and keep it"—Gospel.)

Given all that, Mary is the model of the Church. For Church is only there (beyond all social action) where people are moved by Jesus Christ, where they live for him and put his desires at the center of their lives, as did Mary.

"I Make All Things New." Mary, as the archetype of the Church, went along with her Son on the path of earthly life. It was for her—as it was for him—a way of the cross, with tears, grief, lament, and distress (Reading). The Gospel speaks of the sword that pierced her heart. Yet by God's grace Mary then entered into fulfillment with God in the new heaven and the new earth, where all pain came to an end for her.

We, as Church, in faith-filled union with her and her Son in glory, are still on the path of our earthly life. Part of our lives (in the Church and in everyday life) is still taken up with a considerable amount of tears, grief, lament, and distress. And death awaits us all. Mary, as archetype of the Church, who has entered into fulfillment with God, gives us hope that God will wipe away each tear from our eyes too and will make all things new for us (Reading).

Petitions

Lord Jesus Christ, we plead with you for mercy:

Make the Church your living home among people . . .
Enliven in the faithful their fellowship with you and with each other . . .
Let men and women, in all their pain, now feel something of your new heaven and new earth . . . .

For yours is the kingdom and the power forever and ever.

Transfiguration of the Lord (August 6)

A LAW OF LIFE

Introduction

When at Mass, how often are you able to be really and completely present? The moments in which we succeed in this or repeat it are rare. For long periods our religious activity is a more or less successful effort to come before God in faith, but without us feeling his presence. In this experience we touch upon a principle that shapes all of human life, as well as our life in faith.

Penitential Rite

Jesus Christ, Son of the living God, image of the Father, ray of eternal light: Lord, have mercy . . . .

Jesus Christ, Prince of peace, Father of the future, our King: Christ, have mercy . . . .

Jesus Christ, bread by which we live, light by which we see, way by which we go: Lord, have mercy . . . .

Talk

A Law of Life. Parents and children are living together in a family. In daily life, irritation abounds. The parents scold the children and the children complain against the parents. There is little of mutual love and respect to be seen. And yet this family lives under the burdens of everyday life with strength from the precious hours (mother's day, birthdays, an illness, after a particularly rough fight . . .), in which the children feel the love of their parents and the parents feel the affection of their children quite clearly. From these light-filled hours there falls light on the gray everyday, which can conceal the reality of mutual love and affection.

A man and a woman are following the same life path. Their lives are influenced for the most part by the demands of their occupations and by serious concern for their family. Their common path too is obstructed by the quarrels of daily life. They get on each other's nerves. They have repeated doubts about each other, and mistrust insinuates itself. Yet somewhere they recognize that they can indeed rely on each other, because they at some time have experienced beyond all doubt (in a happy or a difficult hour) how they know each other to be mutually responsible in love.

A Law of Faith. This law of life also manifests itself as a law of faith. In our communion with God, there are also long stretches of humdrum living and only few precious moments in which we clearly feel God's presence.

We say too glibly that prayer is conversation with God. The light-filled hours come seldom in which we really sense God in our prayer and hear his answer clearly. For the longest time, our prayer is honest effort to direct ourselves inwardly toward God. We often do not succeed in it at all, because we are not able to recollect and concentrate ourselves. And when we do succeed, we find ourselves not rarely before a kind of incomprehensible darkness into which we speak without receiving any answer. Yet we continue in our attempts at prayer because at some time we have experienced that we rightfully address God as the great "thou" of our lives.

We say that the eucharistic celebration is an encounter with the Risen One. At some Eucharist each one of us was once moved by his presence. Yet normally it is hard for us to stay with our thoughts. And when for once we are really and totally there, we feel little of the presence of Christ. Yet we share again in the Mass faithfully and regularly, since the experience of the past has taught us that HE is truly there. We trust that he will at some point reveal his presence more clearly to us.

Transfiguration and Daily Life. That which we experience in human life and in the life of faith is what the disciples of Jesus also experienced before and after Easter. In the earthly circle of disciples, their faith lived from the hour of revelation (whether on the mountain or elsewhere), wherein they clearly recognized his mystery. After Easter, they lived from the light-filled hours of their encounter with the Risen One, who shone forth into their everyday Christian lives like "a lamp shining in a dark place" (Reading). It gave them courage to venture their lives with him.

Petitions

Great God, you reveal the mystery of your Son on the mount of transfiguration.

Give to all who are weary and burdened the sense of your presence . . . .
Reveal your mysterious reality to all who seek and question . . . .
Let the question of your Son arise among shallow and indifferent people . . . .

For he is your beloved Son, to whom the whole world should listen. You who live and reign forever and ever.

St. Sixtus and Companions (August 7)

"IN THE EYES OF THE FOOLISH, THEY ARE DEAD..."

Introduction

Sixtus had been bishop of the Roman congregation for only a year. In the persecution under Decius (who took aim mainly at community leaders in order to deal Christianity a lethal blow), he was arrested in 258 at a worship service in a catacomb and immediately beheaded. The legend is concerned more with his deacon Lawrence (cf. August 10) than with him. Still, his name appears in the Roman Canon. Thus, together with him, we confess Jesus Christ in this Eucharist, whose death and resurrection we proclaim until he comes in glory.

Penitential Rite

Lord Jesus Christ, you have destroyed the power of death. You are the resurrection and the life: Lord, have mercy . . . .

You sit at the right hand of the Father and will come again to judge the living and the dead: Christ, have mercy . . . .

You are our advocate and mediator with the Father, so that we may gain forgiveness for our sins and attain everlasting life: Lord, have mercy . . . .

St. Sixtus and Companions (August 7)

Talk

An Accounting of Our Hope. Since the earliest times, Christians confess in the Apostles' Creed: "I believe in the resurrection of the body and life everlasting." Martyrs like Pope Sixtus and his companions have testified by their deaths that this was not mere lip-service for them. During their lifetimes they attempted to understand what was meant by this article of faith, and were able to express it in many tongues.

Some years ago, the German Synod published a document entitled "Our Hope." They intended to provide an accounting of our faith in the present day. Let us adopt this intention and briefly give an account of our hope for everlasting life, which we express in every eucharistic liturgy.

In God's Hand. The people of the Old Testament were deeply imbued with trust in the God who had sealed the Covenant with them and who had promised them his faithfulness. Even now we use their words in the Psalms and in their other poetry, in order to express our trust in God (cf. GL 289;291;302).

Beyond Death. With faith in God's love and faithfulness, the holy ones of Israel in the late Old Testament period asked themselves the question whether God's care for human beings could cease with death. Their believing and trust-filled answer was: God in his love must also look after man even on the other side of death. Man in death cannot fall outside of God's hand. In the last book of the Old Testament, this conviction is stated in this way: "The souls of the just are in the hand of God, and no torment shall touch them . . . they are in peace . . . because God tried them and found them worthy of himself . . . the Lord shall be their King forever . . . and the faithful shall abide with him in love" (Reading).

Hope of Resurrection in Jesus Christ. The first Christians (who, after all, came out of the pious Judaism of Jesus' time) knew about this trusting hope in the fulfillment of human life with God. To them the Lord, who died on the cross and rose again, revealed himself. In their encounter with him they became certain that God's faithfulness had endured beyond Jesus' death, and that it would also endure beyond the death of a Christian. And they confessed as every generation of Christians through all time have confessed: "I believe in the resurrection of the body and life everlasting."

Based on the Resurrection of Jesus. Christians have always known (despite all heartwarming and edifying images of "eternal life") that this fulfillment with God escapes human understanding. Just as God himself is a mysterious reality, so also is the permanent life of man with God (cf. Reading) "unimaginable": it is and remains a mystery, into which we, with our human concepts, can barely enter.

As Christians, therefore, we believe "in the resurrection and everlasting life" not because we clearly know what awaits us beyond death, but because we trust in God, from whose hands no sparrow falls (Gospel) and in whose hand we ourselves, at the moment of death and throughout its dark wave, remain sheltered.

Petitions

God and Lord of the living:

Be near to those whose lives are endangered . . .
Console the dying with faith in your faithfulness that goes beyond death . . .
Open the ears of the desperate to the Good News of the Resurrection . . .
Let our dead remain with you always in love . . . .

For the living and the dead are protected in your hand, who live and reign forever and ever.

St. Cajetan (August 7)

IN CONTRAST TO THE RENAISSANCE

Introduction

"I am not lying when I say that there are people of good will who are ashamed to be seen at Confession or at Holy Communion." This remark was made by St. Cajetan (1480–1567) concerning religious conditions in Venice on the eve of the Reformation. Similar conditions still exist today. For that reason, the great goal of this saint is still valid today: "I will not rest until I see Christians rush like starving people to the priests in order to let the selves be filled with the Eucharist, and regard this not as a disgrace but as a great honor."

Penitential Rite

Who has trusted the Lord and been put to shame?
Who has hoped in him and was abandoned?
Who calls upon him, and he hears him not?
For gracious and merciful is the Lord, he forgives sins and helps those in need.

Have mercy, Lord our God, have mercy . . . .

Talk

Forces of Renewal. Around 1500 Rome was the center of European cultural life. The most renowned artists were in the employ of the papal court. Yet Rome at that time was also "sinful Babylon." A frivolous outlook on life and a pagan life-style were common. Loose morals and abuses abounded.

At the same time, there were stirrings of religious renewal among papal officials and church dignitaries. Clergy and laity came together in the "Brotherhood of Divine Love." They bound themselves to a regular religious life (regular prayer, daily participation at Mass, monthly communion . . .) and to the care of the sick in Roman hospitals. Their goal was "to sow and plant the love of God" in people's hearts.

Cajetan. Cajetan of Thiene, a northern Italian and a doctor of canon and civil law, came as an official of the papal administration into contact with these reform circles and actively worked in the Brotherhood.

After being ordained a priest (Cajetan was then thirty-seven), he had to return to northern Italy for family reasons. In the years that followed, he dedicated himself to the establishment and cultivation of similar reform movements in Vicenza, Verona, and Venice. He remained committed to a conscious religious life (in contrast to secularizing tendencies in his age)—and to the care of people with incurable or particularly repulsive illnesses (in contrast to the "ideal" human image of the Renaissance).

During these years, Cajetan reflected on the question of what further direction his priestly service should take. He prayed over it for a long while, until in 1524 he took the decisive step forward. He went ahead and founded a community of priests, whose members led a very purposeful apostolic life and, in contrast with the avarice and vanity of the period, expressly renounced every kind of property, income, and benef-

St. Cajetan (August 7)

ice. They wanted to live from alms alone. Their affirmation of poverty was stated by Cajetan in a letter to his relatives: "I see Christ poor and me rich, him despised and me honored. I want to come a step closer to him and have thus decided to give up all that I still possess of earthly good."

The small group of priests of mature age aroused attention in Rome. Its members made such an impression by their conscious religious life that their name of "Theatines" (taken from the bishopric of their general superior) became synonymous with piety, justice, and strictness in living.

Our Contrasts. Cajetan of Thiene worked for the religious renewal of his age by very consciously acting out contrasts against the contemporary spirit of the times. He was not interested in mere protest, but rather in an undiminished life in the Spirit of Jesus Christ.

What contrasts are current nowadays? I believe that even today we have to attach new value to regular and faithful prayer. A modest standard of living would be a contrast to the excessive consumption of our society. And the particular care for sick and elderly people could give witness, in a society that recognizes the young and the healthy almost exclusively, that even the "weak" and the "unproductive" are beloved of God.

Petitions

God our Father, you call us to trust in you and your help. We pray to you:

For all who endanger their faith by the neglect of their prayer life . . .
Lord, have mercy . . .
For all who become neglectful of religion in their material prosperity . . .

For all who are hardening into religious self-sufficiency and do not see the need of their brothers and sisters . . . .

God our Father, give us all the power to renew our lives in the spirit of the Gospel. You who live and reign forever and ever.

St. Dominic (August 8)

HIS DESIRE: SOLID PREACHING

Introduction

Francis of Assisi and Dominic, a Spaniard, were contemporaries. They both flourished around the year 1200. Both gave in their lives and work an answer to the needs of the Church in their times. Since these two saints were distinct one from another, the answers, by which they gave help to the Church, were distinct.

Penitential Rite

Lord Jesus Christ, you call men and women to imitate you: Lord, have mercy . . . .
You give them the task of proclaiming God's Kingdom: Christ, have mercy . . . .
You want them to accept this task with all their strength: Lord, have mercy . . . .

Talk

An Eye Open for Necessary Things. A student interested in spiritual matters who sold his books (which in those times were invaluable rareties) in order to help the hungry with the proceeds: that was certainly no tavern-crawler avoiding the hard realities of life. This was

Dominic in his younger years. He explained his deed (imitated by others at the university) with the words, "How could I study from these dead books when I know that living people are starving?"

In this anecdote a characteristic of St. Dominic comes to light. He was a man of study and of prayer. He loved his books and the still hours of prayer. He gave this motto to the brethren in his order: *"Contemplata aliis tradere,"* "Bring to others what you contemplate." In plainer English we could say: let your preaching bring out what you yourself have already thought through and have reflected upon in your prayer.

At the same time, he was a man of action who sought to meet the religious needs of his time as a priest and pastoral worker. On that account, he worked to take out of his religious community a troop that could work without much baggage wherever it was needed.

Priest for Preaching. Dominic found his field of work on assignment by the pope in southern France. There the unity of the Church was endangered by the Albigensians and the Waldensians. The nobility and the greater part of the gentry were particularly critical of the official Church.

In this situation papal legates, who went about like high lords, achieved little. Dominic took another approach. He went through the country as a poor and humble preacher. He sought out critical and alienated people and entered into relingous discussions with them. Hostility and misunderstanding did not discourage him.

As time went on, the humble wandering preacher found men joining him. The bishop of Toulouse gave the group the specific charge to preach in his diocese and instruct the people. Yet Dominic also envisioned a worldwide community of itinerant preachers. He sent his brothers forth from Toulouse into other cities and countries and established his own residence in Bologna, Italy.

In establishing his order, the saint knew well how necessary suitable preaching was for the emerging town dwellers. He was convinced that his brothers needed quiet and solitude in order to prepare themselves for preaching. For that reason, he authorized them (unlike Francis with his brethren) to hold as common property modest cloisters and the necessary books, even if they went through the country as poor wandering preachers living from alms. For that reason, from the start he valued a fitting theological education (again, unlike the layman Francis).

His Work. Dominic died on August 6, 1221 in Bologna. Only in 1217 did the expansion begin of the Preaching Brothers, or Dominicans, beyond their first house in Toulouse. Yet the community grew and gave to the Church in the following decades men like Albert the Great and Thomas Aquinas, who substantially furthered the intellectual exchange of Christiantiy with the influences of the age. St. Dominic himself receded behind his work. In this point as well he was different from St. Francis of Assisi. No legends or anecdotes swarm around his image. He speaks to us above all in his achievement, which is still living in the Church today.

Petitions

Lord Jesus Christ, you have sent us your Spirit, who teaches us to understand and appreciate your Good News.

Bless the work of the Dominicans in their various areas of apostolate . . . .
Be near to the Dominican congregations of Sisters in their service at home and in the missions . . . .
Help all preachers and liturgical readers to prepare themselves by study and prayer for proclaiming the Word on Sundays . . . .

For you want to come to the people of today through our mediation. You who live and reign forever and ever.

St. Lawrence (August 10)

A MATCH FOR ANY SITUATION

Introduction

The memorial of a martyr named Lawrence, observed on August 10 on the spot of a church named after him can be traced back to the early fourth century—proof enough that this feast is really that of a Christian killed for his faith. More specific details of his life and suffering are lacking to us. Pious tradition has seen him as a true Roman who patiently endured martyrdom and overcame his pagan judge by his inner peace and by his penetrating irony.

Penitential Rite

"Jesus, accused by false witnesses, rejected by the high council, condemned to death": Lord, have mercy . . .

"Jesus, stripped of your garments, nailed to the cross, counted among criminals": Christ, have mercy . . .

"Jesus, laid in the tomb, descended into the realm of the dead, risen in glory": Lord, have mercy . . . (GL 766,4).

Talk

The Renowned Martyr. The tradition sees in Lawrence the archdeacon of Pope Sixtus, who was executed on August 7, 258 in Rome. His first assistant endured martyrdom a few days later.

The tradition—transmitted by Bishop Ambrose of Milan—develops the image of the "renowned martyr" in the scene of parting between Bishop Sixtus and Deacon Lawrence. Ambrose first has the deacon speak: "Where are you going, Father, without your son? You have never offered the gifts without your servant. You have entrusted to him the consecrated blood of the Lord, a share in the celebration of the mysteries. Will you now deny him a share in your own blood?"

To this, Sixtus (facing immediate martyrdom) replies, "No, my son, I do not leave you behind. Greater battles remain for you. As an old man I am going through the gauntlet to an easier battle. A glorious victory over the tyrant awaits you, the young man. You will follow me in three days. It is not fitting for you to win at the side of the teacher, lest it appear that you needed a helper. Poor students can go ahead of their teacher, but good students follow him. They win without the teacher, for they no longer need his instruction."

This bravery that was undaunted by death, together with irony and inner clarity, shows itself also in the deacon's sufferings as depicted by Ambrose: he was being roasted alive on a grill, and while he lay in flames, he said to the executioner, "The roast is ready, turn it over and eat."

I believe that we should not be discouraged by this ideal sketch of a martyrdom if we are worried about a serious moment of witnessing the faith in hard circumstances. After all, Jesus Christ did not die like a proud Roman. He experienced anxiety in the face of suffering on the Mount of Olives, and anxiety in the face of death on the cross. Irony did not befit him in his last hour, when he could only cry out loudly. He clung fast to the Father in his human poverty and became victor in the resurrection.

The Treasure of the Church. Another aspect of the tradition surrounding Lawrence's death is picked up in today's Reading. When the pagan judge demanded that the deacon surrender the treasures of the Church, Lawrence led all the poor, lame, and blind people into the imperial palace and declared, "These are the Church's everlasting treasures."

This is a striking interpretation of the Church's basic mission. Her real treasures are not the funds that she collects; not the art works produced by believing generations; not the church buildings nor other valuable properties; her real treasures are not even the believers themselves. Her everlasting treasures are the people whom she selflessly aids; for whom she herself diminishes, for whom she is available, even when she gets no thanks or no response. To put it in another way: we enrich the Church when we give of ourselves to the poorest of the poor. And—a point which is brought home to us on the feast of the martyr Lawrence—our lives thus become the most genuine witness for Jesus Christ.

Petitions

Lord Jesus Christ, we call upon you for the members of your mystical Body who carry the cross of persecution along with you:

Give them the strength for fearless witnessing . . .
Strengthen those under imprisonment and torture . . .
Forgive the persecutors of the Church . . .
Receive the victims of unjust violence into your Kingdom . . . .

Grant us these things through the intercession of all the holy martyrs. You who live and reign forever and ever.

St. Clare (August 11)

FOR THE SAKE OF POVERTY

Introduction

An eighteen-year-old girl, embroiled in conflict with her parents, leaves their house against their will: a case like this is not new to history.

It was done in 1211 by St. Clare of Assisi. On the night of March 18, she secretly left her parents' home and joined the movement of her compatriot Francis of Assisi (whom some of his contemporaries would have called a hippie, had the word already existed then). How did this affect Clare?

Penitential Rite

Lord Jesus Christ, knowing you surpasses all things: Lord, have mercy . . .
Through faith in you we are saved: Christ, have mercy . . .
You have touched us deeply: Lord, have mercy . . . .

Talk

Noble Background. Clare grew up in a noble family. Her youth was clouded by the turbulent struggles between the dominant nobility and the upcoming bourgeois. Under her mother's supervision, she acquired a good practical and academic education. The family was counting on her to marry a nobleman someday and thus make her contribution to the growth of the power of her clan.

Encounter with Francis.
In Assisi, Francis and his novel religious movement had been the topic of news for some time. The townsman's son returned from his journey to Rome in 1210 with his companions. The great Pope Innocent III had given him canonical permission for his new living pattern of radical poverty and of lay preaching.

Clare heard the preaching of St. Francis calling for penance and conversion. The words would not let her alone. She went to Francis and discussed with him how she as a woman could take part in the Franciscan movement. After talking with him, she secretly left her parents' home. With one of her childhood friends, she received from Francis at the chapel of the Portiuncula in Assisi the grey penitential habit that she would wear for the rest of her life.

Battle for an Ideal.
The two first Franciscan nuns then took refuge in a Benedictine convent. They soon had to leave this haven, since the nuns feared reprisals by Clare's relatives. At last the little sisters' community found a permanent home in San Damiano.

Still, Clare's battle for her Christian ideal was not yet over. She wanted radical poverty for her community. The community of poor sisters of San Damiano was not to have its income secured by property (which was then normal for all male and female cloisters). To depend entirely upon gifts and begging was even more revolutionary for a female than for a male community. Till the end of her life, Clare fought for the papal privilege that she not be forced by anyone to accept property. Two days before her death on August 11, 1253, the rule of her order was approved. It was the hour of her greatest joy.

Her Personality.
Clare must have been a very independent person, seeing how she set her own course against her family's will and against the church traditions of her age. The radical attitude of this

charming woman, radiant with goodness and affection (as portrayed by people who knew her), led her in her younger years to excessive penitential practices that ruined her health, causing Francis to intervene and moderate them. For the last thirty years of her life she was mainly sick in bed, and yet led her sisters with motherly care and conducted her convent through all difficulties with astounding energy.

Truly, Clare must have been an energetic personality. Yet her life was more influenced by the fact that, for her, the knowledge of Jesus Christ was absolutely central, and her main concern was, above all, to gain Jesus Christ. Her entire life was spent moving toward this goal (cf. Reading).

Accordingly, she made a great impression during her life on the faithful and upon leading churchmen. She was then canonized as a saint only two years after her death.

Petitions

Lord Jesus Christ, you call men and women to imitate you, and you give them the strength to tread new paths in the Church.

> Give the Church the strength for a credible witness to evangelical poverty . . .
> Guide religious organizations in their efforts to adapt to the times . . .
> Let the hidden prayers and sacrifices of contemplative convents bring forth good fruit for the Church . . . .

For you have freed us through the path of self-denial and poverty. You who live and reign forever and ever.

Sts. Pontian and Hippolytus (August 13)

TRIALS—THE MOST NORMAL THING IN THE WORLD?

Introduction

The first exact date by month and day in the history of the papacy is September 28, 235. On that day Pope Pontian, a prisoner in the mines of Sardinia, resigned his office, in order not to leave the Roman community without orderly leadership capable of functioning. This bishop of Rome later died (as did the Roman priest Hippolytus) as a slave laborer far from Rome. In Rome itself (and in all other Christian communities) the trials through inner and outer difficulties went on, spoken of in today's Reading: Do not be frightened by trial, for "it should not catch you off guard."

Penitential Rite

> "O Lord, you will not withhold your compassion from me.
> For I am beset with evils too many to be counted.
> My sins have fallen upon me and my sight fails me.
> O Lord, come to my rescue, Lord, come to my aid" (Ps 40:12,13a,14).
> Have mercy, Lord our God, have mercy . . .

Sts. Pontian and Hippolytus (August 13)

Talk

Encouragement. The Bible can sometimes be unbearably direct. The Reading today tells us that we should not be surprised if we as Christians encounter resistance and hardship and are tripped up by obstacles. It goes on to say, "Rejoice, instead, insofar as you share Christ's sufferings. . . ." It then continues, "Happy are you when you are insulted for the sake of Christ, for then God's Spirit in its glory has come to rest on you."

In other words, this means that if the Christian is really in communion with God, it will be shown by the magnitude of obstacles and hardships that he has to deal with. The more disturbed and endangered is his life, then so much closer is he bound to Jesus Christ.

Applied to the Church, this means that if she lives in a sort of peace, she must ask herself whether she still lives in imitation of Jesus Christ or has rather bought herself a false peace by being untrue to the Good News. If she, however, must search out her way through inner and outer hardships, she can then be certain that God in his Holy Spirit is with her on the way.

Let us take a hard look at this blunt utterance from the Reading. It is not the respectable place of the Church in public life, nor her well-developed organization, nor even her internal harmony free from factionalism and tensions, that tell whether the Church is in God's grace. In the presence of internal difficulties (theological quarrels, policy struggles, lack of priests . . .), under attack, suspicion, and slander from all sides, she then shows that Jesus Christ walks along with Christians through time.

Time Is Always Full of Distress. A look into history shows clearly that the Church was never without the presence of Jesus Christ. For "a trial by fire" (Reading) has burned since the first days of Christianity without ever being quenched. Each generation has experienced the Church of its time as the tested and endangered Church. And each age has felt in its burdens and hardships of faith that God's Spirit rests on it. Each age can justifiably say, "The time is full of distress, the cause of Christ is locked in mortal combat. And yet never has Christ moved more powerfully through earthly time, never was his coming clearer, never was his presence more palpable, never was his care more precious than now!"

Our Time. Our time as well has its share of inner and outer burdens upon our faith and our ecclesial life. They are also a sign for us that Christ moves powerfully through our time. In tune with the author of the Reading, we are not surprised by this. We will not be ashamed to belong to a Church that has to struggle with problems for which she still does not have solutions. Yes, we will perhaps still find strength to do good unto others amid all our trials (Reading). Above all, we will always "entrust" our "lives to a faithful Creator" in prayer (Reading).

Petitions

Lord Jesus Christ, you have gone before your Church on the way of the cross and have called upon her to follow you:

Be present to all who are reproached for the sake of your name . . . .
Protect bishops and priests from weariness and resignation when they are hindered in their ministry by secular restrictions . . . .
Strengthen the trust of all who have been left insecure by the Church's internal controversies in recent years . . . .
Remind all who feel that the renewal of the Church is not going fast enough, of the mystery of the cross . . . .

You who live and reign forever and ever.

The Assumption of Mary into Heaven (August 15)

ASSUMPTION, NOT ASCENSION

Introduction

"More life," "greater quality of life"—the open theme of political parties and the secret theme of effective advertising today. From all sides a "fuller life" is recommended and offered to us. Are we aware that Jesus Christ in a special way offers us more life? The feast of the Assumption of Mary into Heaven makes us conscious of the fuller life that God wants to bestow on all men and women.

Talk

Nearness of Death and Desire for Life. Externally, our world seems to be in order despite the threat of environmental pollution and the energy crisis. Seen from outside, most people in Europe and North America seem happy. Never before could they afford for themselves what they do now, and they thoroughly exploit the opportunities of the free world. Yet what goes on under the shiny surface?

Many older people saw much of death in wartime, through trenches and bombing raids, on the refugee trail or in the hunger and misery of postwar years. They wake up even now in a cold sweat because of nightmares. Young people are afraid of being shortchanged by life because they cannot afford what those modern saints, the idols of show business and of the jet set, dangle in front of them as a normal living standard. Others detect that a high standard of living and material wealth do not guarantee a fulfilled life, and they feel themselves to be defrauded out of authentic life precisely by our society of abundance.

And everyone is looking for "more life," a "better life," greater "quality of life." They are struggling for a higher standard of living. They work until they collapse with the purpose of being able to afford more. Or, they turn their backs on our industrial society in order to find happiness in the simple life of hippie-style movements. The pothead or the junkie goes tripping in order to expand the mind so as to experience more life. Meditation today is the style. People go to masters of meditation in west and east in order to discover hidden zones of their lives and to experience complete life. And many attempt it in a totally new way even with Jesus of Nazareth, whom the Gospel of John presents as saying: "I came that they might have life, and have it to the full" (Jn 10:10).

Fulfillment of Life in God. Why do more people not look to Jesus Christ in their search for fulfilled life? Why do so many see a threat to life in his message rather than the promise of true life?

For Jesus Christ understood himself to be the answer to the basic human question: where do I find more life? By the example of his life he showed us human beings that we attain selfless love if we strive to live more happily with one another. However, in his death and resurrection he also showed that the longing for fullness of life is fulfilled only beyond death.

On Easter, on every saint's feast, and particularly today, we proclaim in the communion of the Church that the human longing for more life is not a cruel delusion. Death does not prove it to be a great illusion. It finds its fulfillment in God. Since today we are celebrating the bodily assumption of Mary, the belief is uttered that in life with God the whole man comes into fulfillment. In him every human longing for life is fulfilled.

The Assumption of Mary into Heaven (August 15)

Assumption—not Ascension. To be sure, this fulfillment of life in God is realized in a different way than we may expect. We readily look for examples from our human experience to express what Jesus Christ has brought to us by way of fulfillment of life. On Easter, we look at new-blooming nature that does not stay in the grave of winter. We see a metaphor in a seed that dies in order to make new life possible.

Yet these comparisons can lead us to false conclusions. They give us the impression that life in God is the natural fruit of our present life. Yet, by the letter of today's Reading, Jesus Christ did not "rise," he was "raised up." Some people mistakenly see this feast as Mary's ascending into heaven, whereas the liturgical texts speak of it as her assumption.

In these formulations, the biblical conviction is expressed that our life does not attain its fulfillment by its own power, but rather that God intervenes to bestow this fulfillment on mortal man. This basic conviction is perhaps expressed better by this comparison: in farm fields during these late summer weeks we see hay—withered dead grass. Fulfillment in God is as if someone were to fill this destroyed grass with life again, a life that does not develop like a new plant out of the dying seed.

Mary—Archetype of Life. Our reflection today is on the bodily assumption of Mary into heaven. In Mary—taken up in body and soul into complete communion with God—is revealed to what end God has called all human beings. The longing for a fulfilled life is no deception. Life with God is complete human life. Yet it is also something new that God gives to us. On this feast we proclaim our faith that Jesus Christ has come so that we might have life and have it more abundantly (cf. Jn 10:10).

St. Stephen of Hungary (August 16)

USING HIS TALENTS

Introduction

Each of us has daily tasks and duties. Each of us has specific gifts and capabilities which can be applied to the performance of everyday responsibilities. We are not the king of Hungary as St. Stephen was. We also do not have the vast resources that he commanded. From God we have received our circumstances of life and our talents. Eventually we must also give an accounting of what we do with these gifts. Do we make use of them? Or do we bury them?

Penitential Rite

"O Lord, turn your ear to my cry.
Do not be deaf to my tears.
In your house I am a passing guest, a pilgrim, like all my fathers.
Look away that I may breathe again before I depart to be no more" (Ps 39:13,14a).

Have mercy, Lord our God, have mercy . . . .

Talk

Scenes from the Years 955 and 1000. In 955 nomadic pagan hordes on horseback from Hungary were threatening (once again) the west and its Christian culture. They were slaughtered on a battlefield south of Augsburg in Germany.—On Christmas Day, 1000, King Stephen of Hungary received by authorization of the pope the anointing as Christian king; with it, he received the royal right to establish dioceses and to appoint bishops. Much was accomplished in Hungary during this brief period.

Task and Goal. The Hungarians are a "foreign people" in Europe—their language demonstrates it even to this day. They are related neither to the Slavs (in Poland and in the Balkans) nor to the Latins (in Rumania) nor to the Germans (in the west). In the second half of the tenth century they sought union with western Europe. They accepted Christianity in its western form (and not—as the Slavs—through the mediation of Byzantine missioners). Obviously, the politically motivated acceptance of Christianity by the royal household did not consolidate the faith throughout the country. King Stephen actively collaborated in this long-term process, without being able to see it completed with full success by the end of his life (he died in 1038).

King Stephen. Stephen was baptized together with other members of the royal family in 973 or 974 at the age of four or five. Western European missioners shaped his religious life. He married Gisele, the sister of the German emperor.

His goverment's policy was to unite Hungary by establishing a strong monarchy and to protect the independence of his country from east (Byzantium) and west (the German Empire), from north (Slavic kingdoms) and south (Muslim influences) through clear alignment with the west. His battle against paganism and his commitment to the Church were tightly bound up with these political goals. This, however, did not mean that his devotion to Christianity arose only out of political considerations.

As monarch, King Stephen was concerned mainly for the organizational development of the Church. He founded monasteries as centers of missionary and spiritual life. He erected dioceses and provided for their material welfare through generous endowments. He had beautiful churches constructed in the centers of his kingdom as well as many simple chapels in the open countryside. He called in missioners from Bavaria and Bohemia, from Italy and Byzantium to his country to handle the necessary local work. At the same time he carried the Hungarian presence to other countries: he founded a Hungarian Benedictine monastery in Jerusalem, built a Hungarian pilgrims' hostel in Rome, and constructed a Hungarian church in Byzantium.

By way of securing his country's independence, he arranged that the Hungarian Church be directly subject to the pope; in this way, its organization remained independent from the Church in the German Empire.

Through his commitment, King Stephen decisively advanced the Christianization of Hungary. He transformed Hungary into a western country and gained respect for it throughout the whole known world. Christianity has influenced the country right up into our own times—even though the Church had had much difficulty there in recent decades. The Hungarians themselves honor King Stephen as their national saint, and his memorial day (August 20) is still observed as a public holiday, although now under the name of "Constitution Day."

Petitions

Let us pray for Christians in Hungary. God our Father:

Grant to Hungarian Christians courage and joy in their faith . . .
Strengthen the appropriate cooperation between the Church and other social powers . . .

St. Stephen of Hungary (August 16)

Give to Christian communities zealous pastors and competent workers in parishes . . . .

Hear our prayer through the intercession of St. Stephen and of all Hungarian saints. You who live and reign forever and ever.

St. John Eudes (August 19)

UNDERSTANDING THE LOVE OF CHRIST

Introduction

Is our basic religious attitude determined by fear of a punishing God—or more by grateful amazement over God's unfathomable love? With the first attitude, my most important question is: what *must* I do (so that God will find in me no grounds for punishment)? With the second attitude I will always ask: what *can* I do in everything (so that I can respond generously to his generous love)? With the first, my religious life will be unhappy and troubled. With the second, people will always notice the joy of faith in me. Along with St. John Eudes, have I understood something of the love of Christ that surpasses all understanding (Reading)?

Penitential Rite

"Come to me, all you who are weary and find life burdensome, and I will refresh you."   (Silence)   Lord, have mercy . . . .
"Take my yoke upon your shoulders and learn from me, for I am gentle and humble of heart."   (Silence)   Christ, have mercy . . . .
"For my yoke is easy and my burden light."   (Silence)   Lord, have mercy . . . .

St. John Eudes (August 19)

Talk

"For My Yoke Is Easy, and My Burden Light"? Is it our experience that a life with Jesus Christ is relatively easy and involves no heavy burdens? In the case of John Eudes (1601–1680) it seems—as it does in our lives—to have been, when seen from outside, something else altogether.

His religious path in life led him in 1623 into the community of the Oratory. He cherished his confreres as they did him. He took on responsible posts within the community. In 1643 he was dismissed from the community because he was clinging to his plan for establishing a seminary. Did this parting of ways come easy to him?

From 1632 to 1675 John Eudes worked tirelessly as a mission preacher. He would stay two or three months with his assistants in a given parish, would preach at least twice daily, heard confessions, and made peace among the people. Through his work he came to recognize how necessary a thorough religious and theological education was for future priests. Since, in his opinion, the traditional priestly training left much to be desired, he founded a community of priests that established seminaries at the same time as they worked in parish missions in various cities of France. To counteract the ill effects of prostitution, he founded a community of women who would look after "fallen girls" (as they were then called): from this foundation there developed the Sisters of the Good Shepherd, who still work in this spirit for the care of girls and women.

Along with an incredible amount of work and cares, his efforts also brought him strong hostility, calumny, and even rejection.

"Rooted in Love and Founded on It." And yet John Eudes did not collapse under the burdens of his life. At the same time, he was able to affirm completely the saying from the Gospel: ". . . for my yoke is easy and my burden light." The central message of Jesus was overwhelmingly clear to him, that his and our Father is the God of unselfish love. In the suffering and death of Jesus he did not see the face of a God who demands cruel satisfaction for offenses committed against him. He saw in the open heart of Jesus the symbol of the love by which God gave himself over for us even to the last breath and the last drop of blood. For this reason, John Eudes developed a deep personal devotion to the Heart of Jesus, and spread it in his pastoral work.

Since John Eudes knew himself to be hidden in this love (". . . rooted in love and founded upon it . . ."—Reading), he found it easy to bear the real and present toil and burden of his life and service, and not to lose heart in the midst of difficulties. Since he understood at least something of the love of Christ "which surpasses all understanding", it went without saying that he was to pass this love on tirelessly through his own life.

Would not things be easier in our lives if we were to count firmly on God's unfathomable love for us, and if we were to try to put this love into practice at least now and then?

Petitions

Father, from whose name every generation in heaven and on earth draws its name:

Grant that all Christians may grow in their hearts through your Spirit in power and strength . . .
Let Christ live by faith in their hearts . . .
Grant that they might know your love and understand it ever more deeply . . . .

God and Father of our Lord Jesus Christ, let us become more and more like you and thus come into our perfection. You who live and reign forever and ever.

St. Bernard of Clairvaux (August 20)

A MONK WHO LEFT AN IMPRINT ON HIS AGE

Introduction

Tourists in middle European countries very often stop for visits at old monasteries. Some are impressed by the massive castle-like monasteries of the baroque period in southern Germany and Austria. Others admire more the medieval cloisters of the Cistercians in Eberbach in Rheingau, in Maulbronn near Mühlacker, or in Heiligenkreuz near Vienna. In these edifices they are seeing foundations that go back to the origins of the Cistercians. Their amazingly rapid spread was indissolubly connected with the life of St. Bernard of Clairvaux.

Penitential Rite

Lord Jesus Christ, we follow many paths that lead us into error; you call us onto the way that leads to life: Lord, have mercy . . . .

We hear many words that are lying and deceitful; you speak the word of truth to us, by which we may live: Christ, have mercy . . . .

We see many lights that disappoint us and lead us astray; if we follow you, we will have the light of life: Lord, have mercy . . . .

Talk

Improbable Facts. In 1112, Cîteaux in Burgundy, France, was a poverty-stricken monastery that couldn't be compared with the great Benedictine abbeys of that age. The few monks there led an externally hard life of penance and mortification. The community was in danger of dying out because of a lack of vocations.

Then, suddenly, thirty academically trained respected clerics entered the abbey in order to share the hard life of the monks. Their leader was Bernard, a twenty-one-year-old nobleman. He had convinced his friends and brothers (even the married ones!) to undertake this new life along with him.

The thirty novices brought others in by their example. Three years later, two new foundations had to be established. At the age of twenty-five, Bernard became the abbot of the new abbey of Clairvaux. The influx of novices soon led to new foundations out of Clairvaux as well. Up until Bernard's death in 1153, sixty-eight daughter foundations derived from Clairvaux with hundreds of monks. They led a hard and simple life in which prayer and manual labor (and, increasingly, spiritual work) predominated.

New Upsurge of Faith. What meaning did this avalanche-like spread of new monastic life have? Reform circles in the Church had come to realize how worldly the Church had become and how little of the Spirit of Jesus Christ could be found in her. Even monasteries were rich, and monks were comparable to secular nobles in their life-style. The call grew loud in the Church for a Gospel-inspired life, and people concerned with religion sought—by the standards of their times—to live in greater faithfulness to Jesus Christ through the return of monasticism to simplicity of life.

The Cistercians evolved this ideal into livable form. The monks themselves were once again obliged to manual labor (the Benedictines had their serfs or their lay brothers for that purpose). The churches in the new cloisters could have only a small turret (and no tower). The liturgy was markedly sober and simple.

The Monk Who Guided World History. Bernard, as abbot of Clairvaux, was the soul of the Cistercian movement, which rapidly extended beyond the abbey and left its mark on all of western Europe. He went out from his monastery time and again to get involved in the issues of the times. He had to defend his monastic community against the attacks of the Benedictines. In internal church controversies he aligned himself with the legitimate pope and helped his cause toward success. He took a stand against heretical movements among the people and among theologians and did not spare even the conditions at the papal court in Rome from vehement criticism. Caught up in the ideals of his time, he won all of Europe over to a new crusade by his fiery preaching. The crusade, however, failed and brought on much suffering in Europe.

In all his political activity and in all his pastoral work, Bernard remained a monk whose major goal in life was to seek God. He found God in the God-man Jesus Christ and tirelessly led his monks and Christians of his time into a deeper Christ-centered piety through his preaching and writing.

Petitions

Merciful God, we humbly pray to you for your holy Church everywhere:

Fill her with truth and peace . . .
Cleanse her where she is corrupt . . .
Protect her from error . . .
Lift her up where lack of faith has brought her down . . . .

Father, hear our prayer through Jesus Christ our Savior, who lives and reigns with you forever and ever (cf. GL 27,1).

St. Pius X (August 21)

"FOR YOU BECAME VERY DEAR TO US"

Introduction

"I am incompetent and unworthy. Forget me!" Thus did Cardinal Sarto answer his fellow cardinals in the summer of 1903, when they elected him pope by a great majority. As he finally accepted the election, he urgently cried out to them, "Help me, I beg you, help me!" As Pius X, this pope did not always have a skillful hand in dealing with political problems of the universal Church (Modernism!). His strong points lay more in his work to revivify Christian living.

Penitential Rite

Lord Jesus Christ, patient and merciful: Lord, have mercy . . .
Lord Jesus Christ, generous to all who call upon you: Christ, have mercy . . .
Lord Jesus Christ, fountain of life and holiness: Lord, have mercy . . . (GL 768,2).

Talk

Pastor with All His Body and Soul. Joseph Sarto, son of a farmer, made his way through hardships to the priesthood. Beginning in 1858, he went through his famous nine-year cycles as curate, as pastor, as vicar general and theology professor, as bishop of Mantua and as cardinal of Venice, until his election as pope in 1903. Pastoral work remained throughout at the center of his interests. As pope, he still remained a master of speaking to the people in their own idiom (he kept the custom of giving a plain talk on the day's Gospel to the faithful every Sunday in the Vatican gardens).

Restore All Things in Christ. While his predecessor Leo XIII had concentrated his attention primarily on the outward life of the Church—above all, on the necessary balance between the modern world and Christian tradition—for the new pope the main goal was the internal renewal of the Church. In his first encyclical he wrote, "The guiding principle of our papal work is to restore all things in Christ, so that Christ might be all in everything."

Toward this goal were oriented several organizational measures: the revision of canon law, the reform of the Roman central offices of the Church, new editions of the Roman Breviary, and the Roman Missal. . . .

The revision of the breviary and the missal were aimed at the pope's central concerns: he knew that the Church could only be renewed if she lived by the mystery of the Eucharist. The reform of the liturgical books was to help priests and ordinary faithful "not to pray *in* the Mass, but to pray the *Mass,*" as he once expressed it. He also coined the term, the "active participation of the laity" in the eucharistic celebration (by this he clearly meant, beyond the common praying and singing, the inner share in the basic meaning of the Eucharist).

When the pope spoke of the "active participation" of the faithful in the Mass, he was concerned primarily with the reception of Holy Communion. At the beginning of our century it was still the custom to receive Holy Communion only on certain major feast days (Easter, All Saints, Christmas, church dedication . . .)—and then only after confession. Pius X set forth the principle for this practice: "No one, who sees himself to be in the state of grace and who approaches the holy table in the right spirit, should stay away from it." On the same principle, he also urged that children should be allowed to make their first Holy Communion as early as possible.

The Church clearly grasped the ideas of this saintly pope, insofar as the external full participation in the Mass through reception of Holy Communion is concerned. Yet we must still make a new appraisal of what it means to "approach the holy table in the right spirit": do we take our share in the Lord's Supper seriously enough? Do we let ourselves be consciously drawn into the love of Christ? Is our life shaped by the eucharistic celebration?

"For You Became Very Dear to Us." I believe that we first really take part with all our heart in the Eucharist when love for all people grows in us because of it; it is described in this way in today's Reading and Gospel, and shaped the life and work of Pope Pius x.

Petitions

Let us pray:

For the holy Church of God throughout the whole world. (Silence) For our Holy Father, Pope_____ . . .
For our bishops and priests . . .
For all the faithful . . .
For all people who, aware of it or not, are seeking after Jesus Christ . . . .

God our Father, let your face shine upon your servants, and lead them on the way of salvation. You who live and reign forever and ever.

Queenship of Mary (August 22)

"HAIL, HOLY QUEEN"

Introduction

Since the eleventh century Christians pray, "Hail holy Queen." This ancient prayer and its various versions still belong to our treasury of prayers. Today's memorial of the Queenship of Mary was first observed in 1954. We can ask ourselves whether our modern image of a queen carries the same meaning that Christians of earlier generations wanted to express when they gave Mary the title of queen. Perhaps we can learn from the text of this prayer what we might consider when we pray in the rosary, ". . . Jesus, who crowned you, O Virgin, in heaven."

Penitential Rite

Lord Jesus Christ, victor over death and the grave: Lord, have mercy. . .
You are always close to your Church: Christ, have mercy. . .
You will come again in glory: Lord, have mercy. . . .

Talk

Blest by God. For the Church, Mary is, from the very first, ever queen of God's grace. Her place in salvation history begins with her finding favor before God, who is with her (Gospel) and does great things for her (Magnificat). Her assumption into heaven and her crowning as queen are the final consequences of the fact that God took her into service as mother of the Redeemer—and enabled her to render this service. In her as queen God's grace shines forth.

"...Our Sweetness..." It is a source of gladness for the Christian that Mary was full of grace. "Hail our sweetness," says the prayer. What does this mean?

Let us look at everyday experiences for comparisons. Football fans are glad for their team when it wins. Rock fans are moved to tears when their idol is cheered. A parish is proud if its pastor becomes bishop. In these (and many similar) cases we rejoice with someone who stands out with excellence, because we have a special tie with him or her. On the one hand there is selfless rejoicing; on the other hand, something of the glory of the football team or the rock star or the pastor falls on us.

Something similar befalls the Church in relation to Mary. The Church knows herself to be united with Mary beyond Mary's death. She rejoices in Mary, who was chosen by God in a special way and brought to perfection in him. At the same time, we as Church are rather proud of our tie with her and that we bask in something of the light that falls on her (to put it in very human terms).

"Our Hope." If we look at old lives of saints, we will always find the same trait attributed to queens and princesses (e.g., Kunigunde, Matilda, Hedwig, Elizabeth): as ladies of high station their hearts were open to simple and lowly people and to the sick and the needy, and they gave them direct aid (in today's terms, they cut through the red tape to help them).

Now, in the "Hail, Holy Queen," the Church pictures herself in this way: "To you do we cry, poor banished children of Eve; to you do we send up our sighs, mourning, and weeping in this vale of tears." We are thus like the great host of the poor and needy that were found in every land in times past. Mary is similar, in her perfection with God, to those queens and princesses, and has the good qualities of these women in the fullest measure. As "Mother of mercy," she turns her "eyes of mercy" toward us. She stands before the Father as an intercessor for us and helps us where she can. She is (as the faithful of earlier ages really saw her) our last hope for uncomplicated and rapid help.

Show Us Jesus! Mary, blessed by God and fulfilled in God, is one in whom we rejoice. She has her eyes upon us, supports us and intercedes for us. She is Queen: she has this central place in the economy of salvation through Jesus Christ—and she uses this position only to "show us the blessed fruit of [her] womb, Jesus," and to lead us home to him.

Petitions

Heavenly Father, you took up Mary into heaven and gave her to us as a powerful intercessor. Hear our prayer:

Awaken joy in the Church over Mary's calling and perfection . . .
Strengthen in Christians the readiness to give themselves over to your plan of salvation after Mary's example . . .
Let the poor and the sick find help for their needs through her intercession . . .
Give the world peace through her mediation . . . .

For you desire to lead the whole world through her collaboration to Jesus, the blessed fruit of her womb. You who live and reign forever and ever.

St. Rose of Lima (August 23)

PATRONESS OF LATIN AMERICA

Introduction

It is possible nowadays that a young girl might shear her hair off to ward off her parents' marriage plans for her. But for a young girl to stick her hand into quicklime in order to disfigure herself physically, for her to wear a heavy chain around her body her whole life long, and to whip herself regularly, for religious reasons: these are things we learn about without at first any comprehension of them. Yet perhaps we can make the effort to grasp what kind of religious life lay behind these barely understood practices that we read about in the life of St. Rose of Lima.

Penitential Rite

Lord Jesus Christ, you are the treasure in the field for which it is worth selling everything else: Lord, have mercy . . .

You are the pearl worth our putting everything else for sale: Christ, have mercy . . .

You have gifted us with your fellowship as the valuable treasure and the fine pearl: Lord, have mercy . . . .

Talk

Shocking Radicalism. Again: this was a girl who whipped herself regularly, who slept on two planks, and who lived in a cabin built by herself in her parents' garden. She also was fasting most of the time

St. Rose of Lima 355

and prayed and meditated twelve hours a day in her humble hovel. We can leave aside the question whether this life-style manifests mental abnormality. Nor do we entertain any thought that we should imitate these forms of religious life.

Yet maybe our attention will be gained when we consider that this saint, known for her "religious excesses," strongly influenced the religious life of her home city of Lima, Peru.

In the Service of the Church in Pioneer Country.

Less than a hundred years had passed between the discovery of America and the birth of Rose in Lima in 1586. Her country was the "wild west" of that age. Rose belonged to the "master race" of the Spaniards who, on the backs of the bloodily conquered and oppressed Indians, set up a pleasant colonial life-style for themselves. Her austere personal life-style has to be seen against the background of much injustice perpetrated by her countrymen, for which she wanted to do penance.

Against this background we can first understand her constant service to the poor and needy. In the dispossessed and despised she saw Jesus Christ himself and thus served them with all her strength.

Another great concern of her life was mission work among the oppressed Indians. As a woman in the existing circumstances, she could not go to the aborigines in the forests and mountains of Peru. Yet she stirred the consciences of priests in Lima by her words and expressly challenged them to pastoral work among the Indians.

Living in her parents' garden as a hermit, the saint also founded the first nuns' cloister in her home town, to allow women in that pioneer country to lead a contemplative life in the service of the Church and for the spread of the faith.

Unconditional Discipleship.

Rose of Lima was not a woman who tortured herself in misled piety. Rather, she was a human being who was not enough for herself, who found Jesus Christ (just as the man in the Gospel found his treasure, and the merchant his pearl), who directed everything toward her union with Jesus Christ (hard penances, hours-long prayer . . .), and thereby became able to serve her neighbor. Her religious austerities were a sign of her uncompromising readiness to imitate Jesus Christ. Upon considering the life of this saint, I am reminded of a line that I read someplace or other: When I really want something, I am ready to pay the price for it.

Certainly there was much "imprudence" in the life of St. Rose of Lima. She died at thrity-one, because she had ruined her health by her penitential practices. Yet considering her radicalism, we have to ask ourselves what price will we pay for our faith? How much time do we allow for worship services? What sacrifices do we accept so that we might safeguard the treasure and the pearl of faith? Where do we put into practice our fellowship with Jesus Christ in service to our fellow man?

Petitions

God our Father, look upon the countries of Latin America. Hear our prayer by the intercession of St. Rose of Lima:

Awaken social responsibility among the wealthy . . .
Guard the poor from hatred and bitterness in their struggle for their rights . . .
Let rich and poor find one another in their common faith in the Good News of your love . . . .

For you want us to live together as your sons and daughters in your Spirit already in this world. You who live and reign forever and ever.

St. Bartholomew (August 24)

"A TRUE ISRAELITE"

Introduction

Apart from his name, the Gospels have little to tell about him. According to ancient traditions, he worked primarily in India and Armenia. His skull's crown is venerated in the cathedral of Frankfurt. Michelangelo presented him in the Sistine Chapel as a martyr whose skin had been removed (and portrayed himself on the separated skin). Bartholomew the apostle falls among the unknown apostles, who nonetheless—along with the better-known ones—built up the Church at the beginning as the circle of Jesus' disciples.

Penitential Rite

"Happy the man whose offense is forgiven, whose sin is remitted.
O happy the man to whom the Lord imputes no guilt, in whose spirit is no guile" (Ps 32:1f).

Have mercy, Lord our God, have mercy . . . .

Talk

The Twelve—Archetype of the Church. The faith of the Church rests upon the witness of the apostles who shared in Jesus' public life and who became certain that he lived in God when they saw the Risen One after the disaster of his death. In our Catholic tradition, we too readily see the twelve apostles as just predecessors of our bishops (and priests). Yet the count of twelve clearly derives from the twelve tribes of the people of the Old Testament. The number clearly tells us that Scripture sees in the circle of Jesus' disciples the basic cell of the whole Church of Jesus Christ (and not just of the hierarchy).

Thus much of what the Gospels tell us about the circle of the twelve apostles is applicable to all Christians and not just to bishops and priests. We can accordingly apply the story of the calling of Nathanael (whom many exegetes believe to be identical with Bartholomew) to our own way to Christ.

Can Anything Good Come from Nazareth? Nathanael was not impressed with Jesus of Nazareth. He was skeptical, and expressed his reservations. Yet he was also ready to approach this unusual man about whom everybody was talking and to make his acquaintance. He evidently accepted Philip's invitation to "come and see."

We find ourselves in good company when we have questions and problems regarding our faith—and express them openly. An unquestioning faith tends to be the exception in the spiritual climate of our age. If we, amid all our critical reservations and questions (regarding faith, church life, theology . . .) are prepared to rely on Jesus Christ in the Church that we know (and to allow ourselves to be inspired by him), then we, like Nathanael, are on our way toward him.

And when we see people who—like Nathanael—at first demonstrate their skepticism over the Christian faith, we should not write them off too soon. We can invite them, as Philip invited his friend, and thus lead them on to Jesus Christ.

Rabbi, You Are the Son of God. Nathanael went out of curiosity, but also with an open mind, to Jesus. The wandering preacher from Nazareth spoke to him. In this encounter, the future apostle was captivated by the mystery of Jesus. He confessed, "Rabbi, you are the Son of God, you are the King of Israel."

St. Bartholomew (August 24)

"You Will See Much Greater Things." As the Gospel of John describes it, Nathanael thus took only his first step toward Jesus. He joined him. Yet it was only in the course of his association with the earthly Jesus and in the course of his lifelong mystical communion with the Risen One that Nathanael grasped that God himself had come to humankind in Jesus of Nazareth. This Jesus was completely human and also completely divine. That is the real meaning of the metaphor of the angels of God ascending and descending on the Son of God.

We also find ourselves again in good company if we experience ourselves as growing in faith, and if we find that we are understanding ever more deeply the mystery of Jesus Christ in the course of our own lives. Since Jesus was patient with Nathanael, we too will be patient with every Christian who at first sees in Jesus Christ only a great man and who has yet some way to go before recognizing Jesus' mysterious communion with God.

Petitions

Let us pray with confidence in the intercession of St. Bartholomew:

For all those who are critical of the Christian message: Christ, hear us . . .
For all Christians who have particular problems of faith . . .
For those who proclaim the faith in parishes and schools . . . .

God our Father, hear our prayer through Christ our Lord.

St. Louis (August 25)

HOLINESS ON THE ROYAL THRONE

Louis XIV, the Sun King of France, is reputed to have said, "I am the State." We can scarcely imagine this statement as ever coming from the mouth of Louis IX (1214–1270). During his long reign (beginning in 1226) he was guided by the word of Jesus: You shall love the Lord your God with all your heart, and you shall love your neighbor as yourself.

Penitential Rite

"Release those bound unjustly, set free the oppressed, break every yoke." (Silence) Lord, have mercy . . . .
"Share your bread with the hungry, shelter the oppressed, clothe the naked." (Silence) Christ, have mercy . . . .
"Remove from your midst oppression, false accusation, and malicious speech." (Silence) Lord, have mercy . . . .

Talk

Personal Life. The young king remained at first under the direction of his mother (until 1252). She was a capable politician, yet also a zealous mother. Her anxiety was lest her son should become independent, and she repeatedly interfered in the young king's marriage, even in its most intimate areas. Did he, under this burden, learn the patience that made him so famous among his contemporaries?

St. Louis (August 25)

Louis and his wife were happily married. She had eleven children, of whom nine survived childhood. He and his wife were in harmony in the simple and religious structure of their daily lives. The king participated in daily Mass. He prayed regularly the Liturgy of the Hours. He put aside all luxury in his clothing. He took on corporal penances (completely in line with the taste of his times): he fasted, he whipped himself, and he wore a penitential belt.

Service to the Kingdom. His fasting fits in well with today's Reading. Yet the other side of his austere personal way of life was his effort to rule his country with awareness of his responsibilities. True, he was still a child of his time, and not all of his measures would meet with our approval (such as his policies toward blasphemers, heretics, and Jews). He not only served the poor personally (and was repelled not even by lepers), he also undertook many attempts to bring peace and tranquillity to his country. He carried out legal reforms and curbed the arbitrary powers of regional lords. He forbade duels and mandated a forty-day armistice for all cases of quarrels among his vassals (they were accustomed to resorting to force). Defendants and plaintiffs both had free access to him, as far as possible. He supported the foundation of the University of Paris, and the country had him to thank for a great number of charitable institutions.

His efforts to rule in the spirit of the great commandment of love was manifest in his foreign policy as well. He renounced some conquests that his grandfather had achieved, and freely gave back the territories. People trusted his integrity so greatly that they called him in as arbiter in disputes throughout Europe.

His Crusades. True to the mentality of his times, the holy king turned his gaze toward the Holy Land. While political motives predominated for other European rules, religious motives prevailed in Louis' mind and led him to initiate two campaigns, with heavy losses and little success, in Egypt and Tunisia. It was his love for Jesus Christ, whose humanity was being taken seriously again precisely during that period.

It was the desire of Christianity to convert the Moslems and to possess the land in which Jesus had lived, so as to have a tangible remembrance of him, one more important than all the relics that people were collecting at that time in Europe.

The first time, Louis sojourned from 1248 until 1252 in Egypt and Palestine. After initial successes he was captured and had to pay a heavy ranson to free himself and his soldiers. In 1270 he set out once again. This time, however, he reached only Tunis in North Africa with his forces. By the walls of this city he fell victim to the pestilence that was epidemic among his troops.

When Pope Boniface VIII canonized King Louis of France in 1297, he was not just playing politics; he comprehended the veneration that France felt for her dead king.

Petitions

Almighty God:

Strengthen the solidarity of bishops and faithful in France . . .
Aid the dialogue between progressive and conservative groups in the French Church . . .
Bless the efforts of French laypeople and priests to give credible witness to the Good News among the working class. . . .

For it is your will that the Church proclaim your love in word and deed. You who live and reign forever and ever.

St. Joseph Calasanz (August 25)

YES TO THE WILL OF GOD?

Introduction

"Father, your will be done," we pray each time in the Lord's Prayer. An old familiar phrase can become stale for us to the point that we no longer think on it. How do we pray the Our Father when we have to make decisions for our own future? Do we hold to it if we, because of difficulties and burdens, have doubts about the love of God? St. Joseph Calasanz (1556–1648) tried to keep this phrase of the Lord's Prayer at the center of his life. He once said, "We must let God act. All that is important is that we know and do his will."

Penitential Rite

"O Lord, do not rebuke me in your anger; do not punish me, Lord, in your rage.
My guilt towers higher than my head; it is a weight too heavy to bear.
O Lord, do not forsake me!
My God, do not stay afar off!
Make haste and come to my help, O Lord, my God, my savior!" (Ps 38:2,5,22f).

Have mercy, Lord our God, have mercy . . .

Talk

Lord, What Is Your Will? Joseph Calasanz, of Spain, looked for a long time until he found his true task as a follower of Christ. After being ordained a priest in 1583, he was soon appointed vicar general of his home diocese in northern Spain. His career advancement in church administrative work seemed assured.

Yet, after nine years, he resigned his post. He gave away nearly all of his considerable fortune and went to Rome. There he led an unusual life over the next five years. Every day he arose at midnight and, by dawn, would visit all seven principal churches in Rome. During the day he would help the poor and the sick wherever he could (Reading).

During these years, he became more and more aware of the need of so many children wandering around the streets of Rome homeless and abandoned. Joseph attempted to move the "establishment" (Roman pastors, Jesuits, Dominicans) to take some action against this need. When he failed in this (everyone pleaded "overwork"), he himself founded the first tuition-free school in Europe in 1597 with the help of like-minded people.

In this way the priest from northern Spain found his place for life. His school grew rapidly. With his confreres he formed the Order of Piarists in 1621 which soon spread beyond Rome.

"We Must Let God Act." Joseph Calasanz looked for a long time before he realized what life's work God had for him. In the second half of his life, God strengthened him for something of trials. His school was attacked by hostile students from other (church) schools. A group of confreres sought to depose him as founder. They slandered him, had him arrested, and spared him no trick or humiliation. A lady relative of the reigning pope was enraged that her confessor (a confrere of St. Joseph Calasanz) was transferred to another city. She got the pope to dissolve the society (in 1646). Thus, shortly before his death, the ninety-year-old founder stood by the ruins of his life's work. He expressed

his attitude through all these unhappy years in this way: "It is not wise to concentrate on secondary causes and not see God, who sends us these things for our greater benefit." (Footnote: Eight years after the founder's death, the Piarists were once again recognized as a religious society.)

"Father, Your Will Be Done." All that is important is that we know and do his will." Joseph Calasanz lived by this motto. He recognized his life's calling in the signs of the times. He saw the need, and gave himself over to it energetically. God's will in our lives reveals itself generally in the same way. Where (in personal relations, in the parish, in public life . . .) do tasks await me? Where is God waiting for me?

If difficulties occur as we work at our tasks, we—like today's saint—will know that God does not abandon us and does help us, even in these hours, to do his will: to fulfill his mandate with trust in his help.

Petitions

Let us pray with confidence in the intercession of St. Joseph Calasanz:

> For understanding and patience on the part of parents who have growing children. (Silence)
> For responsible awareness and kindness on the part of teachers in our schools . . .
> For joy in faith and love for people on the part of all who give witness to the faith in school and religious instruction . . . .

God of kindness, help the Church through word and deed to pass on the faith to young people. You who live and reign forever and ever.

St. Monica (August 27)

A MOTHER WAITS

Introduction

Mothers and their sons—they are an inexhaustible theme in human history. Mothers who are proud of their sons. Mothers who suffer on account of their sons.

So many mothers suffer today because of their growing children, concerned for their religious path—as Monica did 1,600 years ago over the religious development of her son Augustine. She prayed her whole life long for the conversion of her problem child.

Penitential Rite

Lord Jesus Christ, you are patient with your disciples: Lord, have mercy . . .

You accept sinners with full understanding: Christ, have mercy . . .

You forgive over and over again: Lord, have mercy . . . .

Talk

Patience with her Husband. Monica was raised in a Christian family. She then married a pagan. For years she put up with his unpredictable bad temper and his marital infidelity; she sought to win him for the faith more by the witness of her life than by a stream of words. At long last her husband became a catechumen and was baptized on his deathbed.

Patience with her Son. Monica had her son Augustine accepted as a catechumen shortly after his birth and took charge of his religious education. In her family, infant baptism was apparently not the norm.

Her son grew apace. Monica could be proud of his accomplishments in school. Yet in the religious area her Augustine went off the track. As a young student he was a follower of the Manichaean heresy for a time. He lived with a woman and made no arrangements to marry her. He soon had an illegitimate child to care for.

Even when Monica could not approve her son's ways, she still loved him. When Augustine, as professor, was moving from Carthage to Rome, she wanted to go with him. The mother's nearness was burdensome to the son. He deceived her in order to be able to sail away without her. One can imagine Monica's disappointment!

Yet she soon found ways and means to travel after her son. She found him in Milan, where he had established contact with St. Ambrose. At age thirty-three, Augustine drew an end to his life as he had lived it till then. He had himself baptized, and in the ensuing years of his life became more and more a great man of faith and a theologian. Shortly after the conversion of her son, Monica died during the return trip to Africa in 387.

Augustine brings out in an overview of his mother's life that she drew the power for a life of active love for neighbor and for her patient waiting for his conversion from her regular participation in the Mass and from her intensive life of prayer. He also relates that on one occasion a bishop said to his mother, "It is impossible that the son of so many tears should perish."

Waiting in Patience and Praying. Monica prayed for the conversion of her husband. He accepted baptism on his deathbed. She cared for the welfare of her son and was able at last to rejoice at his conversion.

"Too beautiful to be true," some of you may be thinking. You may have been putting up for decades with the fact that your husband has no religious interest. You have been waiting a long time for your daughter to return to the Church and for your son finally to be married in the Church. And you still see no sign that your prayers have been heard.

Let us calmly consider the fact: children today follow different paths than their parents in the area of religion, and they do not always find their way back to the religious values of their family of origin. This causes great pain to many of you. What stance should you take? Excessive pressure will yield nothing. Yet you will not decline to speak a prudent word of invitation or advice at the right moment. And you will carry your children (and your husband) in prayer to God. If you remain bound, waiting and praying, to your children, then it will also prove true for your children that "it is impossible that the child of so many tears should perish"—even if this child does not find God along the lines of the visible Church.

Petitions

God, we call you our Father. You have given parents the responsibility for their children.

> Let children grow up into a deep and lively faith in the fellowship of the Church . . . .
> Help them in their search for their vocations and their life partners . . . .
> Grant that they may, throughout their glad and bitter life experiences, become attentive to you and to your Good News . . . .

For restless are our hearts, until they rest in you.

St. Augustine (August 28)

GOD STANDS AT THE END OF THE ROAD

Introduction

"Great are you, O Lord, and exalted beyond all praise. And yet man will praise you, this tiny particle of your creation. You yourself urge him on: for you have created us for yourself, and restless are our hearts until they rest in you." The great Augustine, who wrote these lines in his *Confessions*, felt this unrest of the human heart over God in the errors and mistakes of his youth, and in the theological work and pastoral practice of his adulthood.

Penitential Rite

"O Truth! You, light of my heart! I lost myself in earthly things and became darkness unto myself." (Silence) Lord, have mercy . . . .

"I detected your voice behind me inviting me to return, yet I could hardly hear it over the noise of the unruly." (Silence) Christ, have Mercy . . . .

"I do not want to be my own life. I have done evil out of myself, I have become death to myself. Now, however, I live in you." (Silence) Lord, have mercy . . . .

(Augustine)

Talk

Errors and Mistakes. Augustine (354–430) had a lively mind. He was unusually temperamental, excessively sensitive, and all too aware that learning came easy to him. He was able to pursue his studies only with aid from a patron, who provided money for his tuition and lodging. At sixteen, the money was no longer available to him. He had to interrupt his studies, and soon joined a group of young rowdies who made trouble throughout his hometown of Hippo, in North Africa. When he went to Carthage to continue his studies, he took a girl as his mistress and had a son by her.

Success in studies made the young intellectual proud, and arrogant. Not yet baptized yet still officially enrolled as a catechumen, he mocked his mother's piety. Yet he was also driven by an inner unrest and by his quest for the meaning of life and of truth. He looked for the answers to his questions from Greek and Roman philosophers and from the Christian sect of Manichaeans. He even turned to the Bible but was turned off by its mediocre translation into Latin.

Conversion. Augustine experienced his definitive conversion at the age of thirty-two in Milan, where he had a position as professor. His studies and his encounter with Ambrose, the renowned bishop of Milan, had prepared him. He discovered Christ as the center of his life—and after this experience he could hardly grasp why he had taken so long to break through to the truth of revelation. Looking back on his life, he wrote in his *Confessions:* "Too late have I loved you, O Beauty, ever old, ever new—late have I loved you. How could this be? You were in me, and I myself was outside of myself. You called me, and your cry pierced through my deafness; you shone forth, and your brightness banished my blindness; you emitted your fragrance, I breathed it in, and now I sigh for you; I tasted you, and now I hunger and thirst for you; you touched me, and I was aflame for the peace that you give."

St. Augustine (August 28)

Theologian and Pastor. Augustine was baptized on Easter of 387; shortly thereafter he returned to his home town of Hippo in North Africa. He sold his property and founded a monastic community; other interested men, who dedicated their lives to prayer and study, joined him. The faithful soon called upon him to be their priest; then, in 396, he became bishop of Hippo. As priest and bishop, he considered himself as servant of the ordinary people of his diocese [Gospel]. He was able to speak directly to his people and to inspire them, something we can clearly see in the many homilies by him that have come down to us. At the same time, he participated in the Church's internal controversies in those times as a leading theologian. In his great work, *The City of God,* he sought to explore the meaning, in the light of faith, of the great turmoil of his age, of the decline of the Roman Empire, of the disorder of the tribal migrations, and of the emergence of new centers of power among the Germanic tribes. He died in 430 while his see city was under siege by Germanic Vandals.

God Stands at the End of the Road. "Sing and walk about, for God stands at the end of the road," Augustine often said. He went down many wrong paths until he discovered Jesus Christ and God in him. Following his conversion, he did not tire of penetrating even more deeply into the mystery of God. Yet he always realized that God was already acting in him by the Holy Spirit. And he often prayed as we today can pray with him:

> Breathe in me, O Holy Spirit, that all my thoughts may be holy.
> Act in me, O Holy Spirit, that all my works may be holy.
> Draw me, O Holy Spirit, that all I love may be holy.
> Strengthen me, O Holy Spirit, that all I guard may be holy.
> Guard me, O Holy Spirit, that I may never lose what is holy.

The Beheading of John the Baptist (August 29)

CAN WE TRUST IN GOD?

Introduction

"For whoever relies upon God, him God will not abandon" (GL 295,3). Can we really abandon ourselves to God? Does he protect us in dangers and hardships? How does he protect us? What experience with God's help do we have in our lives?

Penitential Rite

God speaks: "When he calls, I shall answer: 'I am with you.' I will save him in distress and give him glory. With length of life I will content him; I shall let him see my saving power" (Ps 91:15ff).

Have mercy, Lord our God, have mercy . . . .

Talk

Jeremiah. ". . . For I am with you, to deliver you, says the Lord" [Reading]. Jeremiah, filled with anxiety, received this promise when he was called to be a prophet. What did this deliverance involve?

Jeremiah fulfilled God's mandate as best he could. He quickly learned that his religious opponents would fight him; yet did he also

The Beheading of John the Baptist (August 29)

learn that they would not overcome him since God was with him? [Reading]. He had to defend himself in court against the charge of blasphemy (chap. 26). He was arrested, flogged, and placed in stocks (chaps. 19–20). He had to disappear in order to escape his adversaries (chap. 35). He was imprisoned as a threat to soldiers' morale and as an archtraitor (chap. 37). He was cast into a clammy cistern, where he was supposed to perish in torment (chap. 38); however, he was rescued at the last minute.

True, Jeremiah did make it through all these perilous situations with his life. But is this what God's deliverance really is?

John. What do we see in the fate of John the Baptist, on whom there was the hand of the Lord (Lk 1:66)? He brought to his people the "knowledge of salvation" (Lk 1:77), yet God did not shield him from the hatred of Herodias. Herod had him arrested at her instigation. She had to wait a long time for her hour, but she finally gained the prophet's murder [Gospel]. Again: is this God's deliverance for those to whom he promises it?

We Ourselves. Surely a few of us have been rescued in our own lives out of dangerous situations. One may have stayed alive amid mortal dangers in wartime. Another, as if by a miracle, may have gotten out safe and sound from a totally demolished car after a traffic accident. Still another may come through a dreaded cancer operation successfully, and feel as if new-born. . . By faith, we will see in these life-situations of ours the love of God in action, who never abandons us and walks with us throughout our lives (cf. Gl 295,3).

Yet we also clearly realize that God does not shield his faithful ones from every difficulty. He did not protect Jeremiah and John from enmity and pain. He did not spare his son, Jesus Christ, from his disciples' lack of understanding nor from the hostility of the Pharisees. He did not rescue him from the way of the cross nor from death on the cross. Jesus of Nazareth, in all faithfulness to God and in all the love of his Father, had to drink from the cup of suffering, just as Jeremiah and John had to drink it. Should we then wonder if God does not protect us in our lives from every hard hour, and does not keep us away forever from sickness and death?

But then, where can we see this help of God who stays with us to deliver us? [Reading]. We too know, along with Jeremiah and John, in the dark hours of our lives, that we are not alone. We draw strength from our conviction that God is with us, even if we cannot understand what good it is for us.

With our faith in the death and resurrection of Jesus, we know, more profoundly than could Jeremiah and John as men of the Old Testament, how God delivers us [Reading]. God was with Jesus of Nazareth during his life and in his death, and is with him beyond death. He did not abandon him on the cross; he delivered him into unending life. This is where God's care for us will be finally evident: God, in whom we place our trust, will not abandon us at the hour of our death and will give us everlasting life. Knowing of this final deliverance we can, with Jeremiah and John and all believers, place our trust completely in God.

Petitions

Let us pray to God, our almighty Father:

Let us pray for all who, carried away by their passions, bring down injustices upon other people . . .
For all who have to bear with the moods and demands of others . . .
For all who cause trouble for others by reason of their own recklessness and insecurity . . . .

Almighty God, let everyone feel your presence. Protect them in the perils of this life and give them at last eternal joy with you. You who live and reign forever and ever.

St. Gregory the Great (September 3)

THE LAST ROMAN ON THE PAPAL THRONE

Introduction

War, natural catastrophes, pestilence, uprooting—these were so much a part of the normal order of things in Italy at the time of Pope Gregory the Great (540–604), that a contemporary gladly praised everyone who died for leaving behind forever the catastrophes of this earth. The pope himself had gained the appellation "the Great" not for his contributions to church music ("Gregorian chant" is named after him) but rather for his effective and practical dedication to the Church and to all of Italy.

Penitential Rite

"I kept it secret and my frame was wasted. I groaned all the day long. But now I have acknowledged my sins; my guilt I did not hide. I said: 'I will confess my offense to the Lord.' And you, Lord, have forgiven the guilt of my sins" (Ps 32:3,5).

Have mercy, Lord, our God, have mercy. . .

Talk

Total Service and Longing for Solitude. As a young patrician, Gregory set out on the career of state official. At the age of thirty, he became (in our terminology) Rome's mayor. His term of office was remembered favorably by the Roman populace, and contributed to his election twenty years later as pope.

However, the successful civil administrator withdrew suddenly into the quiet of his ancestral home, which he converted into a monastery. His secret desire was for monastic life in solitude. During his whole life he stood in tension between his heart's inclination and the demands of his times. He resolved this tension with this principle: "We ought indeed to long for silence with our hearts, and yet defer it until tasks have been accomplished."

This basic readiness for service to all led him to accept the office of deacon in one of the seven sectors of Rome, giving him responsibility for administration and charity. His openness to service led him, as papal envoy to Constantinople, to the seat of the emperor, who at that time was governing Rome as well. It finally led him to accept, with a heavy heart, his election as pope.

A Practical Man. In 590 (the year of his election to the papacy), the political and social structures of Italy were shaken to their depths by the storms of the tribal migrations. Natural catastrophes worsened the situation. As a practical man, Gregory directed his efforts to where they would do some good. He had a clear perception of what would be possible here and now. At the same time, he looked after not only the Church but also all of Italy, which was left without political leadership.

Gregory the Great, by his talent for practical matters, put the finances of the Roman Church into order and channeled the surplus into the care of the many refugees fleeing to Rome away from the Germanic hosts. He sought contact with the leaders of the Germanic migratory tribes, even though they were anything but Christian rulers or were adherents of Arianism. He was able and willing in some instances to secure peace by massive financial resources, and to secure the liberty of prisoners with ransom money.

His literary activity—he is also venerated as a doctor of the Church—also had a thoroughly practical purpose. His letters give evidence of his tireless concern for the souls entrusted to him. His other writings had the aim of putting faith into living practice.

Servant of the Servants of God. In this manner, Gregory carried out his service as pope in the spirit of today's Readings. He did not give in to discouragement, and he won the respect of his contemporaries by proclaiming the truth openly (Reading). In all that he did, he was everybody's servant (Gospel). So strongly was this the inner attitude of the great pope, that he expressly rejected the title of "universal pope" flatteringly accorded to him. Rather, he assumed the title that is still born by the popes: *servus servorum Dei*—servant of the servants of God.

Petitions

Let us pray for our Pope,————. . . .

Protect him with your power and guide him with your love. . . .
Provide him with aides who are responsible and understanding. . .Christ, hear us. . . .
Strengthen him with your power in all his cares and disappointments. . . .
Let him, together with all Vatican authorities, advance the vitality and the unity of the Church. . . .

For you, O Lord, are the shepherd and guide of all the faithful. You who live and reign forever and ever.

The Birth of Mary (September 8)

DAWN OF SALVATION

Introduction

The loveliest dawn does not shed light of itself. It takes its glowing light from the sun that it precedes. Christian piety has made use of this image to describe the mystery of Mary. She is called the "dawn of salvation." She draws her light only from Jesus Christ, the true sun. Her birth, which we celebrate today, has meaning only because she was called, in the Holy Spirit, to be the Mother of Jesus (Gospel).

Penitential Rite

"The Lord is kind and full of compassion, slow to anger, abounding in love.
How good is the Lord to all, compassionate to all his creatures.
All your creatures shall thank you, O Lord, and your friends shall repeat their blessing" (Ps 145: 8–10).

Have mercy, Lord our God, have mercy . . . .

Talk

The Birth of the Mother of Jesus. Following the death and resurrection of Jesus, the young Church at first had little interest in his early years of life or in his family circumstances. Only the later Gospels

The Birth of Mary

of Luke and Matthew include an infancy narrative in their presentation of the public life and suffering of Jesus. Their first concern was to show that Jesus of Nazareth was the Messiah "from the beginning" (and not just from the baptism in the Jordan onward) and was the one who would "free his people from their sins" (Gospel). Jesus' parents are spoken of only marginally: Matthew portrays Joseph as the archetype of a God-fearing man; Luke presents Mary as the archetype of the Church, understandable only as coming from Jesus Christ.

Only afterwards did pious legends dwell more closely on the person of Mary. In a writing from the second century (the so-called "proto-gospel of Jesus"), accounts were given of the miraculous birth of Mary. This source, however, does not provide historical information free from uncertainty. Following the pattern of many Old Testament tales, the story is told how God, by a miraculous intervention, creates the woman whom he has destined for the task of being the Mother of God. Joachim and Anne (Mary's parents) were childless. In their pain, they prayed to God, who then promised the already aged couple a child—and the miracle of the pregnancy took place. The child stood out from the beginning by reason of her special piety, and thus gave the best forecast for the fulfillment of her future task.

Mary, "Dawn of Salvation": these pious legends present Mary in this way in speaking of her birth and childhood. They see Mary only in relation to Jesus Christ and to God's work of salvation. In the manner of her birth the care of God for men shines forth, and by her birth God is glorified.

In the belief that "Mary, the Virgin Mother of God, was conceived without original sin" (the title of the feast for December 8), we confess the same conviction, on another level, as the pious legends from the early Church: God prepared Mary in a special way for her task of being the mother of the Redeemer; in her special charge, the love and greatness of God shine forth.

God with Us. Thus is the birth of Mary placed in the whole history of our salvation. The God who revealed himself in the burning thornbush as the God who is with his people; who showed his concern for his people in handing down the Law on Mount Sinai, and in the trek to the Promised Land; who himself saw to it that his people had the necessary leaders in the course of their history (e.g., by the miraculous birth of Samuel): this God showed his intention to be "God with us" (Gospel) also by calling John the Baptist to be the forerunner of Jesus (made evident by the sign-filled circumstances of his birth) and by enabling Mary, through preservation from original sin (also made evident by the sign-filled circumstances of her birth) to be the mother of his Son. Seen in this way, the birthday of Mary is a sign indicating Jesus Christ, in whom God clearly reveals that he is the God who will remain with us forever.

Petitions

Gracious God, in your special favor toward Mary, the mother of your Son, you reveal to us that your love holds true for all men and women:

> Help your Church to do your will in love . . . Bind the destinies of nations to peace and salvation . . . Teach the rich to share with the poor . . . Make us credible witnesses to your love . . . .

For you intend to be God with all men through us. You who live and reign forever and ever.

St. John Chrysostom (September 13)

ONE WHO STANDS UP FOR SOMETHING SETS HIMSELF APART

Introduction

Chrysostom—a name seldom found in the baptismal registers of our parishes. It is a name that we can more easily imagine as borne by members of religious orders. Today's saint himself did not receive the name at baptism. As an addition to John, his baptismal name, his contemporaries gave him the name "Golden Mouth" on account of his powerful preaching which greatly influenced his listeners.

Penitential Rite

Lord Jesus Christ, your Word directed to us often lands "on the footpath" and thus cannot grow: Lord, have mercy. . . .

It often lands "on rocky ground" and thus can take no deep root: Christ, have mercy. . . .

It often lands "among thorns" and is choked off by our selfish desires and anxieties: Lord, have mercy. . . .

Talk

Quotations. "If you fear someone, you will also be despised by him." "There is nothing worse than conformity. It robs people of reasoning reflection and gives them a name for dullness, yes, and goes so far as to make them completely unreasoning." "If we are conversing about light matters and notice that someone in the group is not paying attention, we consider it an insult. Yet we do not think that we are disrespectful to God when, while he is speaking to us of important matters, we nonetheless are not attentive to his words and turn our minds elsewhere."

These are a few quotations from John Chrysostom. When he preached, it was not boring for his listeners. Who was this man? What was his destiny?

A Long Path to Priestly Service. John was born in 350 in Syria, and was baptized around the age of twenty. He first studied law and classical rhetoric. After completing this education, he made a thorough study of theology and received minor orders. He then retired to the mountains for a long time, to live as a monk (which at that time was "in" among young people). Yet it became clear to him in solitude that Jesus Christ was calling him to service in the community. He returned to his home city of Antioch to become a deacon at age thirty-four and a priest only when he was thirty-nine. Among his own he worked in the following years as pastor, preacher, and writer.

Bishop of Constantinople. In the capital of the empire, people learned of the preacher from Antioch and of his ability to move men and women by the force of his words. The emperor used subterfuge to lure the simple priest to come out of the province to Constantinople and made him the bishop of the Capital.

Yet the new patriarch did not address the upper class of the metropolis and of the imperial court only with his mouth. He himself led a strict and simple life. He spoke up for the poor and admonished the rich. He labored for church renewal. At times he became hard, unbending, ironic, and sarcastic in his pastoral zeal. He was not spared the rejection, hate, and enmity of all whose unchristian life he forthrightly denounced. When he became a victim along with other bishops in the empire of internal church controversies (against which his calling as

St. John Chrysostom

bishop of the Eastern Roman capital did not help), his fate was sealed: Chrysostom was packed off into exile. The bishop was seized during the Easter services in his cathedral and deported to the empire's frontiers. Because he continued his pastoral work and preaching in his new place of residence, he was finally banished to the distant shores of the Black Sea. On his way there, which the ailing bishop had to traverse by foot, he died on September 14, 407.

One Who Stands Up for Something Sets Himself Apart. Chrysostom dedicated himself as priest and bishop to the Church. It may have been that his temperament sometimes got the best of him, which earned him the criticism and enmity of many people. Yet he never doubted God's faithfulness. He died after saying these words: "Glory to God for everything. Amen."

Petitions

Lord Jesus Christ, hear our prayer:

We pray for all bishops, priests, and lay people, who give service by proclaiming the Word. (Silence) Christ, hear us. Christ, graciously hear us.
We pray for all those who, in giving witness to their faith, run into misunderstanding and hostility. . .
We pray for all who, in their devotion to the Church, are burdened with the cross. . . . .

Lord, let their trust in you not be shaken, and let them not become discouraged in their dedication to your cause. You who live and reign forever and ever.

The Triumph of the Cross (September 14)

IN THE CROSS THERE IS SALVATION

Introduction

Crosses on church steeples and in cemeteries. Crosses in our streets and in our fields. Crosses in our churches and in our homes. Crosses around our necks—made of silver or wood. Gothic crosses and baroque crosses, images of the cross in traditional and contemporary forms . . . Do we see the cross of Jesus Christ, raised up at that time on Golgatha, in all these crosses? What does the cross on the altar mean? The sign of the cross, with which we began this Eucharist?

Penitential Rite

"Jesus, burdened with the cross, like a lamb led to the slaughter, fallen under the weight of the cross": Lord, have mercy. . . .

"Jesus, nailed to the cross, cast into abandonment, dead on the cross": Christ, have mercy. . . .

"Jesus, laid in the tomb, descended into the realm of the dead, risen in glory": Lord, have mercy . . . (GL766,4).

Talk

"Triumph of the Cross"? We have not hurled the wood of the cross from Golgatha away like garbage into the dump of world history. We have preserved the cross of Christ as the center of our faith and have

placed it in the middle of our communities. The persecuted Christians of the first centuries engraved it into their tombstones. Later generations displayed it in the openness of churches and of everyday living. Artists gave expression to their devotion in touching scenes of the crucifixion. Believers had the cross fashioned as a symbol of salvation with gold and gems.

We have glorified the cross in its triumph. Yet have we not also obscured its true message? Who sees the bond of the bishop's gold cross or the silver cross around one's own neck with Jesus' crucifixion? How many people, in museums and churches, admire the cross merely as an interesting object in art history, without reflecting on the reality it is intended to symbolize? Is my purchase of a cross only a matter of artistic taste, or is it primarily a matter of faith (which does not exclude a reasonable awareness of style)?

A Sign of Jesus' Death and Resurrection. In the cross there is only salvation and life for us (GL205,1), if we look through the signs (more or less artistically done) to the cross on Golgotha. When on Golgotha, we look upon him who died on the cross for us, who thereby returned home to God and opened for us the way of fulfillment. Not in the wood of the cross, but rather in him who suffered and died on the cross, is there salvation, life, and hope (GL205,1). For that reason, it is good that we normally have in our Catholic tradition of piety the image of Jesus on the cross (and not the empty cross used in part of the Protestant tradition).

"God So Loved the World . . . " We rightly understand the suffering and death of Jesus on the cross when we see in him, according to the Gospels, the revealing of God's love.

In the past, we talked glibly of offending God and of necessary atonement for the sins of the world. Many people imagined that God demanded death on the cross for his Son as satisfaction for all offenses that people had committed against him. They can therefore see in the cross only the face of an unmerciful God insisting on punishment (his goodness becomes evident in that he lays this punishment not on each individual person, but on his own Son as representative for all).

The Gospel sees the sense of the crucifixion differently. God (even as the disappointed and offended one) loves the people who have strayed from him. He does not want to condemn them, but to rescue them. He comes after man in his Son, Jesus Christ. Jesus accepts toil, suffering, cross, and death in order to make certain that, with a love unto the end on his part, no one should perish and everyone should have eternal life. Seen in this way, the face of the Good Shepherd, who lays down his life for his sheep, is revealed in the crucifixion of Jesus.

In this eucharistic celebration, does the cross of Jesus Christ appear to us here in this sense? Can we, in our sacramental encounter with the Risen One, who bears the wounds, sing: "O what a love, Lord Jesus Christ, / is here for mankind to see! / We who taste it here and now / will live for all eternity" (GL547,4)?

Petitions.

Lord Jesus Christ, by your death on the cross you have redeemed the world.

> Have mercy on those children who never come to know the sign of the cross either at home or at school. . . .
> Have mercy on those adults who see the cross only as an object of art history or custom. . . .
> Have mercy on those people who misuse expensive and elegant crosses as charms around their necks. . . .

Lord, reveal your love on the cross to all people, that they might attain to salvation and life through you. You who live and reign forever and ever.

Our Lady of Sorrows (September 15)

TO SUFFER OUT OF LOVE

Introduction

The cultural image of women has shifted greatly in recent decades. One aspect that remains: if a woman becomes a mother and consciously takes on a mother's responsibility, she accepts the same things as did mothers of earlier generations. This includes that which Mary, as Mother of Sorrows, took upon herself: to suffer out of love, so as to enable others to live.

Talk

To Be a Mother. To be a mother means: to enable a person to have life, to give life, to take responsibility for this life, to care for this life with tireless effort. Whether it is a mother with a woolen kerchief and rough hands or a mother with designer jeans and manicured nails, the responsibility is always the same.

A mother experiences great joy with her child (or children): joy at birth, at growing; sharing in the children's successes; satisfaction when the children move on to find their own place in life. . . .

A mother, however, also experiences much toil, suffering, and pain on account of her children. It is not so much a matter of the burden of pregnancy and the pangs of birth; medical care can help to alleviate these. It is also not primarily a matter of daily work in house and kitchen, with the washing machine and the vacuum cleaner; the future (or the family's financial situation) may bring about a reduction of work. A mother's suffering and pain come mainly from her care for her children, leading to sleepless nights and sometimes tears. Will the child overcome his or her illness? How is he doing in school? Is she too going downhill? Will the growing son keep the faith of his parents? Will the twenty-year-old daughter separate herself entirely from her family?

Every mother experiences this in a fully personal way: love for a child contains the readiness to suffer on the child's account. Yet, she also realizes that only in this love that is open to suffering can she enable the child to live a truly human life.

Love and care for a specific person includes always and everywhere the readiness to suffer on account of that person. This is a basic principle that holds true for the love of a parent for a child as it does for the love between a man and a woman and for every kind of deeper human encounter.

Mary. It must be understood that, proceeding from this principle, Christians have always looked upon Mary and have seen in her the model of love that is ready to suffer.

Mary loved her Son. She took part in his life. She experiences joy and pain with him, as does every mother with her child. Still more did she suffer in a special way because of her son's singularity which resulted from his mission. The Seven Dolors of Mary (Simeon's prophecy, flight into Egypt, loss of the Child in Jerusalem, encounter on the way of the cross, Mary at the foot of the cross, the body of Jesus in his Mother's arms, the burial of Jesus) which were meditated upon over and over again in faith by the devotion of past decades and years, give specific emphasis to this aspect of Mary's suffering on account of her Child.

Mary, as Jesus' Mother, loved all mankind as he did. She thus suffered, as he did, on account of people beloved to her; on account of their lack of interest in the Good News, of their lack of understanding, of their resistance to the love of God. . . .

Mary loved her Son and, with him, she loved people with her whole heart. She loved as a human being who, precisely because she loved, was especially vulnerable. She suffered therefore in a special way in this love for her Son and for all people. At the same time, she did not let herself be separated from her love by her suffering, and discovered for herself that suffering love brings forth life.

We Ourselves. To suffer one another out of love! Think of your own life. Parents in relation to their children and vice versa. Married people in their life together. Relations with a beloved person for whom you are responsible for, with whom you have a personal bond. What is there to suffer with one another? Personality differences, faults, incomplete understanding, disappointment with one another. . . .

Let us say it calmly: in this suffering with each other, we are tempted to break off with one another. We are tempted to say, "It's all useless! Why should I try to understand when I am always misunderstood? Why should I forgive, when I am always being abused? Why should I be the one always to put up with someone else's rotten moods? Why should I leave myself open to suffer on account of this person?"

Should we not ask ourselves, if our thoughts are running this way, that the suffering of Mary and Jesus was not in vain? Mary as Mother of Sorrows, made possible the life of Jesus Christ. She has, as Mother of Sorrows in shared suffering with her Son on account of the world, made true life possible for us men. Since Jesus Christ was ready to suffer out of love, and since Mary suffered with him out of love, the "resurrection and life everlasting" (Creed) are available to us.

And when suffering for a beloved person gets us down, it is then a good idea to speak to Mary, the Mother of Sorrows, about our need concerning this person and to pray, "Mary, you suffered for us men and women and thus made eternal life possible for us. Obtain for us the strength to love our fellow human beings even when we suffer on their account, so that we might make possible for them true human life and life in fellowship with your Son."

Sts. Cornelius and Cyprian (September 16)

BISHOP IN TIME OF TRANSITION

Introduction

What would become of us if a persecution against the Church broke out overnight? If parish offices could no longer continue functioning and if church periodicals were banned? If there were serious disadvantages involved in declaring oneself a Christian? Let us think in this connection not only of Christians in countries new to the Church, let us think also about ourselves.—St. Cyprian was bishop of Carthage in North Africa when, after a fifty-year period of peace, Christians were suddenly subjected to violent persecution in the year 250. How did he manage with his community (i.e., his diocese) during this period?

Penitential Rite

Jesus Christ, victim for the world, source of grace, our nourishment: Lord, have mercy . . .
Health of the sick, consolation of the sorrowing, strength of the dying: Christ, have mercy . . .
God and Man, bread of life, our hope: Lord, have mercy . . .   (GL 767,2).

Talk

Rapid Advance. In his home city of Carthage, Cyprian belonged to the upper class. He was a professor and a lawyer, and his prosperity allowed him a comfortable life. Yet he never was free from the feeling of an inner void. He made contact with convincing Christians and was baptized, apparently in the year 240, at about forty years of age. The seriousness with which he took the "new life" was shown when he donated a great part of his wealth to the poor, dedicated himself to celibacy, and left aside his treasured pagan books to study sacred Scripture. Is it any wonder that the community of Carthage wanted him soon as a priest and elected him bishop in 248?

Continual Danger of Death. The auspicious beginnings of his episcopal service were interrupted in 250. In the last eight years of his life, Cyprian stood accused time and again before the pagan judge, until he was executed on September 14, 258. During this period he led his community out of hiding and kept appearing in public during the times between the specific waves of persecution. While the plague raged from 252 to 254, he organized an extensive ministry to the sick and the needy, which gained him the regard even of many pagan neighbors (although certainly the aroused common people blamed the Christians for the plague and demanded their persecution).

Internal Church Problems. We can imagine how, under the sudden onset of persecution, many Christians denied their faith, whether by expressly defecting to paganism, or by making the prescribed sacrifice in a pro-forma way, or by merely acquiring a certificate (through good connections) attesting their participation in official worship. When these fallen-away members (and they were considered to be such) wanted to be public participants again in the Church during calmer times, the question arose as to how the community of steadfast believers should deal with them. Cyprian demanded from them stiff penance before official reconciliation with the Church. Specifically, he insisted that they be excluded from the sacraments for a long term and that they had to show by their change of life how seriously they took their return.

On this matter, he held a famous correspondence with Pope Cornelius in Rome, which showed the concern of the Church at that time to maintain contact with Rome and to attune pastoral practice to that of the Roman community.

In Carthage itself, the question produced divisions—at one time the North African metropolis had three (Catholic!) bishops. In consideration of a threatening new persecution, Cyprian retreated from his strict demands and gave the instruction that all the fallen-away people who were disposed to do penance should be immediately reaccepted into full communion with the Church. He justified his action in this way: "How are we then to enable them to drink the chalice of suffering [in a new persecution] if we do not first give them the chalice of the Lord to drink in the Church according to the law of the community?" In this way the great bishop, who demanded much of himself, pursued the path of understanding of human weakness in regard to his fellow Christians—and thereby the path of Jesus Christ as well, who came to seek out what was lost (cf. Lk 19:10).

Petitions

Jesus Christ, you came to seek out the lost ones and rescue them. We call upon you:

For all those who betray their own convictions out of fear and false consideration . . . Christ, hear us . . .
For those self-righteous Christians who judge others harshly and uncharitably and condemn them . . .

For all who place higher demands upon others than upon themselves. . . .

For you are the Good Shepherd who pursues the lost sheep and rejoices when he has found it. You who live and reign forever and ever.

St. Robert Bellarmine (September 17)

THEOLOGY PROFESSOR AND PAPAL ADVISOR

Introduction

"Bellarmine is loved because of his great goodness. However, he is a scholar who lives only among his books, and has no grounding in practical questions. He would not be a good pope, because he thinks exclusively of the Church's interest, and does not take the claims of secular princes into consideration. He has doubts, too, as to whether he should accept certain presents." Perhaps Cardinal Robert Bellarmine (1542–1621) was not qualified to be pope (in the conclave of 1605 he was a prominent candidate), but the Roman diplomat who penned the above quotation gave us the portrait of a man who, in his scholarly activity, lived in the Spirit of Jesus Christ and labored tirelessly for the Church.

Penitential Rite

"Revive us now, God, our helper!
Put an end to your grievance against us.
Will you be angry with us for ever, will your anger never cease?
Will you not restore again our life that your people may rejoice in you?" (Ps 85:5–7).
Have mercy, Lord our God, have mercy. . . .

Talk

Theologian in the Controversies of His Time. Robert Bellarmine found in the imitation of Christ the authentic meaning of his life in his studies, in his activity as professor of theology, and in his writing. The brilliantly endowed young Italian became a Jesuit, studied at Louvain in Belgium, and became professor at the Jesuits' Roman house of studies (the present-day Pontifical Gregorian University).

There he found his place, in which he carried out a fruitful scholarly activity. Yet even though Robert Bellarmine lived mainly among his books, he influenced the Church of his time with his theology. A section of his major work (the theological controversy with Protestantism) was placed on the Index (and yet was soon removed). His general superior thought it wise to appoint the embattled theologian as provincial superior in Naples so that the turmoil in Rome could die down during his absence. A few years later (Bellarmine had resumed his teaching activity) the pope sent him as bishop into the provinces, because he did not agree with his theological views.

During the last fifteen years of his life, the famous theologian was an unassailed authority in Rome. After his death, another member of the college of cardinals said of him, "Nearly all of us cardinals followed him, so great was the weight of his knowledge, his steadfastness, and his authority among us."

His Theological Work. Along with his theological controversies with Protestants, Robert Bellarmine took part as well in other contemporary theological disputes. When the pope insisted upon a rapid decision in the question of the cooperation between divine grace and human freedom, Bellarmine explicitly warned him against any hasty determination—and, for this theological forthrightness, he was forced to go out to the boondocks as bishop. (It is worth noting that this theological problem still remains open even today!)

Bellarmine played a decisive part as well in the famous trial of Galileo. As a theologian, he was of the conviction that, between sacred Scripture and the verified observations of the astronomer, no contradiction could exist. Yet, along with all his scholarly sincerity, he was so entrapped in traditional viewpoints that he could only conclude that Galileo had to be mistaken in his observations. Thus he informed Galileo of the Roman demand that he cease discussing the disputed question (whether the sun moves around the earth or the earth around the sun).

Still, our theology professor did not concern himself with general theological questions alone. He knew that, before God, only one's life counted (and not brilliant theological knowledge and extensive scholarly books). He did his theology as an aid to authentic Christian living. His last work, completed a year before his death, embodied this line of thought. Its title: *The Art of Dying Well*. The wisdom (Reading) of his theology was not confined to his elaboration of theological systems. It came into effect in consciously living and dying with Christ upon whom he built his life's house as a "prudent man" [Gospel].

Petitions

Almighty God, you send forth your Spirit of truth to your Church:

Increase in Christians the recognition of your vast goodness and love . . .
Fill theologians with unconditional love for your wisdom . . .
Further the dialogue among Christian communions and among distinct theological systems . . . .

For you are the guide of wisdom and you keep the wise on the right way. You who live forever and ever.

St. Januarius (September 19)

AGAINST WEARINESS AND RESIGNATION

Introduction

It may be that God, in his miracles, takes into account specific ethnic traits. The miracle of the liquefying blood of St. Januarius in Naples (he is said to have been bishop of that city and to have been executed under Diocletian) would be out of place, in a way, in northern Europe or North America. Such events make us feel rather awkward. We see them as having little religious utility for a critical modern world. We lean more toward the opinion of the French worker-priest Henri Perrin: "Longing for God will awaken again if people can see and experience Christians who truly give witness to Christ."—Am I one of those Christians?

Penitential Rite

> Jesus, bread by which we live: Lord, have mercy . . .
> Jesus, light by which we see: Christ, have mercy . . .
> Jesus, the way on which we go: Lord, have mercy. . . .

Talk

Bitter Experiences. A young couple begin their common way in life with the enthusiasm of great love. They really want to be there for each other in love. They use their imaginations and always look for new ways by which to display their mutual love.

Yet on the gray streets of everyday life, routine sets in more the longer it goes on. Each one gets used to the other. The excitement of the new and the unusual disappears. They live a dull life even under better material conditions. And one day the two of them realize that "everything has changed from what it used to be." The wine of mutual enthusiasm has become heavily diluted with the water of everyday living and of habit.

Maybe this development was necessary. Maybe their mutual love is now more genuine and realistic than at its beginning. Yet maybe this development is also the beginning of the end. Maybe both must do something to breathe new life into their love.

Things are like this in every area of human life: initial enthusiasm does not maintain itself for any long period. It gets lost on the long way of carrying out good intentions. Weariness and resignation endanger the accomplishment of even the most ideal plans.

Similar Experiences in Faith. The Letter to the Hebrews, in today's Reading, reminds us that our life of faith proceeds by the same measure. Already in the early Christian generations there were community members who, after withstanding harsh persecution with enthusiasm, became weary in years of relative peace and lukewarm in their faith. Perhaps even in those times, when people thought in concrete terms of the daily coming of Christ in judgment, the waiting simply lasted too long—and they lost faith and hope. The Letter to the Hebrews warns, "Do not, then, surrender your confidence; it will have great reward. You need patience to do God's will and receive what he has promised" (Reading).

Trust and Perseverence. How do our own experiences seem to us? Three years ago we used to pray regularly at table when at home—how does it go today? Before, we never even dreamed of missing Sunday mass—and now? Then we could always find time for a couple of minutes in the church—and now something else is always more important. . . .

Yes, even our faith can become dormant. It can be lost, as a handkerchief can be lost, without really being noticed. It can become so ordinary to us that it no longer impresses us, and we can forget it. We can overlook it, just as we no longer notice something old and familiar.

We are Christians who truly give witness to Christ (cf. the above passage) only if our faith is alive, if in our lives there is something to notice of our trust in God, of our hope for fulfillment in him, and of our patience in love.

Here in the eucharistic celebration is the place where we can let ourselves ever again be newly enthused (in the truest sense of the word) by Jesus Christ for the wearisome everyday way of faith. It is on this way that we seek to fulfill the will of God until he comes again in glory and until we firmly receive what he has promised.

Petitions

Let us pray:

For all those in whose lives God's Word cannot take root (Silence). . . .
For all those who, in distress and under persecution, have become weary in their faith . . .
For all those who, in the midst of their abundance and external security, forget the Gospel . . .
For all those whose faith is blocked up in routine and mere fulfillment of duty. . . .

Lord Jesus Christ, prepare the earthly kingdom of human hearts so that the faith can take root and grow. You who live and reign forever and ever.

St. Matthew (September 21)

FROM TAX COLLECTOR TO APOSTLE

Introduction

In our Church we exclude from reception of the Sacraments "public sinners" who do not live according to the Church's system of values. As a basis for this we invoke the practice of the early Church as described by Paul in I Cor 5:1-13. Yet are we aware that these measures are supposed to help such Christians to change to the full fellowship of the Church? That Jesus, who called the "public sinner" Levi to be an apostle, also expects the religious renewal of an "excommunicated" Christian (and, consequently, that we must not impede by our prejudices the Lord's work of renewal in the community)?

Penitential Rite

Lord Jesus Christ, you take to yourself prostitutes and tax collectors: Lord, have mercy. . . .

You called the "public sinner" Levi into your circle of disciples: Christ, have mercy. . . .

You are always ready to forgive us again: Lord, have mercy. . . .

Talk

Jesus Mingles with Sinners. The Palestinian society of Jesus' time had its outsiders too, people "with whom no respectable person would be seen." Tax collectors belonged to this category.

Jesus of Nazareth "had a heart" for these borderline characters. In his controversy with the overly-pious of the established Jewish society, he made it clear to these despised people, who before God really had a great burden of misdeeds, how even the most pious person basically stands before God: empty-handed, dependent on God's merciful love.

Yet Jesus did not use these outsiders merely as teaching aids. He did not just work for their rehabilitation. He mingled with them. He accepted invitations from them, he feasted with them—and was promptly lumped together with them by the respectable society of his time (cf. Gospel).

Jesus went still one step further. He called Levi into the circle of the apostles. He entrusted to this tax collector—who, on account of his past, had a bad reputation among his countrymen even after his encounter with Jesus—the responsibility for the Good News that proclaimed the God who had come in Jesus Christ "to call, not the self-righteous, but sinners" (Gospel).

The Transforming Power of Jesus. It must be noted that, even though Jesus mingled with sinners, he did not make light of their past. He affirmed to the adulteress that she had indeed sinned. He did not say to the tax collector Zacchaeus that his previous crimes were "only half bad." Even in the calling of Levi, it is nowhere stated that Jesus had said that Matthew was basically a good fellow whom people should hold in respect. Jesus was clearly aware of his past (and of his main character traits). However, where we normally expect actions ("First show me that you've really changed!") before we trust someone, Jesus trusted Levi the tax collector in the hope that his trust would lend him the strength to change and to lead a life in imitation of him. Jesus gifts sinners with his unconventional love in the hope that they might become able to respond to him with the same love.

We and Levi. We can leave aside the question whether the Gospel of Matthew was really written by the former tax collector Levi, called Matthew by the other evangelists (scholars still discuss the question).

We can also leave aside the question where and how the life of the apostle Matthew came to an end (we have no certain information).

More important is that we recognize ourselves in the figure of Levi. For it is not only the Pharisees, but we ourselves as well who, with all our piety, before God resemble prostitutes and tax collectors who have no clean garments and who depend upon God's mercy. Are we really convinced of this?

We also, however, resemble Levi the tax collector, who was unconditionally loved by Jesus and thus gained the strength to change his life and to follow his Master. Do we wonder enough at God's unconditional love and do we see our lives as a response to the love with which God has first loved us?

And are we ready to deal with everyone after the example of Jesus? With our relatives and acquaintances, but also with the marginal characters of our society? Are we ready to love them unconditionally and thus to help them to change themselves?

Petitions

Lord Jesus Christ, head of your Church, we pray to you:

Call young people into your following and your service . . .
Let all whom you have called know your will . . .
Give them the strength to respond with their whole lives by trusting in your grace. . . .

For with the calling you also send the strength to meet the requirements of your service. You who live and reign forever and ever.

Sts. Cosmas and Damian (September 26)

HELPERS TO THE SICK AND SUFFERING

Introduction

Their relics are venerated in the cathedral of Hildesheim and in the bishop's church of Essen (both in Germany), yet they themselves are more legend than fact: the brothers Cosmas and Damian, who as physicians helped the sick at no charge. Their worldwide veneration makes manifest the oppressive burden of illness and pain that mankind bears. At the same time it also shows the Christian dedication to the sick and the suffering, to which the Church in her imitation of Jesus Christ has always felt herself obliged.

Penitential Rite

Jesus Christ, your Father sent you into the world for our salvation: Lord, have mercy . . .

You have come into the lowliness of our human existence in order to heal our sicknesses: Christ, have mercy . . .

You strengthen us by the Holy Spirit in our bodily frailty with never-flagging strength: Lord, have mercy . . . (after GL 76).

Talk

Savior of the Sick. "After sunset, as evening drew on, they brought him all who were ill, and those possessed by demons. . . . Those whom he cured, who were variously afflicted, were many, and so were the demons he expelled" (Mk 1:32f). This summary report is placed at the beginning of the Gospel of Mark. Jesus of Nazareth is the Savior of the sick and the suffering—each chapter of the Gospels demonstrates it again.

After the healing of the man born lame, the Acts of the Apostles states: "The people carried the sick into the streets and laid them on cots and mattresses, so that when Peter passed by at least his shadow might fall on one or another of them. Crowds from the towns around Jerusalem would gather, too, bringing their sick and those who were troubled by unclean spirits, all of whom were cured" (Acts 5:15f).

Church for the Sick. The Church has remained true to this tradition. Ancient Christian bishops had already organized care for the sick (within and beyond the limits of the community). Ordinary Christians (like Cosmas and Damian, representative of many others) took over the care of the sick as a matter of course. Medieval monasteries developed hospitals and built their apothecaries. In the nineteenth century, a number of religious congregations were founded that bound themselves explicitly to the service of the sick and the suffering. Catholic congregations opened hospitals. Finally, Christian missions have brought preventive and curative medicine to developing countries.

Church for the Sick Today. The modern developed state has in our times assumed much responsibility for what the Church used to do for sick people. We need not lament and miss this past administrative and organizational task.

We could use the new-found opportunity to serve the sick in a very different way. Jesus of Nazareth came to Peter's mother-in-law as an individual and helped her (cf. Mk 1:31). Peter and John looked the man born lame right in the eye as an individual and healed him (cf. Acts 3:4–8). Our modern medical care threatens to become impersonal. The sick see themselves increasingly faced by machinery and organization that care for them. They look, however, for someone to be close to them in their pain. Herein lies a task for the Christian physician and the believing nurse, for the church social worker and the sympathetic relatives: to reach out to the sick person so as to let him know that people suffer with him and want to help him personally. . . .

Sign of Final Healing. Yet perhaps the sick require still more. In a contemporary poem we hear:

> Just believe that you they need,
> the people who with you go.
> They need your goodness and understanding,
> and that which they most lack:
> your knowledge of light everlasting   (Maria Nels).

All our care for the sick ultimately cannot overcome death. Ought not the sick, then, to be able to see that we "believe in the Resurrection and life everlasting"? Do we not thus render them an important service as we do with all physical aid?

Petitions

Lord Jesus Christ, you look after the sick and the suffering:

Give the sick relief from their pain and, if it is your will, give them prompt healing as well . . .
Guard them from discouragement, embitterment, and ingratitude toward their circumstances . . .

Bless the work of physicians and nurses . . .
Give all helpers of the sick kindness and patience. . . .

For you choose to work your marvels on sufferers through our service. You who live and reign forever and ever.

St. Vincent de Paul (September 27)

SAINT OF CHARITY

Introduction

"I have respect and love enough to give to an entire world." We can accept these words as being those of Vincent de Paul, a plain peasant's son, who in Paris enjoyed the trust of the highest levels. He founded charitable groups in many French cities that were to take care of the poor. He brought a group of priests into being that was to work in parish missions for the religiously neglected country folk. All the groups of "Sisters of Charity" (by whatever name they go now) trace their origins to him; without them, church life during the last one hundred and fifty years is unimaginable.

Penitential Rite

"God has chosen the foolish to confound the wise." (Silence) Lord, have mercy. . . .
God has chosen the weak of this world to confound the strong." (Silence) Christ have mercy. . . .
God has taken what is nothing to overcome what is something" (Silence) Lord, have mercy. . . .

Talk

A Mediocre Priest. The simple peasant couple from southern France had definite material reasons for letting their son Vincent become a priest: he could make his living in a church career. The young cleric lived with this attitude, and was ordained a priest at the age of nineteen. He looked for a secure post, and at first found none. He went over his head into debt, and sank without paying off his creditors. In 1610—he was about thirty—he was in Paris in search of a church post that would provide him with a comfortable living. There, however, he met with people associated with the famous Bishop Bérulle. And there he underwent a profound conversion. He forsook his selfish plans and saw himself more and more as a priest for others.

Simple Priest with Great Influence. As a "priest of the people," Vincent held mainly the position of house chaplain for noble families during the ensuing decades of his life. This gave him unrestricted access even to the members of the royal family in Paris. Yet he did not limit himself to pastoral activity among the upper class. He had come to know the unimaginable spiritual and material need of many people in France. He accordingly employed his contacts to relieve need wherever he could.

To the extent that his time allowed, Vincent worked time and again in direct pastoral care in parishes, in which he established the above-mentioned charitable groups. He was able to move his powerful patrons to soften the lot of galley slaves. He accepted money from nobility and used it to establish a congregation of priests (the Vincentians). They soon were working fruitfully in France and overseas. He gave this confreres the mandate to provide good priests by running seminaries. He also regularly set up conferences and training days in order to help priests fulfill their pastoral tasks in the Spirit of Jesus Christ.

In Paris he succeeded, along with St. Louise de Marillac, in founding the Daughters of Charity; in them the practical direction of St. Vincent became manifest in a special way: he had brought together a group of noble ladies who were ready to use their money for the care of the poor, and yet were not in a position to help the poor directly through hard labor. For this reason he founded a community of ordinary girls and women who were closer to the poor and the abandoned with their background and their education: they brought the rich ladies' money to the people by their service.

Great in Simplicity. Vincent de Paul died in 1660 at the age of seventy-nine. He was not a social revolutionary. He did not basically change the society of his time. As a child of his time, he couldn't even conceive of it. And yet "he rendered respect and love to the whole world" (cf. quotation in the introduction). This he did insofar as he used his practical judgment to do whatever a situation showed him was God's will. He did this as an ordinary priest, and, amid all honors, was surely laughed at by some high-placed people in Paris. In him we see revealed the truth of the Reading: God over and over chooses the unlikely and the weak to accomplish great things.

Petitions

Lord Jesus Christ:

You have proclaimed the Good News to the poor: let us be joyful messengers of your love in word and deed . . .
You took the sick to yourself and worked wonders for them: let us perform for them the miracle of your love . . .
You accepted sinners out of love: let us show to sinners the way to your love. . . .

Thus let us fulfill your command, so that we can be cleared in your court. You who live and reign forever and ever.

St. Wenceslaus (September 28)

GERMANS AND CZECHS

Introduction

Duke Wenceslaus of Bohemia counts among the figures (Stephen of Hungary, Canute, Eric, and Olaf from the northern European countries . . .), who come at the beginning of the civil and ecclesiastical history of their countries and who are venerated both as saints and as national heroes. Often little is known of their lives. This is especially true of Duke Wenceslaus, who was murdered on September 28, 929, when he was barely twenty years old. He was a victim of cold-blooded people who were ready to sacrifice someone else's life in order to push through their own plans. Sometimes we suffer (in a milder form) like Duke Wenceslaus. Sometimes we resemble (in a milder form) his murderers.

Penitential Rite

Jesus Christ, you are the resurrection and the life: Lord, have mercy . . .

You sit at the right hand of the Father: Christ, have mercy . . .

You are our advocate and mediator before the Father: Lord, have mercy. . . .

Talk

Historical Fact. Wenceslaus grew up in a Bohemia that was still widely pagan, brought up by his grandmother Ludmilla, who was venerated as a saint. After the death of his father, he became duke of his country while still a young boy. Governmental affairs were at first conducted by his mother. In the then current controversies among his country's various political powers, Wenceslaus was the symbol for the Christian party. This group was dedicated to, along with acceptance of Christianity, a cautious opening to the west—i.e., inclination toward the German kingdom. The pagan party (which had won over his mother and brother to its side) looked more toward national independence and rejected Christianity along with western influence. Duke Wenceslaus finally fell victim to a conspiracy of his religious and political adversaries. He lost his life not only as a believing Christian, but also as a defender of peaceful contacts between Czechs and Germans.

Czechs and Germans. Christianity implanted itself in the Czech people after the death of Wenceslaus. Germans and Czechs found themselves confessing the same faith.

Yet they still did not cease to fight with one another and to harm each other. I don't know if the German settlement in wide areas of current-day Bohemia took place always by peaceful means. I don't know if Germans and Czechs lived together for centuries in peace and mutual respect, or if in the jointly settled areas one part of the population was oppressed and unjustly treated by the other. I only know about all the pain and injustice that Germans and Czechs brought upon each other in the context of the last war: occupation of Czechoslovakia by Nazi Germany and destruction of its state, expulsion of millions of Germans, unimaginable cruelties on both sides. . . .

Perhaps among us there are some refugees from Bohemia and Moravia who experienced this outbreak of hate on their own bodies. Is not the memorial day of St. Wenceslaus an occasion finally to forgive one's tormentors of that time and to pray now once more with full awareness: Our Father . . . give me the strength to forgive as you always forgive us . . . ?

The German Church and the Czech Church. One can remember on St. Wenceslaus' day that the Czech Church was founded out of Germany. German missionaries labored in Bohemia and Moravia, long before German settlers came there.

This historical relation binds Germans to a solidarity with the Catholic Church in Czechoslovakia, which at this time is going through a dark period of its history. The Church is severely limited in her life by the atheistic state. Upright Christians are liable to harassment in the workplace. Nuns (who are active in state hospitals or in factories) are prevented from living and praying in community. . . .

Our solidarity (by our interest, our prayers, personal signs of association . . .) will also serve those who, as a kind of civil rights activists in a Christian spirit (whether or not they call themselves Christians) campaign for the respect of the dignity of the individual and for the defense of self-evident human rights in their country.

Petitions

God and Lord of all the world, we pray for the people of Czechoslovakia:

Grant to the authorities of state and society the readiness to promote whatever serves the peace and prosperity of all . . .
Grant to the Church the necessary freedom for fulfilling her task . . .
Give courage and inner constancy to all who dedicate themselves to the cause of human rights in their countries. . . .

Lord, look with grace upon the people of Czechoslovakia. Bless their way in our time, that it might become a way to salvation. You, who live and reign forever and ever.

Sts. Michael, Gabriel, Raphael (September 29)

CREATURES OF GOD

Introduction

"Through Jesus Christ we praise your mercy now and forever and sing with the choirs of angels in praise of your glory." With these or similar words closes the preface at each Mass. What does it mean to me that we celebrate the Eucharist in communion "with the choirs of angels"? It is a fitting question on the memorial day of the archangels Michael, Gabriel, and Raphael.

Penitential Rite

"Lord, our sin is the sin of our fathers: we have done wrong, our deeds have been evil.

O Lord, remember me out of the love you have for your people.

Come . . . that I may see the joy of your chosen ones, and may rejoice in the gladness of your nation" (Ps 106:6,4,5a).

Have mercy, Lord our God, have mercy. . . .

Talk

Variations in the History of Devotion. The early writings of the Old Testament speak little of angels (they tend more to dwell on *the* angel of God). They become mentioned more frequently in the latest

OT works. There we even see names (Michael, Gabriel, Raphael), similar to the New Testament. The Christian doctrine on angels evidently found more response in faith among Christians of the past than is the case today. In any event, earlier generations lived with them more assuredly than is possible for many people today.

I don't know what opinions many of you might have on the question of angels. Some of you may be saying to yourselves that the Church's doctrine on angels has scarcely any meaning for your personal religious lives. Others of you, in your honest opinion, might believe that there are no spiritual creatures found between God and man, and that any mention in the Bible simply serves the literary purpose of bringing out in vivid imagery the mystery and otherness of God. If you think along these lines, then you are granting that you have no special interest in angels—or else you are indicating your personal inquiry into current trends in theology—without worrying about being heretical or slipping out of religious belief. Still, try to listen, with an open mind and without prejudice, to what the Christian tradition declares in its doctrine on angels.

"God's Deputies." In today's preface this doctrine is summed up: "In praising your faithful angels and archangels, we also praise your glory, for in honoring them, we honor you, their creator. Their splendor shows us your greatness, which surpasses in goodness the whole of creation." The angels, then, are creatures of God. God's greatness shines forth from them. God's power works through them in our lives. God himself is glorified in their veneration.

The angels stand as "the side of God turned to us," as "God's deputies" in our world and our lives. We comprehend the real intent of this teaching correctly only when our attention is turned through veneration of them toward God, when we grasp more deeply through them God's power and greatness—and God's loving care for us. There are certainly other ways to come before the God who reveals himself to us in Jesus Christ (cf. Gospel), but a properly understood devotion to angels also leads to this goal.

Michael, Gabriel, Raphael. The three archangels of today's memorial are also figures pointing to God.

Michael is spoken of in holy Scripture in the context of God's battle against evil. He is a sign that God himself enters the fight against evil—and wins (cf. Reading 2). This is a consoling message for us in our often seemingly hopeless battle against evil and for goodness.

God himself speaks to men and women through *Gabriel* (as he did to Zachary and Mary). God himself calls us to service and wants us to work for his Kingdom. Are we open enough for him—even when he shows us his plans and unexpected ways?

Raphael accompanied Tobias on his journey abroad and protected his relatives from evil spirits. It is God himself who everywhere (at home or away) holds us in his hands and guards us from evil. Through the angels, God himself is our true guardian angel.

Petitions

Almighty God, you work through angels as well in your history among humanity:

Strengthen all people of good will in their battle against evil and in their devotion to goodness . . .
Reveal your will to all who seek sincerely to know it . . .
Be near to all who need protection and help . . .
Grant relief from their need to the sick and the suffering. . . .

Lord, let us experience your greatness and love in all the events of our lives, and let us become your messengers to our fellow men and women. You, who live and reign forever and ever.

St. Jerome (September 30)

A DIFFICULT CONTEMPORARY

Introduction

Jerome was a "gifted but difficult, undisciplined, and arrogant student . . . he possessed an extremely sensitive, passionate, mistrustful, and envious character." During his lifetime these unfavorable traits burdened the great exegete. They made it hard for him and other people to live together in peace. And yet this impulsive, irritable, and sarcastic man rendered a priceless service to the Church. This is a sign for us that Jesus Christ can perform through us—with all our limitations and weaknesses—important and worthwhile things for the life of the Church.

Penitential Rite

"It is you, O Lord, who are my hope, my trust, O Lord, since my youth.
Do not reject me now that I am old; when my strength fails do not forsake me.
O God, do not stay far off: my God, make haste to help me" (Ps. 71:5,9,12).

Have mercy, Lord our God, have mercy. . . .

Talk

Between Extremes. Jerome (347–420) lived during the time of the decline of Roman paganism and of the rise of the early Church. During his student years in Rome, the young man from the province of Dalmatia (Yugoslavia) knew how to amuse himself by all the rules of skill. Yet at the age of nineteen he very deliberately had himself baptized. He soon began to long for monastic life, which was being talked about everywhere. He joined a group of monks in Italy and soon after journeyed to the east in order to lead a strict ascetic life.

Yet, with his classical education, he was soon repelled by the low intellectual level of many monks. He went back to the city, allowed himself reluctantly to be ordained a priest, and continued his studies. He returned to Rome in 382. Pope Damasus there made him his secretary and asked him to produce a new Latin version of the Bible. At the same time he did pastoral work with various groups of noble Roman ladies (and when people criticized him for this, he replied in his sarcastic way, "I would speak less with women if men asked me more about the sacred Scriptures").

After the death of the pope, he could stay in Rome no longer. With his beloved books and manuscripts (which he had collected or completed in work that took years), he relocated permanently in the east. He settled in Bethlehem, where he founded a monastery and assumed its direction. A group of his female admirers from Rome followed him and established a convent nearby. Jerome dedicated the remaining decades of his life to the complete translation of sacred Scripture from the original languages (Hebrew and Greek) into Latin, and to the commentary on different books of the Bible. His translation soon became the official version of the Church's use and remains so in the Catholic Church even today.

God's Power in Human Weakness. During his whole lifetime, the universally recognized scholar made life hard for himself and for others by his intemperate manner. At every opportunity he flaunted

St. Jerome

his trilingual ability (Latin, Greek, Hebrew). He collided headlong with others because of his uncontrolled behavior. He wounded friends and enemies by his sarcasm. He stuck his nose into everything and tried to make comments (or a fight) about everything.

On the other hand, it is evident how much Jerome suffered from his shortcomings of character and with what disarming openness he admitted his faults (even if, with this knowledge of self, he still did not have the strength to overcome his weaknesses).

The great scholar of sacred Scripture had learned in his own life how God's power becomes effective in human weaknesses. He gives us courage so that we will not weary in our dedication to the Church, even if time and again we feel our limitations and obscure the witness of our life of faith by our personal faults.

Petitions

Lord Jesus Christ, you speak to your Church through sacred Scripture:

Grant us joy and consolation in your Word . . .
Grant that we may understand your Word correctly . . .
Let us hear the Word that helps us to live as you command us to live. . . .

Grant us this through the intercession of St. Jerome. You who live and reign forever and ever.

St. Theresa of the Child Jesus (October 1)

MY VOCATION IS LOVE

Introduction

She was a woman born over a hundred years ago (1873). She grew up in a bourgeois family influenced by religion. When she was fifteen, she entered the Carmelite convent in which two of her sisters were already living. Barely twenty-four-years old, she died in 1897 of tuberculosis. In 1923 she was beatified. Her canonization followed in 1925, and Pope Pius XI declared her patroness of world missions.

We call this woman "little St. Theresa"—and somehow infer the image of "lowly," "naive," "childlike." Does this girl from a sheltered home, who spent the short years of her life in a cloister, have something to tell us for our Christian life?

Penitential Rite

Lord Jesus Christ, you reveal to us the Father's unconditional love: Lord, have mercy. . . .

You draw the humble and the little to yourself: Christ, have mercy. . . .

You want us to pass love along in our lives: Lord, have mercy. . . .

Talk

"The little Saint Theresa." That her image has a partly sugary stripe for us may be due to the fact that she wrote down her religious experiences in the contemporary flowery style of the outgoing nineteenth century. Under closer scrutiny, however, it is evident that this girl was deeply penetrated with the essence of the Gospel.

Jesus Christ, the Center. Theresa had a living relationship with Jesus Christ. She wanted to love him "more than he has ever been loved." She would deny him nothing. She would rather have died than have ever committed the slightest voluntary fault.

To Become a Child before God. This enthusiastic love for Jesus was tied up with the experience of her inadequacy truly to forget her own self. This made her grow in the awareness that being a Christian begins with letting oneself be enriched by God with full trust in him. She grasped that God is not the strict Lord before whom people must demonstrate their religious accomplishments. For her, God was better compared with a mother, who cares for her children [cf. Reading]. Thus Theresa could become like a child before God. She understood this state of childhood before God in the scriptural sense: to be helpless, to have no particular rights, to be unable to rely on one's own accomplishments, and yet to entrust oneself fully to his hands.

Vocation of Love. In a period in which religious life in an order was considered to be a way of saving one's own soul, Theresa discovered more and more that, in the Christian life, it is a matter of love, and that love for God must show itself in love for neighbor. At thirteen, on Christmas of 1886, she understood that the call of Christ is a call to brotherly love. She told her confessor, "It should be heaven on earth for me to do good." When fourteen, she prayed incessantly for the conversion of a murderer and criminal sentenced to death. Her prayer was heard. A year later, she entered the Carmel of Lisieux, "with no illusions," she wrote, "to rescue souls, and above all to pray for priests." Toward the end of her life, she summed up once again the meaning of her existence as a Carmelite in this sentence: "My vocation is to love."

In readiness to love people as Jesus loves them, she also repeatedly accepted the darkness of faith, the bitterness of which she felt right to the last days of her life.

The Little Way. To live with Jesus Christ, to let oneself be enriched by God, to love all men and women as Jesus loves them: in order to demonstrate this one need not, consonant with Theresa, wait for momentous chances; like her, one can try in the most unlikely life circumstances. She tried it in the small world of a Carmel. We stand in the small world of our everyday duties and tasks at home and at work. Would there not be more of the presence of God to feel in our environment if we seriously attempted to follow the "little way" of the saint from Lisieux?

Petitions

God, you are the Creator and Father of all people. You want us to treat all people as you have treated us in Jesus Christ.

> Let all Christians acknowledge your boundless love and put it into practice in their lives. . . .
> Grant that the members of non-Christian religious communities may come closer to you. . . .
> Awaken in everyone the question of the meaning of life and the readiness to examine themselves accordingly. . . .

For it is your will that all men and women be saved and know you. You who live and reign forever and ever.

Guardian Angels (October 2)

"LET ANGELS ALWAYS ATTEND US"

Introduction

St. Frances of Rome (she lived from 1348 to 1440) related that, during the last twenty-three years of her life, she constantly saw her guardian angel at her side; she described this angel in detail; in the light radiating from the angel, she could read and write even at night. . . . Who among us can claim to have a similar inner relationship with a guardian angel?

Penitential Rite

"O God, you know my sinful folly; my sins you can see.
This is my prayer to you, my prayer for your favor.
In your great love, answer me, O God, with your help that never fails" (Ps 69:6,14).

Have mercy, Lord our God, have mercy. . . .

Talk

Extremes. For many contemporary Christians, the traditional teaching about angels has become a problem. They ask themselves why there should still exist between God and man particular spiritual beings and whether God needs special "executive agencies" for our protection. They take into account that the tasks of angels in other parts of the Bible are ascribed to God himself. Thus they do not deny the Church's doctrine on angels, but they keep their distance from it in their own religious lives.

On the other hand is the nearly sectarian current in our Church, known as "Work of Angels." These fellow Christians maintain that every human being, every nation, each day, has its own angel. They can also give the names of all these angels. They demand a special act of consecration of oneself to the angels and see the future of the Church secured only if we again "turn to the holy angels."

For Our Consideration. How should we evaluate these extreme positions (which both may have adherents within this assembly)?

Well, the future of the Church lies with Jesus Christ (and not with the angels), who promised his presence even to the end of this world's time (cf. Mt. 28:20). In his Holy Spirit he journeys with his Church and gives her the strength for her path into the future (cf. Jn 16:5–15). We are dedicated to him through our baptism (and thus do not specially require consecration to the angels). On our way through life with him, it is necessary to turn every day to him(and not to the angels). A veneration of angels that obscures this basic truth does not lie within church tradition, which sees angels as creatures, servants, and messengers of God, in whom God's greatness and might shine forth (cf. GL 605).

Moreover, we should guard against neglecting the Bible's restraint in its statement concerning angels. All imaginative speculations about the "heavenly hosts," their ranks, their plans of service, their names, and their characteristics have no foundation in revelation and avail for nothing. They belong to the fables to which people turn when they are no longer content with sound doctrine, but will seek stories that tickle their ears (cf. 2 Tim 4:3f.).

In addition, God is a God of fullness. He has the whole world in his hand. And yet, according to what faith teaches us, he seriously accepts human beings as co-workers in creation and redemption. He does not do everything by himself, but leaves much for people (and takes away from them neither work nor responsibility). What speaks against the fact that this God of fullness also created other beings and allows them to cooperate in creation and redemption? Their existence and cooperation diminish God's greatness and power just as little as our human existence and cooperation do.

"Guardian Angels." Even if someone at present has difficulties in believing about angels, he can be reminded by the Church's teaching on personal guardian angels that God is not a God of masses, but rather the God who knows, understands, cares for, and protects each individual human being. The belief in guardian angels reminds me that, before God, I am not a number. Before him, I have an unmistakable face. He loves me personally. He accompanies me with his interest in my entire personal life course, in order to prepare for me a totally personal everlasting happiness.

Petitions

Kind Father, you send your angels to guard us in all our ways:

Protect your Church amid the storms of our time. . . .
Reveal to her your holy will. . . .
Give her the power to give witness to goodness. . . .
Be close to each man and woman on his or her personal way through life. . . .

Almighty God, be our shield and protection through your angels on all our ways. You who live and reign forever and ever.

St. Francis of Assisi (October 4)

"PRAISE TO YOU, MY LORD"

Introduction

"We do well to thank you, Holy Father, It is right to praise you." Each preface begins with these or similar words. Is the Eucharist for us (including any penitential rite at the beginning and any petitions at the end of the liturgy of the Word) in the first place a celebration of joy over our communion with God? An expression of joy over God's greatness and majesty, and of thanks for the great things that he does for us and through us? A prayer has been handed down to us from St. Francis of Assisi (1181–1226) which can inspire us to give praise along with him to "the Father, the Lord of heaven and earth" [Gospel].

Penitential Rite

Lord Jesus Christ, you go about doing good deeds: Lord, have mercy. . . .

You shatter the fetters of the grave and rise victorious from the dead: Christ, have mercy. . . .

You will come again and awaken all flesh from the dead: Lord, have mercy. . . .

Talk

Praising God because of Life. Francis of Assisi did not go through life as a naive optimist who had a happy disposition and saw the reality of life through rose-colored glasses. He knew about poverty and injustice in his world; he knew sickness and pain through his own bitter experience. He sought with full awareness to follow the Crucified One in his own life [Reading]. Yet he had also come to know the goodness of God [Gospel], and since he saw the whole world embraced by God's love, in the midst of this life's shadows he was the happy saint who always found reasons to praise God.

Let us be inspired by his "Canticle of the Sun" (GL 285) to see in our everyday lives as well the occasions for which it is right and just to give praise to God.

God's Greatness in Nature. Sun, moon and stars, wind and air, fair and foul weather, water and fire were occasions for Francis to praise God. The beauty of nature, the laws which inhere in her, the works that humanity performs insofar as they bring creation into service—these are still in our day reasons for astonishment, they still reveal to us God's greatness and power. Do we see the mystery of God shining forth in creation?

Francis also praised God "for our sister, the motherly earth," and for all plants that grow upon her. Here we can include beasts as well and be amazed daily anew over the wonder of life that reveals the fullness of divine life.

God's Greatness in Human Mastery of Life. Francis also found in his fellow human beings enough reason to praise God. He saw many who would forgive and forget in their lives. He was astounded by the inner greatness displayed by many in sickness and distress. He admired all who kept patience in difficulties and problems and who sought peaceable solutions.

Let us open our eyes in order to discover the people in our environment who lend us courage since the power of God and the Spirit of Jesus Christ are active in them. And let us praise God for these people.

Praise of God in the Face of Death. In facing his own death, Francis is reported to have added this last stanza to his "Canticle of the Sun": "Praise be to you, my Lord, through our brother, the death of the body. . . ." He knew that death was a hard thing. Yet he also knew that death could not rip him away from the hand of God, because he had lived according to God's will. That meant he could, despite any fear of eternal death, praise God even in the last hours of his life.

How do we face death? We are burdened by the fact that no living person can escape death. Yet we also believe that we do not fall out of God's hand at the moment of death. Thus, at least on healthy days, we can praise God for death. And if we practice here and now over and over to trust in God's presence, we will perhaps someday be able, like Francis, to praise God with full trust at the hour of our death.

Petitions

God of kindness, you reveal your greatness in Jesus Christ and in creation:

Open people's eyes to your mystery in nature. . . .
Let those discover your grace in everything who display human greatness in sickness and need. . . .
Grant that everyone may feel your presence at the hour of death. . . .
Give us all joy in our communion with you. . . .

Honor, praise, and glory be yours, O most high, almighty, and kind Lord, forever and ever.

St. Bruno (October 6)

IN SOLITUDE FOR THE SAKE OF CHRIST

Introduction

In 1976 there was a television documentary about a Carthusian monastery in northern Italy. The program gave a glimpse into the life, prayer, and work of these religious men. The silent monks themselves provided information on the Christian meaning of their lives in solitude and withdrawal. How do we react today to this form of Christian living?

Penitential Rite

Lord Jesus Christ, to know you comes before all else: Lord, have mercy. . . .

To live in fellowship with you is more important than all else: Christ, have mercy. . . .

Everything depends on your love unto death giving form to our lives: Lord, have mercy. . . .

Talk

Amid Church Life. Bruno, born in 1030 in Cologne, became professor of theology and director of the diocesan schools in Rheims after completing his own thorough education. Around 1075, he also became vicar general of his diocese.

Bruno lived and worked during the times of the great medieval church reforms. The Church was making a great effort to regain her freedom from state control and to root out abuses within her own ranks. Bruno took sides with the reformers and thus ran into conflict with his own bishop, who was finally deposed because of his scandalous conduct in his personal life and in his office.

Call to Solitude. Was it flight from responsibility, or resignation, when Bruno refused to become bishop of Rheims? Was it an inner calling, when he withdrew in 1084 into the mountains with some colleagues in order to lead a life of prayer and penance in solitude?

For the hermits of the high Middle Ages, in whose spiritual world Bruno lived, their love for solitude was concerned very explicitly with Jesus Christ, in the sense of today's Reading. They were ready to forfeit everything so that Christ could be their wealth and they could be in him. They experienced how, with the cares and tasks (and distractions) of everyday life, interest in communion with Jesus Christ can disappear. Therefore, they put everything on one card and left everything else behind them, in order to involve themselves only with Jesus Christ in solitude.

For these hermits, it was not a matter of flight and of undisturbed life, but of life in the Spirit of Jesus Christ. This is clear from the fact that again and again they would voluntarily leave their chosen solitude when the needs of the times and the Church demanded their intervention.

Bruno lived in this spirit. He withdrew into the wild valley of Chartreuse and there laid, with a few companions, the foundations for the Order of Carthusians. Yet when one of his disciples became pope, and wanted him around as his counselor, he left his beloved solitude and went to the papal court. So as to bind together the call to life in solitude with dedication to the Church, he secured permission to continue his hermit's life near the papal court. He died on October 6, 1101.

Message of the Carthusians. Bruno's work has lasted through the centuries. The Carthusians flourished most greatly on the eve of the Reformation. There were then about 195 Charterhouses in western Europe. The order continues today with foundations in Europe and North America.

What effect does the Carthusian form of life have on us Christians today? Maybe at first it arouses internal rejection. However, it certainly raises questions for us. Their life, prayer, and work in silence and withdrawal remind us of the empirical fact that religious life dries up and withers if it exhausts itself in sheer activity. If it is our great goal in life to live with complete awareness in communion with Jesus Christ, in the sense of today's Reading, we will not attain this goal without time for personal reflection and for personal encounter with him in prayer.

Petitions

Lord Jesus Christ, you are close to us in the solitude and turmoil of every day.

> Open, in all who lead a life of prayer in the silence of contemplative cloisters, eyes for the needs of today's world. . . .
> Give to all, who work with energetic dedication for their fellow men, the courage for a personal encounter with you in prayer. . . .
> Let all hidden sacrifice and prayer be fruitful for the salvation of the entire world. . . .

For you want to strengthen your communion with us in the silence of reflection, so that we can bring your love to others. You who live and reign forever and ever.

Our Lady of the Rosary (October 7)

MEDITATING WITH MARY

Introduction

The Feast of the Rosary (or, more precisely, the Memorial of Our Lady of the Rosary), had its origins in war. It was instituted in remembrance of the victory over the Turks at Lepanto (1572), and was extended to the universal Church after the victory at Peterwardein (1716). Given this background, confidence in the power of the rosary stands in the foreground of this feast. In the rosary itself it is also a matter of pondering with Mary the events of our redemption in our hearts (cf. Lk 2:19,51), thus letting the prayer become fruitful in our own lives.

Penitential Rite

Jesus Christ, you sweat blood for us: Lord, have mercy. . . .
You were enchained and crowned with thorns for us: Christ, have mercy. . . .
You bore the heavy cross for us and died for us on the cross: Lord, have mercy. . . .

Talk

Meditation. Meditation is currently "in." Eastern prophets of salvation, who offer their exotic techniques, and church schools, that include courses on meditation in their curriculum, find their public.

Meditation, however, is not only something for people who work halftime and look for secret knowledge. Meditation is something for everyone. Basically, to meditate means to occupy oneself with something without haste, wholeheartedly, with all of one's capabilities in a thoroughgoing way, so that one's own heart is moved and the person feels driven to live within this reality.

Meditation in the Bible. People in the Bible meditated in this way. They looked back upon what Yahweh had done for his people in the past (the exodus from Egypt, the march through the wilderness, the Covenant on Sinai . . .). They reflected over and over (without haste or rush) on these deeds of God. They allowed these events to be engraved on their hearts, they formulated them into prayers (the Psalms), they involved themselves with them with the result that they lived in a certain way in these events themselves. Through this reflection on God's effect in the past, their trust in God's protection and help in the present grew. They found the courage to walk with Yahweh into the open future.

Meditation in the Rosary. We attempt to do the same thing in the rosary. In the many Hail Marys, we unite ourselves with Mary, so as to look with her open eyes and her open heart and her inner concentration on that which God in Jesus Christ has done for our salvation.

In the Creed and in the repeated Our Fathers, we place ourselves with full awareness before the Triune God, whom we confess as our Redeemer.

With the beginning prayers, we make ourselves aware of the purpose of our prayer in the rosary: faith should grow in us, hope should shape our lives more strongly, love should become more alive and inflaming.

In each sentence, we take into consideration, in the grand horizon of God the Holy Trinity—whom we call "Our Father" over and over again in the Lord's Prayer—distinct events in which God's love revealed itself in the history of our redemption. We occupy ourselves for some time with them, we try to understand them more deeply, we let them penetrate our hearts, so that they might shape our lives even more than before.

Moreover, we need not limit ourselves in the rosary to the traditional fifteen joyful, sorrowful, and glorious mysteries of the rosary. In communion with Mary, I can meditate on other events from the earthly life of Jesus (or on his promises beyond death). I can then compose a sentence myself to repeat during the Hail Mary.

Prayer for Our Time. I know that for many people the rosary is no longer "in." Is it because that it really produces no more that multiplication of words? Or is it because many people lack the capability to occupy themselves without haste and wholeheartedly with what God has done for us in Jesus Christ, and thus be moved from within?

Petitions

Almighty Triune God! In union with Mary we pray to you:

Increase the faith of Christians in the uncertainties of our times . . .
Strengthen hope in all who have become discouraged in the battle against evil and for a better world. . .
Ignite love in those people who think only of their own advantage. . . .

For your Son's Kingdom will only grow where people carry out the Good News in faith, hope, and love. You who live and reign forever and ever.

St. Denis and Companions (October 9)

TO BE A LIGHT TO THE WORLD HERE AND NOW

Introduction

In the current climate of German-French friendship, we can see more clearly how close are the church bonds between West Germany and France. Denis, patron saint of many churches in Rhineland, was the pioneer missioner in the area of current-day Paris and was venerated above all in the French capital. His identity has been a touchy point in France right up into our century—and provides us an example of the risk the Church runs of forgetting problems of the present for the sake of idle questions of the past.

Penitential Rite

You are the salt of the earth, here and now. (Silence) Lord, have mercy. . . .
You are the light of the world, here and now. (Silence) Christ, have mercy. . . .
You are the city on a mountain, here and now. (Silence) Lord, have mercy. . . .

Talk

Again, History and Legend. The historical Denis was a missioner and bishop in the third century in the area of present-day Paris. Shortly after 250 he was executed for the faith along with his companions. His grave was reverently venerated by Christians of the locality and later became a place of pilgrimage.

In the centuries that followed, the saint's cult grew, since pious scribes of legends drew a connection between him and a character in the Acts of the Apostles. In Acts 17:33f is the account of how a man named "Denis the Areopagite" converted as a consequence of a homily by Paul in Athens. Then, toward the end of the fifth century, a Christian theologian published his works under that name, in order to lend them (consistent with the custom of the time) more authority. In the ninth century the thesis arose in Paris that the city's founding bishop, the Denis mentioned in Acts, and the writer were all identical (which meant that the Church in Paris was the foundation of a direct disciple of the apostles). This thesis found nearly universal belief in the Middle Ages, and understandably raised the prestige of the Franch capital.

Up until our century it was argued, especially in France, whether this thesis merited belief or not. The matter was not always handled objectively and calmly—often enough waves of emotion over it would crest high in the "eldest daughter of the Church" (as the French Church proudly called itself). Today we can distinguish more objectively between history and legend (and can see in the legend the concern to display faithfulness to the apostolic tradition through the invention of a contemporary circumstance).

To Be Light of the World Today. This idle historical discussion today stands resolved. The French Church knows well that she is true to her long history only when she tries here and now to be salt of the earth, light of the world, a city on a mountain [Gospel].

St. Denis and Companions 437

With the absolute separation of Church and State at the turn of this century, France broke into the post-Constantinian era earlier than other parts of Europe. For over seventy years the French Church has had to live without state support (no church tax, no aid . . .). In these circumstances, how has she fulfilled her task of being a light to the world?

In this century, France has produced a great number of Christian writers (Claudel, Bernanos, Mauriac . . .), who have stamped the age with Christian thought. It was the homeland of renowned theologians (de Lubac, Congar . . .), who prepared for Vatican Council II by their works. With its several pastoral and liturgical institutes, it gave important impulses to pastoral work in other countries. Finally, France is the land of worker priests, of the spirited attempt to live the Christian message with complete awareness in a workers' milieu.

Nowadays, one does not hear much about the French Church beyond the country's borders. Is this because of poor communications, or is it because French Catholics work more outside of public notice, and in plain everyday work try to be salt of the earth, light of the world, a city on a mountain?

Petitions

Let us pray for Christians in France:

For French bishops and priests, who carry out their pastoral service in great poverty. (Silence).
For priests and lay people who want to be salt of the earth and light of the world among workers. . . .
For family groups that try to strengthen themselves mutually in the faith. . . .
For youth who seek to live their faith in convincing ways. . . .

God our Father, bless the Church in France, so that she can give witness to the Gospel as a city on the mountain. You who live and reign forever and ever.

St. John Leonardi (October 9)

FROM PHARMACIST'S ASSISTANT TO FISHER OF MEN

Introduction

"Times change, but our goal does not change: that everything go well in God's field." John Chrysostom composed this sentence in the fourth century. John Leonardi worked toward this goal in the sixteenth century. What are we doing in order that everything goes well in God's field in our times?

Penitential Rite

"O Lord, listen to my prayer and let my cry for help reach you. Do not hide your face from me in the day of my distress.
Turn your ear toward me and answer me quickly when I call" (Ps 102:2ff).

Have mercy, Lord our God, have mercy. . . .

Talk

From Pharmacist's Assistant to Fisher of Men. John Leonardi (1541–1609), from a middle-class family, worked in his youth as a pharmacist's assistant. Around the age of twenty-five he, like

St. John Leonardi 439

the disciples in the Gospel, left behind his previous occupation in order to follow the call of Jesus as a "fisher of men." He completed the necessary studies (secondary school, philosophy, theology . . .) in four years—an astounding accomplishment even in those days.

After ordination to the priesthood (1571 or 1572) he worked in his home city of Lucca under difficult conditions. The confusing effect was still being felt in that city of the switch by a famous preacher over to Protestantism (and of his consequent marriage).

John Leonardi recognized how necessary a suitable religious knowledge was for keeping the faith alive. He therefore gave his countrymen not only his example of active love for neighbor through his work in prisons and hospitals. He also preached tirelessly. He founded a confraternity of Christian doctrine, to which men and women belonged who gave voluntary religious instruction to children and youths (a forerunner of our current efforts to have fathers and mothers share in the preparation of their children for first holy communion and for confirmation). To give these laypeople the necessary instructional material, he wrote his own *Manual for Religious Instruction*. He also founded a community of priests that worked with his vision of a renewed pastoral mission.

Activity in Rome. By his unflagging zeal, John Leonardi commended himself (in the words of today's Reading) "to every man's conscience." Yet he also had to experience that the prophet counts for nothing in his home area. His reforming zeal aroused resistance. People slandered him and threatened him with death. He finally abandoned his native city and moved to Rome. There he worked together with St. Philip Neri (who, jokingly but seriously, said to him at their first meeting, "You really are a saint—but please be careful that you remain one!").

Along with his work for his growing religious community, the tireless priest traveled about on assignments by the pope in the ensuing years. He was entrusted with diplomatic missions. As visitator, he supported the renewal efforts of many religious communities. And he planned (against the good advice of the saintly Philip Neri) for the future. For his pastoral zeal, the whole world was God's field. He wanted to send his confreres out into the whole world. Toward this end, he founded in Rome a mission seminary, out of which (thanks to papal support) the College of Propaganda Fidei developed, which rendered invaluable service to world missions in the following centuries.

This multifaceted founder, diplomat, and pastor died on October 9, 1609, in Rome, because he cared for the sick with his own hands during a plague epidemic and caught the infection. Even as a v.i.p. in church politics, he did not consider himself above humble service to his neighbor. He did not reserve his life for (supposedly) greater tasks, he dedicated himself (like the Good Samaritan) to people who in their illness needed him then and there.

"That Everything Go Well in God's Field." This ending of life for John Leonardi reminds us that our care for God's field in our age can surely include a good number of things (such as collaborating on preparations for First Holy Communion . . .), but also that it is carried out where we do not consider ourselves above the smallest services to our fellow human beings.

Petitions

Lord Jesus Christ, you give your Church the task of casting out the nets in your name. We pray for all in the ministry of proclaiming the Word:

For the authors and publishers of religious books.   (Silence)
For priests and teachers of religion in parishes and schools. . . .
For the volunteer catechists in our communities. . . .

Lord, send them joy in faith along with imagination, so that they can lead people of today to you. You who live and reign forever and ever.

St. Callistus (October 14)

YES, TO THE CHURCH OF SINNERS

Introduction

Should we baptize all children whose parents request it—or should we insist on a certain minimum of religious practice by the parents as a condition for baptizing the children? Should we not decisively concern ourselves with the "community Church" (the small circle of those who are truly interested and involved) and abolish the "national Church" (the great majority of whom are involved at some remove, ranging from occasional visits to Church over to mere paper membership)? These are questions that are again getting discussed within the Church. Similar questions had to be decided in Rome during the time of Pope Callistus (217–222).

Penitential Rite

"Let the greater among you be as the junior." [Silence] Lord, have mercy. . . .

"Let the leader among you be as the servant." [Silence] Christ, have mercy. . . .

"I am in your midst as the one who serves you." [Silence] Lord, have mercy. . . .

Talk

External Menace. In the first half of the third century, the Roman Church faced an uncertain future in its surroundings. Times of relative quiet alternated with persecutions, which were directed above all at the leaders of the community. According to tradition, Pope Callistus fell victim to such a measure by the state.

Yet the uncertain external situation did not spare the community from internal difficulties, with which this pope saw himself to be confronted.

Personal Attacks. Bishop Callistus came from a slave background. He served the Church as a deacon and, as such, was elected pope. The scholarly priest Hippolytus could not accept this. He drew up a hostile letter of reproach against the new Roman bishop. According to many scholars, he even had himself ordained as antibishop. Others think that he is identical with the St. Hippolytus whose memorial the Church observes on August 13 (according to one tradition, he renounced his claims while in forced labor in Sardinia and thereby restored peace to the Roman Church).

Theological Controversies. The theological quarrels of his time also forced the pope to expel a group in the Roman Church that called into question the Christian faith in the Triune God (Sabellianism).

Pastoral Questions. Particularly pressing, however, are questions of practical pastoral care. In all specific questions (norms for confession, marital morality . . .) there is the underlying problem: should the Church lay hard demands on the individual Christian—and exclude everyone who does not meet these hard demands? Or should the Church have patience with her weak members—and attempt to lead them on the way of the imitation of Christ more through encouragement than through punishment?

Pope Callistus took the second opinion. He immediately drew the charge of laxity from his adversary Hippolytus. Yet his approach would be taken repeatedly by the Church in the following centuries. I think that it is the approach of Jesus Christ, who will not crush the bruised reed nor quench the smoldering wick (cf. Mt 12:20). It is the humble yes to the Church as the community of weak and sinful people who live by the grace of Jesus Christ alone.

Pastoral Questions Today. In today's Church we are faced with the same basic decision: should we proceed in our pastoral care like zealous rigorists who make no attempt to understand their contemporaries in their difficulties of faith and their human limitations? Or should we, like Jesus of Nazareth, acknowledge their good will (buried under much rubbish, apathy, and lack of interest) and try to arouse it, in order to lead on even nominal Christians a little further by encouragement? I believe that this approach (write off no one, tie into any trace of interest, recognize the most varied ties to the congregation—even when they are very superficial . . .) is even today the approach of Jesus Christ, in keeping with diocesan norms.

Petitions

Lord Jesus Christ, you do not crush the bruised reed nor quench the smoldering wick. Hear our prayer:

For those baptized who face the Church with no interest. . . .
For those Christians who meet the Church's representatives with criticism and reservations. . . .
For all those who are ready for practical service in the community but have no connection with liturgical worship. . . .

For all of us who, for all our good will, often forget our good intentions. . . .

Lord Jesus Christ, straighten up the bruised reed again and kindle the smoldering wick into living fire. You who live and reign forever and ever.

St. Teresa of Avila (October 15)

"WHEN PARTRIDGE, THEN PARTRIDGE...."

Introduction

"When partridge, then partridge: when fasting, then fasting"—in this phrase passed on to us from Teresa of Avila (1515–1582), a human being speaks who, in the course of her life, learned to live and savor each moment with full awareness; who knew that the imitation of Jesus Christ involves both hours of joy (including exuberant joy) and days of wearisome effort. Do we give both of these factors enough attention in our daily Christian living?

Penitential Rite

"Like the deer that yearns for running streams, so my soul is yearning for you, my God.

My soul is thirsting for God, the God of my life; when can I enter and see the face of God?" (Ps 42:2ff).

Have mercy, Lord our God, have mercy. . . .

Talk

A Person with Rich Gifts. Teresa of Avila was a lovable girl. She was charming and alert of mind. She could maintain a whole party and was always in the center of things. She had the art of bringing people joy and of making them laugh, and knew how to do so right up to the end of her life.

In addition, she also possessed prudence, energy, and perseverance, which explained part of her success in her great work of cloister reform.

From a Mediocre Nun to Serious Religious Life.

Teresa entered the Carmelites of the age of nineteen. Her first attempt to live out the Carmelite life ended in seriously broken health. After her recovery there followed long years of superficial mediocrity in religious life. At the age of forty she experienced her definitive conversion and turned into a religious woman who gave herself over totally to Jesus Christ and to following him. She wrote down her mysterious and profound prayer experiences in the ensuing decades of her life in several books. These books still help religiously concerned people in their attempt to live with God. At the same time she felt impelled to work along with St. John of the Cross for the renewal of the female and male branches of the Carmelite Order. She remained true to this task amid all resistance and suspicion and helped many cloisters to renew themselves in the spirit of their order.

We can determine by what inner attitude she lived and to what end she challenged us in our Christian life from the two following tests that come to us from her.

God Alone.

Nothing should trouble you,
nothing should frighten you.
Everything passes,
God alone remains the same.
Patience wins all.
Whoever has God lacks nothing:
God alone is enough.

Are we as anchored in God as this great woman who, as the reformer of her order, had to overcome many cares and problems and put up with many attacks and calumnies? Who, in her personal religious life, often felt nothing of God, and yet prayed on faithfully as a matter of course?

Soldiers of Christ.

> You who are soldiers under Christ's banner
> sleep not, sleep not,
> for there is no peace on earth.
> Christ himself chose to die a strong captain.
> Let us follow him,
> for we are guilty of his death.
> What fortune to serve in this war,
> sleep not, sleep not!
> God wants the earth, let no coward be found among you!
> Let us risk our lives,
> since he will best preserve it
> who gives it up for lost.
> Christ is our commander and the prize of this war.
> Sleep not, sleep not,
> for there is no peace on earth!

Is there something of this dedicated readiness alive in us as well? Are we sufficiently filled with the conviction that the imitation of Jesus Christ has its price everywhere? Are we ready to pay this price in a consistent Christian form of life?

Petitions

Gl No. 644 (spoken or sung).

St. Hedwig (October 16)

DUCHESS OF GERMANS AND POLES

Do all visitors to Andechs, the holy mountain of Bavaria, make it past the tavern on the way and reach the monastic church on the heights? On top is the castle in which the great saint of Silesia, St. Hedwig, was born.

In our century we have seen the forced expulsion of Germans out of Silesia. Hedwig belonged to a period in which the Polish dukes led Germans into the country, and Duke Boleslaus sought a German wife for his son and successor Henry.

Penitential Rite

Lord Jesus Christ, you told us, "Whoever wants to be the greatest among you, let him be your servant": Lord, have mercy. . . .

You told us, "Whoever wishes to be first among you, let him be the slave of everyone else": Christ, have mercy. . . .

You have not come to be served, but rather to serve: Lord, have mercy. . . .

Talk

Life Data. Hedwig was born around 1174 in Andechs Castle. She received her upbringing and education at the Kitzingen convent near Würzburg. At age twelve she was married to Henry, son of the duke of

Silesia, and went with her husband to the foreign country. She gave life to seven children. Even without direct influence on political matters, Hedwig in her own way made a contribution to the country's development.

Duchess of Germans and Poles. In those days, Silesian nobility had a high regard for Germany. They wanted to uplift their thinly settled country economically and culturally. On that account, they invited German settlers into their country. German towns, German villages, German monasteries sprang up. Understandably, Hedwig felt especially attached to her German countrymen in the foreign land. Yet by her tireless kindness and readiness to help, she gained the respect of her Polish subjects as well. The duchess knew that she was responsible for all.

Effective Love for Neighbor. Hedwig saw Jesus Christ himself in the poor and the suffering (and in this she resembled her niece, St. Elizabeth of Hungary). She saw to the construction of hospitals and leper homes. Her contemporaries were amazed that she would serve the poor and the sick with her own hands, and that she would send her ladies and servants to do only what she could not accomplish all alone. The extent to which she saw Christ in the poor can be seen in the fact that she would always have thirteen poor people near her (to represent Jesus and the twelve apostles). The duchess took care of them herself. They even had to accompany her on her trip throughout the duchy (which for us is an unbelievable whim of noble care for the poor!).

Strict with Herself. The kind and caring woman on the ducal throne of Silesia was strict with herself in her effort to become like the Crucified One. Her austerity in food, clothing, and life-style exceeded all measure. She shocked the ducal court with her "religious extravagances" (as many chose to term them). Yet she continued to pursue further her strict ascetic life.

Under the Cross. Hedwig stood under the cross her whole life long. She suffered from the warlike quarrels within her husband's family. She lived through the deaths of six out of her seven children. She was hardest hit by the death of her son Henry, who was being groomed as his father's successor. In 1241, when the Mongols had invaded Europe and were laying waste to Silesia, the duke engaged them in battle with a small force near Liegnitz. He lost the battle and died right on the battlefield. When Hedwig received word of his death, she was able to console her daughter and daughter-in-law with a phrase adapted from the words of Jesus on the Mount of Olives: "It is the will of God, and whatever he wills and what pleases him must come to pass."

Her Life's End. Till the end of her life, Hedwig knew that her place was at the ducal court, even after the death of her husband. Yet she returned often to the convent at Trebonitz in order to live in the surroundings she had come to know and cherish as a child. There she died on October 15, 1243, and was interred there in the convent church. Germans and Poles soon began to make pilgrimages to her tomb. She was canonized in 1267.

Petitions

Lord Jesus Christ, in your Church there should be neither Jew nor Gentile, neither Greek nor Roman, but only brothers and sisters under your Father.

> Grant that the peoples of the earth may find their way to common ground beyond all cultural, linguistic, and racial differences. . . .
> Let a permanent reconciliation take place between Poles and Germans. . . .
> Free all refugees from any embitterment over the injustice that was done to them. . . .

For you will that all nations and peoples be united in your kingdom. You who live and reign forever and ever.

St. Margaret Mary Alacoque (October 16)

DEVOTION TO THE SACRED HEART

Introduction

These days many important (and unimportant) personalities of our times are glad to speak and write about their remarkable (or trivial) interior life. Of St. Margaret Mary Alacoque we possess only sketches of her life, and that only because her sisters in religion prevented her from destroying her notes during her last illness. In them a human being is revealed who lived by God with heart and soul, and who desired to make his love known to other people. She saw this love in a very particular way in the symbol of the Sacred Heart of Jesus and saw her life's work to be the promoting of this devotion.

Penitential Rite

Lord Jesus Christ, you became poor so that we might become rich: Lord, have mercy. . . .

You healed the sick and revealed to all the power and love of God: Christ, have mercy. . . .

You died for us sinful men, that we might have fullness of life: Lord, have mercy. . . .

Talk

On the Dark Side of Life. The old Christian experience, that people on the dark side of life understand better and accept more willingly the message of Christ, than do those who are sheltered, holds true as well in the life of St. Margaret Mary (1647–1690).

Margaret Mary was often sick during her childhood. When her father died, the family fell into financial hardships. She had to live with an uncle, who treated her like a common servant. Yet, from these experiences of deliberate humiliation by others and of her own personal limitations, there arose within her a totally personal form of religious life. This led her at the age of twenty-four into the Salesian convent of Parey-le-Monial.

Mystical Experiences. Right from her youth, the religious life of St. Margaret Mary was marked by extraordinary mental circumstances. She heard inner voices, and had visions. Her ecstasies bothered her sisters during her novitiate and her later life in community. They took them as a sign of self-importance and dealt with her rudely over them. She herself did not base her prayer life upon these attendant spiritual phenomena. Her genuine religious depth showed its presence thereby, inasmuch as she did not become upset or embittered over the misunderstanding of her sisters, but reacted with tranquil kindness and readiness to serve.

Her personal piety concentrated more and more on the love of God, which revealed itself for her especially in the divine-human Heart of Jesus. She understood that God's love comes to us in the human love of Jesus who enriches us with human warmth and understanding, who (with all his divinity) by human standards consumed himself for us and finally died out of love for us. In one of her great visions, she saw a heart ringed with flames as a symbol of this love.

Devoted to the Sacred Heart. This visionary image ("Sacred Heart of Jesus, burning furnace of charity"—Litany of the Sacred Heart) became the central meditative image of the devotion to the Sacred Heart, for which St. Margaret Mary labored together with her Jesuit confessor. She thus took her place at the beginning of a form of piety which influenced religious life in the Catholic Church, above all in the nineteenth and twentieth centuries (up to our own times). The Feast of the Sacred Heart (Friday after the Octave of Corpus Christi) and the monthly Friday of the Sacred Heart go back to their initiative.

The meditation on the love of God that comes to us in the human heart of Jesus has been set down in many prayers and hymns. The best (old and new) tests are found in *Gotteslob* (549; 552; 553; 780). The images and aspects brought together especially in the Litany of the Sacred Heart are those in which the devotion to the Sacred Heart seeks to know and meditate upon the unfathomable love of God.

"Jesus, meek and humble of heart, make our hearts like unto thine," runs the text of an old short prayer from the devotional tradition. In our Christian life it is no more and no less a matter than whether we recognize the love of God in a special way in the open heart of Jesus or in some other way.

Petitions

Let us pray:

Jesus, full of compassion for people . . . Make our hearts to be like yours. . . .
Jesus, kind to the sick . . . Make our hearts. . . .
Jesus, merciful towards sinners. . . .
Jesus, fountain of life and holiness. . . .

Lord our Savior, let our names be deeply carved into your most Sacred Heart. Let it be our fortune and our honor to live and die in your service. You who live and reign forever and ever (closing after GL 780,6).

St. Ignatius of Antioch (October 17)

BISHOP AND MARTYR IN PASSAGE

Introduction

In the New Testament we have a collection of early Christian writings which the Church considers to be an indispensable witness to her faith. The Gospels and the Epistles, the Acts of the Apostles and Revelation are, however, not the only Christian writings that remain from that early period. There are in addition written testimonies of the life of the early Church, whose (known or unknown) authors came to be called the "apostolic fathers." Among these writings are seven letters of St. Ignatius of Antioch, which he wrote after his arrest en route to Rome, addressing them to various Christian communities in Asia Minor.

Penitential Rite

Lord Jesus Christ, a living unity in your Spirit is not always our concern: Lord, have mercy. . . .

We fear the effort that a life in faith demands of us: Christ, have mercy. . . .

We do not live enough in the joy of our fellowship with you: Lord, have mercy. . . .

Talk

Life and Times. Ignatius was born around the year 50. As he was eventually (somewhere between 100 and 115) condemned to death in gladiator battle in Rome, he must have been a slave in the eyes of Roman law. He might have seen one or another of the apostles on a missionary trip, staying a while in the central city of the Eastern Roman Empire. He later became leader of Antioch's Christian community.

His time was a time of upheaval and troubles from within and from without. The small Christian communities ran into their first conflicts with the Roman state. Even when the police were not hunting Christians down, they still moved in when someone was accused of being a Christian.

Within the Church there were the old tensions between Jewish and gentile Christians and the new questions of the appropriate presentation of the message of Jesus Christ after the death of the apostles. There existed the danger that the Good News would be corrupted and that the communities would split into rival groups.

Faithfulness to Tradition and Unity. During this time Ignatius worked tirelessly for faithfulness to the traditional teaching of the faith and for the unity of the community. He saw in the person of the bishop the guarantor for the uncorrupted shielding of the tradition, and in the fellowship with the bishop the bond of church unity. These thoughts recur time and again in his letters. He wrote in one place, "Where the bishop is found, there should be the community as well, just as where Jesus Christ is found, there too is the Catholic Church." Or: "If the prayer of one person or another has great power, how much more the prayer of the bishop and the community." In another place he praised the community that was bound in heart to the bishop "as the Church with Jesus Christ and as Jesus Christ with the Father."

Readiness for Martyrdom. Ignatius did not view his office of bishop as a post of prestige to be held by authoritarianism. He considered his service as bishop to be a task that he performed with other fellow servants. And he was deeply convinced that he had to give himself up for the community as did Jesus Christ.

This readiness to yield himself up is expressed in those passages in his letters where he speaks of his approaching execution in Rome. After his conviction in Antioch, he was brought to Rome to be cast to the wild beasts. Since people in Rome were openly taking steps to free him, he wrote to the Roman community, "Let it happen that I become the food of wild beasts; through them it will be granted to me to come to God. . . . May I be allowed to take on the sufferings of my God." In the same letter, however, his fear comes out that he might become weak when tested, and he pleads with the Christians in Rome, "Obey me not, even if I call upon you personally; rather, obey what I write. For I write as one who is living and wishes to die."

Petitions

Lord Jesus Christ:

Let mutual respect and comprehension grow among different Christian Churches and communions. . . .
Grant that the various groups in our communities find themselves again and again in common prayer and dialogue on your Good News. . . .
Send the Holy Spirit upon our bishops, that they might lead the Church in faithfulness to you. . . .

For in you alone does the Church have her foundation. You who live and reign forever and ever.

St. Luke (October 18)

A "PAINTER OF MARY"

Introduction

Luke—the author of the Gospel of the same name, and of the Acts of the Apostles—believed, in setting out his writings, that the Church had a long journey through time and that the Second Coming of Christ would be in the even more distant future. In his manner of presenting the story of Jesus and of the young Church, he attempted to help believers keep their faith during the interim period. In this context he also presented Mary, the Mother of Jesus, as the best example of living faith.

Penitential Rite

"They all remained joined in prayer with Mary, the Mother of Jesus." [Silence] Lord, have mercy. . . .

"Mary said, I am the maidservant of the Lord. Let it be done to me as you say." (Silence) Christ, have mercy. . . .

"Mary treasured all these things and reflected on them in her heart." (Silence) Lord, have mercy. . . .

Talk

In this month of the rosary and on this feast of the evangelist Luke, let us talk about the image of Mary, as she is portrayed in his Gospel, and how it affects the imitation of Christ even in our day.

With Mary, the Mother of Jesus. According to Luke, Mary was in complete fellowship with the Church as the Mother of Jesus (cf. Acts 1:14). Along with Matthew and Mark, he emphasizes that family relationship to Jesus is no longer meaningful for the Church: "My mother and my brothers are these who hear the word of God and act upon it" (Lk 8:21). Yet he also pictures the Mother of Jesus as the one who is praised by Elizabeth on account of her faith: "Blessed is she who trusted that the Lord's words to her would be fulfilled" (Lk 1:45).

Praying Faith. This model faith for each follower of Jesus also is evident in Mary's prayer. Christian tradition can only imagine Mary praying at the time of the Annunciation ("Mary was alone, deep in prayer . . .). Luke shows her speaking the Magnificat as an expression of her joy over her calling (cf. Lk 1:46–56) and pictures her united in prayer with the young Church (cf. Acts 1:14). In prayer Mary opens herself to God, in prayer she allows herself to be spoken to and enriched by God. In prayer she responds to God—just as we, as believing Christians, always try to do the same.

Yes to the Will of God. In prayer the Mother of Jesus acknowledges God's plan, in prayer she placed herself at the disposal of God's work of salvation: "Behold, I am the maidservant of the Lord. Let it be done to me as you say" (Lk 1:38). Her confession of faith consists of her letting her life be determined by God's plan, by her serving God's plan of salvation with her whole life—and thus is an example for our faith.

Service to Others. Being "the maidservant of the Lord" takes effect for Mary in her service to her neighbor. Just as Jesus approached people—the very poorest and most abandoned, according to Luke's Gospel—so did Mary go to her relative Elizabeth,—who was in her sixth month (cf. Lk 1:36), and stayed with her for about three months (cf. Lk 1:56). For the Word of the Lord, which she followed (cf. Lk

8:21), is summed up in the great commandment of love for God and love for neighbor (cf. Lk 10:27).

Mary Treasured All These Things in Her Heart. Two times Luke states that Mary "treasured all these things and reflected on them in her heart" (Lk 2:19,51). The Mother of Jesus remembered what God had done in her Son. She reflected upon the incomprehensible fact of redemption over and over—just as the whole Church and each individual Christian must keep and always reflect anew on the awareness of redemption in Jesus Christ.

Believing after the Example of Mary. Luke does not tell us in his Gospel what Mary looked like, how long she lived, where she died. But he does portray her for us as the great believer. We believe as she did, if, in communion with the Church, we are open in prayer to God; if we—especially in the rosary—recall what has come to pass in Jesus Christ with her cooperation, and ponder it again and again; if we in prayer place ourselves at God's disposal and accomplish God's Word through our service to others.

Petitions

Lord our God, in union with Mary, the Mother of your son and our Mother, we call upon you:

Bless the work of theologians in seminaries and colleges . . .
Help preachers to speak convincingly and clearly about your Good News . . .
Give to all the faithful the readiness to ponder your Word in their hearts and to apply it in everyday life . . . .

For you want the Church to give witness to the Good News for all time. You who live and reign forever and ever.

Sts. John de Brebeuf, Isaac Jogues, and Companions (October 19)

MISSION AMONG THE INDIANS

Introduction

Indians in America and Canada were widely exterminated in their encounter with Christian immigrants from Europe. Military actions and diseases brought in by the white man brought down the once-proud masters of the forests and prairies. Now only pitiful remnants lead a life on reservations subsidized by the government. What do we know about the efforts of Christian missioners who tried to win over the "Redskins" for the faith? Today's saints made their contribution in the seventeenth century. They are representative of all before and after them that worked among the Indians of Canada and the United States.

Penitential Rite

"Awake, O Lord, why do you sleep?
Arise, do not reject us for ever!
For we are brought down low to the dust;
our body lies prostrate on the earth.
Stand up, and come to our help!
Redeem us because of your love!" (Ps 44:24,26f).

Talk

Special Problems. Missionaries who wanted to work among the Indians in America and Canada in past centuries found themselves faced with immense difficulties. Their work was first hindered by the struggle between Catholic France and Protestant England, as they fought for their spheres of influence for over two hundred years. Moreover, as European missioners they stood between land-hungry immigrants and justifiably mistrustful Indians, who were unwilling to hand over their land. European Christians also did not always provide shining examples of Christian life. Then too, the missioners had to study the language intensely and accept unimaginable physical hardships on their missionary travels.

John de Brebeuf. In the seventeenth century, Jesuits labored alongside other orders in the eastern border area between America and Canada among the Iroquois and Huron tribes. Among them, John de Brebeuf cut an impressive figure. The Frenchman was forced to interrupt his first mission project when he was captured by the English and packed off back to Europe. Four years later (1633) he went again to Canada. During the next sixteen years he worked under many difficulties with the Indians. He authored a dictionary and a grammar of the Huron language, which he spoke like his own. He was a good organizer and financier. Above all, he left an impression through his goodness and self-possession, which he maintained in all the dangerous situations of his laborious service.

Difficult political circumstances, tensions between Indians and immigrants, differences of opinion among the missioners concerning the correct missionary methods, and illnesses gave John de Brebeuf much to deal with during these years (the Reading is appropriately applied to him), yet he remained true to his vow never to be unfaithful to his missionary task out of a fear of death. In this spirit, he resumed his missionary work among the Hurons in 1649; he was captured by the (hostile) Iroquois and was tortured to death.

The Church and the Indians Yesterday and Today.
Along with John de Brebeuf, we memorialize today seven other Jesuit missioners who met their deaths during that period in North America. As officially canonized saints, they are representative of all unknown missioners whose lives were ended by murder, or who as "martyrs of the cold" (of loneliness, of the hardships of month-long trips) gave up their lives for the Indians (and the Eskimos). In the shifting geographical areas (hundreds of miles out from European settlements), they sought to protect (by the standards of the time) "their" Indians from the white man. They strove for peaceful coexistence between the "sons of the wilderness" and the Europeans—yet they could not rescue the Indians from ruin.

Today public opinion in the United States and Canada is again more clearly aware of the injustices inflicted on the Indians. In the Catholic Churches of these countries the readiness is increasing to work with the Indians (many Catholic) on reservations and to render them help to help themselves.

Petitions

Lord Jesus Christ, with confidence in the intercession of all missioners who have worked in the United States and in Canada, we pray for the Church in North America:

Grant that they may credibly give witness of the Good News to people in our century. . . .
Let them recognize their responsibility for the minority groups of North American society. . . .
Bless the dedication of priests and religious who work among Indians and Eskimos. . . .

You who live and reign forever and ever.

St. Paul of the Cross (October 19)

THE WORD FROM THE CROSS

Introduction

With every sign of the cross that we consciously make (at the beginning and the end of the day, before and after meals, at the beginning and the end of the eucharistic liturgy . . . we place ourselves expressly under the cross of Christ; we acknowledge him who brought us salvation through the cross and demanded of his disciples, "If a man wishes to come after me, he must deny his very self, take up his cross, and begin to follow in my footsteps" [Gospel]. For St. Paul of the Cross (1694–1775), the taking up of the cross was a reality that shaped his whole life. How does the reality of the cross appear in my own life?

Penitential Rite

Jesus Christ, who died on the cross for us by the holy wounds in your hands: Lord, have mercy. . . .

Jesus Christ, who died on the cross for us by the holy wounds of your feet: Christ, have mercy. . . .

Jesus Christ, who died on the cross for us by the holy wound in your side: Lord, have mercy. . . .

Talk

In the Middle of the Enlightenment. Paul of the Cross worked during his youth as an assistant in his father's shop in a small northern Italian town. At the age of nineteen he was so moved by a sermon of his pastor that his life took on an expressly religious direction. Along with his regular job, he gave religious instruction as a volunteer in his parish (and spent seven hours each day in prayer and other pious practices). When he was twenty-six, he received permission from his bishop to live as a hermit and to engage in apostolic work in the diocese. Like-minded people soon joined him; however, they did not last long under the overly strict ascetic. Twenty years passed before the pope approved the founding of the "Passionists" (a religious congregation that held special devotion for the cross and the passion of Christ), after the original rule had been substantially mitigated.

This saint discovered anew for himself personally (and for his generation) the "wisdom of the cross" [Reading], and the call of Jesus in taking up the cross, right in the middle of the century of the Enlightenment and of the triumph of human reason. On that account, he gave his congregation a habit which, for adornment, had only a heart joined to a cross. He saw in the cross the revelation of God's love, which went all the way with us. He grasped through the passion, death, and resurrection of Jesus the "divine wisdom" that the cross is not the way to final destruction, but to a new beginning. He wanted to become like the cross-bearing Jesus in his own life (and saw the path to this goal in an ascetic life with as many renouncements as possible). Through his pastoral activity he wanted to bring people before the love of God, revealed on the cross, and lead them to carrying their own crosses.

The Word from the Cross in Our Lives. Do I place myself under the cross (in every sign of the cross and in each eucharistic celebration) as did Paul of the Cross?

I only stand underneath the cross when I acknowledge the revelation of the love of God (and not the gruesome punishment by a vengeful God) in the passion and death of Jesus. When I learn from Jesus' fate, then my own suffering does not lead inescapably to ruin, but rather, if accepted with him, becomes the way to a new life with God. When I gain courage from recognizing this "wisdom of God," then I can pursue my own way through life (not always easily) with trust in his help.

Insofar as I do this, I also accept my own cross and imitate him [Gospel]. We are rightly astonished today by the austerities and hardships by which the religious radicalism of many saints also became manifest (as Paul of the Cross lived them out for his contemporaries). Yet we are also correct in thinking that, in reference to the matter of carrying the cross, for us "normal" Christians it involves taking on the large and small demands of everyday life, of not buckling under when difficulties and resistance set in and when we have to "bite the bullet" in order to pull through. When we honestly try to do this, we are carrying after Jesus our cross (and his) within our lives.

Petitions

Lord Jesus Christ, you call upon your disciples to take up their cross and to follow you:

Be close to all who have the cross of age and illness to carry. . . .
Give courage to all who are burdened with the cross of failure. . . .
Bless the life of all who take hard things upon themselves in order to do penance for others. . . .

For you will come with your angels in the glory of your Father and will render to each of us according to our deeds. You who live and reign forever and ever.

St. John of Capistrano (October 23)

ENVOY IN GOD'S STEAD

Introduction

A Christian saint is not a perfect human being, but rather a person who seeks to live, with all his or her limitations and weaknesses, primarily with Jesus Christ. Thus, nothing was lacking to the genuine holiness of the most famous migratory preacher of Europe, St. John of Capistrano (1386–1456), when he confessed his pride, self-righteousness, and meanness in his writings and homilies. If we cannot compare with him (or with other saints in their radical seriousness over Jesus Christ), we want at least to be like him in humility, by which we confess our sins before God and call his mercy upon us.

Penitential Rite

"The Lord is compassion and love, slow to anger and rich in mercy. His wrath will come to an end; he will not be angry for ever.
As far as the east is from the west so far does he remove our sins" (Ps 103:8f,12).   (Silence)

Have mercy, Lord our God, have mercy. . . .

Talk

Extraordinary Calling in Hard Times. As the Council of Constance was convening in 1414, for forty years there had been two popes in Europe (and for years a substitute third as well), who battled with each other violently. The unity of the Church was, as a consequence, seriously impaired by fanatic movements (such as the Hussites in Bohemia). The Council succeeded in getting the three popes to abdicate, and in electing a new pope. To a certain extent, this provided the organizational conditions for a renewal of church life. The renewal itself was carried forward by people like John of Capistrano.

John was the son of a Nordic baron who had migrated to Italy. His father fell victim to the troubles of the times, and the family castle was burnt down. After his education in law, John became a judge in Perugia. He became engaged to the daughter of a count from his home area. He then was captured during a military conflict. In the weeks and months of his imprisonment, he went through an interior transformation. This gave him a completely new direction in his life. He dissolved his purely juridical marriage; then he became a Franciscan and developed from 1417 onwards his career as a wandering preacher, which led him into practically every country in Europe.

A distant image of the appearance that John of Capistrano (and other preachers of the period) gave can be seen perhaps in the "preaching processions" of the German Father Leppich in the 1950s. The eloquent Franciscan of the late Middle Ages moved around with a complete group of assistants from town to town. They served him as interpreters (he preached only in Latin), they reproduced his posters, they wrote down his homilies from under his pulpit.

Today we can barely imagine the wide effect of this migratory preacher. For forty years he traveled throughout Europe in order to lead his nations in one faith. He not only renewed church life everywhere, he also contributed markedly to the common effort of the European countries to repel the Turkish threat, which led to the victory at Belgrade, in the year of the saint's death.

Homilies Lived Out. If we inquire what was this tireless pastor's secret of success, the answer would lie partly in that John of Capistrano belonged to the renewal movement among the Franciscans (the "Observants"). These Franciscans were convinced that their preaching was fruitful only if they had lived out what they were preaching. They dedicated themselves therefore to living a consciously exemplary Christian life. As a lawgiver, John gave permanence to this Franciscan line. On his preaching tours, he sought with his aides to put common prayer and exemplary life in the center, amid all external turmoil and all pastoral demands, since he knew that words inspire, but example sweeps people along.

To preach what one is living! Words inspire, but example sweeps people along. This holds true not only for pastoral care. It also holds true for witnessing the faith in one's neighborhood, for religious discussion in public. . . .

Petitions

Let us pray:

For preachers and pastors: that they might live out what they proclaim to others . . . Lord, have mercy. . . .
For mothers and fathers: that they may be examples to their children of what they demand of them. . . .
For all of us, that we might announce the Good News through the witness of our lives. . . .

Lord, our God, speak through our example to the people of our time and lead them on this way to fellowship with you. You who live and reign forever and ever.

St. Anthony Mary Claret (October 24)

MISSIONARY TO THE COMMON PEOPLE, BISHOP, CONFESSOR TO THE QUEEN

Introduction

"With his many thousands of sermons that were extraordinarily popular, Father Claret, a man of unbelievable activity, has re-Christianized all of Catalonia. He accomplished the same feat in the Canary Islands and later in Cuba, where Catholicism was on its last legs. His stay in Madrid was a genuine catastrophe for the Spanish revolutionary movement." This was the judgment of a political and ideological opponent of one of the greatest figures of the Spanish Church in the nineteenth century.

Penitential Rite

Lord Jesus Christ, you proclaim to people the Father's love: Lord, have mercy. . . .

You call people from all races and classes into the service of the Gospel: Christ, have mercy. . . .

You want us to bring to people the Good News of the Father's forgiving love: Lord, have mercy. . . .

Talk

Parish missioner. It was only at the age of twenty-one that Anthony Mary Claret was able to begin the path to the priesthood that he longed for. At twenty-eight, he was ordained a priest as a late vocation. After a failed attempt to become a Jesuit (he had to leave because of illness), he started a fruitful parish mission activity in his Spanish homeland. He knew how to address his countrymen—and often preached six to eight hours a day. He knew how to reach people's hearts in the confessional. Astounding conversions often resulted. For all this he was ruthlessly attacked and slandered by the various civil war parties (times in Spain were unstable).

He had similar success on the Canary Islands, where his bishop sent him, because his life was no longer safe in Spain during the revolutionary year of 1848.

Archbishop of Cuba. Some few weeks after the founding of the parish mission society known as the Claretians, Anthony Mary was unexpectedly named archbishop of Cuba, the Caribbean island that at the time was under Spanish dominion. With a heavy heart, the saint undertook the responsibility for this neglected diocese. True to his own past, he toured his diocese as bishop and missionary to the common people. Success, and opposition, from antichurch circles were not long in coming. While many believers were led to a more aware faith, the bishop several times narrowly escaped death in attempts on his life.

Confessor to the Queen. As the quarrels between the archbishop and his adversaries in Cuba were reaching a high point, the Spanish queen requested the saint to return to Madrid and there to serve her and the royal family as pastor and counselor. Anthony Mary accepted the new mandate. In his new post he was successful not only in reconciling the royal couple with each other, he also exerted influence over Spanish church politics in general and saw to the appointment of worthy and competent bishops. If he was traveling with the royal pair, he would preach to the faithful wherever they stopped. He used his spare time to write a number of religious works that were published in large printings.

It All Depends on Love. When the Spanish king and queen were deposed in 1868, the saint had to go with them into exile in France. He was finally forced to hide himself from vengeful Spaniards in a Cistercian monastery; he died there in 1870 after a long illness.

Anthony Mary Claret had extraordinary gifts and capabilities. Yet he knew what really counted in the imitation of Christ. Something he wrote once for his co-workers has meaning as well for us and for our dedication to the Kingdom of God: "The virtue that an apostolic worker needs is love. He must love God . . . and men. If he lacks this love, then all his abilities will not help him. However, with this love and normal abilities, he will be able to overcome everything."

Petitions

Let us pray to our Lord Jesus Christ:

For all who fearlessly proclaim the Good News   (Silence)   Christ, hear us. . . .
For Christians in Cuba, who under current conditions are striving for a living faith.   (Silence)   Christ, hear us. . . .
For all bishops who are faced with the hard task of providing up-to-date pastoral care in their dioceses.   (Silence)   Christ, hear us. . . .

For you are the hidden life-power of your Church. You who live and reign forever and ever.

Sts. Simon and Jude (October 28)

THE CALL TO DISCIPLESHIP

Introduction

Simon—a terrorist, who met Jesus and became his disciple. Judas (not Judas Iscariot)—who encountered the wandering prophet from Nazareth. Neither is sketched with any more detail in the Gospels. According to legend, they preached in Egypt and Persia and were executed together. The Gospel's description of their calling holds true for our call to discipleship in our current-day Church. Let us open ourselves anew for Jesus Christ, who now prays for us and with us, that he might go forth with us at the end of the Eucharist into our daily lives.

Penitential Rite

Lord Jesus Christ, you prayed the whole night long for your disciples: Lord, have mercy. . . .

You chose the apostles for special tasks: Christ, have mercy. . . .

You went with them to the sick and to those plagued with unclean spirits: Lord, have mercy. . . .

Talk

An Important Moment. Luke uses unaccustomed solemnity in his account of the calling of the twelve. Jesus prayed the entire night, before he chose from the group of people interested in him the ones who were to form the inner circle of his disciples. By the specific emphasis on Jesus' long prayer, there is stressed the importance of this selection for the individual disciples (and for the Church). One's whole life was taken in service to Jesus and his cause. The twelve were to be Jesus' constant companions. In fellowship with him they became the "Apostles" (the ones sent forth), to whom he could later entrust his Good News.

A Wide Spectrum. A glance at the names of the apostles shows that Jesus could use the most diverse types and characters for his circle of disciples: from the law-abiding Peter to the tax collector Matthew even to the terrorist ("zealot") Simon. He spoke to them in their distinctiveness, he made them over into disciples by his closeness, and daring terrorists. They brought their distinctiveness into the circle of disciples and found themselves united in a common enthusiasm for Jesus and his Good News.

He Came Down from the Mountain with Them. Jesus did not allow his disciples to remain with him "on the mountain" of prayerful communion with the Father. He came down from the mountain with them. He went into the plain with them, where many people "from all of Judea and Jerusalem and the coastal region around Tyre and Sidon" were waiting for him. He went with the apostles to the people who were clamoring for him: they wanted to hear him, touch him, be healed by him from their illnesses.

The day came when he sent his disciples forth so that they might, in his authority (and on their own responsibility) "to proclaim the Kingdom of God and to heal the sick" (Lk 9:1–6, cf. Lk 10:1–16). Thereby they also found the people who were looking for them: the cripple at the gate of the temple (Acts 3:1ff); the crowds in Jerusalem and the surrounding cities with their sick and with those afflicted by unclean spirits. . . .

One Call to Discipleship. Baptism as call to discipleship, appointment to specific services within the Church—these are still in our day important moments surrounded with the atmosphere of prayer, in order to make it clear that here there is something important going on between God and man.

Even now Jesus can use the most diverse types and characters for the living disciples. Our congregation, in its variety (and sometimes in its painfully felt contradictions), is the best illustration of this. Do we find ourselves united in a common enthusiasm for Jesus and for his Good News?

Our calling likewise does not have the goal of us being together with Jesus "on the mountain" (in liturgical worship, in prayer). He comes down "from the mountain" with us, that we might put ourselves at the disposal of the people who need us on the "plain" of hard everyday life, in his name and his power; that we might instruct them and heal them of their illnesses. . . . And this "plain" starts again today immediately beyond the church door, which we close behind us after the liturgy.

Petitions

Lord Jesus Christ, you call men and women into your Church to give witness to the Good News:

Grant that the Church might become an ever-clearer sign of your love among the nations. . . .
Bring to her the Spirit of prayer and gladness in the liturgy. . . .
Awaken in young people the readiness to place themselves at the service of the Church with all their hearts. . . .

For you alone give the Church growth in goodness. You who live and reign forever and ever.

All Saints (November 1)

THE SAINTS, "GOD'S CHILDREN"

Introduction

Just ask an average Christian whether he or she is or wants to become a "saint." Many will ward off the question with gestures—and emphasize at the same time that of course they try to live as complete Christians in professional and private life. But "become a saint"? Thanks for asking! Deep attitudes of piety and notions of holiness of previous generations have led to the point where the words "saint," "sanctity," and related categories bring out only unfavorable feelings, and do not manifest to many Christians any ideal of Christian life. On the Feast of All Saints, it is fitting to look over these abused words.

Penitential Rite

"Blest are the lowly; they shall inherit the land." (Silence) Lord, have mercy. . . .

"Blest are they who show mercy; mercy shall be theirs." (Silence) Christ, have mercy. . . .

"Blest too are the peacemakers; they shall be called sons of God." Lord, have mercy. . . .

Talk

Holiness as a Gift. The apostle Paul did not have to contend with our current antipathy toward being a "saint." When, for example, he addressed the Christians in Corinth as "saints" (cf. 1 Cor 1:1), they were certainly proud of the title.

The Christians from Corinth, whom Paul calls "saints," made up a community which was split by factions and conflicts, in which there were abuses that cried out to heaven and required the apostle's personal intervention. They were no showcase of virtue and piety. They did not lead exemplary lives in every respect. Paul did not call them saints on account of any especially pious change in life. For him they are "saints" because Christ has removed them from the dominion of sin through baptism and has brought them into living communion with God. They are "saints" because they are "children of God" [second Reading].

In sacred Scripture, to be a "saint" means principally to be in union with God, to have a share in divine life. Understood in this way, being a saint is not a human accomplishment but rather is God's gift: our sanctification, our share in his divine life is his unfathomable will (cf. 1 Thess 4:3).

We can have no reason for objecting to this meaning of sainthood. It is simply the gift of our faith. To reject it would be equivalent to rejecting God himself and our status as God's children.

Sainthood Obliges. Without question, this gift of sainthood obliges us. Our share in divine life demands from us a godly way of life. Paul never tired of hammering into his Christians, "You are holy, therefore become holy!" Even in this sense Paul said that our sanctification, that is, a godly way of life, is God's will.

All Saints

What This Means. "To become a saint" is thus the life program of every Christian, which results from our baptism and from our call to fellowship with God. No Christian can presume then to say, sainthood is not something for everyone.

However, this "learning program for Christian sainthood" does not involve acrobatic feats of prayer or astoundingly extraordinary deeds. Paul spoke of the above-mentioned demand for a saintly way of life along with simple questions of business and sexual morality, of brotherly love and reasonable work, including a "respectable life" (1 Thess 4:4–12). The Gospel gives the eight Beatitudes as basic attitudes proper to a life according to God's will.

To put it another way: Christian sainthood consists primarily in that we, with the knowledge of our endowed communion with God, show ourselves to be God's servants in our daily duties and tasks. It does not place extraordinary demands on us. The extraordinary thing lies in that we take our communion with God with total seriousness every day. No column sitter and no fasting champion will excite people for Christ today. Only a Christian, who as a workaday saint puts his faith into daily practice, will give clear witness to Christ. All of us are certainly called to this workaday sainthood (whether or not the word "saint" fits us in this context).

Petitions

Holy God, it is your will that all men live by their communion with you. Hear our prayer by the intercession of the saints:

Increase in the Church the gratitude of believers for the gift of sainthood. . . .
Strengthen the hope of Christians amid the difficulties of everyday living. . . .

Grant that Christian communities of faith might become advocates of the dispossessed and the oppressed. . . .

Lord, awaken in the Church the Spirit of the Sermon on the Mount, so that your Kingdom might grow in this world. You who live and reign forever and ever.

All Souls (November 2)

BUT SHE IS STILL DEAD

Introduction

One day an acquaintance found the great actress Adele Sandrock in black clothing on the street and asked what was the occasion of her mourning. "My mother is dead," she replied. The acquaintance responded with amazement, "but that happened two years ago already . . . " The actress answered, "But she is still dead."—Is this all we can know, if we recall our dead today? What comment does our faith make on our own experience that our own dead as well are "still dead" years (or decades) later?

Talk

They Are Still Dead. In these days, you have decorated graves. You have visited them at the cemetery. Your thoughts drift to other graves in other cemeteries, perhaps to graves that no one recognizes anymore: military graves on foreign soil, graves of relatives in other countries. The remembrance of deceased relatives and friends comes alive in you. You think of people who have died just this past year. You think of others whose lives came to an end years or decades ago. And you are aware that they are all "still dead."

Death as Separation. Perhaps the memory of the circumstances of the deaths of our friends and relatives has softened with the passage of time. Perhaps a veil of forgetting has fallen over the pain of the final illness or over the horrible circumstances of the traffic accident. What we always, however, feel over again, what always lives again with us is this fact: whether death comes through a heart attack or in an auto accident, whether life slowly expires through the feebleness of old age or someone dies gradually from a terrible illness, death separates people from one another irrevocably. People who have lived and worked, loved and fought together. People who trusted one another, who felt a belonging to one another, who had fellowship with each other.

This separation is irrevocable. There is no reverse out of death. We feel that over and over as pain. This experience that something is taken away from us by a person's death is all the more lively and painful in proportion to the depth of our relationship.

I Am the Resurrection. We Christians are also not spared this experience of a human relationship definitively destroyed by death. Even our relatives and friends are "still dead" after years and decades. However, let us not despair at their graves in weary resignation.

In the middle of our cemetery there stands a large cross. On many tombstones there is a symbol of the cross. We print a cross on our death notices and adorn the cover of a coffin with a cross. If this symbol of the cross in connection with death is for us not just a venerable custom, then let us express our conviction in faith: since God in his love for us men has gone to death on a cross, we in death will not fall out of the loving hand of God (cf. Wisdom 3:1). Therefore our dead are with the living God.

The hope expressed in the symbol of the cross becomes still clearer if it is presented as the victory banner of the Risen One (as on some tombstones), if next to the cross on the death notices or the condolence cards there appears something close to the words in today's Gospel: "I am the resurrection and the life; whoever believes in me, though he should die, will come to life; and whoever is alive and believes in me will never die" (Jn 11:25ff). That means that even though our dead are "still dead" and there is no return into earthly life, we believe that they live with God in a new way, if they have tried to conduct their earthly lives with trust in Jesus Christ and with fidelity to his demands.

Fellowship To Come. Since we believe that our dead live with God, and since we also believe that we are all called to this life in God, death therefore does not mean any definitive separation for us, despite all of its irrevocability. In our new life with God we will also have fellowship with other men and women, with whom we have lived and worked together during our earthly life. And in this new life our fellowship will be much happier than before.

Our relatives and friends are "still dead." We feel painfully the gap that their deaths have left in our own lives. We are thus struck by the condition of certain death. Yet we believe in "the resurrection and the life" in Jesus Christ. Thus we are consoled, in all our pain over the loss of beloved persons, by the "bright promise of immortality" [Preface of the Dead].

St. Martin de Porres (November 3)

A SAINT OF BROTHERLY LOVE FROM THE THIRD WORLD

Introduction

For us it is fairly easy to live "respectably." Most of us grew up in wholesome circumstances and had the love of our parents from the cradle onwards. We live in a country with no overwhelming social tensions. Our welfare system for the most part guarantees a minimum for existence to (nearly) everybody. St. Martin de Porres (1569–1639) sought to love God and man (Gospel) under very different starting conditions and in a world full of injustice and need that cried out to heaven.

Penitential Rite

"Bear with one another; forgive whatever grievances you have against one another." (Silence) Lord, have mercy. . . .

"Over all these virtues put on love, which binds the rest together and makes them perfect." (Silence) Christ, have mercy. . . .

"In wisdom made perfect, instruct and admonish one another." (Silence) Lord, have mercy. . . .

Talk

Bitter Childhood and Youth. The saint's proud Spanish-born father, who in the newly discovered lands of Central America came to be governor of Panama, lived with a black woman and promised to marry her. The higher he rose in the ranks of society, the more he became ashamed of his companion. He separated from her and sent her back into the slums from where he had taken her. There the mulatto Martin was born and reared by his mother. After a while, the father's conscience bothered him. He asked his former mistress to give the children over to him so that he could provide for their education. When people in prominent circles of Lima remarked that "he always brings those two mulattoes around with him," he sent them again back to their mother.

This simple black woman must have been a worthy person. She gave so much love to her son (and his sister) that he was not embittered by all the impediments he had to experience as a half-breed, but rather put his whole life in the fully deliberate service of all people. She gave him a religious upbringing that influenced his entire life.

In the Service of the Sick. The alert young man acquired wide knowledge as a druggist and "physician." Soon he had a thriving "practice," i.e., the poor, the needy, and the sick came to him from all over the city. He helped many people more by his kindness and love than by his medical arts. Every morning he took part in the Mass and then dedicated himself to his patients with all attention and generosity until nightfall.

Dominican Brothers. His interest in a conscious life with God brought the successful and beloved health practitioner to seek admission into the Dominicans. Since the prevailing law prevented the acceptance of a mulatto as a member in full standing, he was willing with full awareness to become a simple lay brother. He still had to wait nine years until he was at last accepted into the order.

In the remaining years of his life, he divided his time between nocturnal prayer (often throughout the whole night) and his daily service to the sick and suffering members of the monastery community. His care did not stop at the cloister walls. Rich and poor came to him to ask for help in their physical infirmities and spiritual needs. He himself lodged homeless and needy sick people in the monastery. Sometimes his kind-hearted superior would have to uphold the rights of the monastic community against his boundless love. Together with his sister and some friends he founded an orphanage and set up a great number of other charitable works in the whole city.

Model for Today. Martin de Porres, in his period and in his own way, tried to pass on the love of Christ and to break down the social injustice in the young colonial countries. The Latin American Churches today see in him a model for their efforts towards greater justice on their continent. They realize that personal help from one to another is not enough, but that structures must also be changed. Yet they also know that renewal of their society will succeed only if there are as many people as possible with the capacity for forgiveness and the power to love of a St. Martin de Porres.

Petitions

Let us pray in communion with St. Martin de Porres for the nations of Latin America: Lord Jesus Christ:

Shake up the wealthy and the property-holders, that they might see the need of their brothers and sisters. . . .
Guard the poor from embitterment lest old injustice generate new injustice. . . .

St. Martin de Porres

Give bishops and church leaders your Holy Spirit so that they might fearlessly defend the rights of the poor. . . .

For we love you and your Father only when we love our neighbor. You who live and reign forever.

St. Charles Borromeo (November 4)

BISHOP OF THE COUNCIL OF TRENT

Introduction

Destined by his parents to be a cleric, he received clerical tonsure at the age of twelve. At the same time he became the *pro forma* abbot of an abbey whose revenues were at his disposal. At twenty-two he became a cardinal (without being priest or bishop). Along with various posts at the papal court in Rome (his uncle was the pope) he had the archdiocese of Milan to administer from a distance. Behind these biographical data, which sound like those of a luxury-loving ecclesiastical prince of early modern times, lie the great reform bishop of the Council of Trent: Charles Borromeo.

Penitential Rite

Lord Jesus Christ, you are the Good Shepherd: Lord, have mercy. . . .

You know your own and your own know you: Christ, have mercy. . . .

You give your life for your sheep: Lord, have mercy. . . .

Talk

Spirit of Imitating Christ in Traditional Circumstances. The family of Charles Borromeo (1538–1584) belonged to European high nobility, which, intermarried and related to one another, held the reins of power in Church and State. The young noble had a brilliant church career open before him as a matter of course, that gave him right away a life free from care and that did not demand involvement in pastoral work.

As a man of his times, Charles Borromeo at first followed the path laid out for him. Yet from the beginning he did not proceed as a career climber, but as a Christian aware of his responsibilities. He did not take his direction from traditions that had become meaningless and unbending, but rather from Jesus Christ. At age twelve he refrained from using for himself the income he received as abbot; instead, he channeled it to the poor. As a young cardinal in Rome, he chose a deliberately modest life-style. He gave his life a religious orientation and became ordained priest and bishop. Finally, he resigned all his posts at the papal court in order to dedicate himself completely to his diocese as its bishop.

A Model for Many Bishops. The Council of Trent came to an end in 1563. It gave much impetus to the renewal of church life. Charles Borromeo took on with enthusiasm the task of applying the needed reforms in his endangered diocese, bordering as it did on newly Protestant areas of Switzerland.

With numerous laws the bishop sought to reorder religious living. In "Instructions to the People" (in sermons and pastoral letters) he strengthened the faith of the people in his diocese. These laws and addresses were collected and helped other zealous bishops in their own reform activities.

At the same time, Charles Borromeo realized that laws and sanctions alone do not renew a diocese. Accordingly, he followed the directions of the Council of Trent by establishing seminaries to provide for the theological education and the religious formation of future priests.

In addition, the bishop also called for the religious instruction of the faithful; this is a concern still pursued centuries later by the Borromeo Guild with its bookstores. Special study centers were to promote the Christian education of leading laity.

However, the cardinal did not rule merely from his desk. He traveled untiringly in order to visit the parishes of his sprawling diocese. Everywhere he paid attention to the big and small questions of everyday church life. He admonished and punished and—within the practice of his time—resorted to political and military measures.

The Good Shepherd—When It Counted. The extent to which Charles Borromeo was led in his pastoral work by love for his fellow man became evident in 1576, a plague year. As the sickness spread in Milan, even government officials fled from the imperiled city. All care for the sick collapsed. The archbishop stayed at his post and assumed command. He organized the care of the sick and the dying. He personally extended needed service and was available as pastor to the seriously ill.

Thus did Charles Borromeo renew religious life in his diocese, not as a cool administrative manager or as a politician for church renewal, but as a priest and bishop, conscious of having been taken into service by Jesus Christ, and desirous of being a good shepherd for people after the example of Jesus Christ.

Petitions

Lord our God, we pray for our diocese:

Let our bishop _____ guide his flock after the example of Christ . . .
Let everyone who works with him be filled with the Spirit of Love. . . .

Let priests carry out their service in parishes with faithfulness and prudence. . . .
Let many people be ready for service in the Church. . . .

God our Father, let our diocese in communion with the bishop become a sign and instrument of your presence in the world. You who live and reign forever and ever (cf. GL 787,1).

Dedication of the Lateran Basilica (November 9)

"YOU ARE GOD'S HOUSE"

Introduction

The Lateran Basilica in Rome is the earlier cathedral of the pope. St. Peter's Basilica became the Catholic Church's central building only in the late Middle Ages. The Lateran goes back to the Emperor Constantine. Fire, earthquake, war and plundering made necessary its repeated reconstruction and restoration. On this dedication day of this impressive Roman church, our concern should be not so much for the building of stone as for the Church built of "living stones" (1 Pet 2:5).

Penitential Rite

"They are happy whose life is blameless, who follow God's law! They are happy who do his will, seeking him with all their hearts. Keep me from the way of error and teach me your law" (Ps. 119:1f,24).

Talk

Pagan Temple and Christian House of God. There is a substantial difference between a pagan temple and a Christian house of God. The pagan temple is the "house of the deity." Correspondingly, the most important aspect is that it is the "sanctum," the "dwelling" of the god. Therefore, little space was needed for believers in Greek and Roman temples.

The Christian house of God is primarily the "house of the people of God," namely, the place where the community of Jesus Christ assembles. For this reason, the Christian church building is not a further development of the Grecco-Roman temple, but rather of the great halls in which markets traded, assemblies occurred, and courts held sessions. The original form of the Christian house of God was the basilica (which can be readily seen even today upon viewing the Lateran Basilica).

It is only from the Middle Ages, when the eucharistic Species left over from the mass became reserved and reverently honored in the space for worship, that the Christian church building could be (mis)understood as a "house of the deity" in the same sense as a pagan temple.

"You Are the Temple of God." In contrast, the early Church was deeply convinced that the authentic "dwelling of God" in the world was the living community of Jesus' disciples. In this community (and not in a building of wood or stone) Jesus Christ is present in the Holy Spirit in a special way among human beings. It is not with a view to the assembly hall of worship, but rather with a view to the community that the New Testament writings employ the word "temple," formed as it was by prior pagan meaning (cf. New Testament Reading: 1 Cor 6:19; 2 Cor 6:16; Eph 2:21).

Building of Stone, and Living Temple of God. In the ritual of church dedication, the liturgy has always seen the stone building as a symbol of the community of Jesus' disciples. For example, in today's Opening Prayer we pray "for those gathered in your Name" (and not for the church building). All buildings, seen in this life, have their justification in a Christian community context only if they help to form the living temple of God.

Does not this order of things give us something to think about? The church of Jesus Christ is not found in whatever country simply because church buildings are in place (or an organization has been formed). In another country it is still living not merely because there are great church buildings there of the past (preserved as monuments of a great past with subsidies from the state). The "temple of God," the place of God's dwelling in this world, can only be found where Christians live and give witness to their faith with trust in Jesus Christ. Whether they come together secretly in somebody's home, or celebrate the liturgy out-of-doors, or in a provisional building, or in a dedicated "house of God," is all secondary.

At this point, do we have the correct standard in our parish, in our diocese, in the whole Church? How much interest, money, and time do we invest in the renovation of our church buildings? What are we doing to raise up the living temple of God in our parish? To state it more plainly, which is more important for us—the life of faith in our community or the well-maintained building (which certainly are not mutually exclusive)?

Petitions

Lord Jesus Christ, you are the foundation of your Church. On this dedication day of the Lateran Basilica, we pray for your disciples throughout the world:

> For the pope, and bishops and priests . . . Christ, hear us. . . .
> For all their co-workers in pastoral care and proclamation of the Word. . . .
> For the faithful east, west, north, and south. . . .
> For all people who are seeking you. . . .

Lord, be near to your Church. Cleanse her from all half-heartedness and lukewarmness. Send her the Spirit of trust and hope, so that she might announce to all people your presence by her witness to your love. You who live and reign forever and ever.

St. Leo the Great (November 10)

SUCCESSOR OF PETER

Introduction

"What Peter believed of Jesus Christ holds true forever; what Christ established in Peter remains forever too." This quote expresses the mature self-understanding of Leo the Great (died 461). As bishop of Rome he was successor to Peter and thus charged in a special way for the Church throughout the world. He took this charge seriously during his twenty-year reign—and worked energetically for recognition of a certain primacy of the bishop of Rome.

Penitential Rite

Jesus, prophet of the Kingdom of God, Prince of Peace, eternal wisdom: Lord, have mercy. . . .

Jesus, living Word, just judge, father of the future: Christ, have mercy. . . .

Jesus, brother of the poor, friend of sinners, help of the sick: Lord, have mercy. . . .

Talk

Pope in Harsh Times. A look back into history can teach us that things now are not so bad for the Church (or for western civilization) as we may sometimes think. During his twenty-year reign as bishop of

Rome, Leo the Great twice rescued his city and parts of Italy from devastation and pillage, when, in the place of collapsed civil leadership, he brought about a negotiated peace with the Huns and the Goths.

At the same time, he had to deal as bishop and guardian of orthodoxy with the Manichaean, Eutychian, and other heretical movements (now of historical interest only). Moreover, out of a vigilant love for the whole Church, he attended to political affairs both east and west. He did this during an era when rough customs prevailed even among bishops: at the "Synod of Bandits at Ephesus" (449), Patriarch Flavian of Constantinople was so beaten by his fellow bishops that he died a few days later as a result. At the renowned Council of Chalcedon, imperial officials complained about the vulgar shouting as not being proper coming from bishops. . . .

Bishop for the Whole Church. During this time Leo the Great dedicated himself for the whole Church. In his efforts toward the recognition of a certain primacy of the bishop of Rome (which in the prior centuries had been emphasized and recognized here and there), his concern was not so much for power politics as it was for the care of the entire Church. As the successor of Peter, he described his papal self-understanding in this way: "We bear the care together with everyone and take part in each's conduct of office: for people take refuge from all over the world at the chair of St. Peter, and all expect love for the whole Church from the Roman pontiff, as the Lord expected it of Peter."

Love for the Entire Church. The special place of the bishop of Rome in the structure of the Church was set forth in different ways in the centuries after Leo the Great. The current form of Rome's primacy has also gone through historical development and is therefore open to wide-ranging change. Vatican Council II instituted a restructuring of the Church's central administration.

Indeed, the reform of the curia is far from over, in the opinion of specialists. The papal self-understanding of St. Leo the Great could be the guiding principle for all changes: It should become clearer that the pope carries the care of the Church together with all bishops (and faithful), contrary to all solitary Roman decisions; forms for "taking part in each's conduct of office" should be identified that will allow the dialogue between Rome and individual bishops to occur more articulately; the love for the whole Church should become evident even in the awareness and recognition of things that have no place in traditional Roman concepts, yet are alive in specific parts of the worldwide Catholic Church.

"Love for the whole Church, as the Lord expected it of Peter"—I believe that in this context we must think through more thoroughly the relation of the Roman pontiff with non-Catholic Christian Churches. How should the love of Peter's successor for all of Christianity make itself manifest today? Has the right way already been discovered? I think that the entire Catholic Church has a great task to complete here.

Petitions

Lord Jesus Christ, you expect love for the whole Church from the pope and from Roman authorities, just as you expected it from Peter:

> Promote the spirit of dialogue between Rome and the entire Church. . . .
> Arouse in Rome the readiness to become aware of and to recognize the special experiences of individual sectors of the Catholic Church. . . .
> Strengthen the faith of all Christians through the life and service of the pope. . . .

You who live and reign forever and ever.

St. Martin (November 11)

THE OTHER MARTIN

Introduction

"I had a dream: a man came before the Lord's court. 'See, my God,' he said, 'I have observed your law and have done nothing dishonest, evil, or malicious. Lord, my hands are clean.' 'Without a doubt,' answered God, 'but they are also empty.' " On this feast of St. Martin, let us think about this story by a contemporary apostle to lepers, Raoul Follereau.

Penitential Rite

"My soul, give thanks to the Lord, all my being, bless his holy name.
It is he who forgives all your guilt, who heals every one of your ills, who redeems your life from the grave, who crowns you with love and compassion" (Ps 103:1,3f).

Have mercy, Lord our God, have mercy. . . .

Talk

The Known Martin. Martin, the mounted soldier, divided his cloak with a beggar while he was still a pagan. His kindness and humaneness live on in the texts of today's Eucharist and in processions held on this day (in Europe). Yet how can we see there is more to him than horse and rider? What can we do to stimulate ourselves to divide our own cloaks, as Martin did, with the needy?

A word from Albert Schweitzer (the jungle doctor of Lambarene) can help us think (and act) upon the matter: "Open your eyes and look for somebody who needs a little time, a little sharing, a little friendliness. Perhaps it is someone lonely or embittered or sick, for whom you can do something. Perhaps it is a child or an old man. Do not let the opportunity escape to give yourself as a person to people. One thing is prepared for you, if you will only rightly desire it."

The Unknown Martin. Yet Martin was not only the soldier who helped the beggar on a cold winter's night. He was also an important churchman of the fourth century.

In his youth it was gradually becoming customary to become a Christian. Son of a soldier, he evidently did not simply swim along with this wave of custom. At the age of twelve, against his parents' will, he enrolled as a catechumen. At 18 he had himself baptized. Soon thereafter he left the army and entered church service. After a period of solitude on a Mediterranean island near Genoa, he settled as a monk in the area of Poitiers. Over the following decades he became the leading figure of monasticism in the western Church.

Martin was chosen bishop in 371 by the great majority of the people and clergy of Tours. As bishop he tirelessly made the rounds of his diocese in order to cultivate religious living, to make peace, and to help wherever he could.

As bishop, however, he still maintained his life-style of monastic poverty—and ran into conflict in a Church that had made an arrangement with the state. Bishops and priests had gotten used to being considered equals of state officials. The Church held a considerable amount of property, and many churchmen had become accustomed to a comfortable life. In this Church it had to be a shock when Martin carried out the life of a penitent, refused the bishop's throne during the liturgy and used an acolyte's stool, and forbade his monks to accept even the smallest gifts.

Martin became drawn as bishop into the church and political controversies of his time—and learned for himself how difficult it can sometimes be to do the right thing. "Far-right" bishops handed down a death sentence upon some heretical bishops in Spain in 385. Martin (who had condemned their doctrine) traveled to the imperial court in Trier in order to save the lives of his erring brothers in faith. When he saw no other way, he celebrated the Eucharist with the group of firebrands, in order to win by this concession reprieve from the death penalty for the condemned heretics. He was successful—but he asked himself over and over till the end of his life whether thereby he had not given too much support to the agitators.

The unknown Martin. Perhaps this background information will make it clearer to us what was the love of neighbor in this man, which we retell time and again in the story of the divided cloak.

Petitions

Almighty God, you challenge us through the example of St. Martin to love our fellow men as ourselves. We pray:

For children who hear the story of St. Martin dividing his cloak. [Silence]
For adults, that they might learn from the example of Martin the bishop. . . .
For all who try to understand the meaning of the legend of St. Martin. . . .

Lord, give us all open eyes for the needs of our fellow men and give us helping hands to set to work where help is needed. You who live and reign forever and ever.

St. Josaphat (November 12)

ONE LORD, ONE FAITH, ONE BAPTISM

Introduction

In 1960 Pope John XXIII had a solemn mass celebrated in St. Peter's Basilica in the Eastern Rite on the feast of St. Josaphat. It set the tone for the commission meetings preparing for the Second Vatican Council, whose greatest concern was to be the unity of Christianity. Through the council itself, the climate among the various Christian confessions changed decisively. Is the great concern of the "high priestly prayer" that all may be one [Gospel] our own personal concern as well? What are we doing for the unity of Christians?

Penitential Rite

"Be humble, meek, and patient." [Silence] Lord, have mercy....

"Bear with one another lovingly." [Silence] Christ, have mercy....

"Make every effort to preserve the unity which has the Spirit as its origin." [Silence] Lord, have mercy....

Talk

Ecumenical Work, As It Should Not Be Today. Around 1600 there was a renewal movement among Orthodox Christians in eastern Poland which sought union with Rome with retention of eastern liturgy and tradition. A number of bishops accepted communion with Rome and sought to bring their faithful along. Orthodox circles resisted. This resulted in double occupancy of individual bishoprics; religious and ecclesiastical political conflicts were brought down to the people and led to riots, murder, and horrible counterreactions by civil authorities.

Josaphat (1580–1623) came from an Orthodox family. He joined the reform movement in his youth. At the age of twenty-five he entered a moribund monastery and brought it along to a measure of vitality. He was ordained a bishop in 1618.

Ascetic in habit and zealous for souls, the bishop was able in the ensuing years to win over many believers for union with Rome. However, a countermovement developed in 1621. Orthodox circles painted a picture of the bogeyman of "Latinization" of the united congregations and agitated the ordinary people against Bishop Josaphat. Incited masses stormed his residence on November 12, 1623, and struck him dead. The counterblow of the (Catholic) Polish king was fearful. He had twenty townsmen beheaded and hundreds of others condemned to death *in absentia*. We can imagine how the "Josaphat affair" (without any personal guilt on the saint's part) has burdened relations between Orthodox and Catholic Christians up until now.

Ecumenical Work Now.

Josaphat's concern is as current now as it was then: that Christians, who believe in the one God and Father of all, who confess the one Lord, Jesus Christ, who receive the same baptism, be able to form a worldwide communion [Reading] and thus proclaim more convincingly the message of Jesus Christ [Gospel].

Contemporary ecumenical work in the Catholic Church also proceeds from the assumption that the various Christian confessions must learn from each other on the way to one Church. What Paul says in the Reading concerning the various services that are necessary for the upbuilding of the Body of Christ holds true as well in some way for the various Christian traditions. Not even we in the Catholic Church have kept the fullness of Christ. The one Church of the future will be shaped not only by our Catholic traditions, but also by the traditions of other ecclesial groups.

We are also of the opinion that the unity of Christians is not decisively advanced by individual conversions to the Catholic Church (even though personal conversions proceeding from honest conviction deserve respect). We think it is proper that Christians, in their concern for the unity of Jesus' disciples, remain true to their own traditions and work within the different confessions for the Spirit of unity and peace and mutual understanding [Reading].

And, of course, we know that the unity of Christians will grow only where Christians try in the power of Jesus Christ to lead a life worthy of their inner calling, insofar as they are meek and patient in their contact with one another, and accept and bear with one another in their differences [Reading].

Petitions

Lord Jesus Christ, it is your will that all who believe in you be at one with each other, just as you are one with the Father. We pray:

For Christians in the Orthodox Churches.   [Silence]
For the members of the main Protestant Churches . . .
For the members of the various Christian sects . . .
For all of us in the Catholic Church . . . .

Lord, grant to all Christian confessions the readiness to put what is common among them in the center, to acknowledge and bear with differences, and to seek true unity in your Spirit. You who live and reign forever and ever.

St. Albert the Great (November 15)

THE FIRST MODERN SCIENTIST

Introduction

There still exists in many circles the opinion that modern physical science and Christian faith must oppose each other irreconcilably. At the same time, many biologists, physicists, and chemists are overlooked who feel themselves invited to belief in Jesus Christ precisely as modern scientists by dint of the results of their scientific inquiries. This was true also of Albertus Magnus, the great natural scientist of the thirteenth century.

Penitential Rite

Lord our God, "how glorious is your name over all the earth": Lord, have mercy. . . .

"What is man, that you should be mindful of him?": Christ, have mercy. . . .

"You have crowned him with glory and honor and have given him rule over the works of your hands": Lord, have mercy. . . .

Talk

An Active Life. Albert (c. 1200–1280) as a young man set out from Lauingen on the Danube to study in Italy. He joined the Dominicans in Padua, then finished his studies in Cologne, Germany. There he worked as professor; among his students was Thomas Aquinas. As his life advanced, he was professor in Paris, organizer of studies for the German Dominican monasteries and provincial superior of the far-flung German province of the order. He became bishop of Regensburg; having put into order the ruined finances of his diocese, he resigned from his episcopal post after two years. He actively preached for the crusades and was repeatedly entrusted with delicate political and diplomatic tasks. He spent his late years again in Cologne, where he is buried.

Philosopher and Theologian. St. Albert's busy life was filled with intensive studies. This "last universal scholar of the western world" achieved outstanding results on two levels.

Philosopher and theologian, Albertus Magnus was not satisfied with obsolete theological constructs. He discerned that a new mode of thought was spreading throughout Europe and was confronting Christian faith with new questions. He deliberately took up his thought (the philosophy of Aristotle) and sought to make it useful for theology. By doing so he ran into conflict with church tradition, but also prepared the way for the towering theological achievement of his student Thomas Aquinas, which still decisively influences religious thought even now.

Natural Scientist. At the same time, Albertus Magnus is justly called the first modern natural scientist. While his contemporaries contented themselves with teachings of the past in the area of nature study (normal for their time), Albert carried out exact observations of nature and came up with results that put the traditional ideas into question. He was thus the first to use completely systematically the methods that were developed and refined centuries later in natural science.

Believer. With all his philosophical, theological, and scientific inquiry, Albertus Magnus was a deeply pious person, for whom all knowledge had to lead to a deeper awareness of God. This thought is attributed to him: "Man's most excellent faculty is his reason. The highest goal of reason is knowledge of God."

Yet Albert the Great was not content with sheer knowledge of God. He knew that one would take God seriously only when one had directed one's life toward God. Thus he prayed repeatedly: "O Lord, I wish I were a man in accord with your most loving will."

The Greatness of God in Creation. Certainly it was a matter of course for Albert, the great German medieval saint, to perceive and admire the greatness of God in the miracles and mysteries of nature. He lived with a self-evident religious outlook. For us of this modern age (whether we are scientists or scientific laypeople) it is more difficult, since we live in an environment that has widely lost the self-understood religious outlook on the world. Must we not make new use of this outlook, so that all our human inquiry and thought might draw us more deeply into the mystery of God and help us to become "men in accord with the most loving will of God"?

Petitions

Lord, God of the universe, you have wondrously made us and more wondrously redeemed us. We pray:

> Let us see your greatness in the mysteries and marvels of creation. . . .
> Grant us zeal in your service, so that we might praise you in thought and action. . . .
> Free our hearts from all selfishness, that we might always think of your will. . . .

For you have called us to know you and to serve you. You who live and reign forever and ever.

St. Margaret of Scotland (November 16)

SHE TAMED HER HUSBAND

Introduction

The cliché of "happy royal children," which is still maintained today by sectors of the press, was really never accurate. By any measure, St. Margaret of Scotland was an example of how much the lives of crowned heads were controlled—and burdened—by political factors from childhood onward. Her noble background meant that she had to sacrifice herself for her country her whole life long—and thus bear the cross to an extent from which most of us are spared.

Penitential Rite

"Remove from your midst oppression." [Silence] Lord, have mercy. . . .

"Remove from your midst false accusation and malicious speech." Christ, have mercy. . . .

"Bestow your bread on the hungry and satisfy the afflicted." [Silence] Lord, have mercy. . . .

Talk

Settling in England. The father of Margaret (1047–1093), son of the Anglo-Saxon king, was driven out of England, where at that time the Danes held power and the Normans were pressing to take over. He married a Hungarian princess and set himself up comfortably in exile. Around 1057 the Anglo-Saxon party beseeched him to return to England with his family and to have himself proclaimed successor to the reigning king (a childless relative).

Margaret moved with her parents to England. Ten years later she was forced to flee with her mother and her brother (who had been called to be king) from the conquering Normans into Scotland. There Malcolm ruled, whose subjects called him "the Bloody." He had purged his political opponents at home by brutal liquidations. He struck fear into the English on the border area by his plundering attacks.

Queen of Scotland. This brutal ruler took the hand of the English princess who had taken refuge in his country. Margaret yielded to family pressures and married Malcolm. Once again, political considerations took precedence over personal wishes and preferences.

In the following fifty-five years of her life, the true greatness of this woman unfolded. Her influence was felt in the royal family, in the whole country, and above all in the realm of the Church.

Concerning the queen's family life, a contemporary biographer wrote, "Through her influence the king gave up his wild ways . . . She altered her whole environment. . . . No evil word could be uttered within her hearing. . . ." He does not mention, however, how much inner strength and patience Margaret required in order to achieve this change in her husband and in the entire climate of the royal court.

The queen was a true "mother of her country" for the ordinary peasants, as were other saintly princesses (Elizabeth of Hungary, for one). Within the limits of the social order of that time, she tried, in line with today's Reading and as far as possible, to alleviate the consequences of tough everyday politics and to lend unofficial help in many needy situations of ordinary life.

Margaret's personal interest in church matters was highly unusual. In spite of being a woman, she convened a Scottish council and expressed herself on theological matters being handled there.

The last days of this great Scottish queen were still overshadowed with great family pain. Her husband and her eldest son fell in battle against her English homeland. Some days after this unhappy event she herself died. She could not foresee that her youngest daughter would one day marry the son of the Norman king of England (once again for political reasons, of course) and would thereby aid the peaceful coexistence of the English and the Scots.

Female Apostolate. Human and Christian atmosphere in the home, unofficial help where help is needed, concern for church matters—I believe these are areas of apostolate where women today can be doing great things for God and for their brothers and sisters—without excluding professional and political service of "liberated" women.

Petitions

Let us pray to God, our almighty Father:

For women who as wives and mothers work completely for their families. [Silence]
For women who combine professional work with care for family. . . .
For women who work in charitable organizations along with their professional or family duties. . . .

Almighty and gracious God, give to women in the workplace and at home the capacity to cultivate a human and Christian atmosphere. In their service, let them see people always more than things or regulations. You who live and reign forever and ever.

St. Elizabeth of Hungary (November 17)

A STRONG PERSONALITY

Introduction

St. Elizabeth Guild, St. Elizabeth's Hospital, Sisters of St. Elizabeth— these very names are a sign of the appeal of St. Elizabeth even 750 years after her death. It also shows how much she is seen as the saint of charity.

Inquiring into her life produces the impression that this princess from Hungary was a strong personality who lived very spontaneously and often swam against the stream.

Penitential Rite

Lord Jesus Christ, you demand of us: "Love your enemies, do good to those who hate you": Lord, have mercy. . . .

You demand of us: "Do not condemn, and you will not be condemned": Christ, have mercy. . . .

You demand of us: "Be compassionate, as your Father is compassionate": Lord, have mercy. . . .

Talk

A Maladjusted Child. Elizabeth, who was born in 1207, was a daughter of the king of Hungary. At four years of age, she was engaged for political reasons to the eleven-year-old Louis of Thuringia, son of a count, and was brought to Wartburg near Eisenach.

St. Elizabeth of Hungary   509

Elizabeth won approval in her new surroundings. Yet her future mother-in-law observed with growing concern that the foreign child did not adjust without problems to the general way of life. Elizabeth was wild and boisterous. She loved horseback riding more than courtly and demure behavior. To the amazement of people around her, she cultivated cordial relations with serfs. Occasionally, she would stop in the middle of her play in order to pray. If her fiance Louis had not protected her against all criticism and carping, and had not committed himself to her by early marriage, Elizabeth would probably have been sent back to Hungary.

Deep Marital Love. Apart from all political motives, the marriage of Louis and Elizabeth was a marriage of love. The spouses understood each other. Elizabeth would not hesitate, contrary to all courtly etiquette, to express her love for Louis spontaneously. Sometimes she would ride out some distance to meet her homecoming husband and greet him with great affection. For his part, Louis was ready to take her to the castle and, contrary to accepted custom, to eat at the same table with her. The depth of the countess' love for her husband was evident in 1227 when he—Elizabeth was twenty—set out for the crusades. When the news of his death arrived shortly afterwards—Louis had succumbed to pestilence—his subordinates could hardly bring themselves to tell the countess. Beside herself, she stumbled through the corridors of the castle lamenting, "Oh, dear God, now the whole world is dead for me."

Also Maladjusted as Wife and Mother. With all her love for her husband, Elizabeth nonetheless lost nothing of her independence, and maneuvered Louis into all sorts of complications. For example, she would sometimes spend the night on her bedroom's cold floor in order to practice mortification. Or she would sit at table without eating because she had bound herself by a vow to eat nothing that had been demanded unjustly from her subjects. Louis backed Elizabeth up with all his authority when, in the famine year of 1225, she opened up the county coffers and storerooms in order to help the needy.

Voluntary Poverty. After her husband's death, Elizabeth could tell that she could not remain permanently at the county court. Without her husband's protection, they were not about to tolerate her singular way of life. She therefore left willingly and quietly. Since she had already lived consciously with Jesus Christ and practiced active love for neighbor, she now followed the ideal that Francis was propagating everywhere at that time through his disciples.

Elizabeth entrusted her children to other hands in order to provide them an upbringing proper to their station in life. She left Eisenach and went to Marburg, where she spent the remaining three years of her life. Out of her widow's inheritance she had a hospital built, in which she herself served the sick as an ordinary nurse. Her confessor had all he could do to prevent her from giving away her entire fortune and from going begging door to door.

After a short illness Elizabeth died on November 17, 1231, and was buried in Marburg. She was canonized only four years after her death. The splended Church of St. Elizabeth was soon erected over her grave.

Petitions

Lord Jesus Christ, you have approached the sick and the needy:

Be close to all who are at the service of the sick and the elderly in hospitals and nursing homes. . . .
Bless the work of parish visitors and social workers. . . .
Look upon the kindness that is done as a matter of course for the needy in our families and neighborhoods. . . .

For whoever helps the needy helps you. You who live and reign forever and ever.

Dedication of the Churches of Peter and Paul (November 18)

THE CHURCH IN THE STEPS OF PETER AND PAUL

Introduction

Church buildings are expressions in stone of the spirit of faith of past generations. We can feel in them something of the enthusiasm for the faith of past generations. They somehow reveal specific aspects of Christian life. Splendid church buildings of the past (in Rome and elsewhere) can, however, conceal the real substance of faith. They can cause us to forget that with Jesus Christ "we go wandering about homeless" (1 Cor 4:11) and that the Church makes her laborious way through the ages as a community of weak human beings. Peter and Paul, as we find them in today's Readings, make this clearer to us than do the two magnificent Roman churches that bear their names.

Penitential Rite

"The Lord is faithful in all his words and holy in all his works.
The Lord lifts up all who are falling and raises up all who are bowed down" (Ps 145:13b–14).
Have mercy, Lord our God, have mercy. . . .

Talk

"He Preached the Reign of God". "With full assurance, and without any hindrance whatever, he preached the reign of God and taught about the Lord Jesus Christ" [Reading]. With this sentence ends the Acts of the Apostles, which traces the path of the Good News from Jerusalem (center of the Jewish world) to Rome (center of the whole world). With this sentence there also ends Luke's account to us of Paul's contribution to the spread of the Good News throughout the world. Paul used all his energies in the service of the Good News. The meaning of his life was achieved in that he was to be the apostle of Jesus Christ to the gentiles (cf. Acts 22:21).

In the account given by Acts, Paul brought the Good News to the middle of the known world. Yet the Church has the duty to preach the reign of God and to teach with all assurance about the Lord Jesus Christ [Reading]. She lives not necessarily where there are magnificent stone churches (or a well-developed organization), but only where Jesus Christ is proclaimed through preaching and worship and where the Kingdom of God is made real by active love.

Despite Fatigue and Opposition. According to Acts' last sentence, Paul was able to proclaim the Reign of God without hindrance. This was more often a desired condition than a real one. On every page of Acts we see examples of how Paul dealt with waves that battered the ship of the young Church (as well as the ship of his own life) back and forth, and how he had to fight against headwinds with his courage and spirit of initiative [Gospel].

Paul's experience (and that of the entire early Church) has remained the same through the course of church history. The Church's time has always been full of distress. The Church has always faced her demise. She often did not know how she would move onward the next day or the day after. Yet at the same time she also experienced that Jesus Christ was with her in the Church's ship. He was the Lord of the waves and of the contrary winds (even when the wind does not always diminish and we wait in vain for the waves to smooth out). Just as Paul found his way to Rome (in order to die there!) by the power of Christ, so also the Church finds her way through the ages over and over.

Despite Doubt and Failure. Thus she follows the path traced by Peter the apostle, who uttered noble words and took on a great responsibility—and then, lamentably, failed. Peter was an odd "rock." He acknowledged Jesus loudly—but did not understand his true mystery. He promised Jesus half the world—and then ran miserably away. He begged Jesus to accept his faith in the Word—and still doubted.

In all this, the Church on her way through time resembles the first pope. She acknowledges Christ—and, in her members, sometimes does not know what this means. She forms great plans—and soon forgets them again. She talks a lot about faith—and still does not dare to trust wholly in Jesus Christ.

Throughout the ages, then, there remains only one choice on her path: to call out with Peter, "Lord, save me!" She thus is able to experience over and over again that Jesus stretches out his hand and helps her to continue on her way through time.

Petitions

Almighty God, hear our prayer through the intercession of the apostles Peter and Paul:

Help the Church to proclaim the Good News convincingly in our age. . . .
Grant that the servants of the Church not be discouraged by the many contradictions of our times. . . .
Let us all learn from our failures and hope in your aid with trust. . . .

For you lead the Church by the Holy Spirit on her path through time. You who live and reign forever and ever.

The Presentation of Mary (November 21)

"FOR WHOEVER DOES THE WILL OF MY FATHER..."

Introduction

Only Luke among the evangelists speaks in any detail about Mary, the Mother of Jesus. He portrays her as the archetype of the Church: she is open to God, she places herself at his disposition by her answer of yes, she stays in communion with him by prayer, and she cherishes all things in her heart that are accomplished by God. Christian piety has often attempted to develop in legends the somewhat prosaic statements by Luke, and to present Mary in a more impressive way as the first of the redeemed and the archetype of the Church. The pious legend that stands behind this feast of the Presentation of Mary is to be seen in this light.

Penitential Rite

Jesus Christ, conceived by Mary, born of Mary: Lord, have mercy. . . .

Offered up by Mary in the Temple and found again by Mary in the Temple: Christ, have mercy. . . .

Accompanied by Mary on the way of the cross and mourned by Mary while on the cross: Lord, have mercy. . . .

Talk

"Presentation of Mary." According to the so-called Proto-gospel of James (a writing of mainly religious character from the second century), Anne promised in her pregnancy, miraculously enabled by God, to dedicate her child completely to God.

The child herself—Mary—displayed an amazingly precocious maturity. At six months she could already walk. When she turned three, her parents fulfilled their vow and presented their daughter in the Temple to God.

Yet the offering was not simply that of the parents. The three-year-old Mary advances (precisely in anticipation of her Biblical saying, "Behold, I am the maidservant of the Lord") purposefully into the Temple. During the solemn procession into the Temple, Mary does not look back: she keeps her eyes fixed on the torch carried by other girls and "hastens up the fifteen steps to the altar without turning around to look at her parents, as little children are normally wont to do." For the writer of the legend, this is the proof of the voluntary offering of herself by Mary to God from earliest childhood.

As this offering by Mary something else then occurs: she begins "to dance on her feet," and thus gives expression to her joy in God (just as this joy in the Gospel of Luke is expressed in the Magnificat).

In the Temple of the Lord. While the writer of the legend in the second century was content to describe Mary's presentation, a writing from the sixth century (the so-called Gospel of Pseudo-Matthew) was concerned with Mary's life in the Temple. It sketches it as a cloistered life (since it wanted to show Mary as a shining example to the nuns of that time). Thus, Mary was "so assiduous in praising God that others took her for not a child but for a grown person. She prayed with such perseverance as if she were thirty years old." She lived by a set rule of life. Only embroidering interrupted her long hours of prayer. She was admired by her sisters for her piety, "for she was firm, unshakeable, and constant, and progressed in virtue each day."

Image of Mary in the Bible. Without doubt, legends like these helped past generations to grasp more deeply and understand more clearly the biblical message of Mary's cooperation in the Redemption (even if the imagination sometimes naturally became engrossed in useless details). We must still attempt now to seek out the biblical kernel of these legends.

Undoubtedly, Mary received a basic religious upbringing in the traditions of her people. In the years of her childhood and youth her intimacy with God had to become established, out of which her later yes could proceed.

Certainly this yes was practiced from childhood by her living according to God's will, as the Old Testament understood it. Certainly her life in faith was marked from its beginnings (completely within the sense of the Old Testament with its canticles of praise and psalms of thanks) by joy in God.

Finally, from childhood onward she was the one to whom the sentence from the Gospel could be applied: "Whoever does the will of my heavenly Father" is especially close to God.

Petitions

Lord, our God, in Mary you have given us an example of our calling. We pray to you:

Enable your Church to place herself, as did Mary, completely under your Word. . . .
Awaken in Christians a deep joy over their calling to the faith. . . .

The Presentation of Mary

Give aid to all efforts in the pastoral care of children and adolescents in our congregation. . . .

Lord, grant that we, like Mary, may say yes to your will and to fulfill it in our lives. You who live and reign forever and ever.

St. Cecilia (November 22)

PATRONESS OF CHURCH MUSIC

Introduction

From the sixth century onward we know of the veneration of a St. Cecilia in Rome. Whoever it really is behind this name can no longer be known exactly. The legend of the life and death of the saint of this name sketches in the image of this virgin and martyr the ideal image of a Christian life that knows itself to be totally bound to Jesus Christ and that wants to lead others to him.

Penitential Rite

"Be holy, for I, the Lord, your God, am holy." [Silence] Lord, have mercy. . . .

"You shall not bear hatred for your brother in your heart." [Silence] Christ, have mercy. . . .

"Take no revenge and cherish no grudge against your fellow countrymen." [Silence] Lord, have mercy. . . .

Talk

Patroness of Church Music. It was not until the end of the Middle Ages that Cecilia, through an accidental error in translation that

St. Cecilia

made her out to have played the organ at her own wedding, became universally known as the patroness of church music. Church choirs and works of sacred music bear her name. Although Cecilia cannot serve as a model for specific musical accomplishments, nevertheless the pious tale of her life and death can still help church musicians and choir singers (as well as all Christians) to live in the Spirit of Christ and to celebrate the liturgy.

The Legend. The Bible, in the Old Testament and the New Testament, portrays the faith-relationship of man to God through the image of betrothal and marriage. This image was assimilated by the Church, and showed itself in the legend of Cecilia.

Cecilia was a young Christian who wanted to take seriously her communion with Jesus Christ. For that reason, she wanted to belong to no man. After her wedding, forced upon her by custom and family, she revealed to her pagan husband that she wanted to belong totally to Christ and that he should renounce marital companionship with her.

Valerian (her husband) let himself be led by Cecilia to Christ and moved his brother as well, with the help of his virginal wife, to accept Christ. When both were then condemned to death as Christians, Cecilia strengthened them in the faith.

Cecilia herself was finally brought before a judge. She defended her faith so convincingly that hundreds of curiosity seekers were converted to Christ. Before she was executed (three cuts with a sword still did not allow the executioner to hack through her neck), she gave her property over to the Church. Even in death she led her friends to Jesus.

The Message for Us. Cecilia based her life completely on God [Gospel]. Through all persecution and pain she had a secure anchor in him. The basis of her faith, which did not rest in inspiring words alone [Gospel], stayed firm even at the moment of the threat of death. Because she fulfilled the will of God in her life, God stayed with her even in death and gave her eternal life.—Do we in our lives merely say

"Lord, Lord" (or just sing uplifting songs in the liturgy), or does his will really have influence over our daily lives with its demands?

Cecilia showed her love for other people [Reading] in her concern for their faith. By the example of her life, she led her husband, her relatives and friends to Jesus Christ.—Is our neighborliness limited to civil coexistence in church or choir as in common singing of a Latin Mass? Where Christians are together and complete a task together (especially in a solemn liturgical celebration), they must also lead each other to Jesus. There one finds the self-evident witness of daily Christian life. There one has room for theological discussions and religious talks. There one should also find place for common prayer at the beginning of a wine-tasting session or some other gathering.

Is our life and work in the church choir stamped with the Spirit of Faith pictured in the legend of the life and death of St. Cecilia?

Petitions

Let us pray for all who cooperate in the solemn celebrations of our liturgy:

> For composers and organists, that they might perform their service with a lively faith . . . Christ, hear us. . . .
> For the singers in our church choir, that their joy in singing might spring from a deeper joy in faith. . . .
> For all who care for the decoration of our church, that their entire lives be friendly and light in faith. . . .

For you call us to have a foretaste of the joy of the eternal wedding feast in our earthly liturgy. You who live and reign forever and ever.

St. Clement (November 23)

FROM THE LIFE OF THE EARLY CHURCH

Introduction

Rome is the geographical center of the Catholic Church. How did this position of Rome become established? When did Rome pull everything into itself (as some say)?—It is nonetheless significant that in the letter of the Roman bishop Clement, toward the end of the first Christian century, the community of Rome already held a certain primacy. This Roman letter to the Christians of Corinth gives us a glimpse into the life of the early Church, one that can provide us some help.

Penitential Rite

Merciful and gracious God, forgive us our sins and wrongdoing, our trespasses and errors: Lord, have mercy. . . .

Do not charge your servants with all their sins, rather purify them with your truth: Christ, have mercy. . . .

Make our way clear to convert to holiness of heart and to do what is good and pleasing in your sight: Lord, have mercy. . . .

(after the Letter of Clement)

Talk

Scant Biographical Data. Little is known of the life of St. Clement, the third or fourth bishop of Rome. According to ancient sources, he led the Roman community from A.D. 92 to 101. According to legend, he was sunk at sea with an anchor tied to his neck, and thus sealed with his death his witness for Jesus Christ.

The Community's Internal Situation. It follows that the letter bearing his name from the Roman community to the Christians of Corinth affords us a glimpse into the life of the Church around the end of the first Christian century.

The elder authorities, the apostles and their disciples (who still could speak of their contact with the original apostles), or even the unknown missioners who had founded the individual Christian communities, were already dead. Human rivalries and theological differences of opinion endangered the unity of local communities and of the entire Church. As groups built up in various communities, the question arose as to what qualifications were required for someone to lead a local church with the authority of Jesus Christ.

The Letter of Clement answers this question with the principle of apostolic succession: one can lead the community with a mandate from God only if he has been called into this service through the laying on of hands by church officials who themselves were appointed by the apostles or their successors.

The Roman bishop did not tire of urging unity over and over again in his letter. For example: "Our body [the community] should be preserved in Christ Jesus, and each one should be subject to his neighbor according to their respective gifts. The strong should care for the weak, and the weak should pay attention to the strong. The rich man should help the poor, the poor man should thank God for having given him someone to aid him in his need. The wise one should display his wisdom not in words, but in good works. . . ."

The existence of this letter is of great meaning in regard to the early Church's understanding of herself. These small, scattered communities were not sufficient unto themselves. They kept ties with one another in continuity with the personal contacts among their founders, and tried to support one another with words of warning and praise in faithfulness to Jesus Christ. That the bishop of Rome was accorded a special place in this context is shown in the fact that his letter to the Corinthian community was quickly distributed and read aloud in the worship services of many local churches.

Testimony of Early Christian Prayer Life. Along with admonitions and instructions for community life, the Letter of Clement also contains a rather long prayer that gives testimony to the prayer life of the young communities. We have already used a passage from it in the Penitential Rite. Let us join these first-century Christians as we now use their words in our petitions before God.

Petitions

God, we hope in your name. You have opened our hearts to acknowledge you. You are the helper of the endangered and the rescuer of the hopeless. . . . We pray to you: be our help and protection.

> Rescue our troubled ones, raise up our fallen ones. . . .
> Make yourself known to the needy, heal the sick. . . .
> Bring back those who stray from your people. . . .
> Feed the hungry, release the imprisoned. . . .
> Lift up the weak ones, and encourage the faint-hearted. . . .
> Grant to us and all dwellers of the earth concord and peace. . . .

For you alone have the power to accomplish these and still greater good things for us. We praise you through Jesus Christ, through whom glory and majesty be yours now and forever. Amen. (*after the Letter of Clement*)

St. Columban (November 23)

"THE FOXES HAVE LAIRS . . ."

Introduction

"The foxes have lairs, the birds of the sky have nests, but the Son of Man has nowhere to lay his head" [Gospel]. This call to homelessness for the sake of sharing in Jesus' life and work deeply influenced Columban and his Irish contemporaries who labored as missioners in Europe in the sixth and seventh centuries. They were more concerned with giving Christian example than with systematic propagation of the faith or with suitable ecclesiastical organization. These ascetic wandering monks pose the question even for us: do we labor in our times as missioners through the example of our Christian living?

Penitential Rite

"See, O Lord, in guilt I was born, a sinner was I conceived.
From my sins turn away your face and blot out all my guilt.
A pure heart create for me, O God, put a steadfast spirit within me" (Ps. 51:7,11,12).

Have mercy, Lord our God, have mercy. . . .

Talk

A Hard Character. Columban (543–615) was educated at a hard school run by the monks of his Irish homeland. Against the resistance of his parents, he joined a monastic community. Meager food, nearly perpetual silence, extensive times of prayer, hard work on the farm or in the workshop, and the study of the sacred Scriptures all helped to form him.

This hard school favored traits that lay dormant within him. He was a man of energy and decisiveness, as his later life showed. He was also, however, a violent character. In his activity on the continent, he struggled with both sacred and secular authority. He initiated conflicts with the (still mostly pagan) inhabitants. He was hard with his co-workers.

Homeless with Jesus. Columban went out with his companions into foreign territory. Foreign lands for them meant (much more than today) insecurity, menace, and danger. They deliberately chose homelessness because they wanted to live displaced, endangered, and threatened with Jesus Christ. They wanted to prevail in the combat of faith through their wandering and thus become like Jesus.

Columban entered first the western Frankish kingdom. He gained a friendly reception along with his companions. At the edge of the Vosges Mountains three monasteries were rapidly established, which drew their membership from the emigrant Irish as well as the native monks.

The strongly emphasized independence of the Irish foundation from the established local Church, along with Columban's violent temperament, led soon to conflict with Church and State. The king made arrangements to have the Irish monks deported from his borders in order to put them on a ship bound for their homeland. However, they made a timely move over to the eastern Frankish kingdom. Soon thereafter they resumed their missionary work in the area of Lake Constance and in Switzerland. After conflicts with the inhabitants there, Columban had to move on to northern Italy. In the village now called Bobbio, the wandering missioner found rest for the last years of his life, as well as after his death.

Personal Confession of Sin. Through his work and that of his disciples, Columban helped shape the European Church of his time. Through his monastic rule he left his stamp on cloistered life for decades to come. His ideal was the hard ascetic life of Irish monks that had so impressed him in his youth.

One detail of monastic life, as Columban practiced it, that had special meaning for the whole Church was the daily examen of conscience by a monk along with his spiritual father. This had a formative effect on the practice of individual confession.

Proceeding from the background of an underlying practice of public penance, the Irish missioners embodied this practice into general pastoral care. The purpose was to help the faithful to make the ever-necessary turn to new ways in the fellowship of the Church. This practice took root and became a mandatory part of Christian living.

Petitions

Lord Jesus Christ, you call us to follow you and require of us that we set our hand to the plow and not look back:

> Be close to young people preparing themselves for priestly service or for religious life. . . .
> Strengthen priests and religious who find themselves in crisis in the prime of their lives. . . .
> Stay with Christians who are tormented by doubts about their faith. . . .

For you accompany us all on the path of faith, hope, and love. You who live and reign forever and ever.

St. Andrew (November 30)

FISHER OF MEN

Introduction

The Gospels tell us of a particular circle of disciples of Jesus during his public life. They give us the names of twelve men who belonged to this circle. The personalities behind these names remain in obscurity with a few exceptions. The apostle Andrew is included among these exceptions. The Gospels mention him explicitly in some passages—and portray him as a person who found Jesus Christ and led others to him.

Penitential Rite

Lord Jesus Christ, you call men and women into your own fellowship of life: Lord, have mercy. . . .

You call them to take up their cross with you: Christ, have mercy. . . .

You give them the mandate to lead others to you: Lord, have mercy. . . .

Talk

Sparse Biographical Data. Andrew of Bethsaida, a fisher by trade, brother of Peter, disciple of Jesus. "According to tradition, he preached the Gospel along the Black Sea and in Greece and died a

St. Andrew

martyr's death on the cross in Patras in Achaia'' (introduction in the weekday *Schott-Messbuch*). The Gospel of John has nothing about him to add to these sparse data. It does, however, give us the profile of a man who had encountered Jesus Christ and was never to break from him.

Called and Sent. When Matthew, Mark, or Luke speak of the calling of the first disciples (among whom was Andrew), in their view the initiative proceeds entirely from Jesus of Nazareth. Jesus "finds" these fishers on Lake Genesareth. He calls them, and they follow him. John shows Andrew declaring after his encounter with Jesus, "We have found the Messiah" (Jn 1:41). Andrew met this Jesus in connection with the Baptist, followed him, and spent the whole day with him (Jn 1:35–39). Something came forth then with Andrew that did not leave him for the rest of his life.

Andrew made it known that he had found the new center of his life in Jesus of Nazareth. "We have found the Messiah," he declared to his blood brother Simon. He began his missionary work in his own family. He led his brother to Jesus.

Apostle, disciple of Jesus, contact and mediator between the people and Jesus: Andrew is portrayed in two other places. He had an integral role in the miraculous multiplication of bread as recounted by John (6:7f). And he, in company with his neighbor Philip, informed Jesus about the Greeks (God-fearing pagans, or Jews from the diaspora?) who wished to speak with him. After the death and resurrection of Jesus, he dedicated his entire life as a missioner in order to bring people to Jesus Christ.

Preparing the Way to Christ. Andrew belonged to the founding generation of the Church that, in every millenium, has the mandate to give witness to Jesus Christ and to lead men and women to him. We are all members of this Church. We have all—hopefully!—found the Messiah, like Andrew. Especially during Advent we should ask ourselves: What can we do so that Jesus Christ may come to people of our time and that they may find their way to him?

Petitions

Lord Jesus Christ, you call your disciples into a communion of life, work, and destiny.

> Preserve in all who are in the service of the Church a living love for you. . . .
> Let all who proclaim the Good News support their words by the works of their lives. . . .
> Give courage and trust in God to all who run into difficulties in their pastoral tasks. . . .

For you remain with your disciples all the time by the power of the Holy Spirit, until you come again in glory.

St. Francis Xavier (December 3)

"HOW COULD HE DO ALL THAT?"

Introduction

"Mission Society of St. Francis Xavier"—this is the traditional title in some countries of the Pontifical Society for the Propagation of Faith. Today this international Catholic organization is known as "Missio." Even though the name has changed, it still is involved with the same activity carried out some four hundred years ago even to the borders of China by Francis Xavier, a Basque nobleman, as one of the first Jesuits: to give witness to Jesus Christ among people and nations who had not yet come to know him.

Penitential Rite

Lord Jesus Christ, you made a slave of yourself for us in order to free us: Lord, have mercy. . . .

You became weak for us weak ones, in order to win us for yourself: Christ, have mercy. . . .

You become all things to all people, so that all might share in the salvation of the Gospel: Lord, have mercy. . . .

Talk

Missionary Responsibility in a Difficult Period. Around 1540 European Christianity was shaken by the controversies of the Reformation. The Church had her hands full with salvaging in Europe whatever was still to salvage. Yet she did not lose herself in these internal quarrels. She sent forth missioners into the new land only a few decades after their discovery, places where the European powers sought to build up their influence.

Ignatius of Loyola sent out the first two Jesuits to the missions a short time after the founding of his company, without anxiety over splintering their limited powers.

Like a Second Paul. Francis Xavier was one of these two—after another confrere had to be withdrawn owing to illness. He set out in 1541 on his journey to India, and remained tirelessly active in southern and eastern Asia as papal legate and religious superior up until his death in 1552. Sites for his work included the Portuguese settlement of Goa, the coasts of India and Ceylon, various island groups in the Pacific Ocean, and finally even Japan. Toward the end of his life he was planning to found Christian communities even in China. Yet he died alone and abandoned on a small island off the Chinese coast.

"How Could He Do All That?" In our jet age, we can scarcely imagine the physical hardships that the saint accepted on his many trips by sea. In our age of television and worldwide interchange among specific cultures we cannot measure the courage that was needed then to visit strange countries with no knowledge of their language or culture, and to give witness to the faith in an unknown environment. "How could he do all that?" wrote a Protestant author who was studying the life of St. Francis Xavier.

The Readings provide an answer. The great missioner of the beginning of the modern age had discovered Jesus Christ in such a way that he could not help but call people's attention to him. It was not fear of punishment, but rather enthusiasm for the love of God, that would not allow Francis Xavier to rest [cf. Reading]. Aware of the Lord's presence (Gospel) he traveled and preached all over, he tried to become all things to all people, so as to rescue at least some of them.

Let us express in our petitions the inspiration that the patron of world missions gives us.

Petitions

Lord Jesus Christ, you have commended the Church to go forth to the entire world, and to proclaim the Gospel to all creation.

Let the Church in our country not become preoccupied with her own cares and problems, but keep alive within her the bond with the global Church. . . .
Strengthen the young Churches in the developing nations, that they might find the right answers to the many questions that they face. . . .
Be near to the suppressed Christian communities in China, Vietnam, Laos, and Kampuchea in the current dark hours of their histories. . . .

For you remain close to your Church until the end of time. You who sit at the right hand of God and live and reign forever and ever.

St. John Damascene (December 4)

CHRISTIAN VENERATION OF IMAGES

Introduction

John Damascene was the son of a Christian high official in the court of the Moslem prince of his home city. John worked as a theologian during his whole lifetime (c. 650–750) in Islamic territory—a sign that the relationship between Christianity and the Religion of the Prophet was not as tense in the beginning as it became in later centuries. As a theologian, John took special part in the contemporary discussions on proper Christian veneration of images.

Penitential Rite

"You must be strong in the grace which is ours in Christ Jesus." [Silence] Lord, have mercy. . . .

"Guard the rich deposit of faith with the help of the Holy Spirit who dwells within us." [Silence] Christ, have mercy. . . .

"Bear hardship along with me as a good soldier of Christ Jesus." [Silence] Lord, have mercy. . . .

Talk

Religious Works of Art—a Matter of Course. Images of saints and blessed, representations of angels and heavenly hosts, portrayals of Jesus Christ, pictorial representations of the Holy Trinity and of the entire heavenly glory are a matter of course. Frescoes from the Romanesque period, splended carved altars from the Gothic period, and colorful paintings from the Baroque period (along with less convincing imitations done in later times) are all examples of this. Even many Protestant congregations have in their worship areas pictorial representations of God or crosses with Jesus' image.

The Prohibition of Images in the Old Testament. Are we really aware that this appreciation of images (seen also in the icons of the Eastern Church) is something unusual and surprising against the background of the Old Testament? Any representation of God was forbidden to the Jews. They were to abstain from images of God in order to maintain their awareness of God's mysterious otherness. They were not to run the (pagan) danger of taking the images of God to be God himself. They were therefore not to think that they had God in hand and could thus force him to be of service to them.

Devotion through Images in the Early Church. After the revelation of God in the human form of Jesus Christ, people in the early Church represented the Risen One with images and regarded these images with reverence. Images of Mary and of other saints soon appeared as well.

To be sure, there were some wrong developments in the veneration of images within the Church as a result of her encounter with the pagan environment. And certainly, against this background, the total rejection of all religious imagery in the Eastern Church can be understood: around 700, it led to a full-blown conflict over images.

In this controversy, John Damascene took sides as a defender of sound church tradition [Reading]. He recognized the danger that a pious individual could get stuck on an image and could forget what the image was intended to symbolize. Yet he also recognized that man with his senses needed tangible and visible signs so that the divine reality might not slip from the horizon of his life.

Devotion with Images Today. Christian devotion with images survived that controversy. Ways of the Cross, images of the Madonna in our yards, devotional pillars in the marketplaces of European cities and pious images in the solitary countryside are evidence of this living religious tradition. Images, such as a crucifix in the living room or a picture (sometimes maudlin) of the guardian angel in the bedroom, have conducted generations of Christians over and over again to God and to his mystery-filled reality.

Do they still accomplish this? Or do many people today, when they see such images, stop with the picture—since they can see it only as an art (or kitsch) object that no longer points to the divine reality? People then merely admire the "beautiful crucifix" or the "elegant Madonna"—and think not at all of the death of Jesus on the cross or of the interceding care of Mary. But let us leave others be: let us ask ourselves, are religious representations for us simply a matter of art or advertising, or do they lead us on to God and his mystery-filled reality as it is revealed in the life and death of Jesus Christ and in the lives of the saints?

Petitions

Mystery-filled and unfathomable God:

Let the mutual understanding of differing religious traditions grow among Moslems and Christians. . . .
Be near to Christian artists with your inspirations. . . .
Grant that we, in this time before Christmas, may acknowledge in Jesus Christ your incarnate goodness and love of humanity. . . .

For you are near to all people in Jesus Christ. You who live and reign forever and ever.

St. Nicholas (December 6)

COMICAL FIGURE OR SAINT?

Santa Claus is coming to town; we see him in our streets and department stores in these weeks before Christmas. In the character of St. Nicholas we can practically touch the secularization, often pointed out, of originally religious objects. What has happened to this great popular saint of the Middle Ages?

Penitential Rite

Lord Jesus Christ, by your great works performed for those in need, you have witnessed to the Kingdom of God: Lord, have mercy. . . .

You have sent your disciples out to heal the sick: Christ, have mercy. . . .

You give us also the command to prepare for your second coming by works of love: Lord, have mercy. . . .

Talk

Legends. "Historical data on Nicholas, one of the most venerated saints both in the east and in the west, are lacking," says a sober entry in one church lexicon. He was probably bishop of Myra in Asia Minor in the first half of the fourth century (the time during which the Church was becoming a public power more and more).

Around this figure a garland of legends has been fashioned: the bishop who liberated three unjustly imprisoned officers and rescued three innocent young men condemned to death; who rescued three poor girls from a house of prostitution by secret donations of money and enabled them to enter respectable marriages; who came to the aid of sailors in a storm.

These legends clearly augmented the popular appeal of this saint. Innumerable churches bear his name. He was held to be the patron of sailors and of merchants, of prisoners and bakers, of pharmacists and lawyers. He was especially venerated by girls hoping for marriage but with no prospect in sight.

Core of the Legends. There is no Santa Claus in the Nicholas legends. In none of these legends is there anything about a tribunal over good and evil or about punishment or reward for children. The main point of all the legends is the saint's effective and selfless love for neighbor.

Can this core of the Nicholas legend not lead us to a more Christian mode of celebrating this season in our church groups and in our families?

Christmas Parties in Our Groups and Organizations.
How can we celebrate the Christmas season really in a Christian way in church circles? Let us leave aside any visit of Santa Claus. Let us also leave aside any chatter that rips people apart for their weaknesses and faults. Let us start with an Advent reading that will remind us that we are supposed to prepare the way of Jesus Christ to humanity by works of love. We can also retell one of the legends about St. Nicholas. When it is time for refreshments, we can exchange pastries with one another. In this symbol of small gifts we can show our readiness for love of neighbor in everyday life. Perhaps a celebration of this type could be used to open an Advent bazaar put on with the cooperation of parish organizations, with the proceeds going to the Church's charitable works locally or on diocesan or global levels. Or else the sharers in this celebration can get addresses of some elderly or infirm parishioners; they can ex-

tend themselves to care for them in these pre-Christmas weeks, and act in some way like St. Nicholas did.

And in the Family. Do the children lose out on something, if Santa Claus no longer makes his appearance? In a simple candlelit family ceremony, parents can point out and expand upon the revealing of the goodness of God and of his love for humanity, made visible in Jesus Christ, and how we should put this love into practice in our own lives. Small gifts exchanged among parents and children express this love. In one legend, St. Nicholas can be brought out as an example of active love for neighbor. Perhaps parents can also get their children to think of how (maybe in the form of a resolution for Advent) they can act like Nicholas toward other people in this time before Christmas.

Can we then not integrate our celebration of St. Nicholas into our preparation for Christmas?

Petitions

> Lord Jesus Christ, hear our prayer during these days of Advent.
>
> Let people catch a glimpse of your love in every good thing that they receive. . . .
> Help Christians give witness to your kindness and love for mankind even in the many small deeds of each day. . . .
> Open our eyes that we might recognize those people in our surroundings who need our particular help. . . .

For you choose to be present in this world through the love that people mutually extend to one another. You who live and reign forever and ever.

St. Ambrose (December 7)

THE CHRISTIAN GROWS WITH HIS DUTIES

Introduction

We are influenced by the permanent elements of history—and we easily associate the essence of the Church with her traditional laws, a tendency we have seen in the changes of the past four years. Things can be quite different in the Church, however, and nevertheless the Church can still be the Church of Jesus Christ, as we see in the life of St. Ambrose of Milan.

Penitential Rite

Lord Jesus Christ, you let your Spirit blow where you will: Lord, have mercy. . . .

You give to each of us the grace necessary to fulfill our tasks in life: Christ, have mercy. . . .

You accept people with their particular traits and abilities into your service: Lord, have mercy. . . .

Talk

Possible within the Church. Ambrose lived from about 339 to 397. He was born in Trier, Germany, the son of a highly placed family of officials. His mother was a Christian. In keeping with the customs of the time, the children remained just catechumens. At the age of thirty, he became governor of Milan. Up to that point he had followed the career of an honest and competent official, yet he showed no special zeal for the Christian faith.

The bishop of Milan died in 374. The city's Christian community was accustomed to electing the bishop by itself. Since the Christians were divided among themselves over the issue, and trouble was expected during the election, Ambrose entered the cathedral personally in order to see that public order was maintained. Suddenly his name was called from the crowd as a nominee for bishop, and everyone present agreed on his nomination. Ambrose hesitated, but then finally acceded to the will of the people. He was baptized immediately, and was ordained bishop a week later.

The Christian Grows with His Duties.

Up until this point, Ambrose had lived as an average Christian; but now he worked at his new task with all his powers. He gave up his comfortable life-style, distributed his goods among the poor, and led a strict, simple life given over to work and study.

During that era of transition from Roman paganism over to a world shaped by Christianity, the bishop of Milan was in his own way missioner, pastor, and defender of the Church. He made use of his thorough classical education in bringing the Good News to his educated contemporaries. Thus, as a doctor of the Church, he rendered great service to the development of theology. Above all, however, he was a tireless pastor and preacher. He loved the liturgy; for it he wrote and composed popular sacred music.

Amid the upheaval of his times, with its gross contradictions between rich and poor, he declared himself in favor of social justice and castigated the ill effects of money and of excessive property. In one homily he stated, "You give to the poor not out of what belongs to you; rather, you give from that which is his. You have appropriated to yourself that which is given for the use of everybody. The earth belongs to everyone and not to the rich alone. . . ."

Ambrose also engaged in tough controversy with the emperor in Constantinople. After the official recognition of Christianity, the emperor considered himself more and more to be lord of the Church. The Milanese bishop declared clearly, "The emperor is *within* the Church and *not over* her." When Emperor Theodosius unleashed a bloodbath out of revenge and had more than 7,000 people killed, Ambrose excommunicated him—and the emperor undertook public penance in order to gain reacceptance into the full communion of the Church.

We Too Can Grow with Our Duties. Ambrose: an average Christian who, touched by Jesus Christ, assumed a duty within the Church, grew in faith with this duty, and thus became a forerunner of Christ in his time. Does our way to deeper faith perhaps lie through a task in our parish that we decide to accept? Could we not become better forerunners of Jesus Christ if we seriously asked ourselves: Where are we, where am I needed in our parish?

Petitions

Lord, you call whomever you will into your following and your service:

Grant to many people in our communities the readiness to render service in our parishes. . . .
Let all who work in the Church grow deeper in the faith. . . .
Strengthen all those with new trust in God, who have become discouraged in their faithful service to their parishes. . . .

For with the duty you also give the strength to fulfill it properly. You who live and reign forever and ever.

The Immaculate Conception of Mary (December 8)

GOD GIVES GRACE FOR SERVICE

Introduction

"I exult for joy in the Lord, my soul rejoices in God; for he has clothed me in the garment of salvation . . . ." With this opening song on today's solemnity of the Virgin Mother of God conceived without sin, we look with Mary upon God, who dwells at the center of any correctly understood Marian devotion. With her, during this Eucharistic liturgy, we praise God who has called both her and us—although clearly in different ways—into service for his Kingdom and has given grace to us for it.

Penitential Rite

> Lord Jesus Christ, image of the Father: Lord, have mercy. . . .
> Son of the Virgin Mary: Christ, have mercy. . . .
> Herald of the Kingdom of God: Lord, have mercy. . . .

Talk

God Gives Grace . . .   On every Marian feast day we, together with Mary, praise God's kindness and mercy under some special aspect. What is the aspect of today's solemnity?

On this day the Church is not announcing that Mary was conceived without the cooperation of a man. The Church is not even celebrating today the article of faith that Mary conceived Jesus without the cooperation of a man. We confess much more with the tradition of the Church that Mary was endowed by God with sanctifying grace from the first moment of her existence in her mother's body, and was not drawn into the world's alienation from God that we call original sin. God grants us in baptism that which he gave to Mary at her very beginning. He was with her from the start.

. . . for Service. If God is with Mary in a special way, then he has a special responsibility for her.

"The Lord is with you," the angel's greeting heard by Mary, was also uttered as a greeting and a promise for the great figures of the Old Testament. The Lord was with Isaac (Gen 26:3), Jacob (Gen 28:15), Moses (Ex 3:12), Joshua (Jos 1:5), Samuel (1 S 3:19), Saul (1 S 10:7), and David (1 S 16:18). God called these individuals to the leadership and rescue of his people and therefore was with them. As "Yahweh," the God-who-is, as "Emmanuel," God-with-us, he was with the great figures of salvation history, because he wanted to be with his whole people, to bless his people and to rescue them. Their election was a call to the service of God's saving will.

God chose to become man in the fullness of time. As God-who-is, he wanted in an unimaginable way to be God-with-us, God among men. He was with Mary in a special way, he took her up from the beginning into the living communion of his grace to make her capable of cooperating with his plan. As the mother of Jesus, she was called in a particularly important way to cooperate in the rescue and redemption of humankind. Thus, and only thus, was she chosen in her state of grace from among all people. She was especially gifted, so that she might gift the world in God's power with the Son who signified salvation.

We Too Are Given Grace for Service. Today, together with Mary, we praise the redeeming love of God that found its entrance into the world through her and her special calling. Yet Mary is also the

The Immaculate Conception of Mary

archetype and example for our own Christian calling. The basis of her blessedness is also the basis of our life.

God remains over our life as well. He has blessed us in a special way in baptism (in comparison with the unbaptized). Through the gift of the life of grace he is also with us, since through us he wills to be with the world and with all people.

The grace of baptism is not granted to us for our exclusive advantage. We are called to be God's instruments in the world by the power of the grace of baptism. God wants to be God-who-is through us among people. He wants to approach people through the service of our selfless love. We are supposed to give to people (as did Mary, but still in a very different way) his Son, Jesus Christ, in whom they find salvation.

Mary accepted her blessing for service with her yes: "I am the maidservant of the Lord. Let it be done to me as you say" [Gospel]. God can also approach people through us in Jesus Christ only if we, like she, utter our *fiat:* our yes to gift of divine life, to our election; our yes as well to the task of bearing Christ, as Emmanuel, as God-with-us, through our selfless love into the world that awaits him with deep Advent longing.

Petitions

Gracious God, you have given Mary grace for service and want to be with people through us as well in your Son, Jesus Christ:

Give us joy over our calling and our gift of faith. . .
Open our eyes that we might recognize the longing for Christ in people today. . . .
Give us the strength to bring your Son to the people of our time through the witness of our selfless love. . . .

Grant us this through the intercession of Mary, whom you have blessed from the beginning with your presence. You who live and reign forever and ever.

St. Damasus I (December 11)

POPE IN A TURBULENT TIME

Introduction

"His victory was bought too dearly, it required too many police tactics, too much imperial complicity, too many corpses to secure his place. His entire pontificate felt the consequences." Thus writes one serious church historian about Pope Damasus, who was bishop of Rome from 366 to 384. He played upon the conflicts that surrounded his election as pope.

Penitential Rite

"Do not remember the sins of my youth. In your love remember me. Lord, for the sake of your name forgive my guilt; for it is great" (Ps 25:7,11).

Have mercy, Lord our God, have mercy. . . .

Talk

Scandalous Quarrels. The Roman Christian community split into two factions at the death of Pope Liberius. The larger group chose Damasus to be pope, the smaller group the priest Ursinus. The hostile parties gave themselves over to street massacres in Rome right after the election; seven deaths resulted. The pagan authorities had to intervene in order to preserve public order; they sarcastically noted the odd way the Christians had of carrying out the great commandment of love [Gospel]. The antipope ended up exiled from Rome and Damasus, supported by civil authority, exercised his office.

Human Weaknesses and Calumny. The pope himself stood out as an embattled personality in these controversies. He had a bent toward personal vanity and considered himself to be a great poet. His adversaries criticized him for being a guest all too often at parties held by rich ladies. On the other hand, it was determined in court that accusations of all types against him were slanderous (thus, the lack of proof for the charges of murder and adultery was judicially demonstrated).

Originator of the Vulgate. With all his human weaknesses, Damasus was still the bishop of Rome, trying to feed the entire flock entrusted to his care [Reading]. A major concern of his was to have sacred Scripture read during the liturgy in an understandable language. The transition from Greek to Latin in the liturgy had occurred in the Roman Church some time before, but only limping translations were available for scriptural readings. These were repellent to educated folk, both Christian and pagan.

On that account, Damasus gave his secretary (St. Jerome) the assignment of making a new translation of the whole Bible into Latin. As a qualified expert in Greek and (a rarity for his time) in Hebrew, Jerome was the ideal man for the project. Through a lifetime of patient work (first in Rome, later in Bethlehem), he completed the Latin version of sacred Scripture known as the Vulgate, which stood as the official version of the Bible in the Catholic Church right up to our time.

Is it any surprise that this new translation was at first rejected by certain church circles as a departure, and that it earned for the pope and his capable secretary personal attacks and suspicions? Yet, in the end, the new translation did establish itself and influenced church life for centuries.

Damasus and Our Age. Why look at the late fourth century? Our current pope is John Paul II. We have our own problems now. Yet perhaps we can draw some lessons for our time.

For one thing: our time is not the first time that there has been unrest and upheavel in the Church because of new biblical translations and because of strange-sounding passages. Even if human speech itself changed, we would have to rework time and again our translations of sacred Scripture (as well as our prayer in common).

For another: internal church controversies, sometimes poisoned by personal weaknesses and sensitivities (among pastoral workers, between laypeople and priests, between theologians and bishops . . .) are part of the life of the Church. Thank God, these days they are thrashed out less bloodily than at the time of Pope Damasus! We cannot avoid them; we can only attempt to steer away from all suspicions, and to resolve all existing objective differences in the spirit of Christian love with mutual patience and respect—or bear the tensions for some time.

Petitions

God, in your providence you chose Peter to be head of the apostles and you founded the Church upon him:

Protect and bless your servant, Pope⎯⎯⎯. . . .
Give him the strength to be the visible and secure cornerstone of unity among your people. . . .
Be near to him throughout all the disappointments of his office. . . .

You who live and reign forever and ever.

St. Jane Frances de Chantal (December 12)

AN EXTRAORDINARY WOMAN

Introduction

What does a housewife and mother do when the children are grown and taken care of? Can and should she take on another task to give meaning to her life?

Jane Frances de Chantal (she lived from 1572 to 1641, in southeastern France) became foundress of an order after a happy marriage and after providing for her children.

Penitential Rite

Lord Jesus Christ, whoever does the will of your Father is counted among your true relations: Lord, have mercy. . . .

Whoever does good and not evil every day of his or her life is your brother or sister: Christ, have mercy. . . .

Whoever opens his hand to the needy and extends his hands to the poor lives in fellowship with you: Lord, have mercy. . . .

Talk

An Extraordinary Life. Jane Frances grew up in a religiously inclined upper-class family. She married within her class at the age of twenty. She brought six children into the world (two of whom died early). A deep respect and authentic love grew up between her and her husband.

Then, when she was thirty, she lost her husband to an unfortunate hunting accident. It was a hard blow for her. Yet through this experience of deep suffering, levels emerged in her that until then had remained hidden. Her religious life became more serious. With all her dedication to her family and to the upbringing of her children, she was nonetheless restless in the ensuing years as she sought to develop her own religious scheme of life.

In 1604 she met the renowned Bishop Francis de Sales. She placed her trust in him and entrusted her spiritual direction to him. Under his guidance her religious life deepened year after year. Once her own children were provided for, she became the foundress of a religious community adapted to her times (Sisters of the Visitation), intended to be accessible to older women as well. They combined common prayer with the care of the poor and the sick in their own homes. Over the next thirty years, she worked tirelessly to spread and consolidate her community.

Her Religious Profile. What do we know of the interior life of this woman? Jane Frances must have matched very closely that valiant woman whose image is given in the Reading. She sought to deal with all the many large and small problems connected with her household and the rearing of her children. She mastered, with great seriousness, style, and energy, the tasks necessary for the founding and leadership of her religious community.

At the same time, her whole life was ordered toward Jesus Christ. During the years of her religious search, she one day branded the name "Jesus" on her skin with a hot iron, in order to make it clear through this external sign that he would be the center of her life from then on.

Yet this communion in faith with Jesus Christ was no heaven on earth for her. Her faith to her was not a secure property. She suffered greatly because she felt nothing of the presence of God, and because she

St. Jane Frances de Chantal

had to defend herself against doubts regarding faith and needed all her strength to dominate her inner anxieties.

Her Friendship with Francis de Sales. Jane Frances de Chantal entrusted herself as widow and mother in her religious search to the saintly Francis de Sales. He was her "spiritual director" (we would put it more plainly: her ordinary confessor). Between them there even grew an intimate and trusting friendship, within which both learned from each other: the bishop was not the only one with something to give. Jane Frances maintained her self-reliance and was completely able to lead her congregation independently as Francis de Sales purposely limited their contact and then soon died in 1622.

Today? Jane Frances de Chantal found a special task for herself as a widow in the Church. Where do tasks lie waiting in our parishes that could be assumed by married women whose children are grown and out of the house, or by widows living alone?

Petitions

Lord, our God, hear our prayer.

We pray for all housewives and mothers who run the risk of withering under the petty details of their daily duties and chores.   [Silence]
We pray for women who have lost their husbands and suffer the burden of loneliness.   [Silence]
We pray for all those women who spend their spare time in kitchen service for the needy.   [Silence]

Lord God, make the efforts of all those people fruitful who, unnoticed, gain mastery over their lives in the Spirit of your Son, who lives and reigns with you forever and ever.

St. Lucy (December 13)

"BETROTHED TO ONE HUSBAND"

Introduction

Lucy (who died as a martyr probably in 304 in Sicily) belongs to the group of highly venerated Christian virgins of the early Church. She found a place not only in Christian devotion. For centuries her name has also been found in the Roman Canon.—How did it come about that saintly virgins played a special role in the estimation of the early Church? Was it simply because their lives were exemplary—or did the Church see symbolically expressed in them the meaning of each Christian life?

Penitential Rite

The Lord does deeds of justice, gives judgment for all who are oppressed. It is he who forgives all your guilt, who heals every one of your ills, who redeems your life from the grave, who crowns you with love and compassion (after Ps 103:6,3f).

Have mercy, Lord our God, have mercy. . . .

Talk

Symbolism of Virgin and Bride. The nubile betrothed maiden or the bride are celebrated over and over in poetry and folk songs (but also by songwriters of current hits). The theme is sounded of how she now thinks only of her fiance or of her bridegroom, and has no further regard for other young men; how she wants to be completely with her partner; how she remains faithful to him even under difficult circumstances. The betrothed maiden and the bride are thus symbols for love and faithfulness in general.

. . in the Bible. The Old Testament made early use of this human symbol in order to speak about the bond of Yahweh with the people of Israel. God was portrayed as a bridegroom. Israel was seen in the role of a bride who loved her bridegroom and wanted to be completely with him. The high point of this symbolic talk was the Song of Songs, an Old Testament writing in which the bond between Yahweh and Israel is present in overtly erotic terms after the human example of a honeymoon.

The New Testament also uses this symbolic talk. Paul addresses the faith of the community at Corinth in today's Reading when he writes, ". . . I have given you in marriage to one husband, presenting you as a chaste virgin to Christ." He wanted the Christians of Corinth to think only of Jesus Christ, and to cast no more glances at their earlier gods; to desire to belong totally to Christ, and to remain faithful to him even in difficult times.

Also, in the parable of the five foolish and the five wise virgins [Gospel], Christians should be reminded that they should live totally for Christ and should seriously attempt to go forth and meet the Lord as he comes again.

Unmarried Saints as Living Examples.

Further: when the Bible portrays the relationship between Israel and Yahweh, between the faithful and Christ with the image of betrothal or marriage, it is including believers both unmarried and married. Every Christian is called upon to have regard only for Jesus Christ, to desire to belong entirely to him, to hold faith with him, and to meet his return full of hope and joy.

The Church, then, in the course of history, has seen these Christian attitudes especially present in those Christians who remained unmarried for Christian reasons and who dedicated themselves in virginal life to Christ and his Kingdom. In the special veneration of saintly unmarried women, she wanted to point out over and over the necessary "bridal" attitude in each Christian life.

To Go Forth to Christ as a Betrothed Maiden Would.
Seeing matters in this way, the memory of the Sicilian Christian Lucy, relatively unknown to us, also turns into a question for us.

Is Jesus Christ my one and all? Is the relationship with him the most important thing in my life? Do I love him as a betrothed girl loves her fiance (taking into account all the obvious differences between the two loves)?

Do I choose to belong entirely to Christ? Am I ready to act upon his wishes and plans? Am I dedicating myself with all my powers to his Kingdom?

Am I faithful to Christ, even when it sometimes becomes hard to count on his presence in the dark ways of everyday Christian living?

Do I go forth to meet Christ as he comes again (in my own death and at the end of time) with the oil of living faith in the lamp of my life?

Petitions

Lord Jesus Christ, through baptism we are in communion with you:

Strengthen our faith. . . .
Increase our hope. . . .
Ignite your love in us. . . .

Grant that we may come forth to greet you with burning lamps in our hands. You who live and reign forever and ever.

St. John of the Cross (December 14)

FORERUNNER IN THE SIGN OF THE CROSS

Introduction

Advent—memory or reality? In these weeks before Christmas, do we merely recall the longing for the revelation of God that was felt in past ages—or do we too still wait in darkness and deathly night for the final revelation? St. John of the Cross rejoiced in his writings over the unfathomable love of God, yet he also spoke of the "dark night of the soul" experienced by everyone who approaches God along the way of the cross.

Penitential Rite

Lord Jesus Christ, you have said, "If anyone comes to me, he must turn his back on his family and his very self": Lord, have mercy. . . .

You have said, "Anyone who does not take up his cross and follow me cannot be my disciple": Christ, have mercy. . . .

You have said, "None of you can be my disciple if he does not renounce all his possessions": Lord, have mercy. . . .

Talk

Path of a Calling. John (born in 1542) grew up as half an orphan and had to earn his own money for his studies. Upon completing his education, he entered the Carmelites. As a young priest, he met St. Teresa of Avila, who was twenty-eight years his senior. She won him over to her plan to re-establish among the Carmelites the original strictness of the order's beginnings. Till the end of his life—he died in 1591—he worked tirelessly for the reformed community of Discalced Carmelites. In doing this, he did not let himself be discouraged by resistance and hostility.

The Cross in His Life. When he entered the order, the saint chose the name "John of the Cross." His life brought him much toil, many crosses, and much suffering. As instigator of the order's reform, he became entangled in vehement quarrels. He was imprisoned by confreres who were opponents of the reform and confined in darkness, until one day he succeeded in escaping. Even among the proponents of reform he was misunderstood and had to suffer much from them.

Amid all external demands and turbulent controversies, however, the saint's great goal was to penetrate ever more deeply into the mysterious reality of God and live with him in living communion. Through the study of Scripture (cf. Reading and Gospel) and his life experiences, he learned that the way of the cross is alone the way to a deeper knowledge of God. For this reason, he demanded harsh renunciation of himself and of his confreres. He could thus ask God to allow him to continue to live under disrespect and misunderstanding so as to be able to suffer a bit more for him. He could then be content in his prayer life if he felt nothing of God's presence: in the dark night of the soul with Jesus on the cross, he could believe only blindly in the Father's love.

His religious life, nonetheless, was not gloomy. Amid all the strictness and the radicality of his following of the cross, he declared in his

St. John of the Cross

writings his enthusiasm for the love of God and could rejoice with faith in this love even while in prison. Since Jesus Christ and the Father were truly at the center of his life, "earthly values" (Family, beauty of the world, success or failure . . .) played only secondary roles for him.

Preparing the Way for Jesus Christ. This saint, while seeking to restore the original withdrawal from the world and the contemplative character of his order for the sake of radically following the cross, nonetheless wrote this statement: "In the evening of our life, we will be judged according to love." He knew that, for God, sacrifice or renunciation or mystical sweetness in prayer did not count, but that only love would matter for God. He sought to realize this love as a response to the love of God in the life-style of his order (and in untiring pastoral work), knowing that the way to selfless love was the way of the cross.

Our circumstances of life are different. We cannot withdraw into solitude. Our duties normally direct us to care for the family. Yet John of the Cross, perhaps especially now during Advent, is asking us: Is your life and work marked by love of God and men? Are you ready to take the way of the cross in your love for other people? Not to run away from difficulties, not to be discouraged by obstacles, and not to be disappointed by unfair dealings?

Petitions

Mysterious and hidden God!

Be close to those who feel nothing of your presence. . . .
Give courage to all who encounter difficulties in their dedication to renewal in the Church. . . .
Give to those who are suffering a deep joy in your unfathomable love. . . .

Lord, let us now believe in your presence and one day see your glory. You who live and reign forever and ever.

St. Peter Canisius (December 21)

THE SECOND APOSTLE OF GERMANY

Introduction

Many of us can remember the catechisms that were used when we had religious education. [In the United States, we had the various editions of the Baltimore Catechism.—Tr.] Not long ago, the Dutch Catechism attracted much attention. The current books for religious instruction for our children are somewhat differently structured from the old catechisms, in which the most important statements about the faith are compiled together into concise questions and brief answers.

The catechism form that we had historically goes back in the Catholic Church above all to today's saint: Peter Canisius.

Penitential Rite

Jesus Christ, patient and full of mercy: Lord, have mercy. . . .
Jesus Christ, rich to all who call upon you: Christ, have mercy. . . .
Jesus Christ, rescue of all who hope in you: Lord, have mercy. . . .

Talk

The Situation of the Church. Abuses in the Church led to the beginning of the Reformation. Many areas of Europe (including parts that today have a Catholic majority again) separated themselves from

St. Peter Canisius

Rome. This development came as a shock to the battered Catholic Church. New forces were aroused that worked energetically for the internal and external renewal of the Church. The Council of Trent was convened. New religious communities were formed. Among them, the Jesuits especially assumed great importance for the Church's renewal.

Biographical Data. Peter Canisius lived and worked during this period. He was born in 1521 in what is now Holland, then a part of the German empire. Against his father's will, he took up theological studies in Cologne. At age twenty-two he joined the young Society of Jesus. Already at twenty-five he became theological adviser to a bishop of the Council of Trent. After some years in Italy, his community's superior general—Ignatius of Loyola—sent him back to Germany in 1549. He found his life's work there, remaining faithful to it until his death in 1597.

Professor of Theology and Pastor. As teacher of theology and as pastoral worker, he labored tirelessly in the ensuing decades in order to strengthen internally the Church in Germany and to win back the areas that had become Protestant. He gained special influence through the publication of his catechisms, which he had produced in three editions. They were translated into many languages.

Church Politician. His activity was not limited to pastoral work. He maintained letter contact with nearly all the leading figures of the Catholic camp. He was a confidant of both the pope and of Catholic German princes. He thus acquired great influence over the course of events.

Rooted in God. Peter Canisius lived during the time of upheaval, appropriately characterized by lines from today's Reading: "For the time will come when people will not tolerate sound doctrine, but, following their own desires, will surround themselves with teachers who tickle their ears." He proclaimed the Word tirelessly. Again and again he spoke up for the Church "whether convenient or inconvenient". He drew the strength for this from his living relationship with God, in which he had become rooted through the Spiritual Exercises of his society's founder. Steeped in this communion with God, in the menacing situation of the Church at that time he could write, "The anxiety of many people is greater than need be, because they look for human rather than divine help. They look for help for the prostrate Church out of doubt rather than out of holy confidence."—Must we not allow the same to be said in today's Church? Ought we not to strive more for a conscious communion with God in a regular prayer life?

Love for the Church. Along with his living faith, he was gifted with an unyielding faithfulness to the Church. He saw clearly the Church's weaknesses and attacked harshly the abuses in the Church in his time. He suffered the weariness of good people and expressed this pain more than once in this fashion: "Peter sleeps and Judas keeps vigil!" Yet he loved this Church, he remained true to her and at the same time cooperated for her reform from within.—Do we have the same attitude toward the Church amid the troubles and problems of our days?

Second Apostle of Germany. Peter Canisius clearly recognized in his time what was necessary for the Church. He pushed forward whatever was required with tireless effort. He still was able to forego his own favorite ideas and plans; this is evident in his editions of the catechisms, where he summarizes the general doctrine of the Church in a sober and even dry style. He wanted to transmit through them the "sound doctrine" of tradition (Reading) without altering it in the least [Gospel]. In this way he became "salt" for the German Church and a "light" [Gospel] for his contemporaries. He contributed to the renewal of the Catholic Church in Germany in such a measure that posterity has given him the title of Second Apostle of Germany.

St. John of Kanty (December 23)

"YAHWEH HAS HAD MERCY"

Introduction

There are saints whose lives are little known, but whose veneration has taken root in the Church, even though their official canonization did not come about until centuries after their death. Among these was the Polish saint, John of Kanty, who died on Christmas Eve in 1473. Perhaps this unknown saint can help us in these days before Christmas to be aware of what it means for us to live like a saint.

Penitential Rite

Lord Jesus Christ, you are the revelation of the Father's love: Lord, have mercy. . . .

You give us examples in the saints of selfless love: Christ, have mercy. . . .

You want to reveal this love through our lives as well: Lord, have mercy. . . .

Talk

What It Is All About. St. John of Kanty began as a theology professor in Krakow. He later worked in parish ministry. He is supposed as well to have organized pilgrimages to Rome and Jerusalem. In the memory of his countrymen, he lived as a man of deep piety and of great love for the poor. Perhaps what emerges from these scanty bits of biographical information is that, in the life of each saint, it does not so much matter *what* he has accomplished as *how* he has lived and worked in imitation of Jesus Christ. For true holiness manifests itself above all in how a person becomes inwardly like Jesus Christ and more and more feels, thinks, and acts like him in everyday situations. Just as John of Kanty drew inspiration for his Christian life from his patron saint, John the Baptist, we too, in these days before Christmas, can draw upon this Advent personality to learn what happens in our lives if we decide to live as saints.

Prepare the Way of the Lord. John the Baptist was the forerunner of Jesus. He saw God and not himself at the center of the world. He lived and worked that God might come to men in Jesus Christ. He was ready to decrease if his listeners more and more found only Jesus Christ. John of Kanty lived and worked as he did.

Do we live with the same attitude? Is the deepest goal of our care for our neighbor that Jesus Christ come to him and he to Jesus? Or is the point for us, whether overt or covert, yet still above all, that we "arrive," that we be respected and honored, admired and praised? It is human, and therefore not wrong, that we should be glad for an echo of our love for neighbor. We continually need now and then a word of thanks lest we become discouraged. Yet we must also always ask ourselves if our love has something of the selflessness of the Forerunner, who, overjoyed that people were discovering Jesus Christ, was content to be forgotten.

Giving Hope to the Poor. Luke, whose Gospel speaks the most about John the Baptist, is the evangelist of the poor. According to him, the Good News is to be proclaimed specifically to the oppressed and the persecuted. They are to know that God has drawn near to them and that their deprivation is coming to an end. John, as the forefunner of the Messiah of the poor, thus called for social justice (cf. Lk 3:10–14). All

Christian love for neighbor, the centuries-long stream in which John of Kanty stood, has intended to give hope in the widest sense to the poor, to enable them to trust that their need would come to an end.

We cannot change overnight our world's unjust conditions. Yet what can we especially do on Christmas, the love feast, to help everyone who is not on the sunny side of life to be able to experience something of God's love? Is our donation to the missions a sign that we love the poor along with Jesus Christ and John the Baptist? Where can we give a similar sign in our immediate environment?

Yahweh Has Taken Pity. That is how we translate the name "John." John the Baptist knew he could proclaim a new future for the world, since God had sent us this future in Jesus Christ. John of Kanty also lived out this trust in God. Are we aware enough that our hope and strength proceed from this mercy that became manifest in the Incarnation?'

Petitions

Son of God become man, hear our prayer:

Give to Christians the Spirit of selfless love. . . .
Open their eyes to the needs in their surroundings. . . .
Reward with your grace all those who tirelessly do good. . . .

Lord, renew in your Church the Spirit of your merciful love. You who live and reign forever and ever.

St. Stephen (December 26)

THE WORLD ACCEPTED HIM NOT

Introduction

Today is like the second day of Christmas for us; for the liturgy, however, it is the Feast of St. Stephen, the first Christian martyr. We bridge this gap with the Christmas elements of our liturgy today: yesterday we rejoiced over the revelation of God's goodness and love for humanity in the Child at Bethlehem; today we remember a man (first of a countless line) who paid with his life for his joy in this Child. This, however, is not enough. We celebrate the feast of Christ's birth and the memorial of St. Stephen each time that we recall thankfully and joyfully during holy Mass the terrible death of this Child. If we thereby at first glance are joining together irreconcilable elements, our faith-conviction becomes explicit that, for the Christian, there is no joy without suffering, yet also no suffering without joy.

Penitential Rite

Lord Jesus Christ, splendor of the Father, archetype of creation, Son of the Virgin: Lord, have mercy. . . .

Friend of the poor, health of the sick, brother of mankind: Christ, have mercy. . . .

Lamb slain for us, man of sorrows, redeemer and savior: Lord, have mercy. . . (GL 765,2).

St. Stephen 565

Talk

Stumbling Block. "This child is destined to be a sign that will be opposed" (Lk 2:34), prophesied the elder Simeon over the Child in the crib. "Happy is the man who does not lose faith in me" (Mt 11:6), said Jesus of Nazareth later about himself.

Jesus Christ came into the world to bring salvation to men and women. He came into a world that, although it was God's property, closed itself off to his coming. It accepted him not—as the Synoptic Gospels present it in their infancy narratives and as the Gospel of John explicitly states it. The world set itself against God's kindness and love for humanity in this Child—made evident in the resistance of the scribes and the pharisees and of the "Jews" (insofar as the Gospels understand these words) in general.

The rejection of the Child was also directed against everyone who recognized and acknowledged God's love in him. It not only pinned Jesus of Nazareth to the cross; it has also ever sought to silence Christians and to get them out of the way.

Through Suffering to Joy. Can we still rejoice in the birth of the Child of Bethlehem, if this Child ended up on the cross and innumerable people had to suffer and die for his sake?

If we knew only that this Child died a horrible death and brought persecution upon his followers, then we indeed could not rejoice over his birth.

Yet the Child of Bethlehem was not overcome by suffering. He triumphed in his resurrection over suffering (and over rejection by the world). It is a question of the joy and fulfillment of everlasting life. If suffering was not absent from his path through life, it was because it was the passage to glory.

Joy in Suffering. Because we believe that Christ has victoriously overcome suffering through his death and resurrection, we can thankfully celebrate the Eucharist on the feast of his birthday. For the memorial of his death is also the memorial of his resurrection. In the Mass we proclaim that God's goodness and love for humanity have prevailed despite any rejection of the Redeemer by the world.

On that account, even right after Christmas we can recall the execution of Stephen. For we do not rejoice today over the fact that, as a disciple of Jesus, he was persecuted and stoned. Much more do we rejoice with him because God's kindness and love for humanity were effective in him, and because he was able to endure his own (life and) death like Jesus Christ in imitation of Christ. Like Jesus, he could say, "Lord, do not hold this sin against them." Just as Jesus, by the account in the Gospel of Luke, let himself on the cross fall into the Father's hand (cf. Lk 23:46), so did Stephen deliver himself under the hail of stones into the hand of the Risen One: "Lord Jesus, receive my spirit!" [Reading]. With Jesus Christ he thus overcame death and entered for ever into joy with God.

We Are Still On the Way. We are still with Jesus Christ on our way through this earthly life. We are still in conflict with the world that refuses God's goodness and love for humanity in the Child of Bethlehem. This "world" also fails to accept us with open arms as messengers of Christ. Each person has his own striking experiences in this regard. If we come up against lack of understanding for our faith, if we run into resistance and rejection and suffer on that account, we then share in Jesus Christ and in the way of all Christians. On this way there is no joy without suffering, but also no suffering without the believing (and joyful) certainty that the love of God eventually prevails—a truth which the resurrection of Jesus and the faith-filled death of Stephen make manifest.

St. John the Evangelist (December 27)

A "SON OF THUNDER"

Introduction

The character of the apostle John lies under a triple shadow: the shadow of John the Baptist (much better known as a patron saint), the shadow of Christmas (which crowds his memorial day), the shadow of many saccharine images (which make a wilted, weakling "pet" disciple out of "the disciple whom Jesus loved"). Yet he was among the first companions of the earthly Jesus of Nazareth, and is one about whom the New Testament speaks fairly often.

Penitential Rite

Incarnate Son of God, life has appeared to us in you: Lord, have mercy. . . .

In you we are in communion with the Father: Christ, have mercy. . . .

In you we already have new life by the power of faith: Lord, have mercy. . . .

Talk

John in the Synoptics. John worked at his trade of fishing along with his brother James (the Great). He was accustomed to the hardships of life and was not a soft weakling (Mt 1:19f). According to the Gospel of John, he was already one of the disciples of John the Baptist (Jn 1:39f). Jesus called the two brothers "sons of thunder" (Mk 3:17), apparently because of their energy and activity. Even in the religious area they were inclined to make short work of things. Thus, they tried to stop someone who did not belong to their circle, but who drove out devils in the name of Jesus, from doing so (Mk 9:38). They also wanted to call down fire from heaven upon the unfriendly inhabitants of a Samaritan village (Lk 9:52ff). They knew how to advance explicitly their own interests, and could also declare clearly that they were ready to share persecution and suffering with their Master (Mk 10:30–40).

John According to the Acts of the Apostles.

According to Acts, John was among the outstanding figures of the early Church after the death and resurrection of Jesus. He appeared at different times with Peter (Acts 3:1–11; 4:13–22; 8:14–25). Before the Sanhedrin both declared, "We cannot help speaking of what we have heard and seen" (Acts 4:19). According to Gal 2:9, he was one of the "pillars" of the young Church. At the Apostolic Council, he was one who preferred a compromise for the mission to the pagans, and thus opened the way for the Church into a broad future.

"The Disciple Whom Jesus Loved."

Legend has it that John later worked in Ephesus. He is said, in his old age, to have repeated in his homilies during worship assemblies this sentence: "My little children, love one another."

Christian tradition also regards him as the author of the Gospel of John and of the three letters that bear his name. John manifests himself in these letters as a disciple of Jesus who stresses greatly the divine nature and divine sonship of his Master and, in a period of penetrating theological controversies, one who fights for the truth of the faith.

The tradition also considers the mysterious never-named disciple of the fourth Gospel to be the apostle John. John, then, is the disciple who sat next to Jesus at the Last Supper (Jn 13:23); who stood under the cross with Mary, the Mother of Jesus, and was drawn into a special

St. John the Evangelist

bond with Mary (Jn 19:26f); who on Easter morning ran with Peter to the tomb, reached the tomb before Peter, and also came to believe in the Risen One before Peter.

Witness to the Newborn Child. John, at one point in time, discovered Jesus of Nazareth (Jn 1:37f). In being with Jesus, he found himself to be especially loved by him and entered more deeply into the mystery of his Master. It was impossible for him to remain silent before the Sanhedrin about what he had experienced. He had to commit to paper his experiences with Jesus. He stressed unfailingly, in the fourth Gospel and in the letters, that the experience of the nearness of the Risen One remains alive only if we as Christians love our brothers and sisters.

His life, then, was a witness for the God whose life-giving kindness and love for mankind revealed itself in word and deed in Jesus Christ, from birth in the manger to death on the cross and in the resurrection.

Petitions

Lord Jesus Christ, Son of God, become man, hear our prayer:

We pray for all who have not yet come to believe in your divine and human reality.   [Silence]
We pray for all who are spending the Christmas holidays in loneliness and isolation.   [Silence].
We pray for all who do not open themselves at Christmastime to the physical and spiritual needs of their neighbors.   [Silence]

Lord Jesus Christ, let us never forget that we have life only when we believe in you and love our brothers and sisters. You who live and reign forever and ever.

Holy Innocents (December 28)

HOW CAN GOD ALLOW THAT?

Introduction

"Feast of the Holy Innocents"—does it have a clear place in our Christmas mood and merriment? It always brings me back to the harsh reality of this world. In bold print, however, this account of the slaughter of children in Bethlehem states that Herod had innocent children killed for a definite purpose (namely, to put a potential opponent out of the way)—and God allowed it. Yes, it got even worse: God rescued the Messiah—but he let the other small children in Bethlehem go to ruin. What moral can we draw from this story?

Penitential Rite

Lord Jesus Christ, we live in a world full of suffering and injustice and are oppressed by it all: Lord, have mercy. . . .

It is hard for us to believe that you are nonetheless the God of unfathomable love: Christ, have mercy. . . .

We often ask, doubting and accusing, "How can God allow that?": Lord, have mercy. . . .

Talk

Sacrificed Children. Children cold-bloodedly sacrificed for some purpose—that is a problem not confined to the slaughter of children at Bethlehem.

Children cold-bloodedly sacrificed for some purpose—that happens a hundred and thousand times over in today's world. Think of the television images of current scenes of war or of countries with persistent internal political conflicts! How many "innocents" are killed there every day? How many "innocents" are scarred for life each day by horrible experiences?

How many "innocents" are sacrificed for some purpose by their parents, and tortured by it all? They are not supposed to disturb their parents' acquaintances and, consequently, have to remain silent. The mother wants to make much of the academic accomplishments of her (not very gifted) child, and the kid is forced to exert inhuman effort in school. The daughter pulls some stunt, and the injured father pitches her out the door. . . .

Sacrificed People. These innocent children are only a segment of all the people who are tortured and sacrificed for some political or personal goal. How much suffering again and again overtakes innocent people, because political groups or even individual persons pursue their selfish plans in cold blood and fail to consider the suffering of others!

How Can God Allow That? Innocent people sacrificed! This is the hard reality of human history, that we should not forget even in front of the manger scene when we sing, "Son of God, how love laughs in your divine mouth . . ." (GL 145). On Christmas we declare that "the kindness and love of God our Savior for mankind were revealed" (Tt 3:4) in the Child of Bethlehem. Yet how can the God of love allow the suffering of innocent people?

On this memorial of the Holy Innocents, let us ask ourselves that question. Let us not push it aside right away. Let us concede that the experience of innocent suffering by so many people is the direct argument against our Christian faith in the God of love . . . .

Active Battle Against Suffering. And let us also concede that we have no satisfactory answer to that question: how can God allow that? In faith, all we know is this: if God became man in Jesus Christ, if he stayed with us in him for a lifetime and was available to us totally, if he was even ready to die on the cross for the sake of his love for us, then this love must be so great that it somehow still embraces the innocent suffering of human history. Then the innocent one need not go to total ruin, then he must be on the way to the happiness guaranteed by God's love even in his suffering (as Jesus Christ himself).

Certainly this faith-knowledge of the love of the incarnate God, near as well to innocents in their suffering, drives us to lessen the suffering of innocents insofar as we restrain ourselves from sacrificing others to our selfish goals. Therefore we must now ask ourselves the question: where do I behave (in the family, among my acquaintances, in the workplace) like Herod, to the extent that I sacrifice other people in cold blood to my selfish purposes?

Petitions

Mysterious God! In the incarnation of your Son you have accepted the world with all its suffering. We commend to you all who suffer in innocence:

The innocent victims of war and revolutions.   [Silence]
The innocent victims of personal ambition and unrestrained power struggles. . . .
The innocent victims of unjust social conditions in the rich nations and the developing countries. . . .

Lord our God, you are the advocate of the needy and the poor. Let us, with trust in you, faithfully witness your kindness and love for humanity in the struggle against suffering and injustice. You who live and reign forever and ever.

St. Thomas Becket (December 29)

MURDER IN THE CATHEDRAL

Introduction

God has become man. God's salvation grows and takes effect mysteriously in this world. This means too that it grows through the dedication of people who have their limits and faults. Even in the saints, God's power becomes manifest through human weakness. This is clear in the life of the English bishop Thomas Becket, murdered on December 29, 1170, in his cathedral.

Penitential Rite

Lord Jesus Christ, you have become man and dwell among us: Lord, have mercy. . . .

Your Kingdom grows mysteriously among men and women: Christ, have mercy. . . .

Your power is mighty in human weakness: Lord, have mercy. . . .

Talk

An Unusual Career. Thomas came from bourgeois origins. After appropriate schooling, he became an official of town finances. At age twenty-five, he became associated by chance with a group of young clerics who had formed around the archbishop of Canterbury. The aging bishop sent the young man abroad for studies. Later he secured for him the post of chancellor to the young King Henry II.

A deep friendship grew between the young king and his somewhat older chancellor. The two soon became inseparable. The chancellor supported the king's policies completely—even when the king interfered with the rights of the Church. He felt very comfortable in the court's splended environment and cut a good figure with his own display of elegance.

When the archbishop of Canterbury died, the king appointed his chancellor to be the successor. Thomas resisted at first, but then consented.

Human Tragedy. Thomas knew human nature. Accordingly, prior to his appointment he told the king, "Our present great friendship will turn into vehement hate. I know that you will demand from me as archbishop many things that I will not be able to allow with a peaceful conscience. And the envious ones will step between us and inflame an endless strife between you and me."

This strife began when Thomas resigned as chancellor after his ordination as bishop. The king took this as a personal insult. At this time in England there were a number of disputed issues between king and Church that had to be thrashed out. Yet one has the impression that, in these turbulent controversies in the ensuing years, it was not just a matter of substantive questions. There were two people in mutual conflict, each one defending his standpoint rigorously and uncompromisingly, wasting little on polite diplomacy. The king, above all, fought like a man who considered himself (rightly or wrongly) thoroughly disappointed by his friend.

The "envious ones" (from the bishops' ranks) did come forth and aggravate the conflict. After two years Thomas had to flee the country under cover. He betook himself to the pope, who at that time lived in France. He spent some time of this six-year exile at a Cistercian monastery.

Murder in the Cathedral. During these years Thomas repeatedly attempted a reconciliation with Henry II. He wrote him friendly letters which never drew an answer. In 1170 a reconciliation was achieved with the help of the pope. Yet soon after the archbishop's return, the conflict flared up again. Toward the end of the year, Thomas excommunicated some bishops. When they had recourse to the king, and the king passed some harsh remarks about the archbishop, some knights took it as a demand for execution. They invaded the cathedral and slew Thomas during vespers.

The balanced historian must remark that Thomas Becket could have avoided his violent death with more diplomacy and tact. With all his limitations, however, he grew through the controversies in his life to an inner maturity that allowed him to say in his final Christmas homily, "The true martyr is the one who has become God's instrument, who has lost his own will in the will of God. . . ."

Petitions

Lord Jesus Christ, you have become man and dwell among us.

Grant steadfastness and flexibility to the Church's representatives in the controversies of our times. . . .
Help the various Christian Churches in England find their way to unity with the universal Church. . . .
Accompany with your Spirit the efforts of politicians toward a balanced relationship between Church and State. . . .

For it is your desire that your Father's Kingdom grow in our time. You who live and reign forever and ever.

St. Sylvester I (December 31)

POPE OF TRANSITION

Introduction

Sylvester—the last saint of the year. Who remembers that "Sylvester" is the name of a saintly pope whose memory is observed by the Church today? Who among us knows anything about this pope's life and work?

Penitential Rite

"I myself will look after and tend my sheep, and I will give them rest." [Silence] Lord, have mercy. . . .
"The lost I will seek out, the strayed I will bring back." [Silence] Christ, have mercy. . . .
"The injured I will bind up, the sick I will heal." [Silence] Lord, have mercy. . . .

Talk

On the Path into the Future. Tonight we will take part in the parish service marking the year's end. Tomorrow we will begin the new year with holy Mass. Even now this Eucharist is filled with the feeling of rapid changes in human living, as is brought out by the new year observance. New Year's Eve and New Year's Day allow us to reflect that we human beings are creatures of change: we come out of a past in which we have somehow established ourselves; we live in the short moment that we call the present; we are therefore on the path into an open and unknown future that waits to be lived. . . .

Sylvester—a Pope of Transition. It is well that the Church recalls St. Sylvester on this last day of the year. For it was under his leadership (he was pope from 314 to 335) that the Church had to find her way into a completely new future.

Up to that point, the Church had lived as a minority, tolerated in part but often persecuted, in the Roman Empire with its lavish state-supported cults. Under Emperor Diocletian, she had still more to suffer. Sylvester, not yet pope, was able to distinguish himself through courage and steadfastness in confessing this faith during this persecution.

Then Emperor Constantine assured the Church freedom of religion and was baptized himself soon thereafter. The Church was able to leave the catacombs and to grow out in the open. She was now explicitly supported by the state—for example, various great churches in Rome (St. John Lateran, St. Peter, St. Paul . . .) were built at the expense of the state.

This meant that the Church was now in a totally different situation. Many handicaps upon church life disappeared. Yet other problems arose in their place. The emperor sought to speak for the Church, just as he had previously spoken for the pagan priesthood. Many opportunists presented themselves for baptism, since it was now a career advantage to be a Christian. Now that external pressure had diminished, vehement controversies arose within the Church on theological matters (Arianism, etc. . .), and they led quickly to factions and divisions.

Sylvester led the Church of Rome during this time. At the same time, he acted as the successor of St. Peter (in a less developed form than today) in union with the universal Church. For this reason, the decisions of importance in church history took place not in Rome but in the eastern provinces of the Church (thus, the Council of Nicaea was held in the east, and the pope was represented only by legates).

Sylvester worked quietly in Rome. He did not leave his stamp on his age as did later popes. Yet he helped the Roman Church in that time of transition, by his unseen administrative and pastoral work, to hold fast to faith in Jesus Christ and not to betray her Lord and Master [Gospel].

"I Myself Will Pastor My Sheep and Care for Them." Sylvester knew that, on this difficult path into the future, Jesus Christ himself was the shepherd leading and caring for her, in line with today's Gospel. Jesus Christ is also the shepherd who cares for each one of us and leads us into the open (and often seemingly dark) future, brought out so clearly for us by New Year's. Let us trust in him as he says today ever to us: I myself will be your shepherd and will care for you, shepherding you rightly.

Petitions

Lord Jesus Christ, with you we come out of the past, we live in the present, we go into the future:

Reward with your blessing those who have done good to us during this year. . . .
Forgive those who have harmed us as we too forgive them. . . .
Make up to others whatever we deprived them of. . . .

For you are with us as our shepherd on our journey till the end of time. You who live and reign forever and ever.

Index of Names and Dates

Achilleus, St.	May 12	Blase, St.	Feb. 3
Agatha, St.	Feb. 5	Bonaventure, St.	July 15
Agnes, St.	Jan. 21	Boniface, St.	June 5
Albert the Great, St.	Nov. 13	Bridget of Sweden, St.	July 23
All Saints	Nov. 1	Bruno, St.	Oct. 6
All Souls	Nov. 2		
Aloysius Gonzaga, St.	June 21		
Alphonsus Mary de Liguori, St.	Aug. 1	Cajetan, St.	Aug. 7
		Callistus, St.	Oct. 14
Ambrose, St.	Dec. 7	Camillus de Lellis, St.	July 14
Andrew the Apostle, St.	Nov. 30	Casimir, St.	Mar. 4
Angela Merici, St.	Jan. 27	Catherine of Siena, St.	Apr. 29
Ann (with Joachim), St.	July 26	Cecilia, St.	Nov. 22
Anselm, St.	Apr. 21	Charles Borromeo, St.	Nov. 4
Ansgar, St.	Feb. 3	Charles Lwanga and Companions, St.	June 3
Anthony, St.	Jan. 17		
Anthony Mary Claret, St.	Oct. 24	Clare of Assisi, St.	Aug. 11
Anthony of Padua, St.	June 13	Clement, St.	Nov. 23
Anthony Mary Zaccaria, St.	July 5	Columban, St.	Nov. 23
Athanasius, St.	May 2	Cornelius (with Cyprian), St.	Sept. 16
Augustine of Canterbury, St.	May 27		
Augustine of Hippo, St.	Aug. 28	Cosmas (with Damian), St.	Sept. 26
		Cyprian (with Cornelius), St.	Sept. 16
Barnabas, St.	June 11	Cyril (with Methodius), St.	Feb. 14
Bartholomew the Apostle, St.	Aug. 24	Cyril of Alexandria, St.	June 27
		Cyril of Jerusalem, St.	Mar. 18
Basil the Great, St.	Jan. 2		
Bede the Venerable, St.	May 25		
Benedict, St.	July 11	Damasus I, St.	Dec. 11
Bernard of Clairvaux, St.	Aug. 20	Damian (with Cosmas), St.	Sept. 26
Bernardine of Siena, St.	May 20	Dedication of the Lateran	

Basilica	Nov. 9	Innocents, The Holy	Dec. 28
Dedication of St. Mary Major in Rome	Aug. 5	Irenaeus, St.	June 28
		Isaac Jogues (and Companions), St.	Oct. 19
Dedication of the Churches of Peter and Paul	Nov. 18	Isidore of Seville, St.	Apr. 4
Denis and Companions, St.	Oct. 9		
Dominic, St.	Aug. 8		
		James the Apostle, St.	July 25
		Jane Frances de Chantal	Dec. 12
Elizabeth of Hungary, St.	Nov. 17	Januarius, St.	Sept. 19
Elizabeth of Portugal, St.	July 4	Jerome, St.	Sept. 30
Ephrem, St.	June 9	Jerome Emiliani, St.	Feb. 8
Epiphany of the Lord	Jan. 6	Joachim (and Ann), St.	July 26
Eusebius, St.	Aug. 2	John the Apostle and Evangelist, St.	Dec. 27
		John I, St.	May 18
Fabian, St.	Jan. 20	John the Baptist, St.	June 24
Felicity (with Perpetua), St.	Mar. 7	Beheading of	Aug. 29
Fidelius of Sigmaringen, St.	Apr. 24	John Baptist de la Salle	Apr. 7
First Martyrs of the Church of Rome	June 30	John Bosco, St.	Jan. 31
		John de Brebeuf, St.	Oct. 19
Founders of the Servites	Feb. 17	John of Kanty	Dec. 23
Frances of Rome, St.	Mar. 9	John of Capistran, St.	Oct. 23
Francis of Assisi, St.	Oct. 4	John Chrysostom, St.	Sept. 13
Francis of Paola, St.	Apr. 2	John of the Cross, St.	Dec. 14
Francis de Sales, St.	Jan. 24	John Damascene, St.	Dec. 4
Francis Xavier, St.	Dec. 3	John Eudes, St.	Aug. 19
		John Fisher, St.	June 22
		John of God, St.	Mar. 8
Gabriel the Archangel	Sept. 29	John Leonardi, St.	Oct. 9
George, St.	Apr. 23	John Mary Vianney, St.	Aug. 4
Gregory the Great, St.	Sept. 3	Josaphat, St.	Nov. 12
Gregory VII, St.	May 25	Joseph, St.	Mar. 19
Guardian Angels	Oct. 2	Joseph the Worker, St.	May 1
		Joseph Calasanz, St.	May 1
		Jude the Apostle, St.	Oct. 28
Hedwig, St.	Oct. 16	Justin, St.	June 1
Henry (with Kunigunde), St.	July 13		
Hilary, St.	Jan. 13		
Hippolytus (with Pontian), St.	Aug. 13	Kunigunde (with Henry), St.	July 13
		Lawrence, St.	Aug. 10
Ignatius of Antioch, St.	Oct. 17	Lawrence of Brindisi, St.	July 21
Ignatius of Loyola, St.	July 31	Leo the Great, St.	Nov. 10

Index of Names and Dates 581

Louis, St.	Aug. 25	Pancratius, St.	May 12
Lucy, St.	Dec. 13	Patrick, St.	Mar. 17
Luke the Evangelist, St.	Oct. 18	Paul the Apostle, St.	June 29
		Conversion of	Jan. 25
		Paul of the Cross, St.	Oct. 19
Marcellinus (with Peter), St.	June 2	Paul Miki and Companions, St.	Feb. 7
Margaret Mary Alacoque, St.	Oct. 16	Paulinus of Nola, St.	June 22
Margaret of Scotland, St.	Nov. 16	Perpetua (with Felicity), St.	Mar. 7
Mark the Evangelist, St.	Apr. 25	Peter the Apostle, St.	June 29
Martha, St.	July 29	Chair of	Feb. 22
Martin I, St.	Apr. 13	Peter (with Marcellinus), St.	June 2
Martin de Porres, St.	Nov. 3	Peter Canisius, St.	Dec. 21
Martin of Tours, St.	Nov. 11	Peter Chanel, St.	Apr. 28
Martyrs of the Church of Rome	June 30	Peter Damian, St.	Feb. 21
		Peter Chrysologus, St.	July 30
Mary, the Blessed Virgin		Philip the Apostle, St.	May 3
Annunciation	Mar. 25	Philip Neri, St.	May 26
Assumption	Aug. 15	Pius V, St.	Apr. 30
Birth	Sept. 8	Pius X, St.	Aug. 21
Immaculate Conception	Dec. 8	Polycarp of Smyrna, St.	Feb. 23
Immaculate Heart	May 31	Pontian (with Hippolytus), St.	Aug. 13
Our Lady of Mt. Carmel	July 16	Presentation of the Lord	Feb. 2
Our Lady of Lourdes	Feb. 11		
Our Lady of the Rosary	Oct. 7		
Our Lady of Sorrows	Sept. 15		
Presentation	Nov. 21	Raphael the Archangel	Sept. 29
Queenship	Aug. 22	Raymond of Penafort, St.	Jan. 7
Visitation	May 31	Robert Bellarmine, St.	Sept. 17
Maria Goretti, St.	July 6	Romuald, St.	June 19
Mary Magdalene, St.	July 22	Rose of Lima, St.	Aug. 23
Mary Magdalene of Pazzi, St.	May 25		
		(Feast of the) Sacred Heart of Jesus	May 31
Matthew the Apostle and Evangelist, St.	Sept. 20	Scholastica, St.	Feb. 10
Matthias the Apostle, St.	May 14	Sebastian, St.	Jan. 20
Methodius (with Cyril), St.	Feb. 14	Seven Holy Founders of the Order of the Servites	Feb. 17
Michael the Archangel	Sept. 29	Simon the Apostle, St.	Oct. 28
Monica, St.	Aug. 27	Sixtus and Companions, St.	Aug. 7
		Stanislaus, St.	Apr. 11
Nereus, St.	May 12	Stephen of Hungary, St.	Aug. 16
Nicholas, St.	Dec. 6	Stephen, St.	Dec. 26
Norbert of Xanten, St.	June 6	Sylvester, St.	Dec. 31

Teresa of Avila, St.	Oct. 15	Triumph of the Cross	Sept. 14
Theresa of the Child Jesus	Oct. 1	Turibius of Mongrovejo, St.	Mar. 23
Thomas the Apostle, St.	July 3		
Thomas Aquinas, St.	Jan. 28	Vincent, St.	Jan. 22
Thomas Becket, St.	Dec. 29	Vincent Ferrer	Apr. 5
Thomas More, St.	June 22	Vincent de Paul, St.	Sept. 27
Timothy and Titus, St.	Jan. 26		
Transfiguration of the Lord	Aug. 6	Wenceslaus, St.	Sept. 28